STAR TREK
THE NEXT GENERATION™

MAELSTROM

MICHAEL JAN FRIEDMAN

DAVE STERN · MIKE O'BRIEN

PABLO MARCOS · KEN PENDERS

MIKE MANLEY · ROBERT CAMPANELLA

TITAN BOOKS

STAR TREK: THE NEXT GENERATION – MAELSTROM

ISBN 1 84576 318 1
ISBN-13: 9781845763183

Published by Titan Books
A division of Titan Publishing Group Ltd.
144 Southwark St
London SE1 0UP

Originally published by DC Comics as *Star Trek: The Next Generation* #13-18.

A CIP catalogue record for this title is available from the British Library.

This edition first published: September 2006
2 4 6 8 10 9 7 5 3 1

Printed in Italy.

Other titles of interest available from Titan Books:

Star Trek — *To Boldly Go* (ISBN: 1 84576 084 0)
Star Trek — *Death Before Dishonor* (ISBN: 1 84576 154 5)
Star Trek — *The Trial of James T. Kirk* (ISBN: 1 84576 315 7)
Star Trek: The Next Generation — *The Hero Factor* (ISBN: 1 84576 153 7)
Star Trek: The Next Generation — *The Battle Within* (ISBN: 1 84576 155 3)

What did you think of this book?
We love to hear from our readers.
Please email us at: readerfeedback@titanemail.com,
or write to us at the above address.

w w w . t i t a n b o o k s . c o m

THE NEXT PHASE

It's been a while, but LeVar Burton is back in the *Star Trek* game, having just directed *Live Fast and Prosper*, a late sixth season episode of *Star Trek: Voyager*.

"I love *Star Trek*," comments Burton, the *Star Trek: The Next Generation* star who's also made a name for himself by calling the shots on acclaimed episodes of *ST:TNG* (*Second Chances*, *The Pegasus*), *Star Trek: Deep Space Nine* (*Indiscretion*, *The Sword of Kahless*, *To The Death*, *Things Past*, *Behind The Lines*, *The Emperor's New*

Levar Burton interviewed
by Ian Spelling

Cloak) and *Star Trek: Voyager* (*Ex Post Facto*, *The Raven*, *Timeless*). "I love playing in that world. Nobody has to twist my arm to get me to do it.

"In this case, with *Live Fast and Prosper*, the script was terrific. Just the title is great. The central characters in the episode are actually guest stars [Kaitlin Hopkins, Greg Daniel and Francis Guinan, the last of whom also appeared in Burton's first *Star Trek: Voyager* engagement, *Ex Post Facto*], and they are playing a band of thieves, a trio of con artists. And they are out in the Delta Quadrant, running scams on unsuspecting alien populations.

"Meanwhile, the *Voyager* is out there on an Away Mission. What happens is that two of the most world-savvy members of the crew – Neelix [Ethan Phillips] and Paris [Robert Duncan McNeill] – get duped by these aliens. As a result, the con men have gained access to the entire *Voyager* database. Using that information they've gleaned, their newest and latest scam is posing as Captain Janeway [Kate Mulgrew], Tuvok [Tim Russ] and Chakotay [Robert Beltran], and they're selling Federation memberships to unsuspecting aliens.

"One of the first images we see in the episode is two Starfleet officers beaming down," continues LeVar, "and from a distance it looks like Tuvok and Janeway. Upon closer inspection we discover that it's not Tuvok and Janeway at all. It's a woman wearing a wig – the aliens are actually bald – that makes her look a lot like Janeway, and she's sort of the same size and shape as Janeway. One of the funnier aspects of the episode is that the man playing Tuvok (Daniel) thinks of Tuvok as his god, and he won't come out of character. He really wants to believe he's Tuvok and we mine the humour in that situation. So the con men aren't doing imitations, per se, but are trying to capture the essence of Janeway, Tuvok and Chakotay,

"Visually," Burton adds, obviously quite enthused, "we did some cool stuff with the camera. My approach

to using the camera as a storytelling tool is to always try to make the camera moves and the blocking organic to the scene. I believe that there is an organic truth that's trying to be expressed and that there's a perfect place to put the camera to support that truth. We've also got a crane and a hothead [a remote camera mechanism] we could use to invent some new angles you haven't seen before. We actually took the crane into the Engineering section, which had never been done before, and did a couple of interesting things in there."

What, one wonders, is Burton's game plan going into an episode? Does he get a script, read it and form ideas in his mind for camera moves right then, or does everything emerge during the prep phase? Or is it a combination of both?

"It's both, but it comes together first when I'm reading the script," he replies. "Certain things are always suggested to me that, invariably, I end up photographing. Then you start to find other elements when you get the show on its feet. Having spent twenty years as an actor, the rehearsal process for me is as much about where

the movement and dynamic are as anything else. More often than not, the choreography of the scene will really suggest a very elegant way to capture the scene on film. You also have to be open to trying different things on the set."

And it's not just Burton's experience as a veteran actor that pays off for him while helming *Star Trek: Voyager*. His decade-plus spent playing Geordi La Forge on *Star Trek: The Next Generation* and the subsequent features has also paid dividends for Burton, the director. "It's worth its weight in gold because I'm intimately familiar with the *Star Trek* world, with this universe," he notes. "I know the language. And when guest stars come on who aren't familiar with how to push the buttons on the consoles, I can always lend some assistance in that area."

Burton's direction of *Live Fast and Prosper* represents his first time back behind a *Star Trek* camera since *Timeless*, the time-tripping 100th episode of *ST: VOY*. To use the actor-director's word of the day, *Timeless* was 'cool'.

"I thought it turned out very well," he says. "I was really happy with it. Garrett Wang's performance [as Harry Kim] was awesome. It was really very solid work. The art department went above and beyond in terms of freezing the Bridge and then turning the Bridge and corridors and Sickbay – all major, permanent sets – back to normal so we could shoot them as normal for the same episode. [Director of Photography] Martin Rush outdid himself on the show. We had a lot of fun with that technocrane on Stage 16, shooting the opening sequence. The visual effects were terrific. The crash of the ship into the ice planet? Come on! Everybody stepped up."

Expanding his horizons beyond the *Star Trek* realm, Burton has just finished several projects. He recently won a Grammy for his reading of a Martin Luther King audiobook, and has any number of ventures in various stages of development. Last year, for example, he directed *Smart House*, a cable television movie for the Disney Channel.

"I had a great time with that," Burton says. "I was able to get [*Star Trek* veteran] Jonathan West to come shoot it with me. It was a nice little family film. The Disney Channel does a lot of pictures and *Smart House* is one of the most popular they've ever produced. Every time the movie runs, the numbers just go through the roof on the channel. Kids really seem to love it and relate to it, which was our intention. We wanted to make a solid, quality family picture that was fun for kids."

As for those projects in development, they include *The Watsons Go To Birmingham*, a television drama with Whoopi Goldberg and Alfre Woodard that Burton hopes to direct this spring for CBS; *At Water's Edge*, a TV movie with James Earl Jones attached; and *Camp P*, a weekly series for MTV that Burton intends to produce and, when possible, direct. He'd also like to act again.

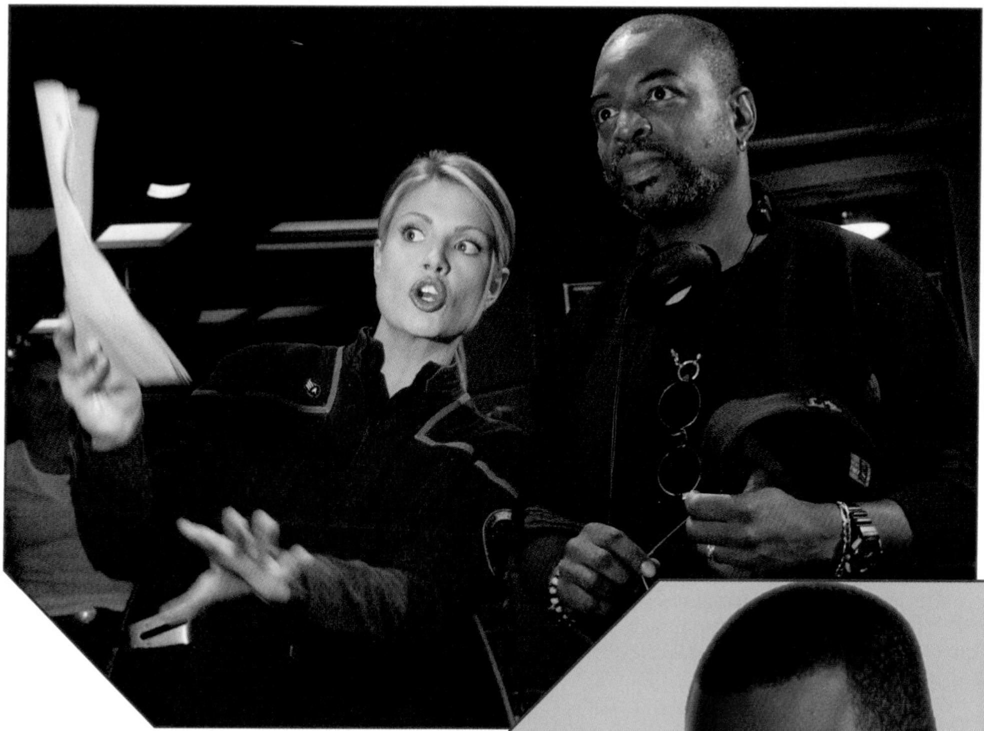

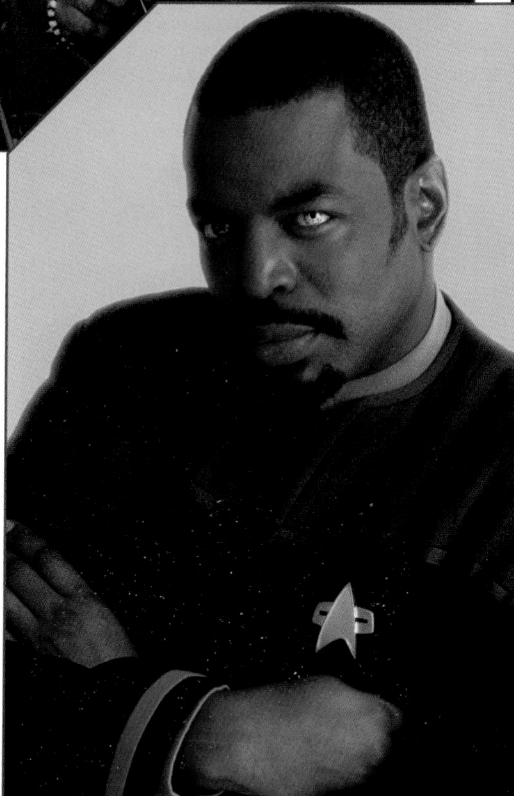

"Actually," he notes, "what I'm really looking for is an opportunity to pull a Michael Landon. What I mean by that is I want to get a series on the air that I'm executive producing, directing quite often and starring on. I've got an idea for a character I want to play that would make for a good opportunity to wear a hat or three. It's a one-hour drama and I'll start pitching that to CBS and the other networks in July, during pitch season."

Lest anyone fear that Burton might one day abandon *Star Trek* entirely, it seems an unlikely prospect. "My company is really busy now," Burton says, referring to his production entity, Eagle Nation Films, "so I have less and less time to devote to *Star Trek*. But it's always been fun for me. As I said, it's like going home for me."

And what is the latest Burton has heard about the future of *Star Trek*? "The latest I've heard is that they are trying to come up with a story for the next film," he responds. "They're working on it. If they're successful at coming up with a story that all the powers that be – the studio, Rick [Berman] and Patrick [Stewart] – are happy with, then I guess we will be shooting it this time next year. I've also heard that they are developing a new series, but I have no information or details on that at all."

Burton can anticipate the final question.

"Would I be interested in directing a *Star Trek: The Next Generation* feature or [episodes of] the new series?" he asks. "Yes. I would be interested in that. Absolutely."

[**Editor's note:** This interview originally appeared in *Star Trek Monthly* #66, cover date June 2000, published in the UK by Titan Magazines. The *Star Trek: Voyager* episode *Live Fast and Prosper* was first aired on 19 April 2000.]

WORF: PAST, PRESENT, AND FUTURE

"A Klingon is proud. He is the ultimate warrior," says actor Michael Dorn, *Star Trek: The Next Generation*'s Worf, as he attempts to explain the complexity of the intense Klingon Security Chief aboard the *U.S.S. Enterprise NCC-1701-D*.

Worf's popularity grew immensely from the first season of the show, when he wasn't much more than a snarling animal. "People see in Worf a strength, a fierceness that's as frightening as it is beautiful," Dorn

Michael Dorn interviewed by Wendy Hall

explains. "A part of us can relate to that, because we all have that same basic animal instinct in us that's covered by the constraints of civility. That animal instinct in Worf is more honest and open. He personifies it, and I believe that most people, though they want to hate him, can't help but like him.

"But," Dorn emphasises, "Worf is not a friendly person. He believes that feelings and closeness are weaknesses that should absolutely be controlled and avoided at all costs. He's not going to let people know him easily. He'll grow subtly through his experiences aboard the *U.S.S. Enterprise* and through his experiences with his crewmates."

Much of the credit for Worf's growth over the series' first seasons he gives to Gene Roddenberry. "In the beginning, I asked Gene exactly what he wanted Worf to be, and he gave me free license to develop him. He said, 'Forget what you've seen in the original show, forget what you've seen in the movies, and forget everything you've ever heard or read about Klingons. Make him yours.' That's what I did."

Dorn adds that this freedom allowed him to let Worf become more than just a make-up job with a deep voice, and because of that, Worf is now more than a figment of somebody's imagination.

"We're talking about a real flesh and blood being," the actor comments. "Whenever you watch an episode, you know that you can count on more than just his physical strength. You can put your trust in his strength of mind, his intellect, as well."

Opportunities for Worf to reveal his many sides are seen especially in episodes where Worf has become a prominent figure. "In *Reunion* [the fourth season episode featuring the return of Worf's lover K'Ehleyr and the first appearance of his son, Alexander], Worf is finally allowed to be the story's focal point," Dorn notes. "Even in *Heart of Glory* [which saw the *U.S.S. Enterprise* up against three Klingons unaware of the

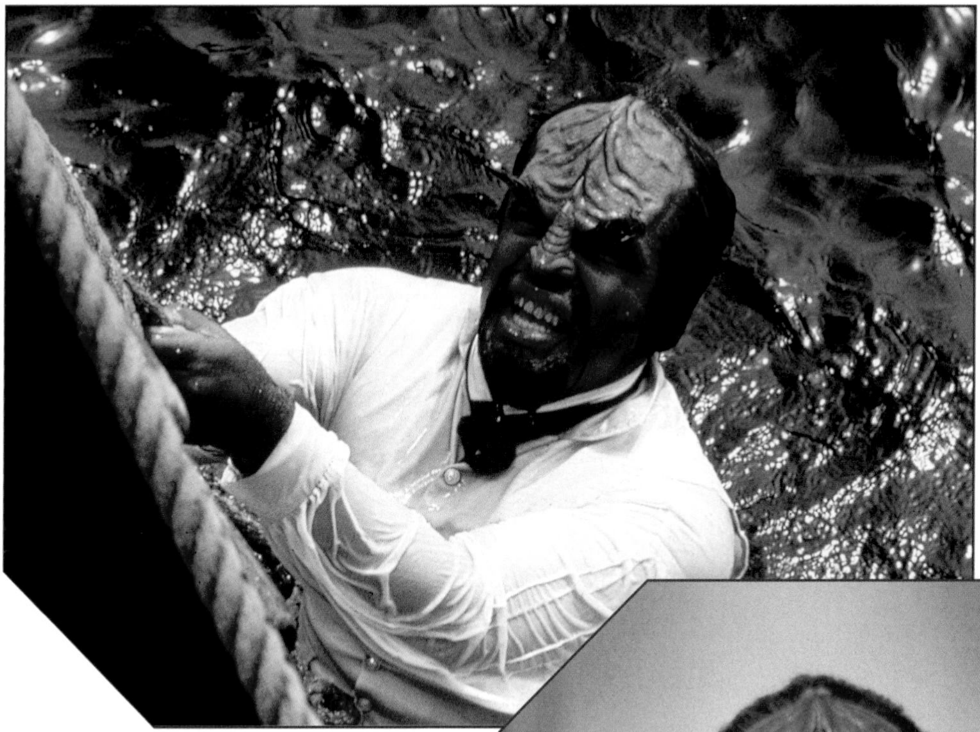

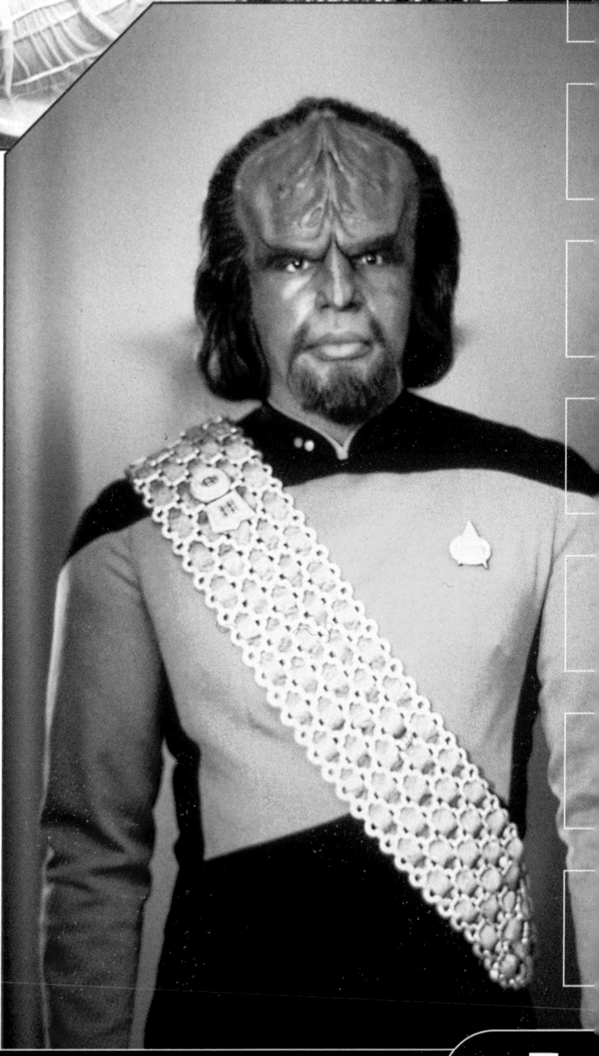

peace between the Federation and their empire] he had to share the limelight with other main characters." And this despite the fact that it is Worf's apparent captaincy of the *U.S.S. Enterprise* that prevents an all-out space battle with the three Klingons.

Despite early problems with the character, stories such as *Reunion* and later episodes such as *Birthright* and *Parallels* confirmed Worf's top-drawer status in the show. But with his popularity also came criticism, particularly about Worf when compared with other Klingons. Some people have argued that the Klingons of the original series and the films were much more ferocious and cunning. Worf has occasionally been accused of being far too docile in comparison.

"If you're expecting a race to remain completely unchanged then you're being rather narrow-minded," Dorn says vehemently. "Even the human race of the 24th Century is different, more evolved than we are in the 20th. Worf considers himself to be the perfect soldier. Regardless of what he may think, he will follow the orders of his Captain – without question – and his Captain is human. He was also raised by humans and that has to have some effect on him."

Some of Worf's fans have also complained that many of the episodes from *Star Trek: The Next Generation* have left plotlines unresolved. "Is life ever resolved?" asks Dorn. "No. You can't sit down in 44 minutes and resolve your life. I think that's what some fans are looking for, a resolution to their own lives. You can't realistically resolve every question. I don't know of anybody who can go into an everyday

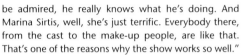

situation and at the day's end say, 'OK, this day has been resolved.'"

For the most part, his developing relationship with Deanna Troi in season seven aside, Worf had very tenuous relationships with the rest of the *U.S.S. Enterprise* crew. "Worf is a loner," Dorn admits. "He's basically a stranger on the ship. To his way of thinking, friendship isn't an option. It's something to be looked down upon, but respect or honour is to be admired."

Although Worf always had problems relating to the other members of the *U.S.S. Enterprise* crew, the actor Michael Dorn had no worries about working with the rest of the team of actors and actresses. "I've never worked with such talented people before," he enthuses. "They're such strong performers with fantastic abilities, and we all seem to complement, instead of clash against, each other. Patrick Stewart is an actor to

be admired, he really knows what he's doing. And Marina Sirtis, well, she's just terrific. Everybody there, from the cast to the make-up people, are like that. That's one of the reasons why the show works so well."

Falling into the role of a Klingon Warrior came fairly easily to Dorn, who admits that he was a fan of the original *Star Trek* series, so he had an edge over the competition during auditions for the part. After a career in two soap operas, a role in television's police action series *CHiPs*, several films, and a time spent with a rock band, that opportunity came. Yet Dorn confides that acting wasn't his original career choice. "When I was in college, my major was in producing and directing. I never gave acting any thought until about 1978 after I received a lot of encouragement from the cast of *The Mary Tyler Moore Show*, where I was a stand-in. Everybody kept telling me how good I was, and that I really should try it out. So, I took some acting classes, and here I am."

All the main performers in *Star Trek: The Next Generation* enjoy some kind of fame – except Dorn. Thanks to the elaborate Klingon make-up, which can take up to four hours to complete, he usually travels about undetected, even by his fans.

"It's a blessing, in a way," Dorn contends. "But then, I don't also get the recognition I need from directors and producers who only see the forehead and the crooked teeth!" Which was why Dorn began his rounds of the convention circuit and began to get to know fans personally. "I've met some wonderful people," he says, "But I never realised the extreme passion that some fans can hold for a show."

Concerning one of his own passions, namely flying, Dorn confesses that he's an avid reader of such publications as *Aviation Week* and *Space Technology* and admits that he would trade his acting career in a minute for a career as a jet fighter pilot. "I almost feel as if I were born too late," he laments. "I would have dearly loved to have been able to have flown with a World War II fighter squadron."

With his feet firmly planted in this half of the 20th Century, however, Dorn must settle with flying his twin engine Cessna 240. "I will only fly a twin engine," he laughs. "That way, if the engine fails, I'll still have another one!"

Perhaps his love of flying and facing the unknown in the sky reveals a little more of Worf, the proud Klingon warrior, in Michael Dorn than he expects. Grinning gently he says, "I don't know how it has happened but I'm beginning to suspect it myself."

[**Editor's note:** This interview originally appeared in *Star Trek Monthly* #2, cover date April 1995, published in the UK by Titan Magazines.]

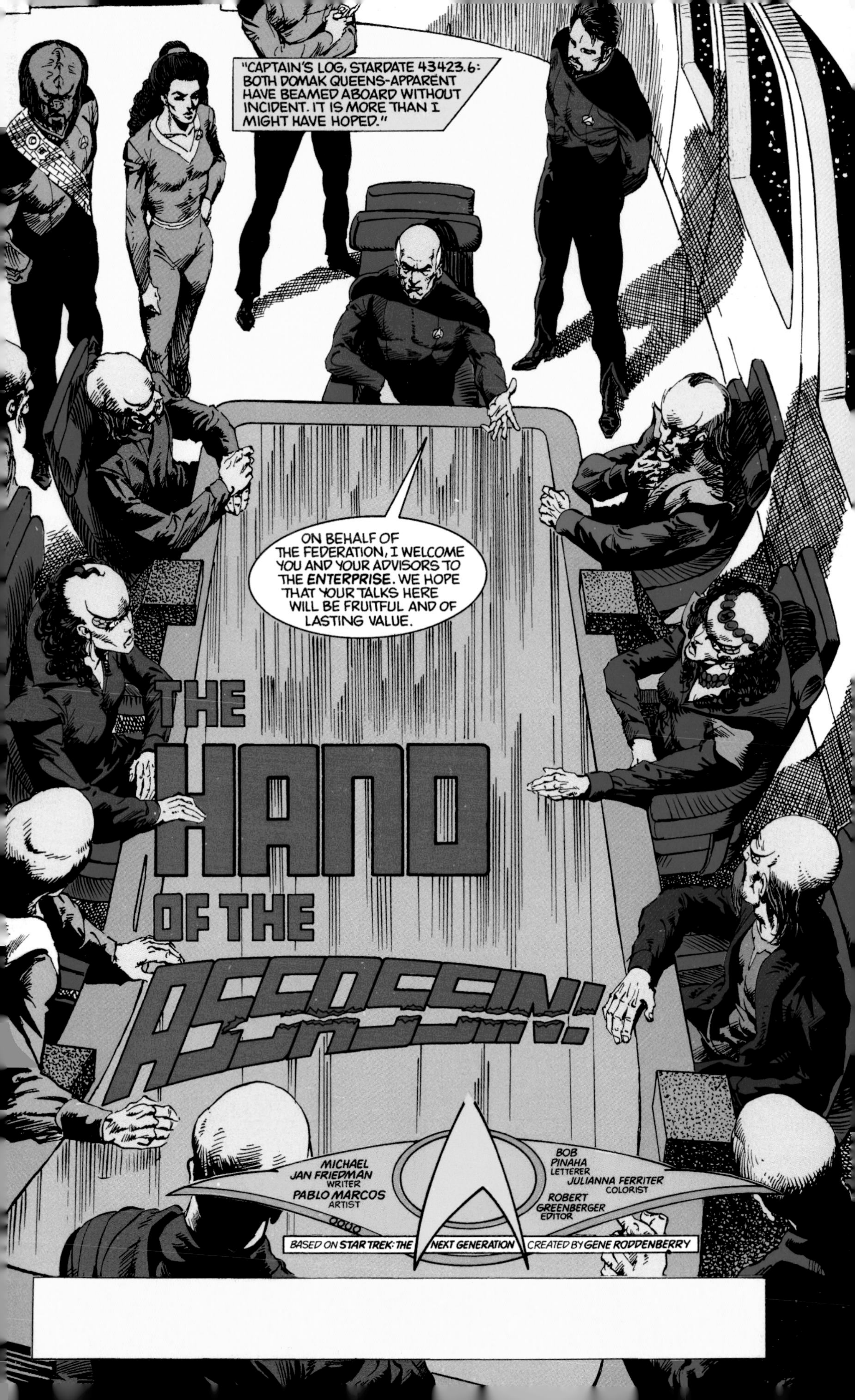
"CAPTAIN'S LOG, STARDATE 43423.6: BOTH DOMAK QUEENS-APPARENT HAVE BEAMED ABOARD WITHOUT INCIDENT. IT IS MORE THAN I MIGHT HAVE HOPED."
ON BEHALF OF THE FEDERATION, I WELCOME YOU AND YOUR ADVISORS TO THE ENTERPRISE. WE HOPE THAT YOUR TALKS HERE WILL BE FRUITFUL AND OF LASTING VALUE.
THE HAND OF THE ASSASSIN!
MICHAEL JAN FRIEDMAN WRITER
PABLO MARCOS ARTIST
BOB PINAHA LETTERER
JULIANNA FERRITER COLORIST
ROBERT GREENBERGER EDITOR
BASED ON STAR TREK: THE NEXT GENERATION CREATED BY GENE RODDENBERRY

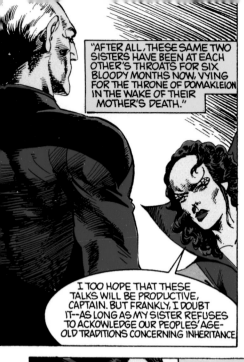

"AFTER ALL, THESE SAME TWO SISTERS HAVE BEEN AT EACH OTHER'S THROATS FOR SIX BLOODY MONTHS NOW, VYING FOR THE THRONE OF DOMAKLEION IN THE WAKE OF THEIR MOTHER'S DEATH."

I TOO HOPE THAT THESE TALKS WILL BE PRODUCTIVE, CAPTAIN. BUT FRANKLY, I DOUBT IT--AS LONG AS MY SISTER REFUSES TO ACKNOWLEDGE OUR PEOPLES' AGE-OLD TRADITIONS CONCERNING INHERITANCE.

"UNDER ITS FORMER QUEEN, DOMAKLEION WAS A STAUNCH ALLY OF THE FEDERATION. IT CAN BE A STAUNCH ALLY AGAIN."

TRUE, THE THRONE WOULD NORMALLY GO TO THE OLDEST, ALLIENA. AND YOU ARE OLDER THAN I. BUT IT WAS OUR MOTHER'S DYING WISH THAT I TAKE HER PLACE AS QUEEN OF DOMAKLEION.

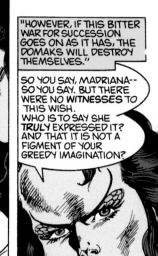

"HOWEVER, IF THIS BITTER WAR FOR SUCCESSION GOES ON AS IT HAS, THE DOMAKS WILL DESTROY THEMSELVES."

SO YOU SAY, MADRIANA-- SO YOU SAY. BUT THERE WERE NO WITNESSES TO THIS WISH. WHO IS TO SAY SHE TRULY EXPRESSED IT? AND THAT IT IS NOT A FIGMENT OF YOUR GREEDY IMAGINATION?

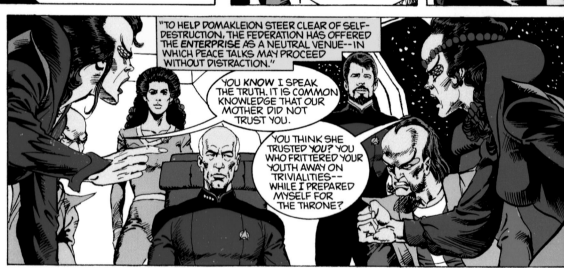

"TO HELP DOMAKLEION STEER CLEAR OF SELF-DESTRUCTION, THE FEDERATION HAS OFFERED THE ENTERPRISE AS A NEUTRAL VENUE--IN WHICH PEACE TALKS MAY PROCEED WITHOUT DISTRACTION."

YOU KNOW I SPEAK THE TRUTH. IT IS COMMON KNOWLEDGE THAT OUR MOTHER DID NOT TRUST YOU.

YOU THINK SHE TRUSTED YOU? YOU WHO FRITTERED YOUR YOUTH AWAY ON TRIVIALITIES-- WHILE I PREPARED MYSELF FOR THE THRONE?

"NATURALLY, NO WEAPONS HAVE BEEN ALLOWED AT THESE PROCEEDINGS. HOWEVER, EVEN WITHOUT DAGGERS AND DISRUPTORS, THE DOMAKS ARE FAR FROM HARMLESS."

YOUR HIGHNESSES-- PLEASE!

"BEING A HIGHLY TELE-PATHIC PEOPLE, THEY ARE CAPABLE OF INFLUENCING OTHERS TO DO THEIR BIDDING. PARTICULARLY THOSE OF OTHER RACES, WHO HAVE HAD NO EXPERIENCE WITH SUCH MANIPULATION."

WE ARE NOT HERE TO FILL THE AIR WITH ACCUSATIONS--BUT TO ENGINEER A RESOLUTION OF YOUR CONFLICT.

2

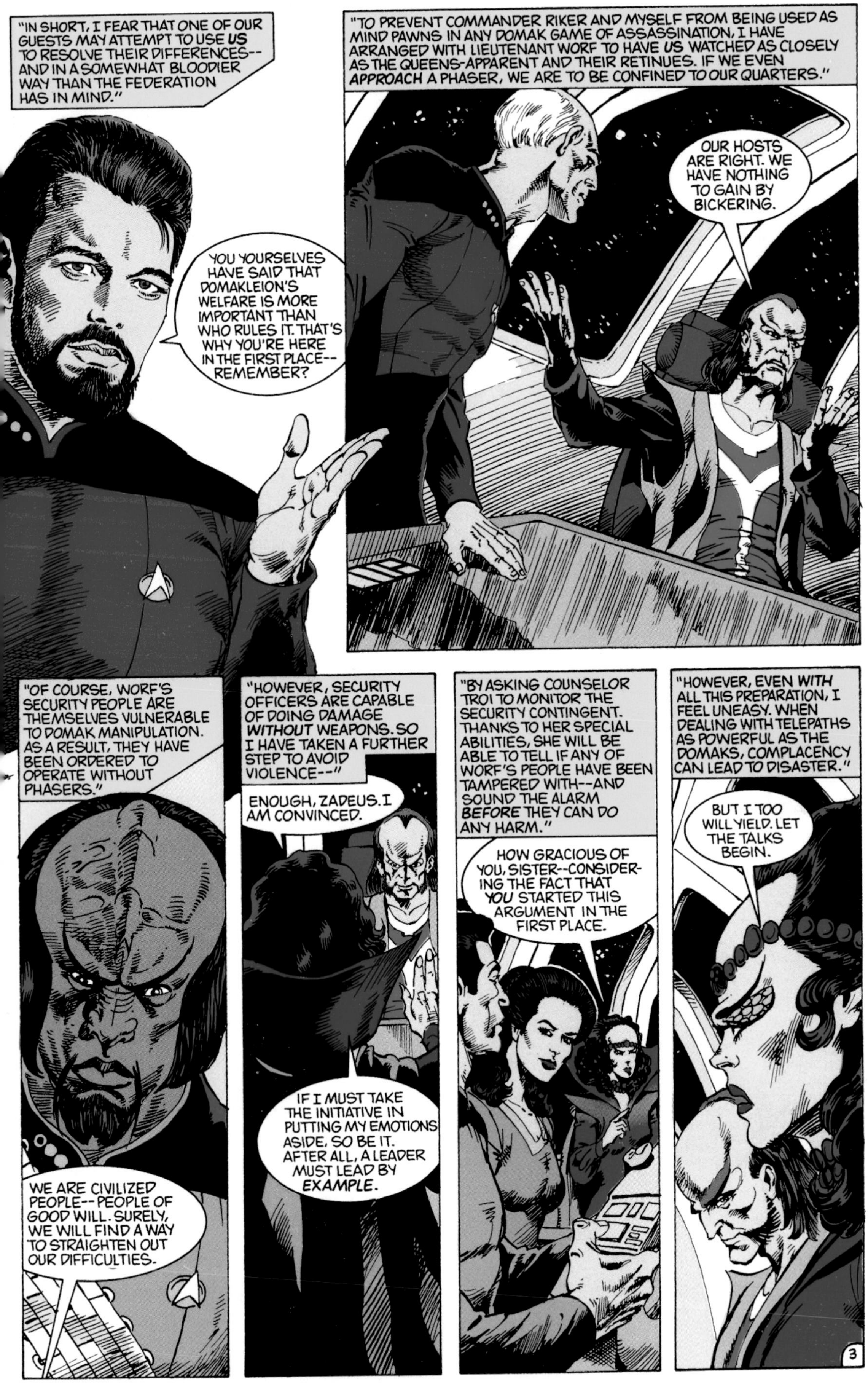
"IN SHORT, I FEAR THAT ONE OF OUR GUESTS MAY ATTEMPT TO USE US TO RESOLVE THEIR DIFFERENCES--AND IN A SOMEWHAT BLOODIER WAY THAN THE FEDERATION HAS IN MIND."
YOU YOURSELVES HAVE SAID THAT DOMAKLEION'S WELFARE IS MORE IMPORTANT THAN WHO RULES IT. THAT'S WHY YOU'RE HERE IN THE FIRST PLACE--REMEMBER?
"TO PREVENT COMMANDER RIKER AND MYSELF FROM BEING USED AS MIND PAWNS IN ANY DOMAK GAME OF ASSASSINATION, I HAVE ARRANGED WITH LIEUTENANT WORF TO HAVE US WATCHED AS CLOSELY AS THE QUEENS-APPARENT AND THEIR RETINUES. IF WE EVEN APPROACH A PHASER, WE ARE TO BE CONFINED TO OUR QUARTERS."
OUR HOSTS ARE RIGHT. WE HAVE NOTHING TO GAIN BY BICKERING.
"OF COURSE, WORF'S SECURITY PEOPLE ARE THEMSELVES VULNERABLE TO DOMAK MANIPULATION. AS A RESULT, THEY HAVE BEEN ORDERED TO OPERATE WITHOUT PHASERS."
WE ARE CIVILIZED PEOPLE--PEOPLE OF GOOD WILL. SURELY, WE WILL FIND A WAY TO STRAIGHTEN OUT OUR DIFFICULTIES.
"HOWEVER, SECURITY OFFICERS ARE CAPABLE OF DOING DAMAGE WITHOUT WEAPONS. SO I HAVE TAKEN A FURTHER STEP TO AVOID VIOLENCE--"
ENOUGH, ZADEUS. I AM CONVINCED.
IF I MUST TAKE THE INITIATIVE IN PUTTING MY EMOTIONS ASIDE, SO BE IT. AFTER ALL, A LEADER MUST LEAD BY EXAMPLE.
"BY ASKING COUNSELOR TROI TO MONITOR THE SECURITY CONTINGENT. THANKS TO HER SPECIAL ABILITIES, SHE WILL BE ABLE TO TELL IF ANY OF WORF'S PEOPLE HAVE BEEN TAMPERED WITH--AND SOUND THE ALARM BEFORE THEY CAN DO ANY HARM."
HOW GRACIOUS OF YOU, SISTER--CONSIDERING THE FACT THAT YOU STARTED THIS ARGUMENT IN THE FIRST PLACE.
"HOWEVER, EVEN WITH ALL THIS PREPARATION, I FEEL UNEASY. WHEN DEALING WITH TELEPATHS AS POWERFUL AS THE DOMAKS, COMPLACENCY CAN LEAD TO DISASTER."
BUT I TOO WILL YIELD. LET THE TALKS BEGIN.
3

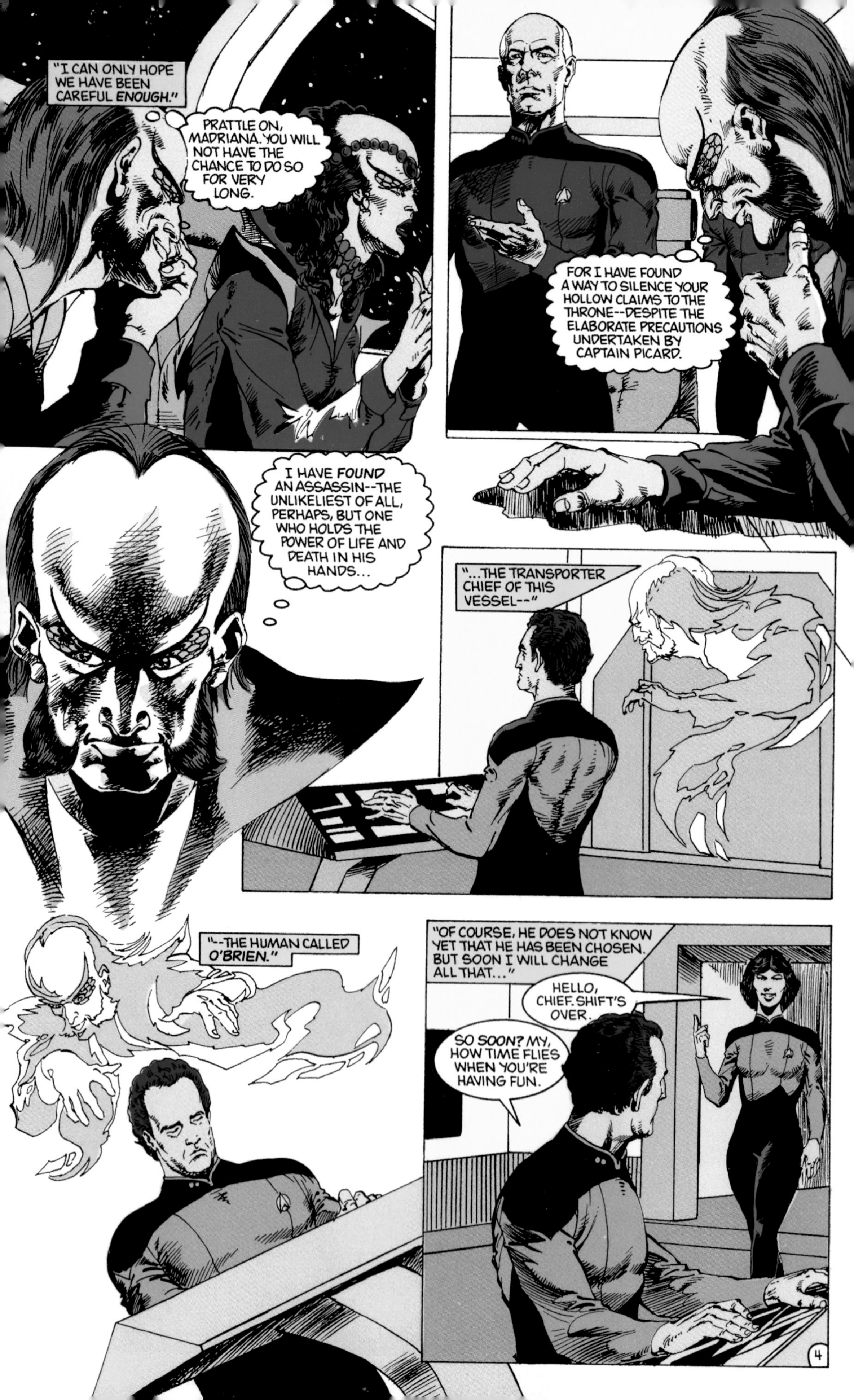
"I CAN ONLY HOPE WE HAVE BEEN CAREFUL ENOUGH."
PRATTLE ON, MADRIANA. YOU WILL NOT HAVE THE CHANCE TO DO SO FOR VERY LONG.
FOR I HAVE FOUND A WAY TO SILENCE YOUR HOLLOW CLAIMS TO THE THRONE--DESPITE THE ELABORATE PRECAUTIONS UNDERTAKEN BY CAPTAIN PICARD.
I HAVE FOUND AN ASSASSIN--THE UNLIKELIEST OF ALL, PERHAPS, BUT ONE WHO HOLDS THE POWER OF LIFE AND DEATH IN HIS HANDS...
"...THE TRANSPORTER CHIEF OF THIS VESSEL--"
"--THE HUMAN CALLED O'BRIEN."
"OF COURSE, HE DOES NOT KNOW YET THAT HE HAS BEEN CHOSEN. BUT SOON I WILL CHANGE ALL THAT..."
HELLO, CHIEF. SHIFT'S OVER.
SO SOON? MY, HOW TIME FLIES WHEN YOU'RE HAVING FUN.
4

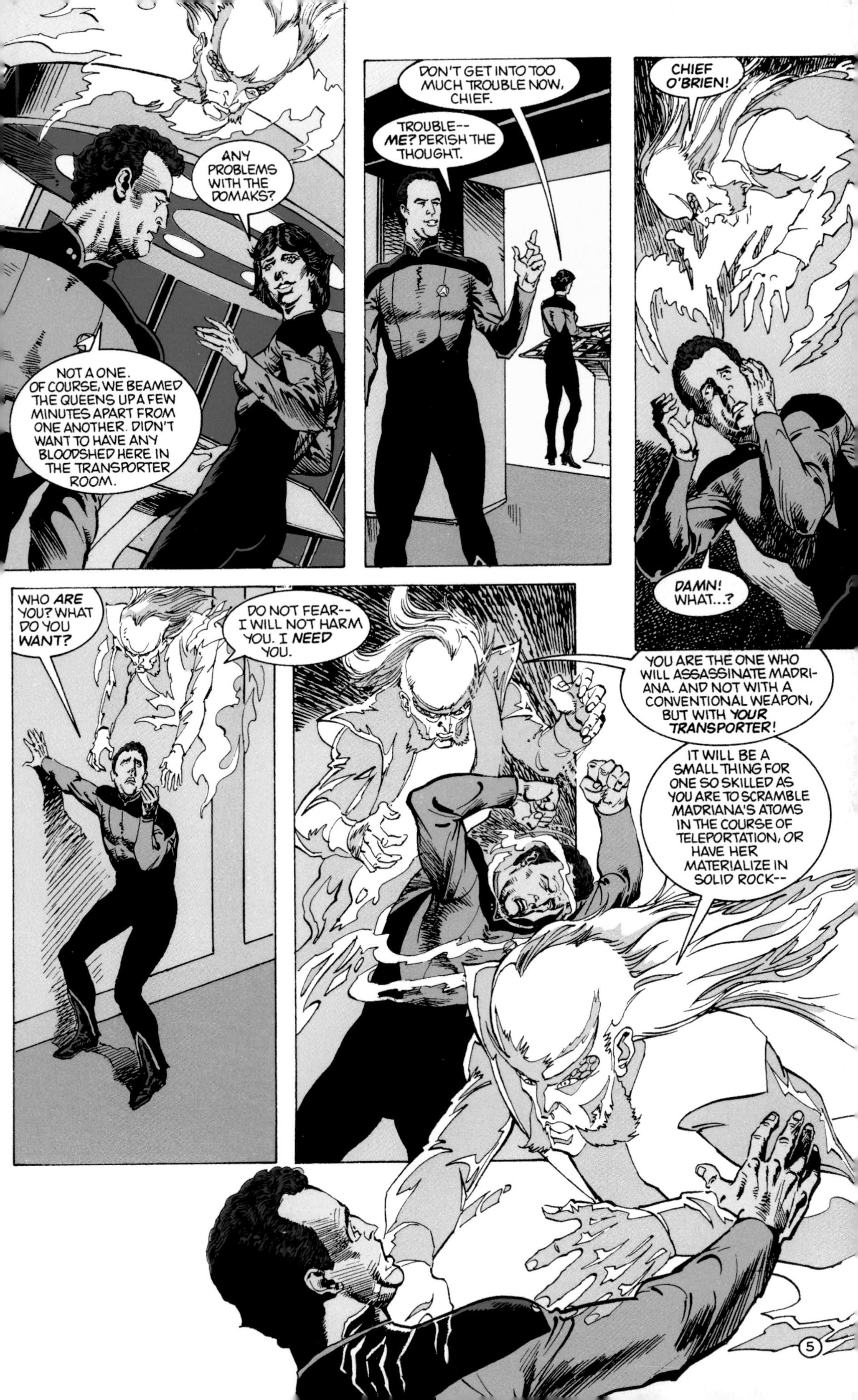
ANY PROBLEMS WITH THE DOMAKS?
NOT A ONE. OF COURSE, WE BEAMED THE QUEENS UP A FEW MINUTES APART FROM ONE ANOTHER. DIDN'T WANT TO HAVE ANY BLOODSHED HERE IN THE TRANSPORTER ROOM.
DON'T GET INTO TOO MUCH TROUBLE NOW, CHIEF.
TROUBLE-- *ME?* PERISH THE THOUGHT.
CHIEF O'BRIEN!
DAMN! WHAT...?
WHO *ARE* YOU? WHAT DO YOU *WANT?*
DO NOT FEAR-- I WILL NOT HARM YOU. I *NEED* YOU.
YOU ARE THE ONE WHO WILL ASSASSINATE MADRIANA. AND NOT WITH A CONVENTIONAL WEAPON, BUT WITH *YOUR TRANSPORTER!*
IT WILL BE A SMALL THING FOR ONE SO SKILLED AS YOU ARE TO SCRAMBLE MADRIANA'S ATOMS IN THE COURSE OF TELEPORTATION, OR HAVE HER MATERIALIZE IN SOLID ROCK--

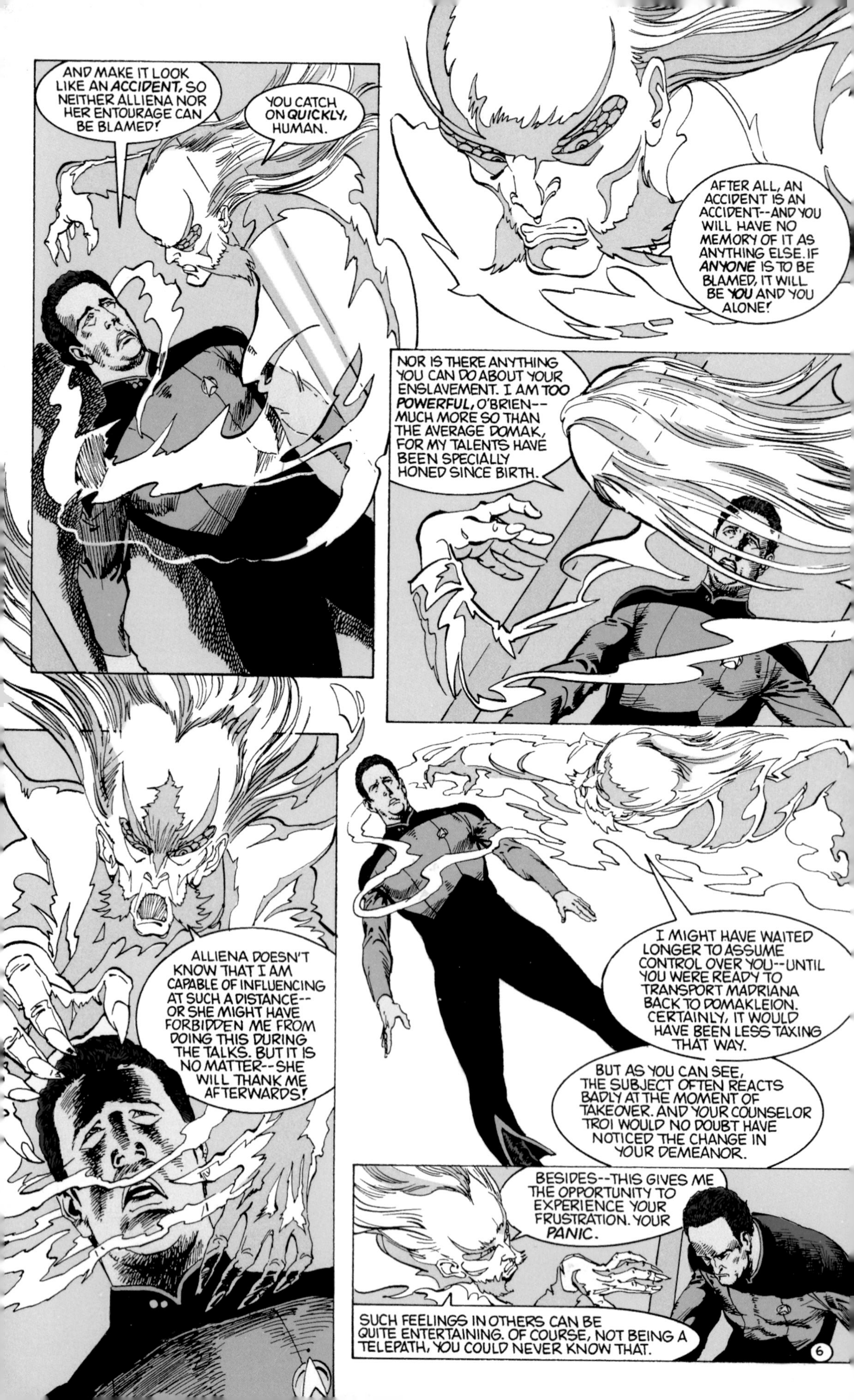
AND MAKE IT LOOK LIKE AN ACCIDENT, SO NEITHER ALLIENA NOR HER ENTOURAGE CAN BE BLAMED!
YOU CATCH ON QUICKLY, HUMAN.
AFTER ALL, AN ACCIDENT IS AN ACCIDENT--AND YOU WILL HAVE NO MEMORY OF IT AS ANYTHING ELSE. IF ANYONE IS TO BE BLAMED, IT WILL BE YOU AND YOU ALONE!
NOR IS THERE ANYTHING YOU CAN DO ABOUT YOUR ENSLAVEMENT. I AM TOO POWERFUL, O'BRIEN--MUCH MORE SO THAN THE AVERAGE DOMAK, FOR MY TALENTS HAVE BEEN SPECIALLY HONED SINCE BIRTH.
ALLIENA DOESN'T KNOW THAT I AM CAPABLE OF INFLUENCING AT SUCH A DISTANCE--OR SHE MIGHT HAVE FORBIDDEN ME FROM DOING THIS DURING THE TALKS. BUT IT IS NO MATTER--SHE WILL THANK ME AFTERWARDS!
I MIGHT HAVE WAITED LONGER TO ASSUME CONTROL OVER YOU--UNTIL YOU WERE READY TO TRANSPORT MADRIANA BACK TO DOMAKLEION. CERTAINLY, IT WOULD HAVE BEEN LESS TAXING THAT WAY.
BUT AS YOU CAN SEE, THE SUBJECT OFTEN REACTS BADLY AT THE MOMENT OF TAKEOVER. AND YOUR COUNSELOR TROI WOULD NO DOUBT HAVE NOTICED THE CHANGE IN YOUR DEMEANOR.
BESIDES--THIS GIVES ME THE OPPORTUNITY TO EXPERIENCE YOUR FRUSTRATION. YOUR PANIC.
SUCH FEELINGS IN OTHERS CAN BE QUITE ENTERTAINING. OF COURSE, NOT BEING A TELEPATH, YOU COULD NEVER KNOW THAT.

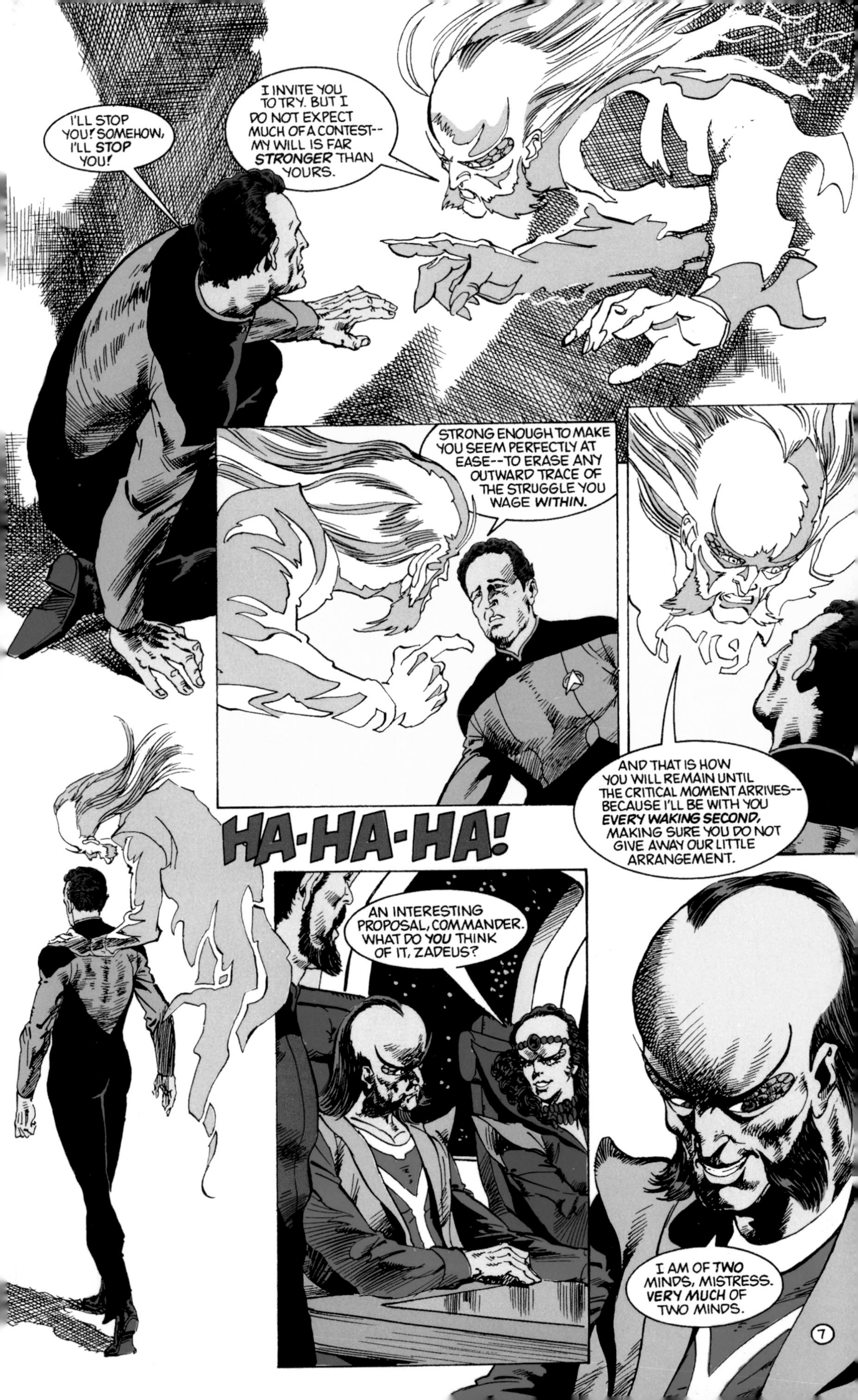
I'LL STOP YOU! SOMEHOW, I'LL STOP YOU!
I INVITE YOU TO TRY. BUT I DO NOT EXPECT MUCH OF A CONTEST-- MY WILL IS FAR STRONGER THAN YOURS.
STRONG ENOUGH TO MAKE YOU SEEM PERFECTLY AT EASE--TO ERASE ANY OUTWARD TRACE OF THE STRUGGLE YOU WAGE WITHIN.
AND THAT IS HOW YOU WILL REMAIN UNTIL THE CRITICAL MOMENT ARRIVES-- BECAUSE I'LL BE WITH YOU EVERY WAKING SECOND, MAKING SURE YOU DO NOT GIVE AWAY OUR LITTLE ARRANGEMENT.
HA-HA-HA!
AN INTERESTING PROPOSAL, COMMANDER. WHAT DO YOU THINK OF IT, ZADEUS?
I AM OF TWO MINDS, MISTRESS. VERY MUCH OF TWO MINDS.
7

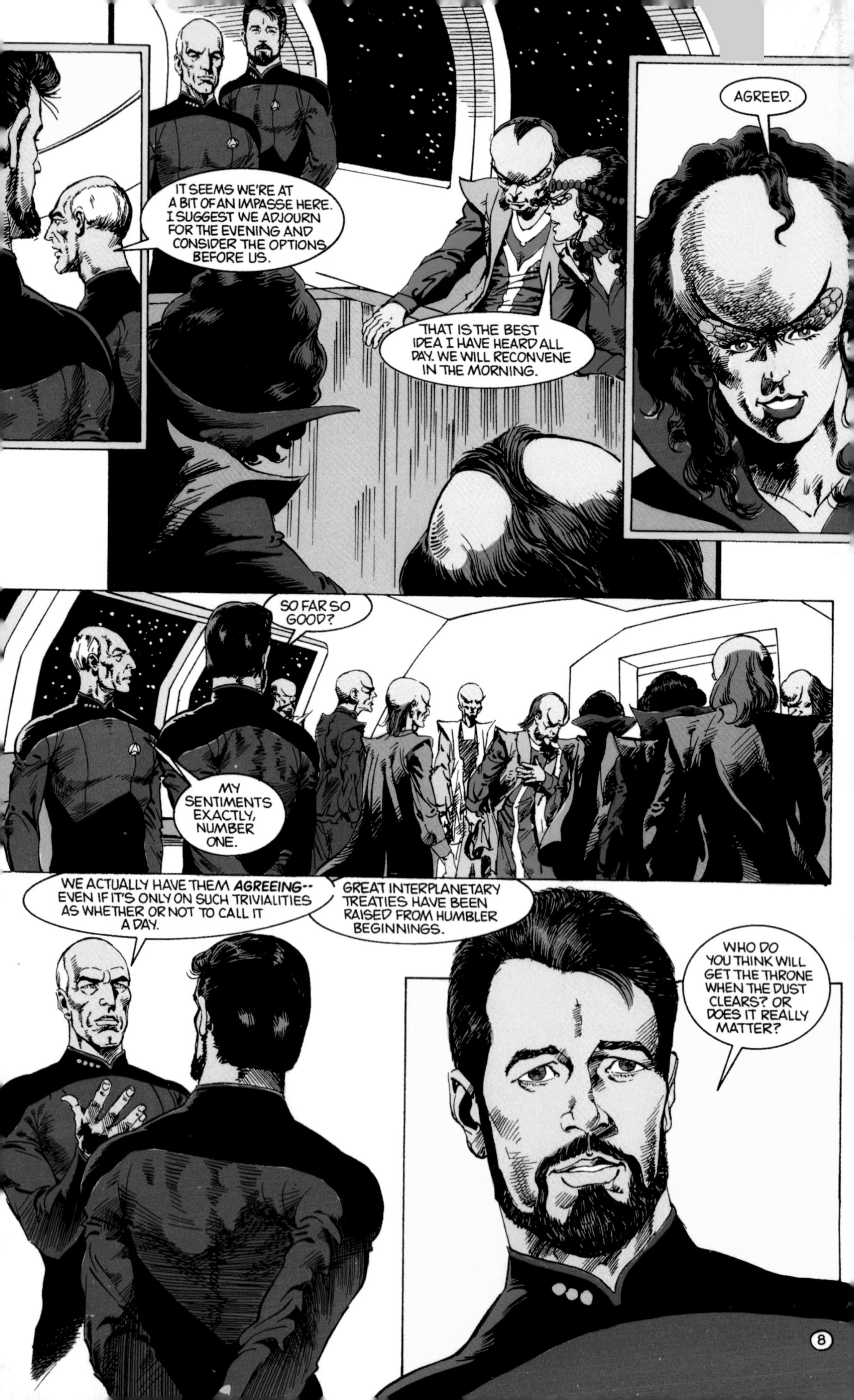
IT SEEMS WE'RE AT A BIT OF AN IMPASSE HERE. I SUGGEST WE ADJOURN FOR THE EVENING AND CONSIDER THE OPTIONS BEFORE US.
THAT IS THE BEST IDEA I HAVE HEARD ALL DAY. WE WILL RECONVENE IN THE MORNING.
AGREED.
SO FAR SO GOOD?
MY SENTIMENTS EXACTLY, NUMBER ONE.
WE ACTUALLY HAVE THEM AGREEING-- EVEN IF IT'S ONLY ON SUCH TRIVIALITIES AS WHETHER OR NOT TO CALL IT A DAY.
GREAT INTERPLANETARY TREATIES HAVE BEEN RAISED FROM HUMBLER BEGINNINGS.
WHO DO YOU THINK WILL GET THE THRONE WHEN THE DUST CLEARS? OR DOES IT REALLY MATTER?
8

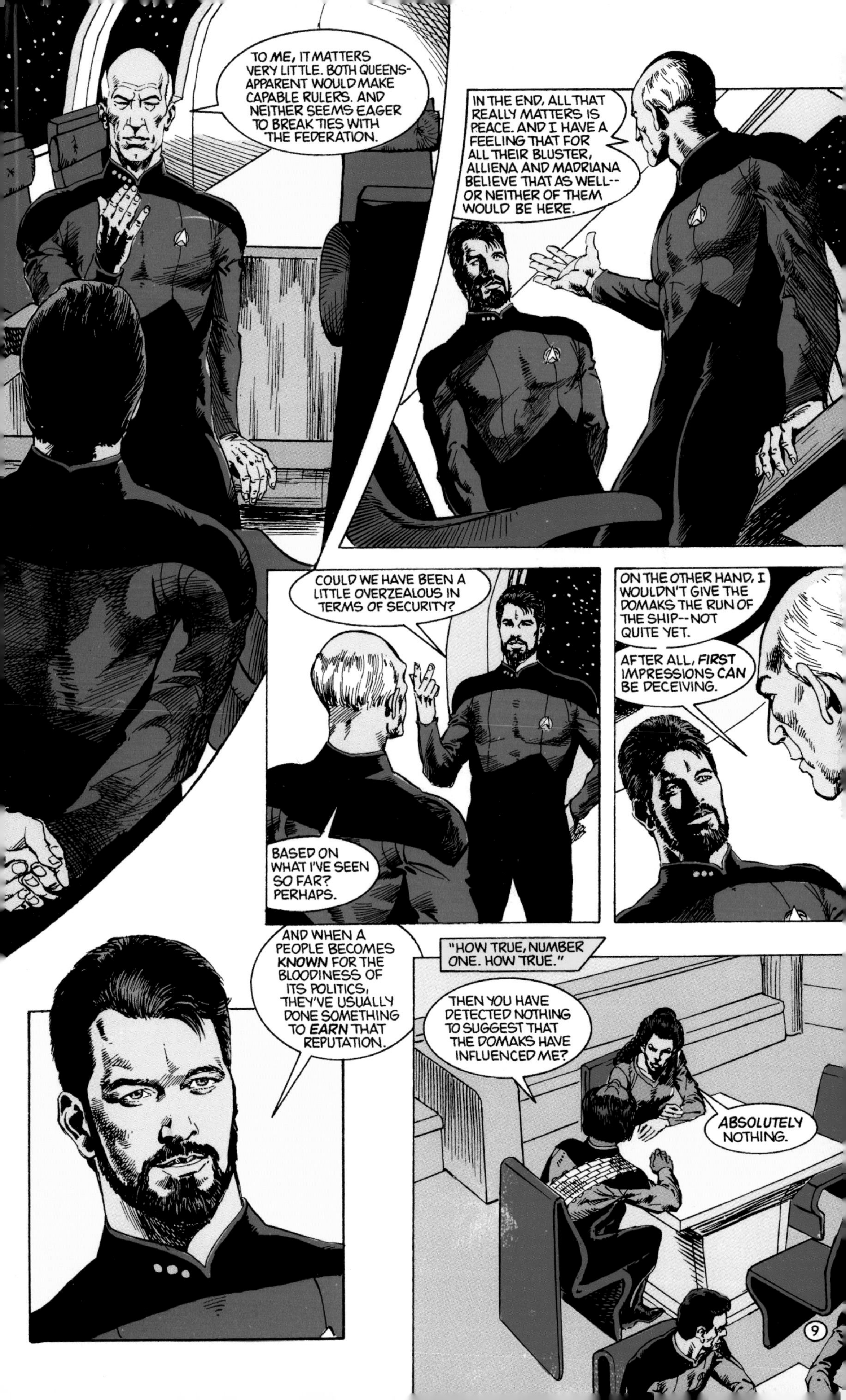

TO *ME*, IT MATTERS VERY LITTLE. BOTH QUEENS-APPARENT WOULD MAKE CAPABLE RULERS. AND NEITHER SEEMS EAGER TO BREAK TIES WITH THE FEDERATION.
IN THE END, ALL THAT REALLY MATTERS IS PEACE. AND I HAVE A FEELING THAT FOR ALL THEIR BLUSTER, ALLIENA AND MADRIANA BELIEVE THAT AS WELL-- OR NEITHER OF THEM WOULD BE HERE.
COULD WE HAVE BEEN A LITTLE OVERZEALOUS IN TERMS OF SECURITY?
BASED ON WHAT I'VE SEEN SO FAR? PERHAPS.
ON THE OTHER HAND, I WOULDN'T GIVE THE DOMAKS THE RUN OF THE SHIP--NOT QUITE YET.
AFTER ALL, *FIRST* IMPRESSIONS *CAN* BE DECEIVING.
AND WHEN A PEOPLE BECOMES *KNOWN* FOR THE BLOODINESS OF ITS POLITICS, THEY'VE USUALLY DONE SOMETHING TO *EARN* THAT REPUTATION.
"HOW TRUE, NUMBER ONE. HOW TRUE."
THEN YOU HAVE DETECTED NOTHING TO SUGGEST THAT THE DOMAKS HAVE INFLUENCED ME?
ABSOLUTELY NOTHING.

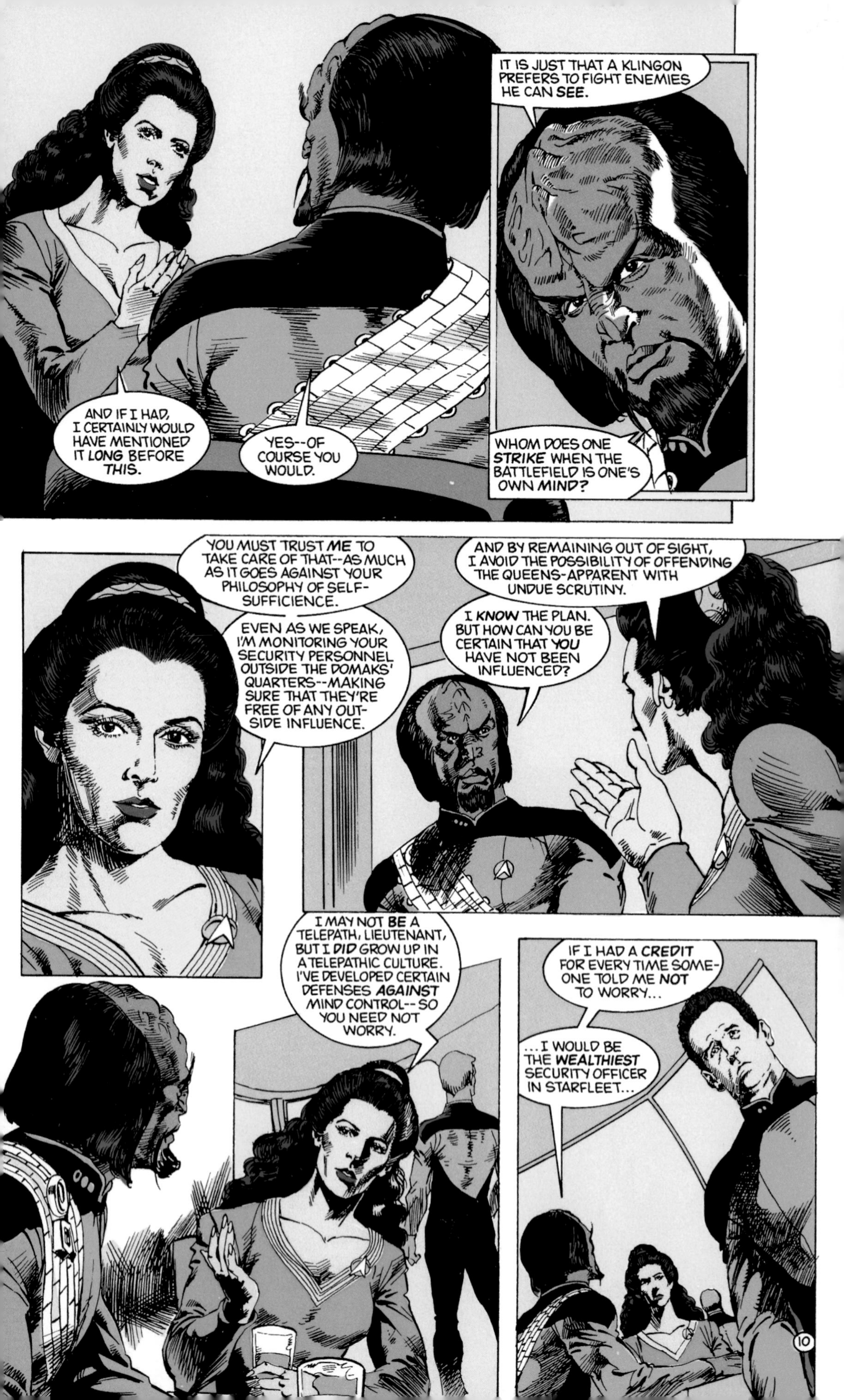
AND IF I HAD, I CERTAINLY WOULD HAVE MENTIONED IT LONG BEFORE THIS.
YES--OF COURSE YOU WOULD.
IT IS JUST THAT A KLINGON PREFERS TO FIGHT ENEMIES HE CAN SEE.
WHOM DOES ONE STRIKE WHEN THE BATTLEFIELD IS ONE'S OWN MIND?
YOU MUST TRUST ME TO TAKE CARE OF THAT--AS MUCH AS IT GOES AGAINST YOUR PHILOSOPHY OF SELF-SUFFICIENCE.
EVEN AS WE SPEAK, I'M MONITORING YOUR SECURITY PERSONNEL OUTSIDE THE DOMAKS' QUARTERS--MAKING SURE THAT THEY'RE FREE OF ANY OUTSIDE INFLUENCE.
AND BY REMAINING OUT OF SIGHT, I AVOID THE POSSIBILITY OF OFFENDING THE QUEENS-APPARENT WITH UNDUE SCRUTINY.
I KNOW THE PLAN. BUT HOW CAN YOU BE CERTAIN THAT YOU HAVE NOT BEEN INFLUENCED?
I MAY NOT BE A TELEPATH, LIEUTENANT, BUT I DID GROW UP IN A TELEPATHIC CULTURE. I'VE DEVELOPED CERTAIN DEFENSES AGAINST MIND CONTROL--SO YOU NEED NOT WORRY.
IF I HAD A CREDIT FOR EVERY TIME SOMEONE TOLD ME NOT TO WORRY...
...I WOULD BE THE WEALTHIEST SECURITY OFFICER IN STARFLEET...
10

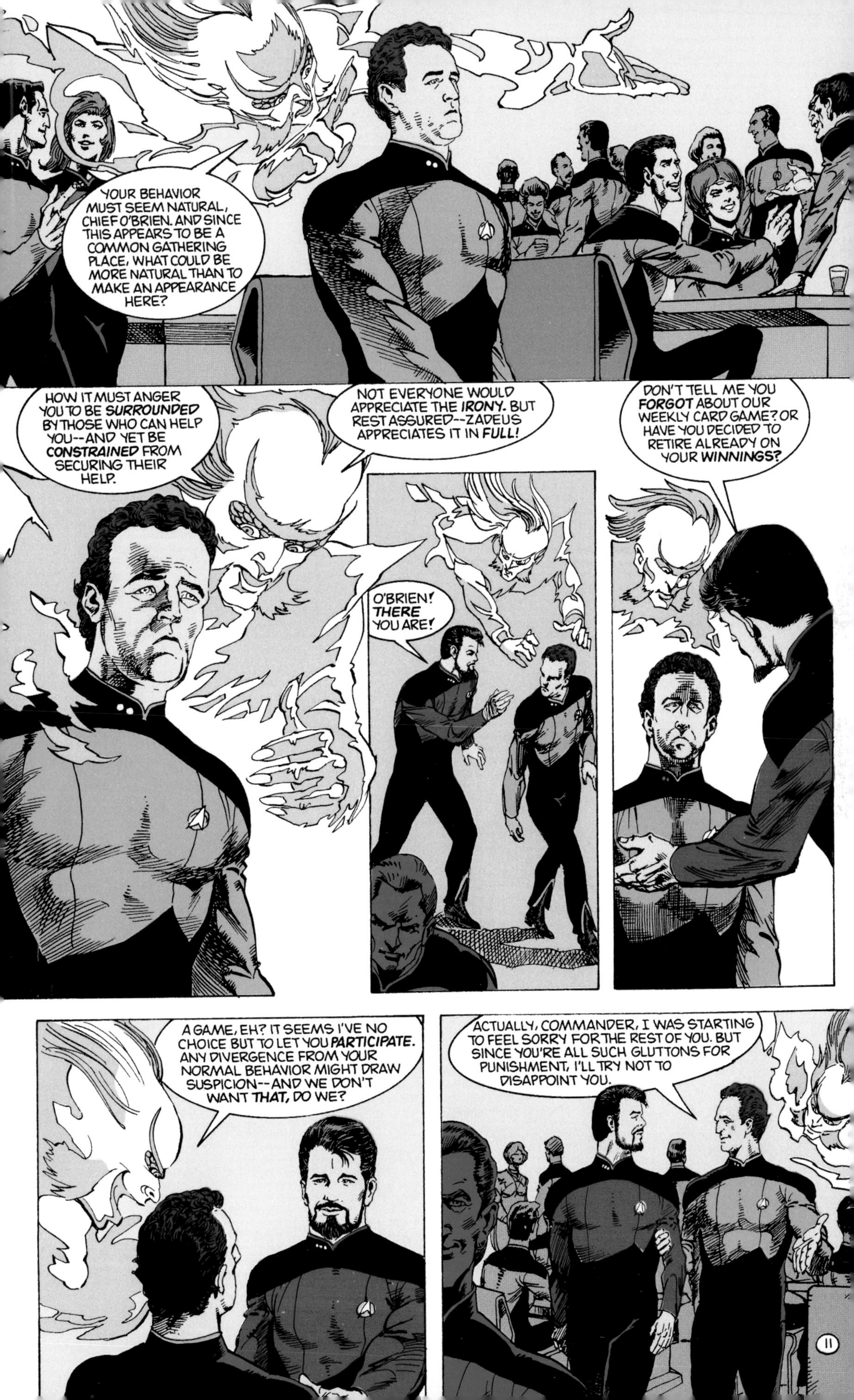
YOUR BEHAVIOR MUST SEEM NATURAL, CHIEF O'BRIEN. AND SINCE THIS APPEARS TO BE A COMMON GATHERING PLACE, WHAT COULD BE MORE NATURAL THAN TO MAKE AN APPEARANCE HERE?
HOW IT MUST ANGER YOU TO BE SURROUNDED BY THOSE WHO CAN HELP YOU--AND YET BE CONSTRAINED FROM SECURING THEIR HELP.
NOT EVERYONE WOULD APPRECIATE THE IRONY. BUT REST ASSURED--ZADEUS APPRECIATES IT IN FULL!
O'BRIEN! THERE YOU ARE!
DON'T TELL ME YOU FORGOT ABOUT OUR WEEKLY CARD GAME? OR HAVE YOU DECIDED TO RETIRE ALREADY ON YOUR WINNINGS?
A GAME, EH? IT SEEMS I'VE NO CHOICE BUT TO LET YOU PARTICIPATE. ANY DIVERGENCE FROM YOUR NORMAL BEHAVIOR MIGHT DRAW SUSPICION--AND WE DON'T WANT THAT, DO WE?
ACTUALLY, COMMANDER, I WAS STARTING TO FEEL SORRY FOR THE REST OF YOU. BUT SINCE YOU'RE ALL SUCH GLUTTONS FOR PUNISHMENT, I'LL TRY NOT TO DISAPPOINT YOU.
11

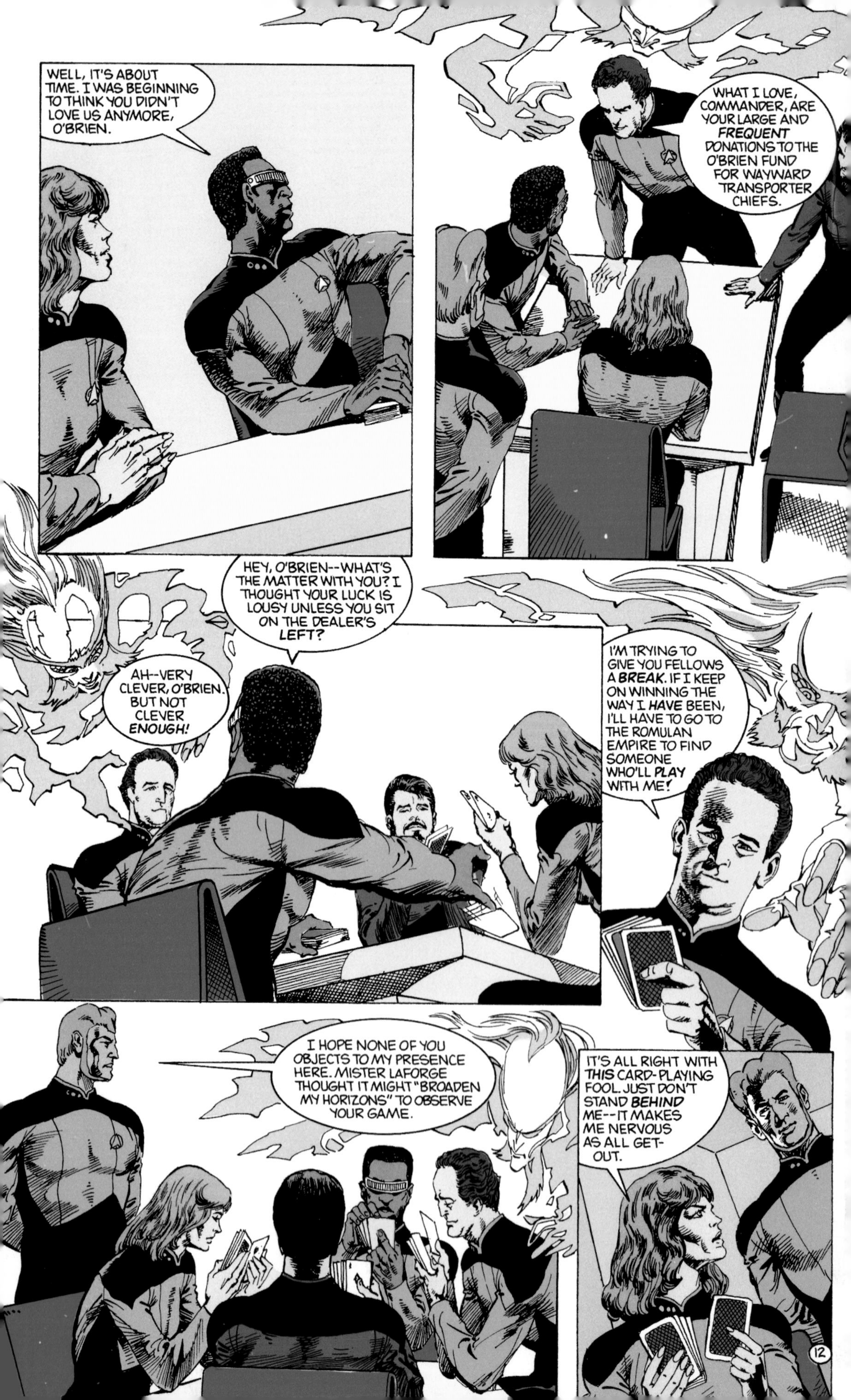

WELL, IT'S ABOUT TIME. I WAS BEGINNING TO THINK YOU DIDN'T LOVE US ANYMORE, O'BRIEN.
WHAT I LOVE, COMMANDER, ARE YOUR LARGE AND **FREQUENT** DONATIONS TO THE O'BRIEN FUND FOR WAYWARD TRANSPORTER CHIEFS.
AH--VERY CLEVER, O'BRIEN. BUT NOT CLEVER **ENOUGH!**
HEY, O'BRIEN--WHAT'S THE MATTER WITH YOU? I THOUGHT YOUR LUCK IS LOUSY UNLESS YOU SIT ON THE DEALER'S **LEFT?**
I'M TRYING TO GIVE YOU FELLOWS A **BREAK**. IF I KEEP ON WINNING THE WAY I **HAVE** BEEN, I'LL HAVE TO GO TO THE ROMULAN EMPIRE TO FIND SOMEONE WHO'LL **PLAY** WITH ME!
I HOPE NONE OF YOU OBJECTS TO MY PRESENCE HERE. MISTER LAFORGE THOUGHT IT MIGHT "BROADEN MY HORIZONS" TO OBSERVE YOUR GAME.
IT'S ALL RIGHT WITH **THIS** CARD-PLAYING FOOL. JUST DON'T STAND **BEHIND** ME--IT MAKES ME NERVOUS AS ALL GET-OUT.

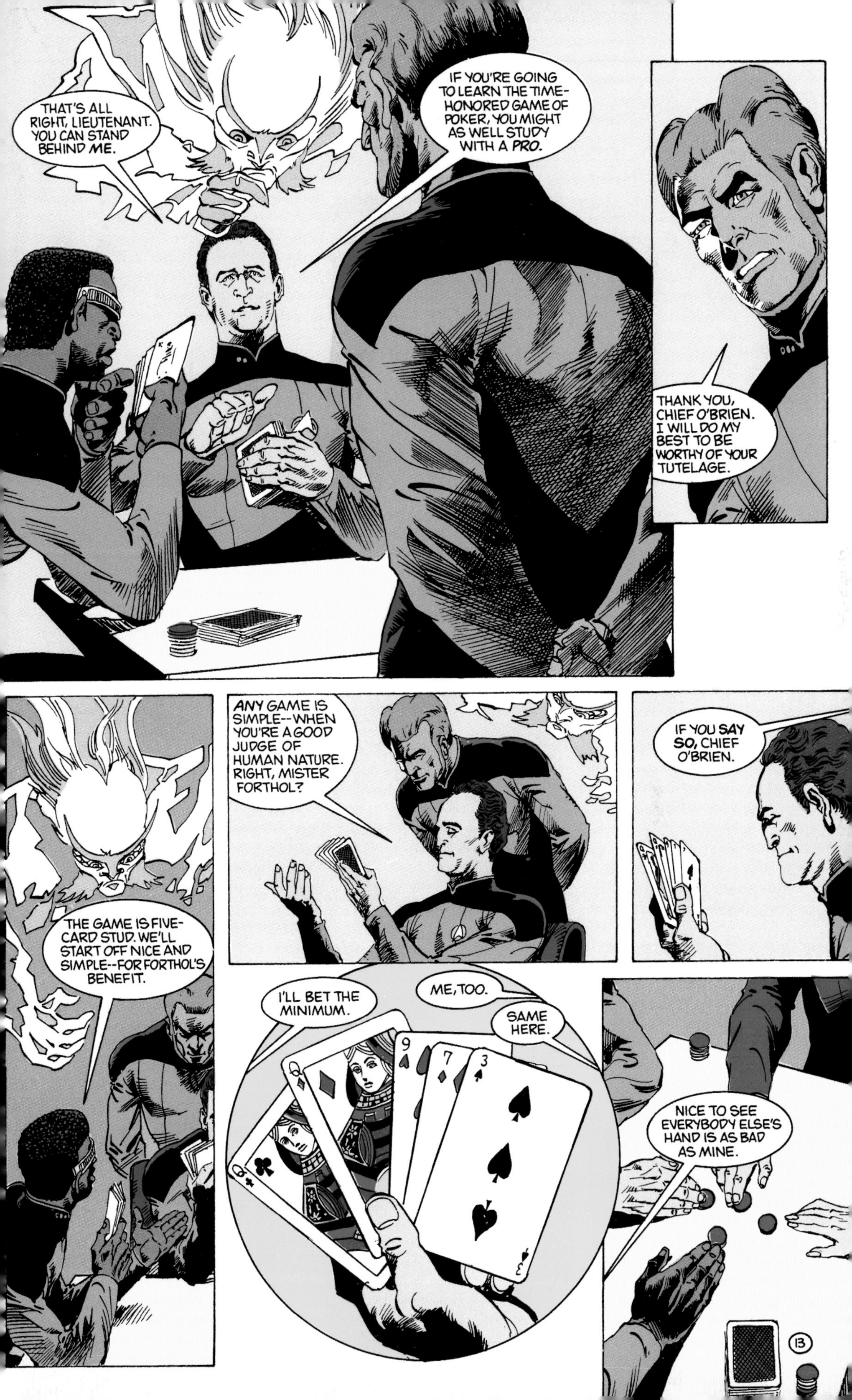

THAT'S ALL RIGHT, LIEUTENANT. YOU CAN STAND BEHIND ME.
IF YOU'RE GOING TO LEARN THE TIME-HONORED GAME OF POKER, YOU MIGHT AS WELL STUDY WITH A PRO.
THANK YOU, CHIEF O'BRIEN. I WILL DO MY BEST TO BE WORTHY OF YOUR TUTELAGE.
THE GAME IS FIVE-CARD STUD. WE'LL START OFF NICE AND SIMPLE--FOR FORTHOL'S BENEFIT.
ANY GAME IS SIMPLE--WHEN YOU'RE A GOOD JUDGE OF HUMAN NATURE. RIGHT, MISTER FORTHOL?
IF YOU SAY SO, CHIEF O'BRIEN.
I'LL BET THE MINIMUM.
ME, TOO.
SAME HERE.
NICE TO SEE EVERYBODY ELSE'S HAND IS AS BAD AS MINE.

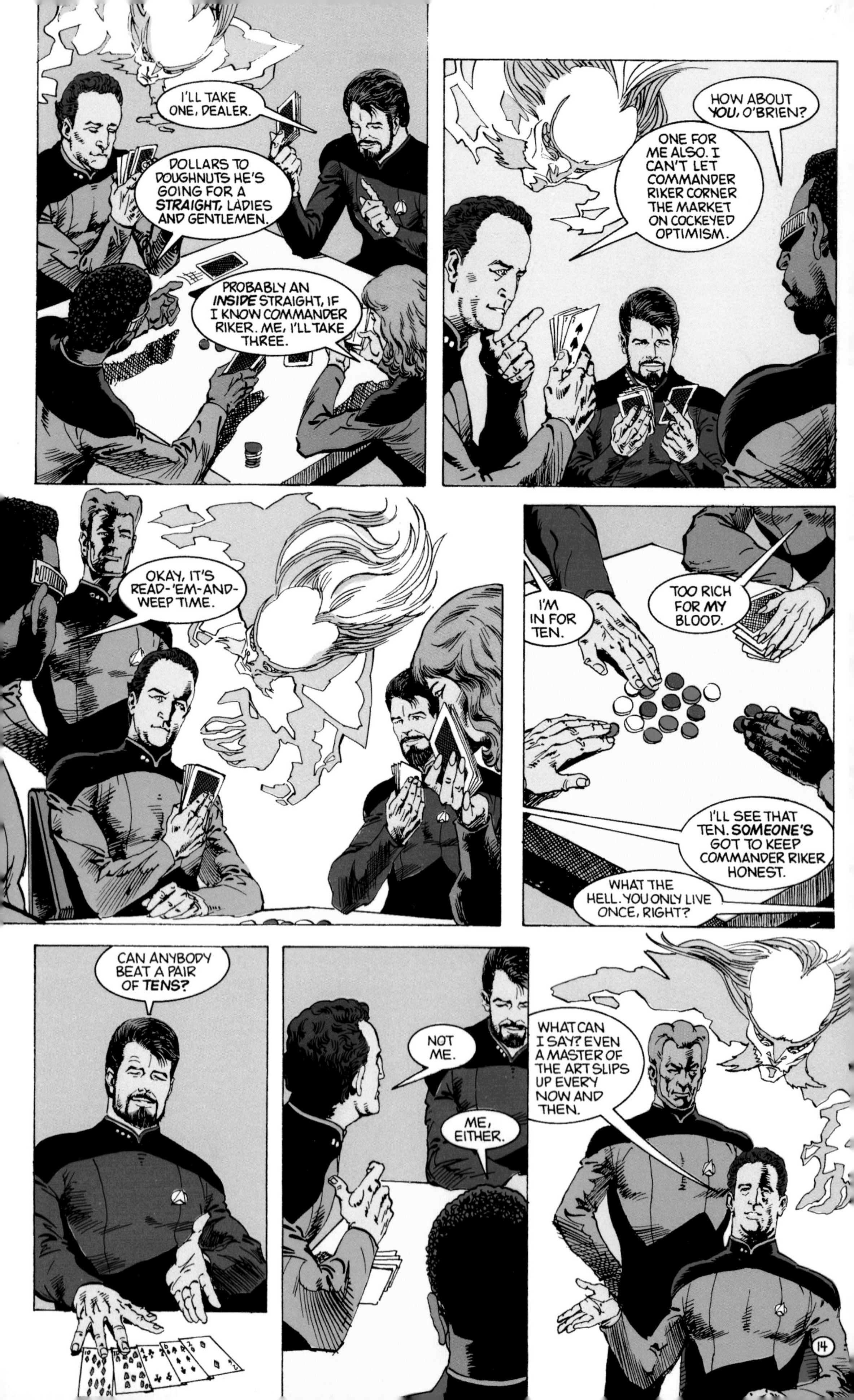
I'LL TAKE ONE, DEALER.
DOLLARS TO DOUGHNUTS HE'S GOING FOR A STRAIGHT, LADIES AND GENTLEMEN.
PROBABLY AN INSIDE STRAIGHT, IF I KNOW COMMANDER RIKER. ME, I'LL TAKE THREE.
HOW ABOUT YOU, O'BRIEN?
ONE FOR ME ALSO. I CAN'T LET COMMANDER RIKER CORNER THE MARKET ON COCKEYED OPTIMISM.
OKAY, IT'S READ-'EM-AND-WEEP TIME.
I'M IN FOR TEN.
TOO RICH FOR MY BLOOD.
I'LL SEE THAT TEN. SOMEONE'S GOT TO KEEP COMMANDER RIKER HONEST.
WHAT THE HELL. YOU ONLY LIVE ONCE, RIGHT?
CAN ANYBODY BEAT A PAIR OF TENS?
NOT ME.
ME, EITHER.
WHAT CAN I SAY? EVEN A MASTER OF THE ART SLIPS UP EVERY NOW AND THEN.
14

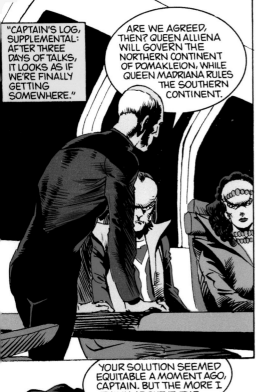

"CAPTAIN'S LOG, SUPPLEMENTAL: AFTER THREE DAYS OF TALKS, IT LOOKS AS IF WE'RE FINALLY GETTING SOMEWHERE."

ARE WE AGREED, THEN? QUEEN ALLIENA WILL GOVERN THE NORTHERN CONTINENT OF DOMAKLEION, WHILE QUEEN MADRIANA RULES THE SOUTHERN CONTINENT.

IF THIS IS SATISFACTORY, I CAN SAY ON BEHALF OF THE FEDERATION THAT WE ARE PREPARED TO ESTABLISH DIPLOMATIC TIES WITH *BOTH* NATIONS -- IF YOU SO WISH.

YOUR SOLUTION SEEMED EQUITABLE A MOMENT AGO, CAPTAIN. BUT THE MORE I THINK ABOUT IT, THE LESS I LIKE IT.

I TOO HAVE SECOND THOUGHTS. IS DOMAKLEION A MELON, THAT IT CAN SO CASUALLY BE CUT IN HALF? WE NEED TIME TO EXAMINE THE RAMIFICATIONS.

AS YOU WISH, QUEEN ALLIENA-- QUEEN MADRIANA. UNDER THE CIRCUMSTANCES, MIGHT I SUGGEST THAT YOU SUSPEND HOSTILITIES PENDING ANOTHER MEETING -- ON THIS OR SOME OTHER SHIP IN, SAY, TWO WEEKS' TIME?

DONE. WE HAVE ALREADY ACCOMPLISHED MORE THAN I THOUGHT POSSIBLE.

YES. MY SISTER AND I HAVE *MUCH* TO THINK ABOUT.

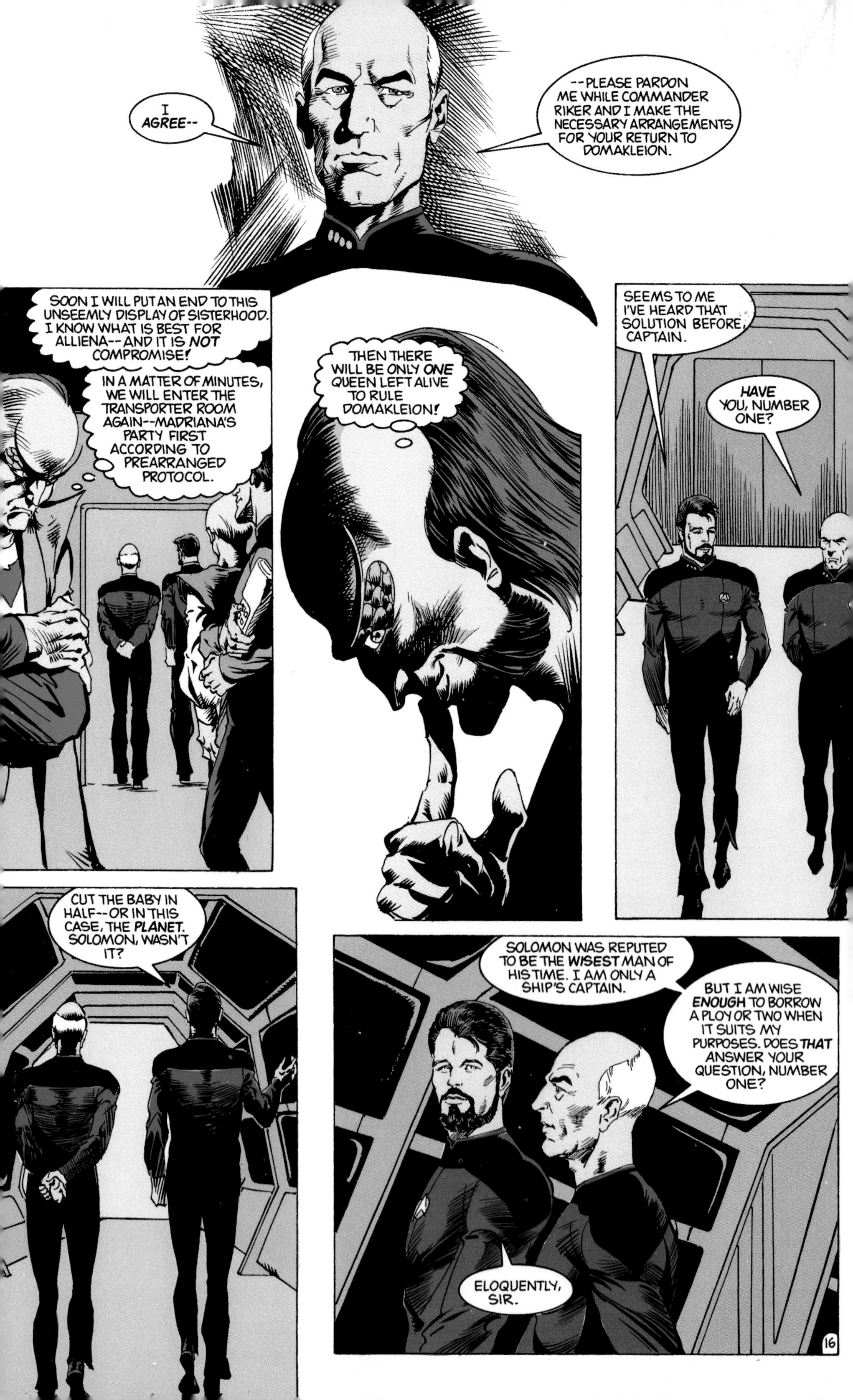
I AGREE--
--PLEASE PARDON ME WHILE COMMANDER RIKER AND I MAKE THE NECESSARY ARRANGEMENTS FOR YOUR RETURN TO DOMAKLEION.
SOON I WILL PUT AN END TO THIS UNSEEMLY DISPLAY OF SISTERHOOD. I KNOW WHAT IS BEST FOR ALLIENA-- AND IT IS NOT COMPROMISE!
IN A MATTER OF MINUTES, WE WILL ENTER THE TRANSPORTER ROOM AGAIN--MADRIANA'S PARTY FIRST ACCORDING TO PREARRANGED PROTOCOL.
THEN THERE WILL BE ONLY ONE QUEEN LEFT ALIVE TO RULE DOMAKLEION!
SEEMS TO ME I'VE HEARD THAT SOLUTION BEFORE, CAPTAIN.
HAVE YOU, NUMBER ONE?
CUT THE BABY IN HALF--OR IN THIS CASE, THE PLANET. SOLOMON, WASN'T IT?
SOLOMON WAS REPUTED TO BE THE WISEST MAN OF HIS TIME. I AM ONLY A SHIP'S CAPTAIN.
BUT I AM WISE ENOUGH TO BORROW A PLOY OR TWO WHEN IT SUITS MY PURPOSES. DOES THAT ANSWER YOUR QUESTION, NUMBER ONE?
ELOQUENTLY, SIR.
16

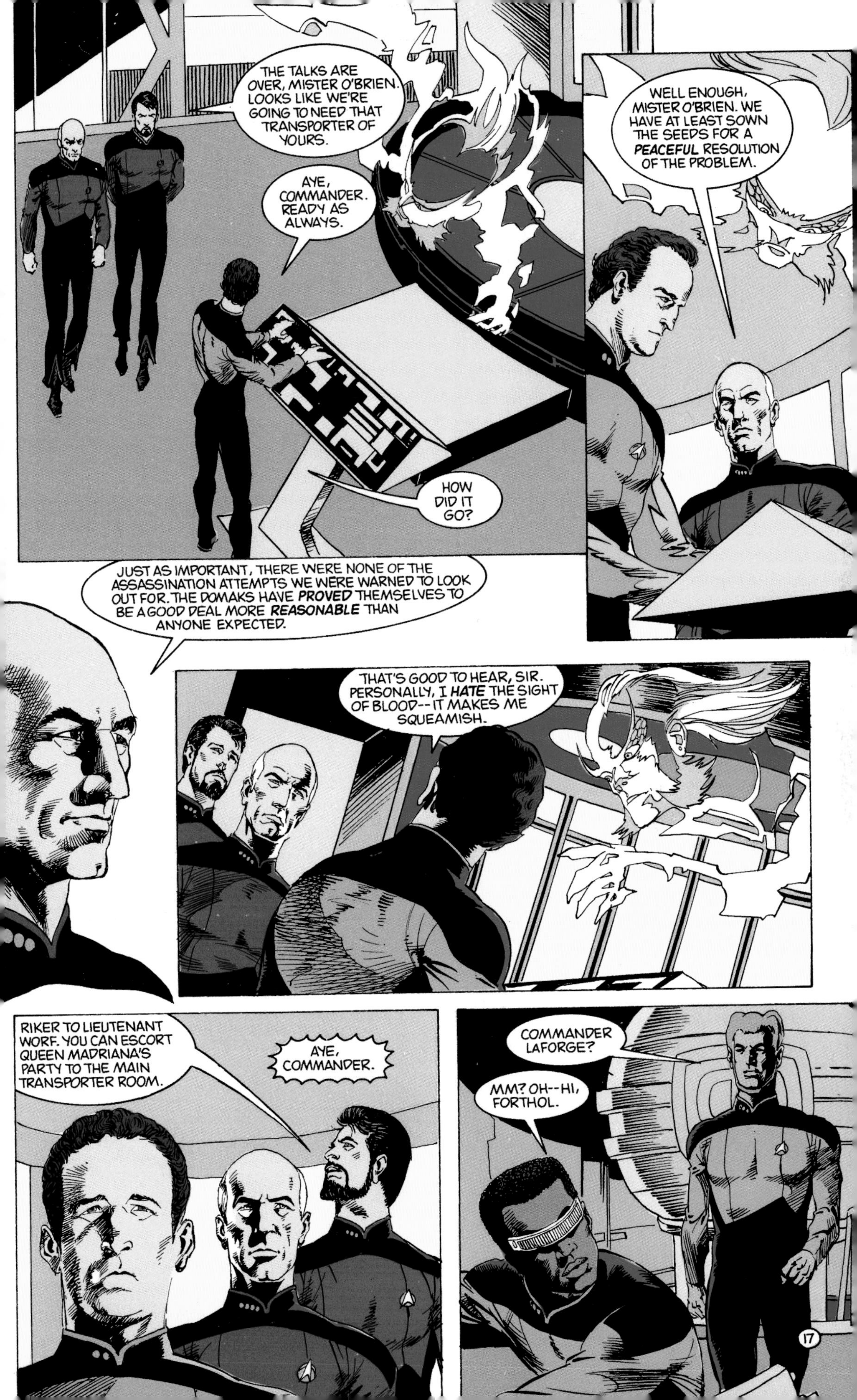
THE TALKS ARE OVER, MISTER O'BRIEN. LOOKS LIKE WE'RE GOING TO NEED THAT TRANSPORTER OF YOURS.
AYE, COMMANDER. READY AS ALWAYS.
HOW DID IT GO?
WELL ENOUGH, MISTER O'BRIEN. WE HAVE AT LEAST SOWN THE SEEDS FOR A PEACEFUL RESOLUTION OF THE PROBLEM.
JUST AS IMPORTANT, THERE WERE NONE OF THE ASSASSINATION ATTEMPTS WE WERE WARNED TO LOOK OUT FOR. THE DOMAKS HAVE PROVED THEMSELVES TO BE A GOOD DEAL MORE REASONABLE THAN ANYONE EXPECTED.
THAT'S GOOD TO HEAR, SIR. PERSONALLY, I HATE THE SIGHT OF BLOOD--IT MAKES ME SQUEAMISH.
RIKER TO LIEUTENANT WORF. YOU CAN ESCORT QUEEN MADRIANA'S PARTY TO THE MAIN TRANSPORTER ROOM.
AYE, COMMANDER.
COMMANDER LAFORGE?
MM? OH--HI, FORTHOL.

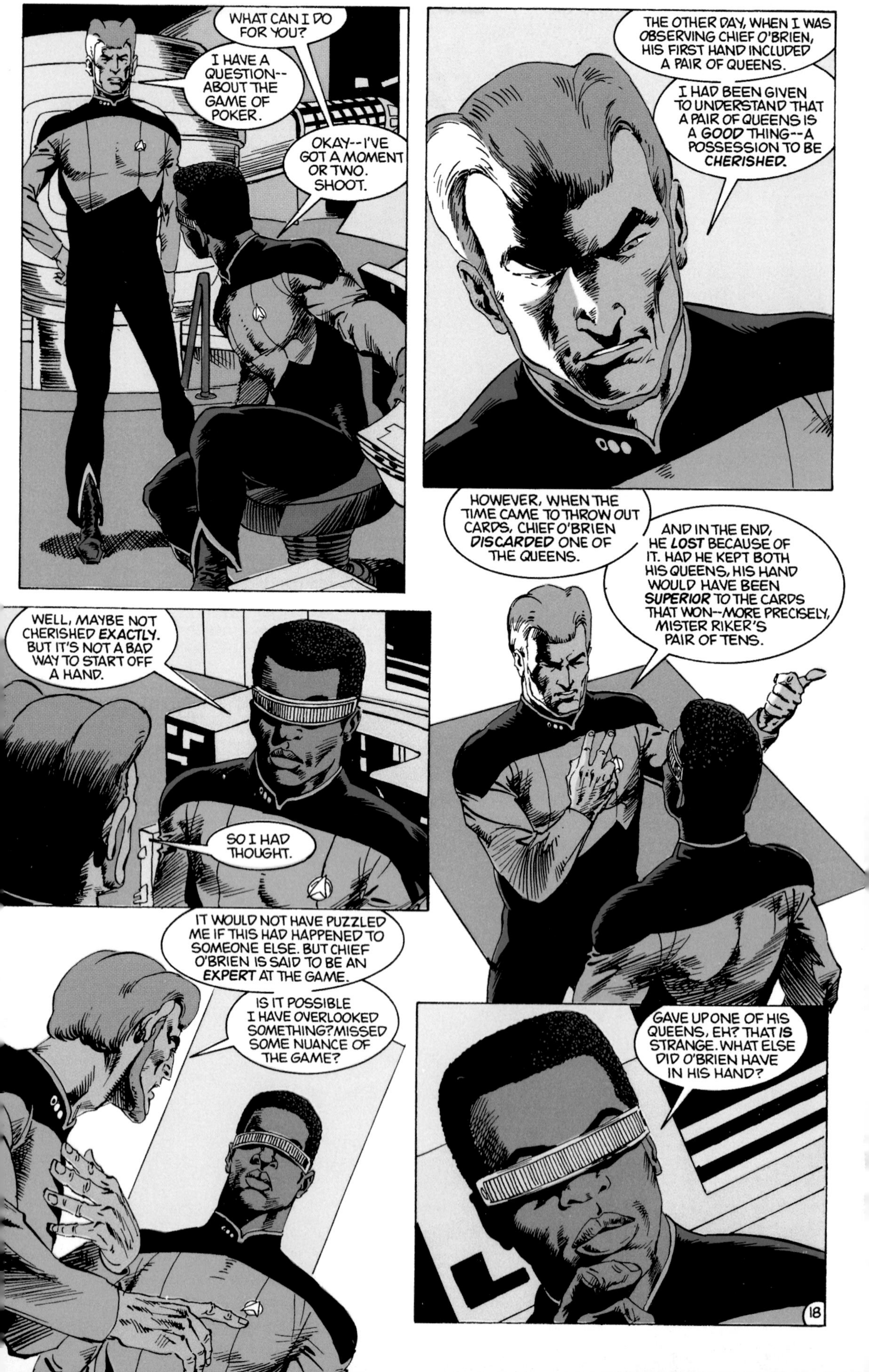
WHAT CAN I DO FOR YOU?
I HAVE A QUESTION-- ABOUT THE GAME OF POKER.
OKAY--I'VE GOT A MOMENT OR TWO. SHOOT.
THE OTHER DAY, WHEN I WAS OBSERVING CHIEF O'BRIEN, HIS FIRST HAND INCLUDED A PAIR OF QUEENS.
I HAD BEEN GIVEN TO UNDERSTAND THAT A PAIR OF QUEENS IS A GOOD THING--A POSSESSION TO BE CHERISHED.
WELL, MAYBE NOT CHERISHED EXACTLY. BUT IT'S NOT A BAD WAY TO START OFF A HAND.
SO I HAD THOUGHT.
HOWEVER, WHEN THE TIME CAME TO THROW OUT CARDS, CHIEF O'BRIEN DISCARDED ONE OF THE QUEENS.
AND IN THE END, HE LOST BECAUSE OF IT. HAD HE KEPT BOTH HIS QUEENS, HIS HAND WOULD HAVE BEEN SUPERIOR TO THE CARDS THAT WON--MORE PRECISELY, MISTER RIKER'S PAIR OF TENS.
IT WOULD NOT HAVE PUZZLED ME IF THIS HAD HAPPENED TO SOMEONE ELSE. BUT CHIEF O'BRIEN IS SAID TO BE AN EXPERT AT THE GAME.
IS IT POSSIBLE I HAVE OVERLOOKED SOMETHING? MISSED SOME NUANCE OF THE GAME?
GAVE UP ONE OF HIS QUEENS, EH? THAT IS STRANGE. WHAT ELSE DID O'BRIEN HAVE IN HIS HAND?
18

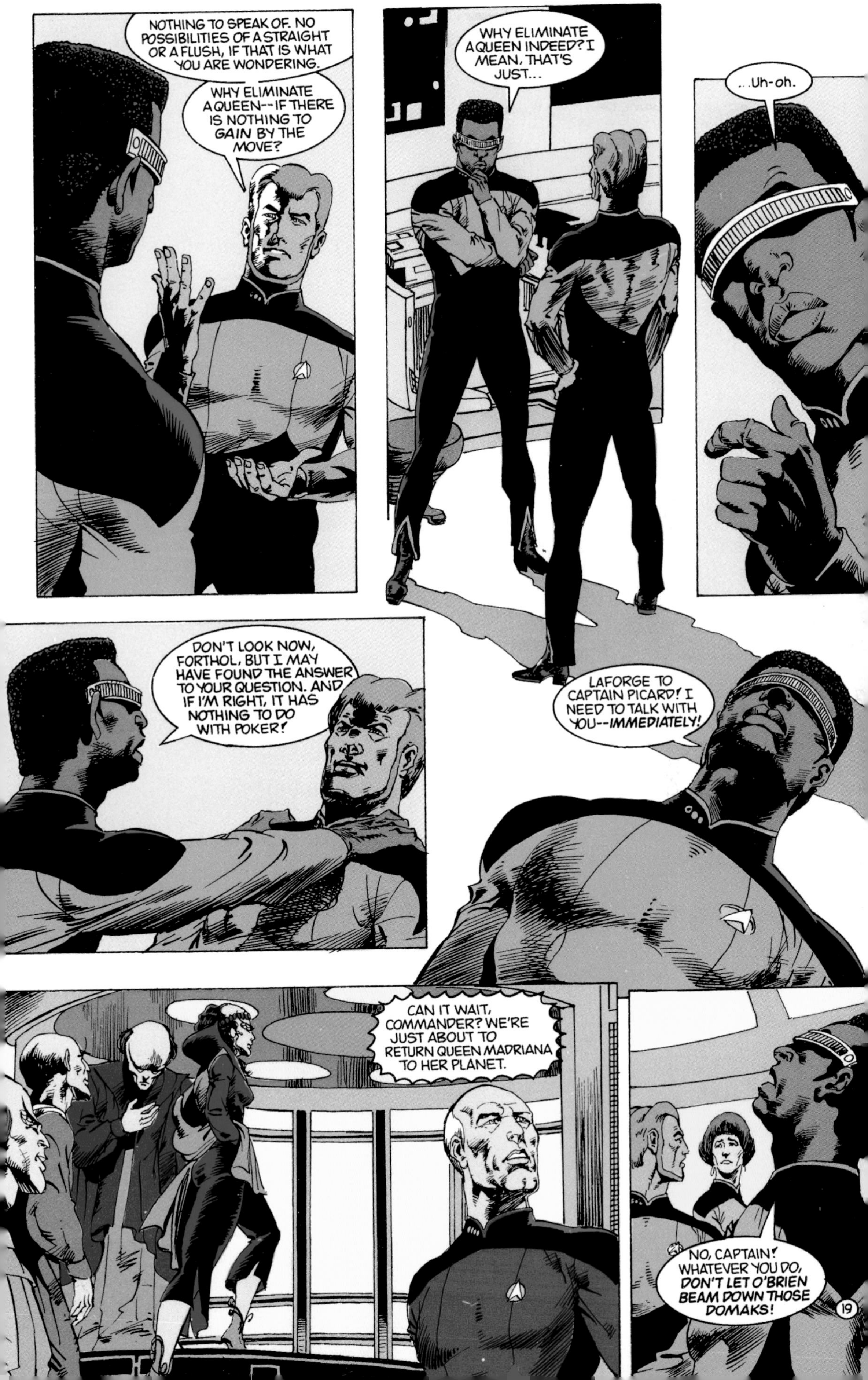
NOTHING TO SPEAK OF. NO POSSIBILITIES OF A STRAIGHT OR A FLUSH, IF THAT IS WHAT YOU ARE WONDERING.
WHY ELIMINATE A QUEEN--IF THERE IS NOTHING TO GAIN BY THE MOVE?
WHY ELIMINATE A QUEEN INDEED? I MEAN, THAT'S JUST...
...Uh-oh.
DON'T LOOK NOW, FORTHOL, BUT I MAY HAVE FOUND THE ANSWER TO YOUR QUESTION. AND IF I'M RIGHT, IT HAS NOTHING TO DO WITH POKER!
LAFORGE TO CAPTAIN PICARD! I NEED TO TALK WITH YOU--IMMEDIATELY!
CAN IT WAIT, COMMANDER? WE'RE JUST ABOUT TO RETURN QUEEN MADRIANA TO HER PLANET.
NO, CAPTAIN! WHATEVER YOU DO, DON'T LET O'BRIEN BEAM DOWN THOSE DOMAKS!

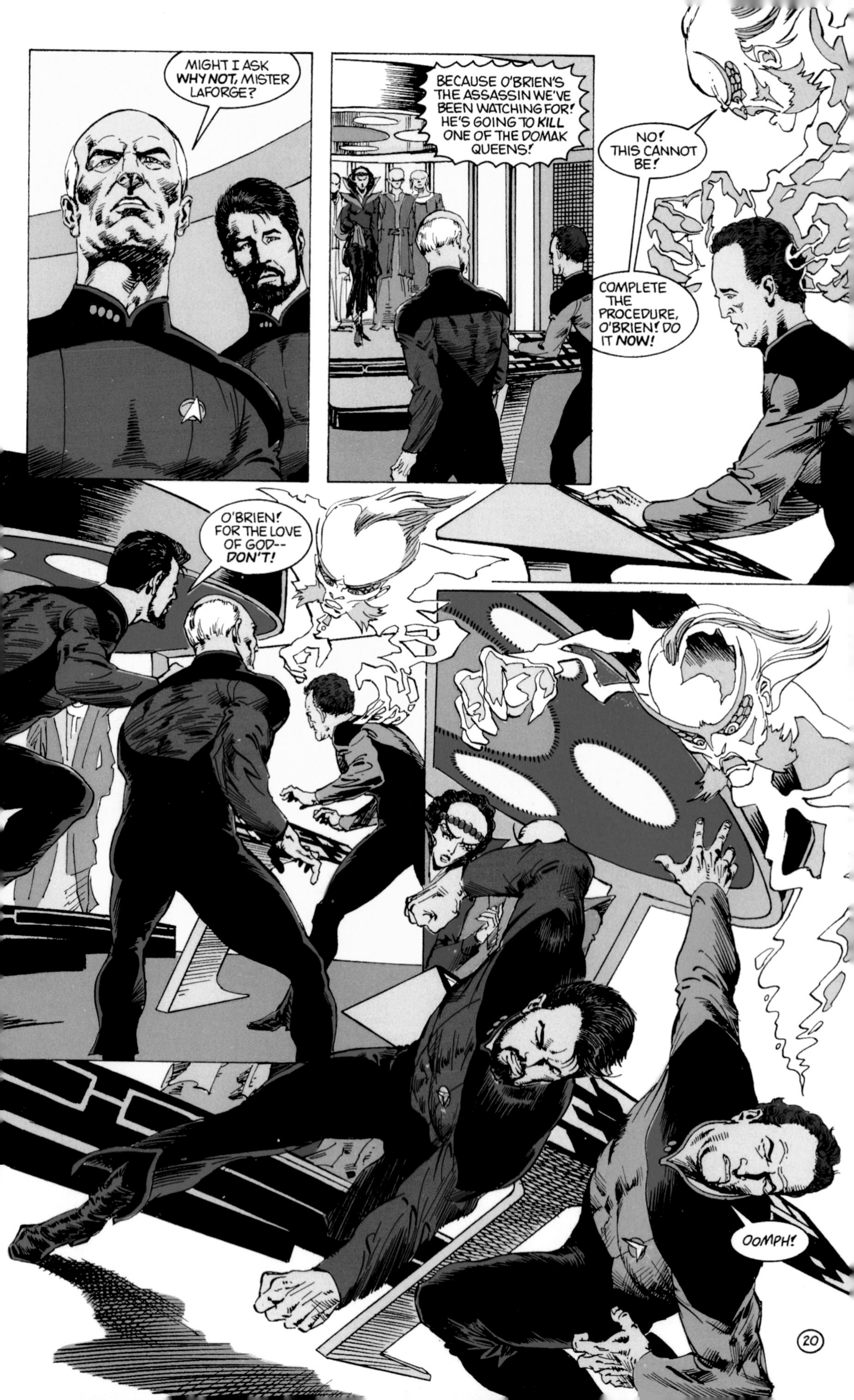
MIGHT I ASK WHY NOT, MISTER LAFORGE?
BECAUSE O'BRIEN'S THE ASSASSIN WE'VE BEEN WATCHING FOR! HE'S GOING TO KILL ONE OF THE DOMAK QUEENS!
NO! THIS CANNOT BE!
COMPLETE THE PROCEDURE, O'BRIEN! DO IT NOW!
O'BRIEN! FOR THE LOVE OF GOD-- DON'T!
OOMPH!

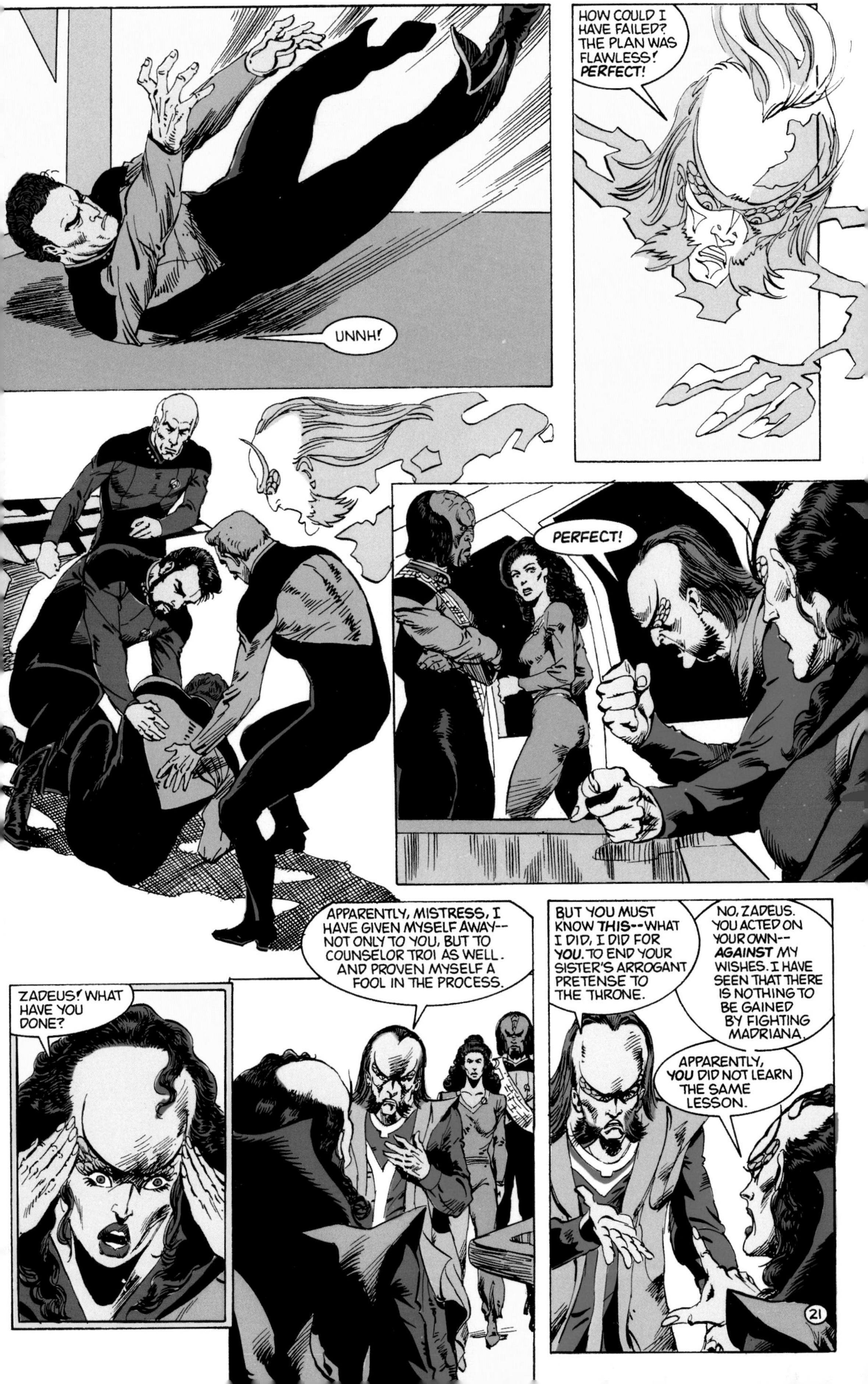
HOW COULD I HAVE FAILED? THE PLAN WAS FLAWLESS! PERFECT!
UNNH!
PERFECT!
ZADEUS! WHAT HAVE YOU DONE?
APPARENTLY, MISTRESS, I HAVE GIVEN MYSELF AWAY-- NOT ONLY TO YOU, BUT TO COUNSELOR TROI AS WELL. AND PROVEN MYSELF A FOOL IN THE PROCESS.
BUT YOU MUST KNOW THIS--WHAT I DID, I DID FOR YOU. TO END YOUR SISTER'S ARROGANT PRETENSE TO THE THRONE.
NO, ZADEUS. YOU ACTED ON YOUR OWN-- AGAINST MY WISHES. I HAVE SEEN THAT THERE IS NOTHING TO BE GAINED BY FIGHTING MADRIANA.
APPARENTLY, YOU DID NOT LEARN THE SAME LESSON.

DID WE STOP HIM IN TIME?

IT SEEMS WE HAVE, MISTER LAFORGE. BUT I'D LIKE AN EXPLANATION-- AND I'D LIKE IT NOW.

ACTUALLY, IT ALL STARTED WITH MISTER FORTHOL HERE. HE WAS AN OBSERVER AT OUR POKER GAME THE OTHER DAY WHEN HE NOTICED SOMETHING STRANGE.

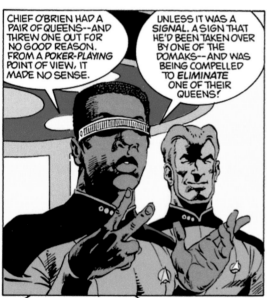

CHIEF O'BRIEN HAD A PAIR OF QUEENS--AND THREW ONE OUT FOR NO GOOD REASON. FROM A POKER-PLAYING POINT OF VIEW, IT MADE NO SENSE.

UNLESS IT WAS A SIGNAL. A SIGN THAT HE'D BEEN TAKEN OVER BY ONE OF THE DOMAKS--AND WAS BEING COMPELLED TO ELIMINATE ONE OF THEIR QUEENS!

I'LL ADMIT IT WAS A LONGSHOT--

AS FAR AS I'M CONCERNED, COMMANDER, IT STILL IS.

WE'VE GOT NO PROOF THAT MISTER O'BRIEN WAS TAMPERED WITH. WE'VE GOT NO PROOF THAT ANYONE WAS TAMPERED WITH.

THAT'S NOT QUITE TRUE, SIR. ZADEUS IS GUILTY-- I READ IT IN HIS EMOTIONS ONLY A MOMENT AGO. JUST AS QUEEN ALLIENA READ IT IN HIS MIND.

THOUGH WE HAD NOT THOUGHT TO SCAN HIM UNTIL, IN HIS DISAPPOINTMENT, HE CRIED OUT AND DREW ATTENTION TO HIMSELF.

ONE MIGHT SAY HE TIPPED HIS HAND.

22

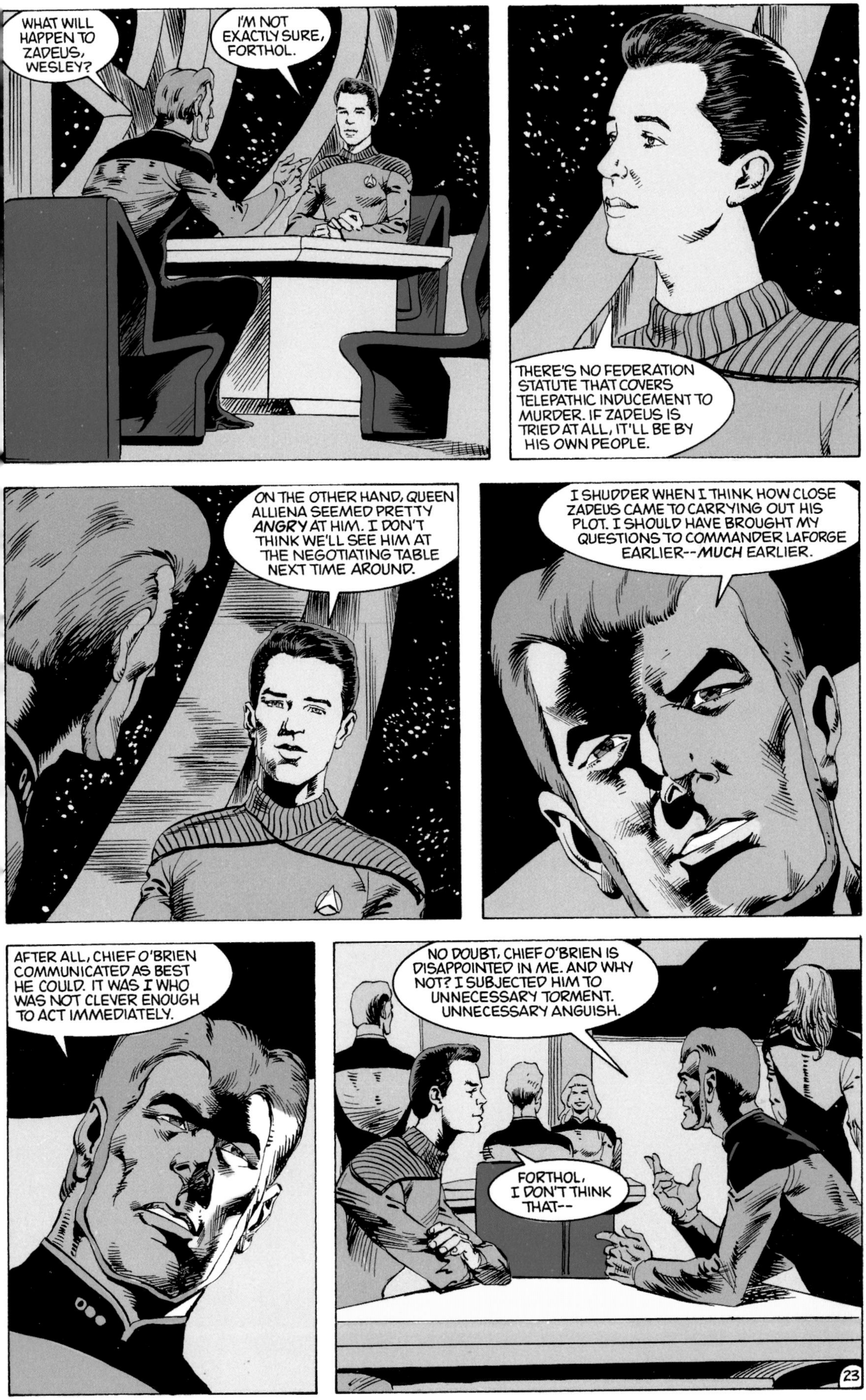
WHAT WILL HAPPEN TO ZADEUS, WESLEY?
I'M NOT EXACTLY SURE, FORTHOL.
THERE'S NO FEDERATION STATUTE THAT COVERS TELEPATHIC INDUCEMENT TO MURDER. IF ZADEUS IS TRIED AT ALL, IT'LL BE BY HIS OWN PEOPLE.
ON THE OTHER HAND, QUEEN ALLIENA SEEMED PRETTY ANGRY AT HIM. I DON'T THINK WE'LL SEE HIM AT THE NEGOTIATING TABLE NEXT TIME AROUND.
I SHUDDER WHEN I THINK HOW CLOSE ZADEUS CAME TO CARRYING OUT HIS PLOT. I SHOULD HAVE BROUGHT MY QUESTIONS TO COMMANDER LAFORGE EARLIER--MUCH EARLIER.
AFTER ALL, CHIEF O'BRIEN COMMUNICATED AS BEST HE COULD. IT WAS I WHO WAS NOT CLEVER ENOUGH TO ACT IMMEDIATELY.
NO DOUBT, CHIEF O'BRIEN IS DISAPPOINTED IN ME. AND WHY NOT? I SUBJECTED HIM TO UNNECESSARY TORMENT. UNNECESSARY ANGUISH.
FORTHOL, I DON'T THINK THAT--
23

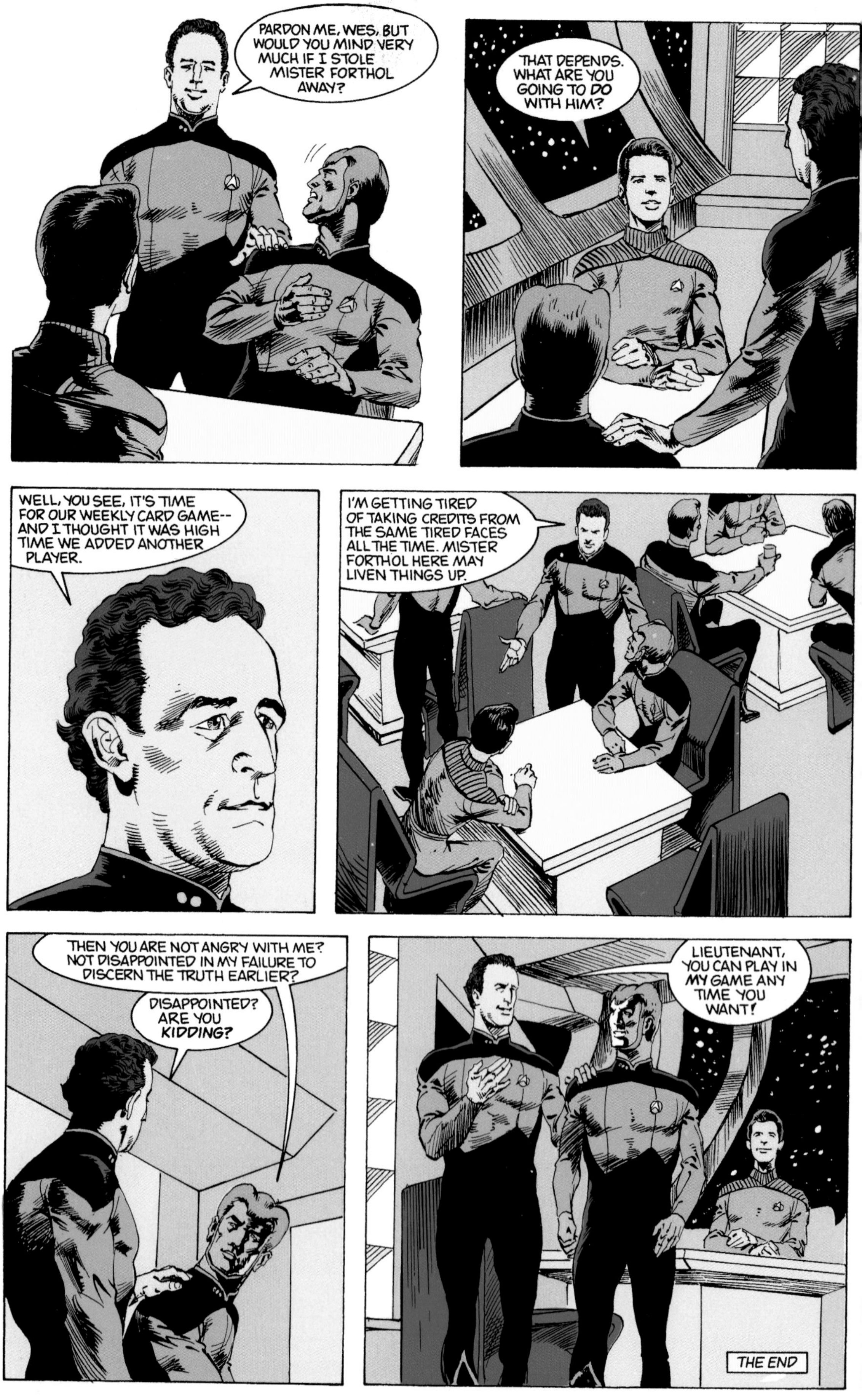
PARDON ME, WES, BUT WOULD YOU MIND VERY MUCH IF I STOLE MISTER FORTHOL AWAY?
THAT DEPENDS. WHAT ARE YOU GOING TO DO WITH HIM?
WELL, YOU SEE, IT'S TIME FOR OUR WEEKLY CARD GAME--AND I THOUGHT IT WAS HIGH TIME WE ADDED ANOTHER PLAYER.
I'M GETTING TIRED OF TAKING CREDITS FROM THE SAME TIRED FACES ALL THE TIME. MISTER FORTHOL HERE MAY LIVEN THINGS UP.
THEN YOU ARE NOT ANGRY WITH ME? NOT DISAPPOINTED IN MY FAILURE TO DISCERN THE TRUTH EARLIER?
DISAPPOINTED? ARE YOU KIDDING?
LIEUTENANT, YOU CAN PLAY IN MY GAME ANY TIME YOU WANT!
THE END

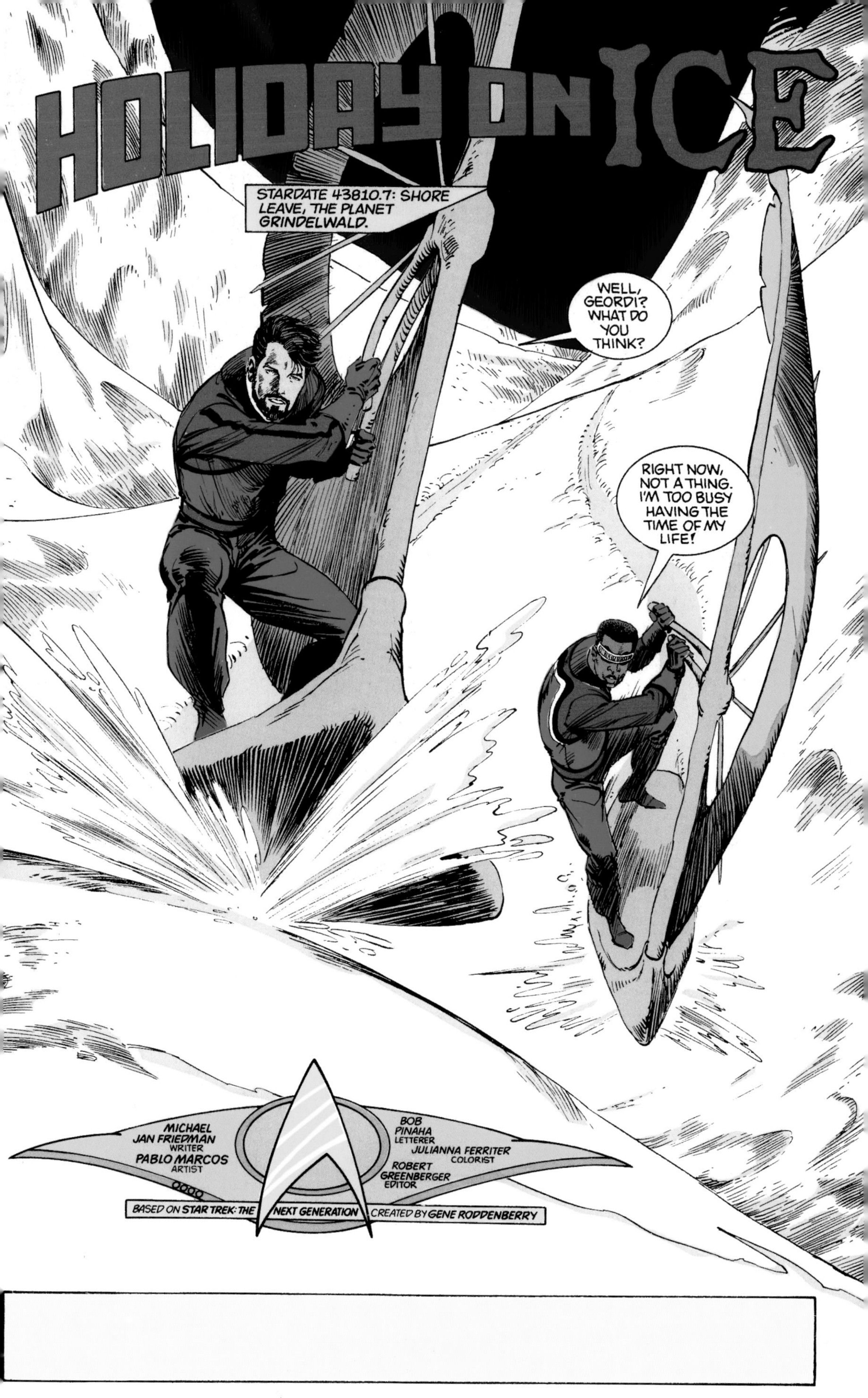
HOLIDAY ON ICE
STARDATE 43810.7: SHORE LEAVE, THE PLANET GRINDELWALD.
WELL, GEORDI? WHAT DO YOU THINK?
RIGHT NOW, NOT A THING. I'M TOO BUSY HAVING THE TIME OF MY LIFE!
MICHAEL JAN FRIEDMAN WRITER
PABLO MARCOS ARTIST
BOB PINAHA LETTERER
JULIANNA FERRITER COLORIST
ROBERT GREENBERGER EDITOR
BASED ON STAR TREK: THE NEXT GENERATION CREATED BY GENE RODDENBERRY

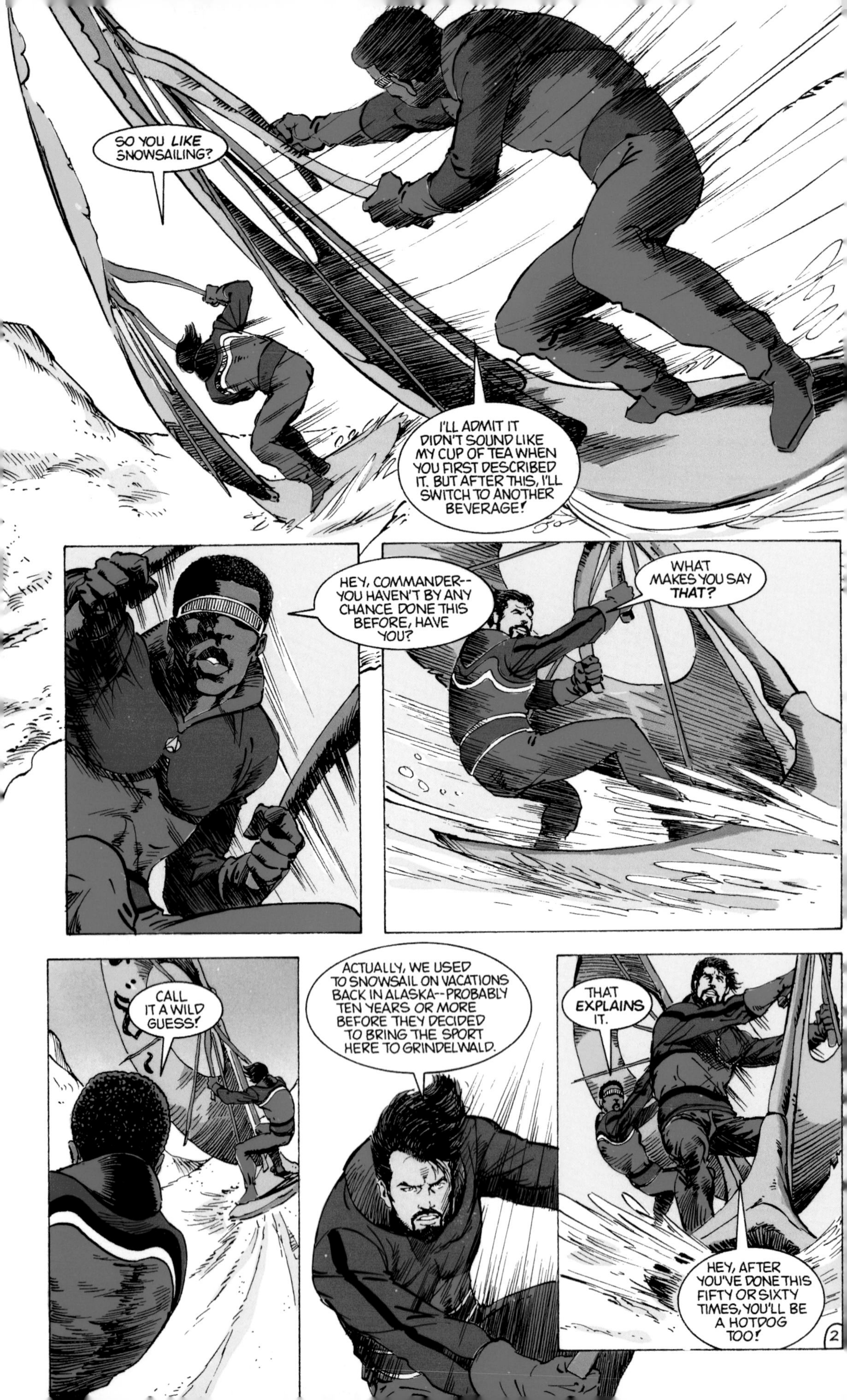
SO YOU LIKE SNOWSAILING?
I'LL ADMIT IT DIDN'T SOUND LIKE MY CUP OF TEA WHEN YOU FIRST DESCRIBED IT. BUT AFTER THIS, I'LL SWITCH TO ANOTHER BEVERAGE!
HEY, COMMANDER-- YOU HAVEN'T BY ANY CHANCE DONE THIS BEFORE, HAVE YOU?
WHAT MAKES YOU SAY THAT?
CALL IT A WILD GUESS!
ACTUALLY, WE USED TO SNOWSAIL ON VACATIONS BACK IN ALASKA--PROBABLY TEN YEARS OR MORE BEFORE THEY DECIDED TO BRING THE SPORT HERE TO GRINDELWALD.
THAT EXPLAINS IT.
HEY, AFTER YOU'VE DONE THIS FIFTY OR SIXTY TIMES, YOU'LL BE A HOTDOG TOO!
2

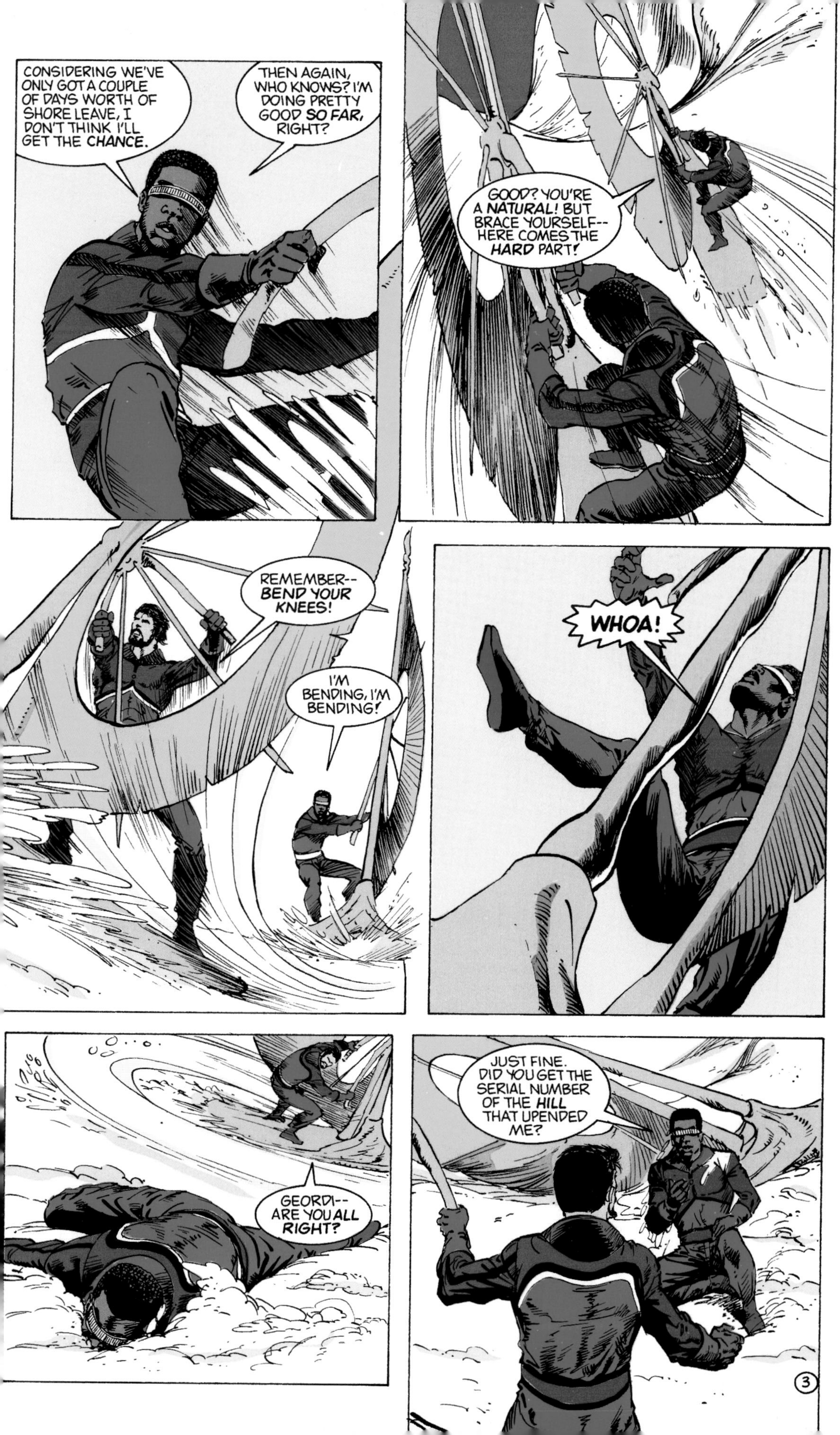

CONSIDERING WE'VE ONLY GOT A COUPLE OF DAYS WORTH OF SHORE LEAVE, I DON'T THINK I'LL GET THE CHANCE.
THEN AGAIN, WHO KNOWS? I'M DOING PRETTY GOOD SO FAR, RIGHT?
GOOD? YOU'RE A NATURAL! BUT BRACE YOURSELF-- HERE COMES THE HARD PART!
REMEMBER-- BEND YOUR KNEES!
I'M BENDING, I'M BENDING!
WHOA!
GEORDI-- ARE YOU ALL RIGHT?
JUST FINE. DID YOU GET THE SERIAL NUMBER OF THE HILL THAT UPENDED ME?

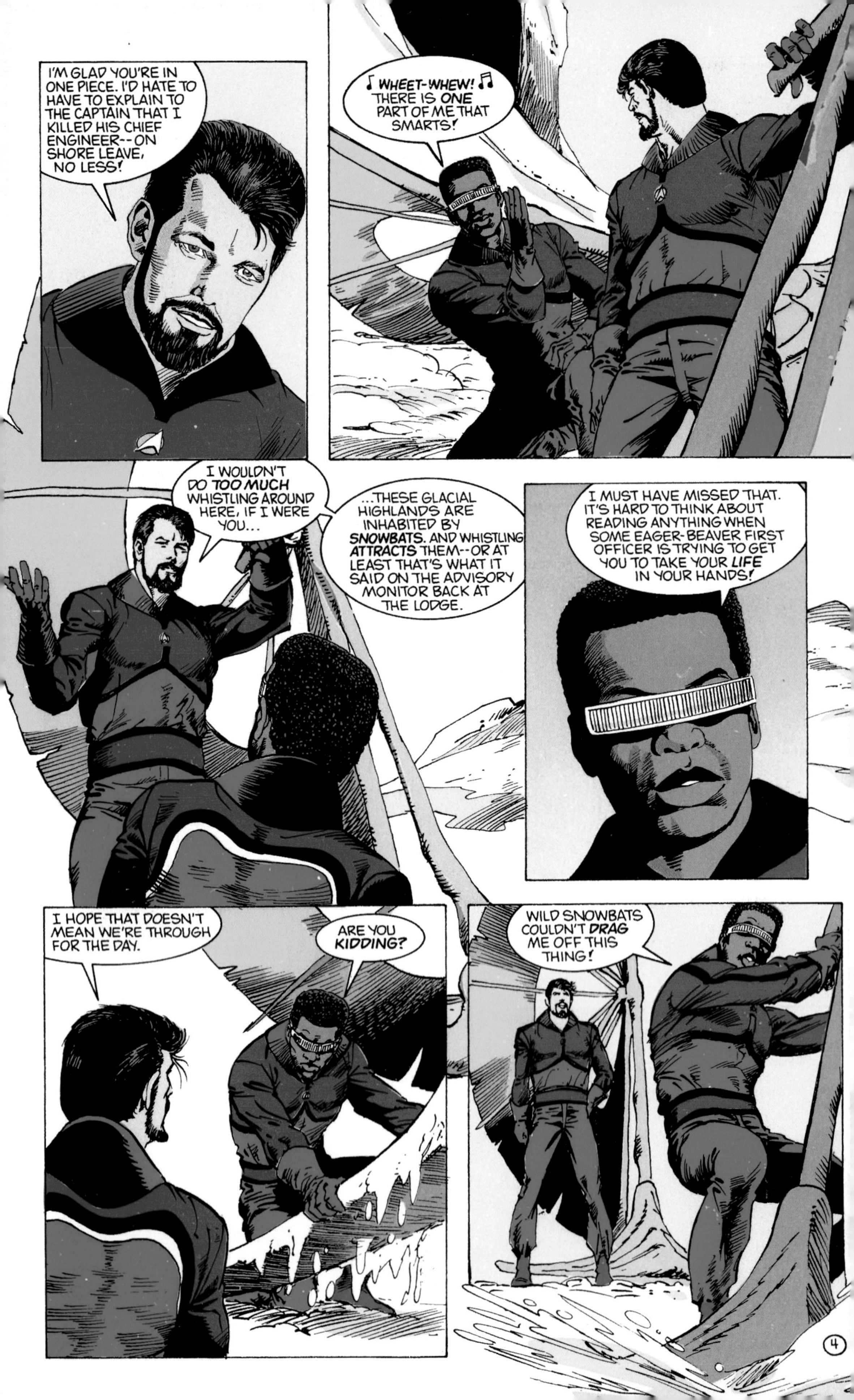
I'M GLAD YOU'RE IN ONE PIECE. I'D HATE TO HAVE TO EXPLAIN TO THE CAPTAIN THAT I KILLED HIS CHIEF ENGINEER--ON SHORE LEAVE, NO LESS!
♪ WHEET-WHEW! ♫ THERE IS ONE PART OF ME THAT SMARTS!
I WOULDN'T DO TOO MUCH WHISTLING AROUND HERE, IF I WERE YOU...
...THESE GLACIAL HIGHLANDS ARE INHABITED BY SNOWBATS. AND WHISTLING ATTRACTS THEM--OR AT LEAST THAT'S WHAT IT SAID ON THE ADVISORY MONITOR BACK AT THE LODGE.
I MUST HAVE MISSED THAT. IT'S HARD TO THINK ABOUT READING ANYTHING WHEN SOME EAGER-BEAVER FIRST OFFICER IS TRYING TO GET YOU TO TAKE YOUR LIFE IN YOUR HANDS!
I HOPE THAT DOESN'T MEAN WE'RE THROUGH FOR THE DAY.
ARE YOU KIDDING?
WILD SNOWBATS COULDN'T DRAG ME OFF THIS THING!
4

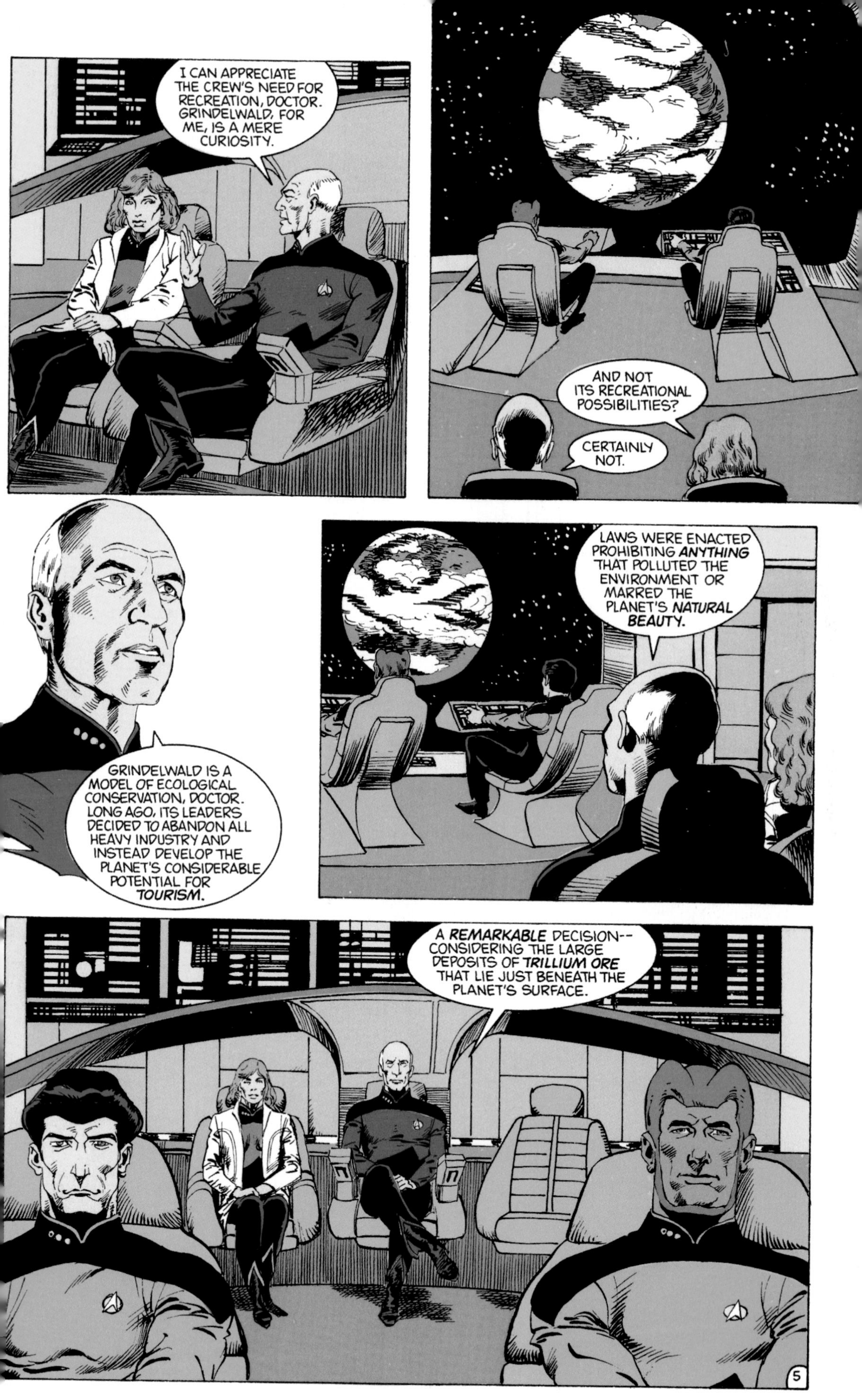
I CAN APPRECIATE THE CREW'S NEED FOR RECREATION, DOCTOR. GRINDELWALD, FOR ME, IS A MERE CURIOSITY.
AND NOT ITS RECREATIONAL POSSIBILITIES?
CERTAINLY NOT.
GRINDELWALD IS A MODEL OF ECOLOGICAL CONSERVATION, DOCTOR. LONG AGO, ITS LEADERS DECIDED TO ABANDON ALL HEAVY INDUSTRY AND INSTEAD DEVELOP THE PLANET'S CONSIDERABLE POTENTIAL FOR *TOURISM*.
LAWS WERE ENACTED PROHIBITING *ANYTHING* THAT POLLUTED THE ENVIRONMENT OR MARRED THE PLANET'S *NATURAL BEAUTY*.
A *REMARKABLE* DECISION-- CONSIDERING THE LARGE DEPOSITS OF *TRILLIUM ORE* THAT LIE JUST BENEATH THE PLANET'S SURFACE.
5

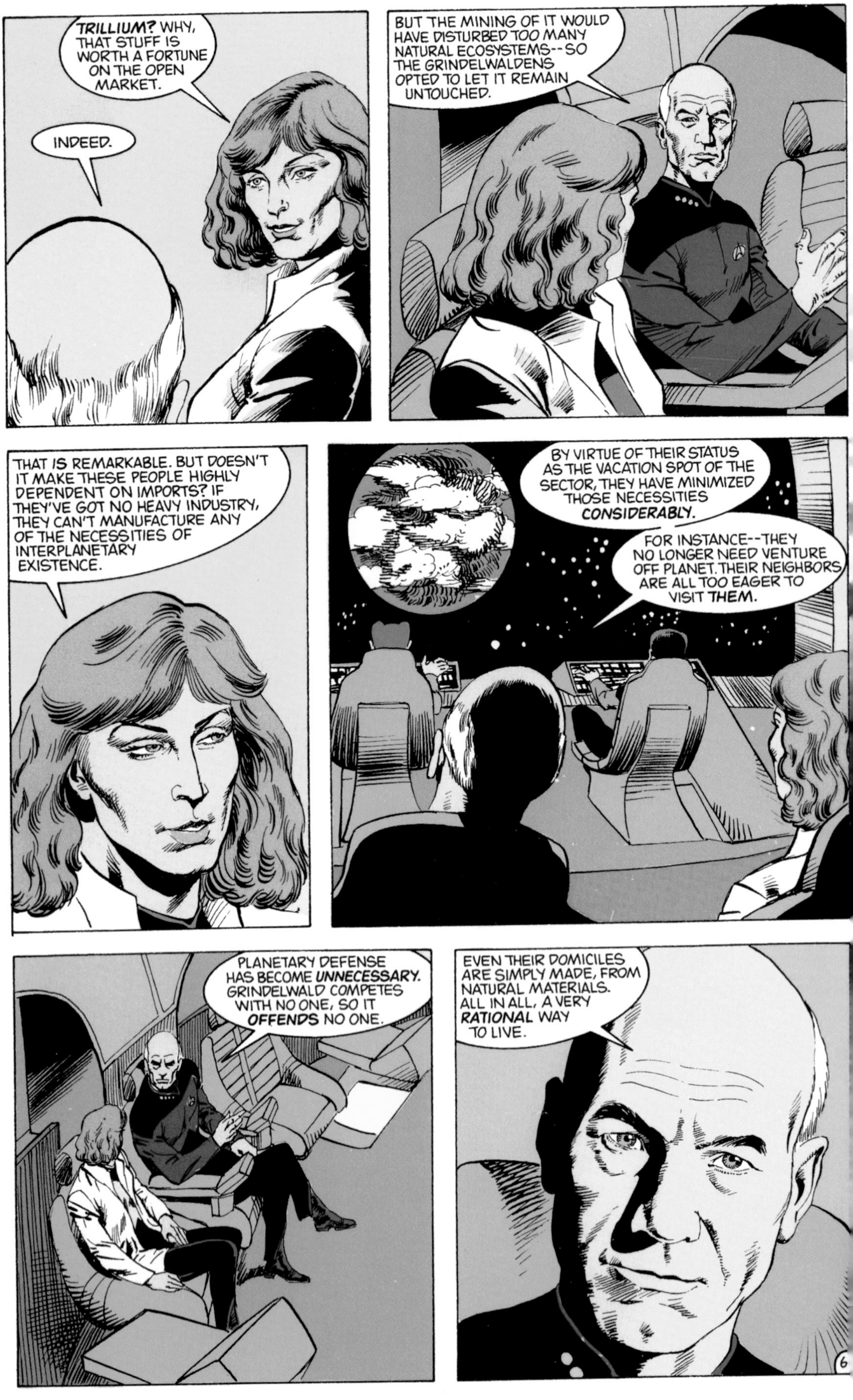
TRILLIUM? WHY, THAT STUFF IS WORTH A FORTUNE ON THE OPEN MARKET.
INDEED.
BUT THE MINING OF IT WOULD HAVE DISTURBED TOO MANY NATURAL ECOSYSTEMS--SO THE GRINDELWALDENS OPTED TO LET IT REMAIN UNTOUCHED.
THAT IS REMARKABLE. BUT DOESN'T IT MAKE THESE PEOPLE HIGHLY DEPENDENT ON IMPORTS? IF THEY'VE GOT NO HEAVY INDUSTRY, THEY CAN'T MANUFACTURE ANY OF THE NECESSITIES OF INTERPLANETARY EXISTENCE.
BY VIRTUE OF THEIR STATUS AS THE VACATION SPOT OF THE SECTOR, THEY HAVE MINIMIZED THOSE NECESSITIES CONSIDERABLY.
FOR INSTANCE--THEY NO LONGER NEED VENTURE OFF PLANET. THEIR NEIGHBORS ARE ALL TOO EAGER TO VISIT THEM.
PLANETARY DEFENSE HAS BECOME UNNECESSARY. GRINDELWALD COMPETES WITH NO ONE, SO IT OFFENDS NO ONE.
EVEN THEIR DOMICILES ARE SIMPLY MADE, FROM NATURAL MATERIALS. ALL IN ALL, A VERY RATIONAL WAY TO LIVE.
6

YOU SOUND ALMOST *ENVIOUS* OF THEM.

I AM, DOCTOR, I AM.

PEACE, SIMPLICITY AND THE CHANCE TO OBSERVE NATURE IN ALL HER SPLENDOR. A DAILY ROUND OF CAREFREE GOOD CHEER.

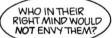

WHO IN THEIR *RIGHT MIND* WOULD *NOT* ENVY THEM?

I'M SURPRISED, CAPTAIN. I'VE ALWAYS THOUGHT OF YOU AS THE RESTLESS TYPE--*TOO CURIOUS* ABOUT WHAT'S AROUND THE NEXT BEND TO STAY IN ANY ONE PLACE FOR VERY LONG.

THAT IS THE WAY I'VE SEEN *MYSELF* AS WELL.

BUT IT DOESN'T KEEP ME FROM ENVYING THOSE UNAFFLICTED WITH *MY FORM OF MADNESS!*

7

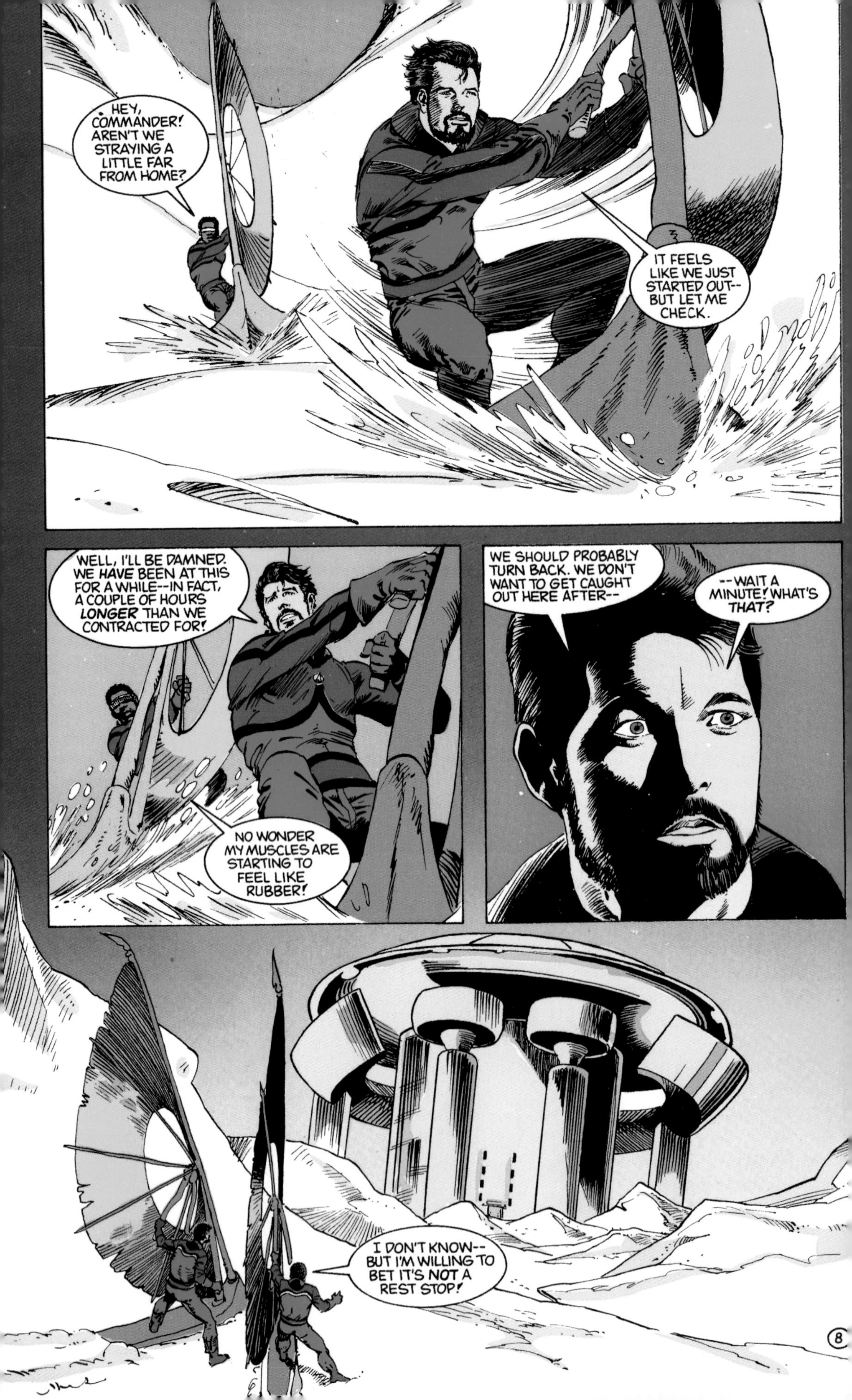
HEY, COMMANDER! AREN'T WE STRAYING A LITTLE FAR FROM HOME?
IT FEELS LIKE WE JUST STARTED OUT--BUT LET ME CHECK.
WELL, I'LL BE DAMNED. WE HAVE BEEN AT THIS FOR A WHILE--IN FACT, A COUPLE OF HOURS LONGER THAN WE CONTRACTED FOR!
NO WONDER MY MUSCLES ARE STARTING TO FEEL LIKE RUBBER!
WE SHOULD PROBABLY TURN BACK. WE DON'T WANT TO GET CAUGHT OUT HERE AFTER--
--WAIT A MINUTE! WHAT'S THAT?
I DON'T KNOW--BUT I'M WILLING TO BET IT'S NOT A REST STOP!

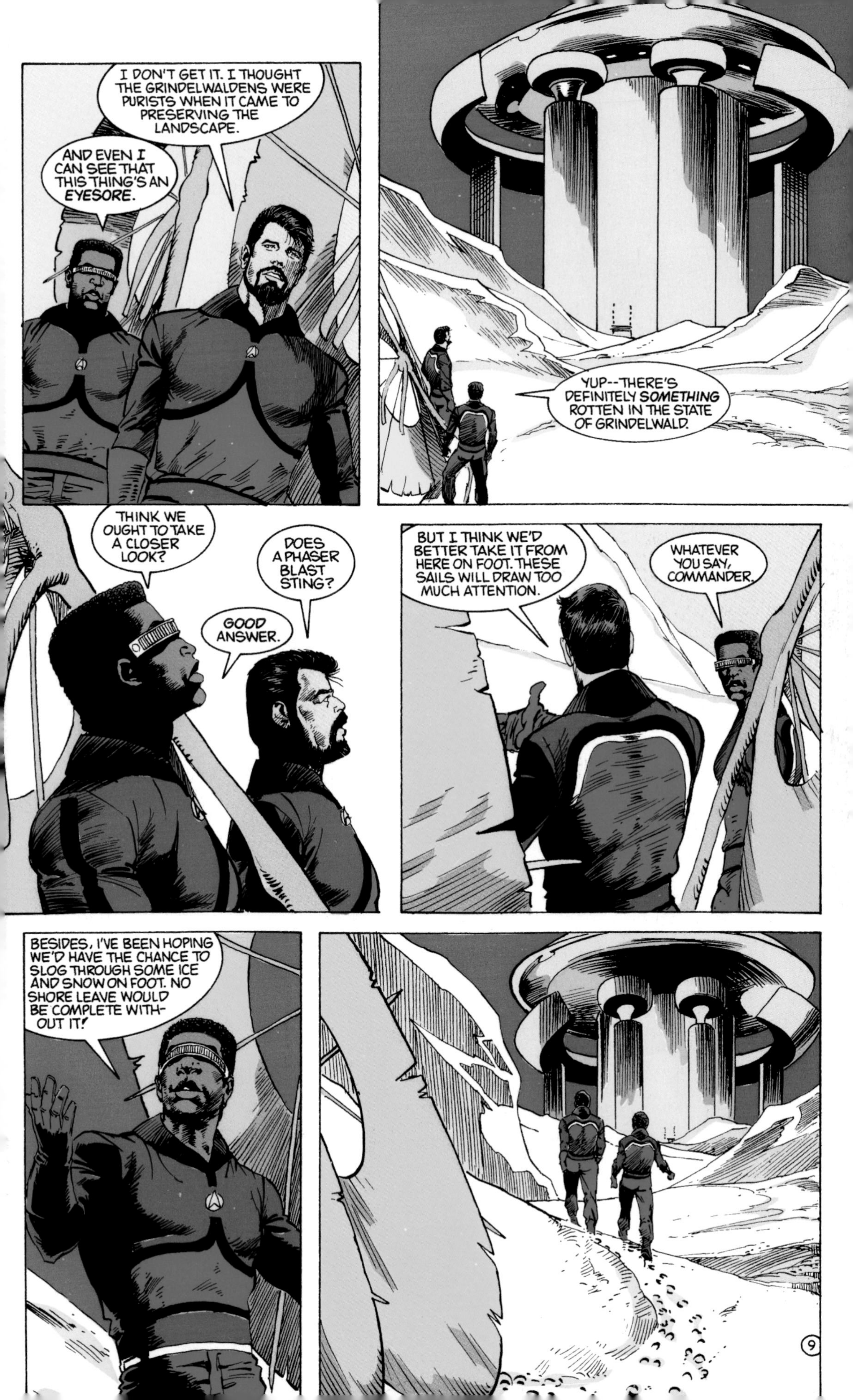

I DON'T GET IT. I THOUGHT THE GRINDELWALDENS WERE PURISTS WHEN IT CAME TO PRESERVING THE LANDSCAPE.
AND EVEN I CAN SEE THAT THIS THING'S AN *EYESORE*.
YUP--THERE'S DEFINITELY *SOMETHING* ROTTEN IN THE STATE OF GRINDELWALD.
THINK WE OUGHT TO TAKE A CLOSER LOOK?
DOES A PHASER BLAST STING?
GOOD ANSWER.
BUT I THINK WE'D BETTER TAKE IT FROM HERE ON FOOT. THESE SAILS WILL DRAW TOO MUCH ATTENTION.
WHATEVER YOU SAY, COMMANDER.
BESIDES, I'VE BEEN HOPING WE'D HAVE THE CHANCE TO SLOG THROUGH SOME ICE AND SNOW ON FOOT. NO SHORE LEAVE WOULD BE COMPLETE WITH-OUT IT!

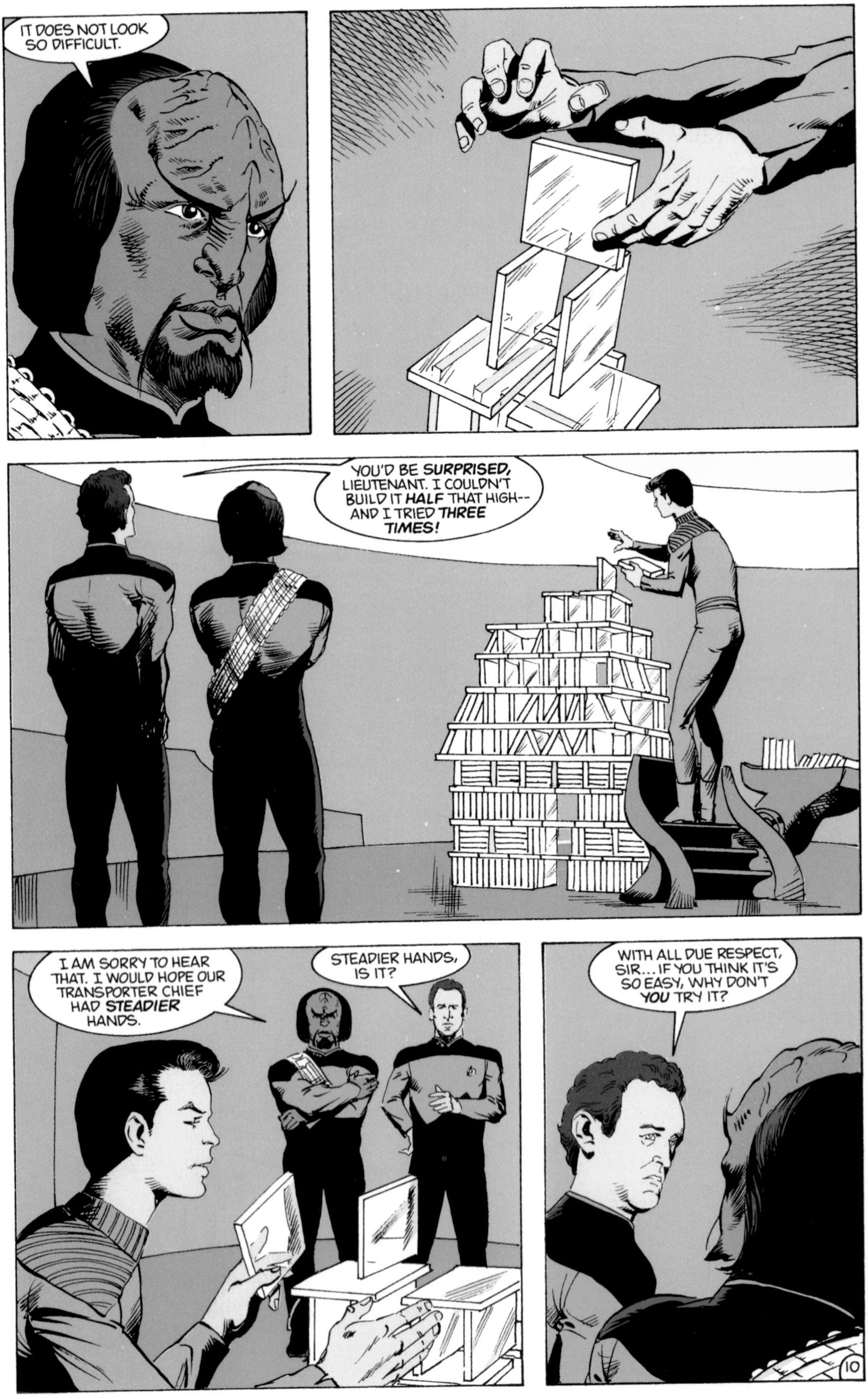
IT DOES NOT LOOK SO DIFFICULT.
YOU'D BE **SURPRISED,** LIEUTENANT. I COULDN'T BUILD IT **HALF** THAT HIGH-- AND I TRIED **THREE TIMES!**
I AM SORRY TO HEAR THAT. I WOULD HOPE OUR TRANSPORTER CHIEF HAD **STEADIER** HANDS.
STEADIER HANDS, IS IT?
WITH ALL DUE RESPECT, SIR... IF YOU THINK IT'S SO EASY, WHY DON'T **YOU** TRY IT?
10

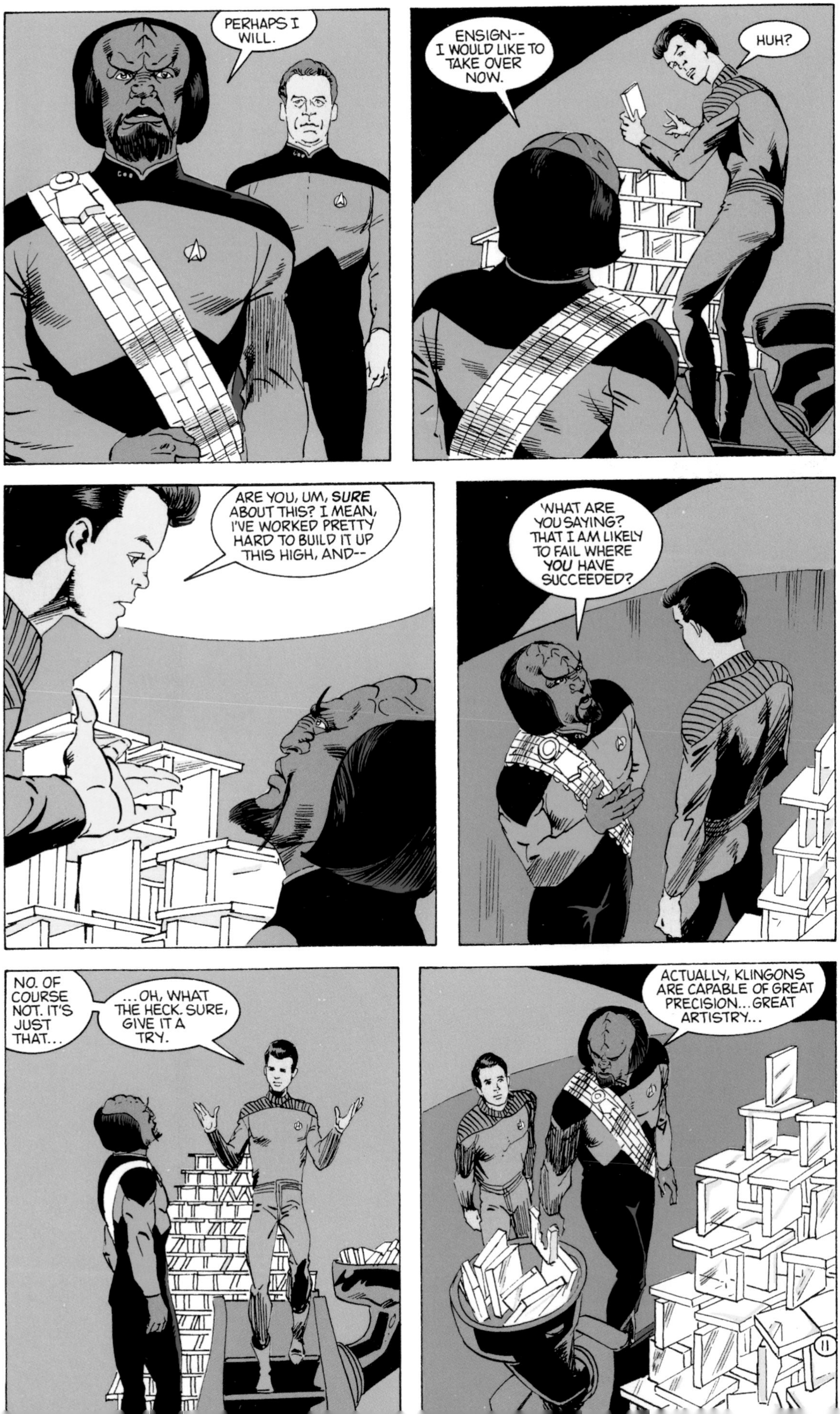
PERHAPS I WILL.
ENSIGN-- I WOULD LIKE TO TAKE OVER NOW.
HUH?
ARE YOU, UM, SURE ABOUT THIS? I MEAN, I'VE WORKED PRETTY HARD TO BUILD IT UP THIS HIGH, AND--
WHAT ARE YOU SAYING? THAT I AM LIKELY TO FAIL WHERE YOU HAVE SUCCEEDED?
NO. OF COURSE NOT. IT'S JUST THAT...
...OH, WHAT THE HECK. SURE, GIVE IT A TRY.
ACTUALLY, KLINGONS ARE CAPABLE OF GREAT PRECISION... GREAT ARTISTRY...
11

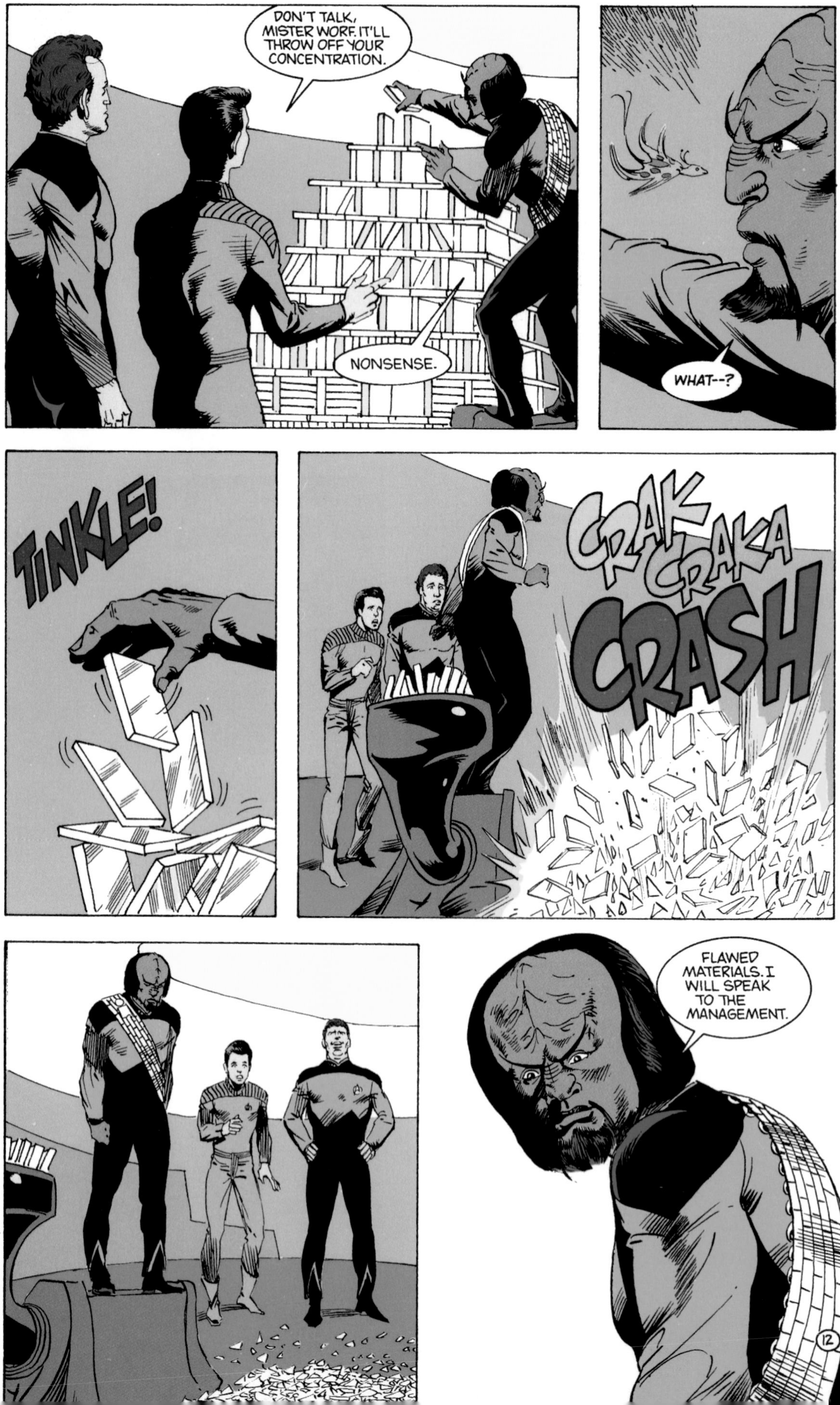

DON'T TALK, MISTER WORF. IT'LL THROW OFF YOUR CONCENTRATION.
NONSENSE.
WHAT--?
TINKLE!
CRAK CRAKA CRASH
FLAWED MATERIALS. I WILL SPEAK TO THE MANAGEMENT.
12

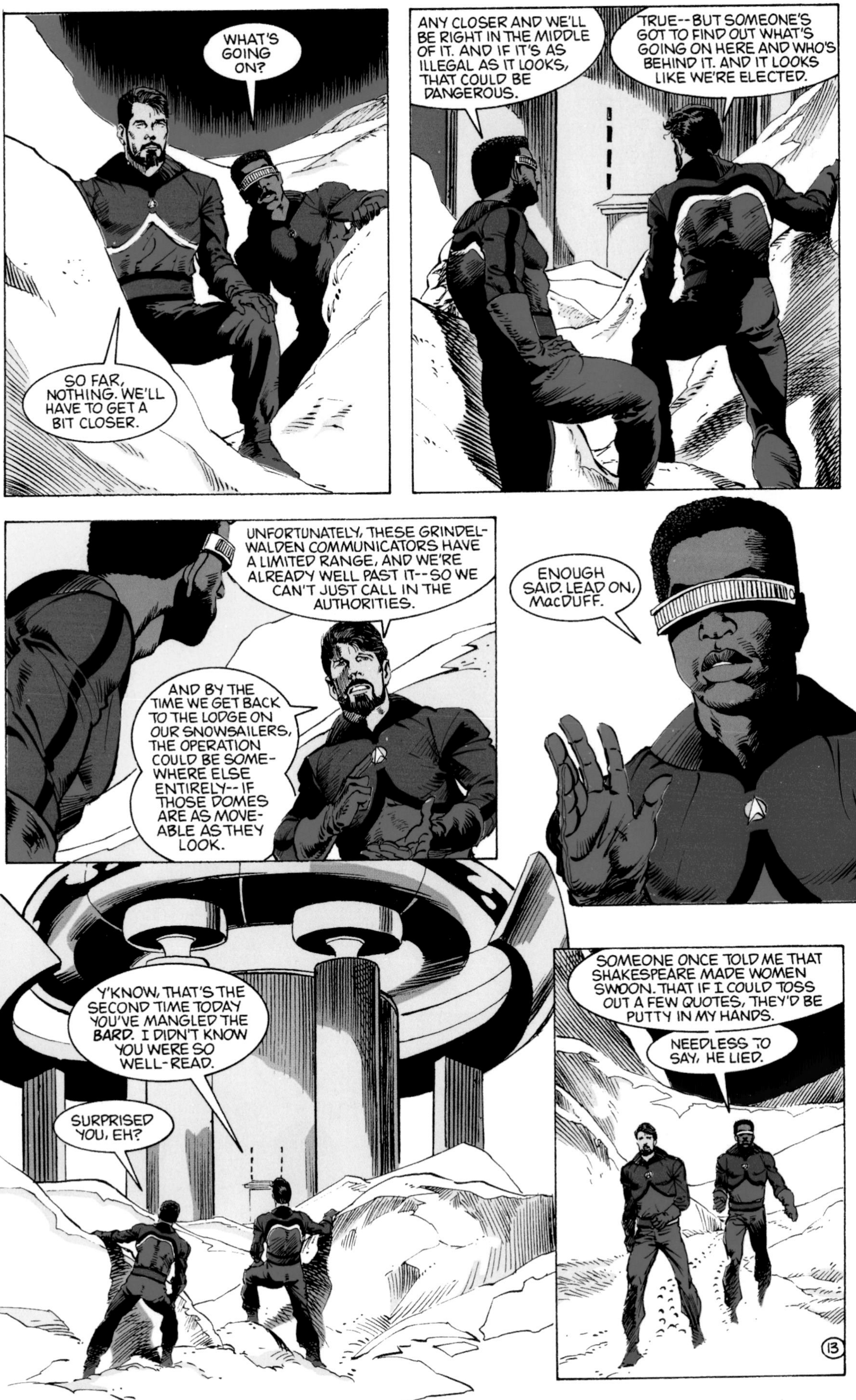
WHAT'S GOING ON?
SO FAR, NOTHING. WE'LL HAVE TO GET A BIT CLOSER.
ANY CLOSER AND WE'LL BE RIGHT IN THE MIDDLE OF IT. AND IF IT'S AS ILLEGAL AS IT LOOKS, THAT COULD BE DANGEROUS.
TRUE--BUT SOMEONE'S GOT TO FIND OUT WHAT'S GOING ON HERE AND WHO'S BEHIND IT. AND IT LOOKS LIKE WE'RE ELECTED.
UNFORTUNATELY, THESE GRINDEL-WALDEN COMMUNICATORS HAVE A LIMITED RANGE, AND WE'RE ALREADY WELL PAST IT--SO WE CAN'T JUST CALL IN THE AUTHORITIES.
AND BY THE TIME WE GET BACK TO THE LODGE ON OUR SNOWSAILERS, THE OPERATION COULD BE SOME-WHERE ELSE ENTIRELY--IF THOSE DOMES ARE AS MOVE-ABLE AS THEY LOOK.
ENOUGH SAID. LEAD ON, MacDUFF.
Y'KNOW, THAT'S THE SECOND TIME TODAY YOU'VE MANGLED THE BARD. I DIDN'T KNOW YOU WERE SO WELL-READ.
SURPRISED YOU, EH?
SOMEONE ONCE TOLD ME THAT SHAKESPEARE MADE WOMEN SWOON. THAT IF I COULD TOSS OUT A FEW QUOTES, THEY'D BE PUTTY IN MY HANDS.
NEEDLESS TO SAY, HE LIED.

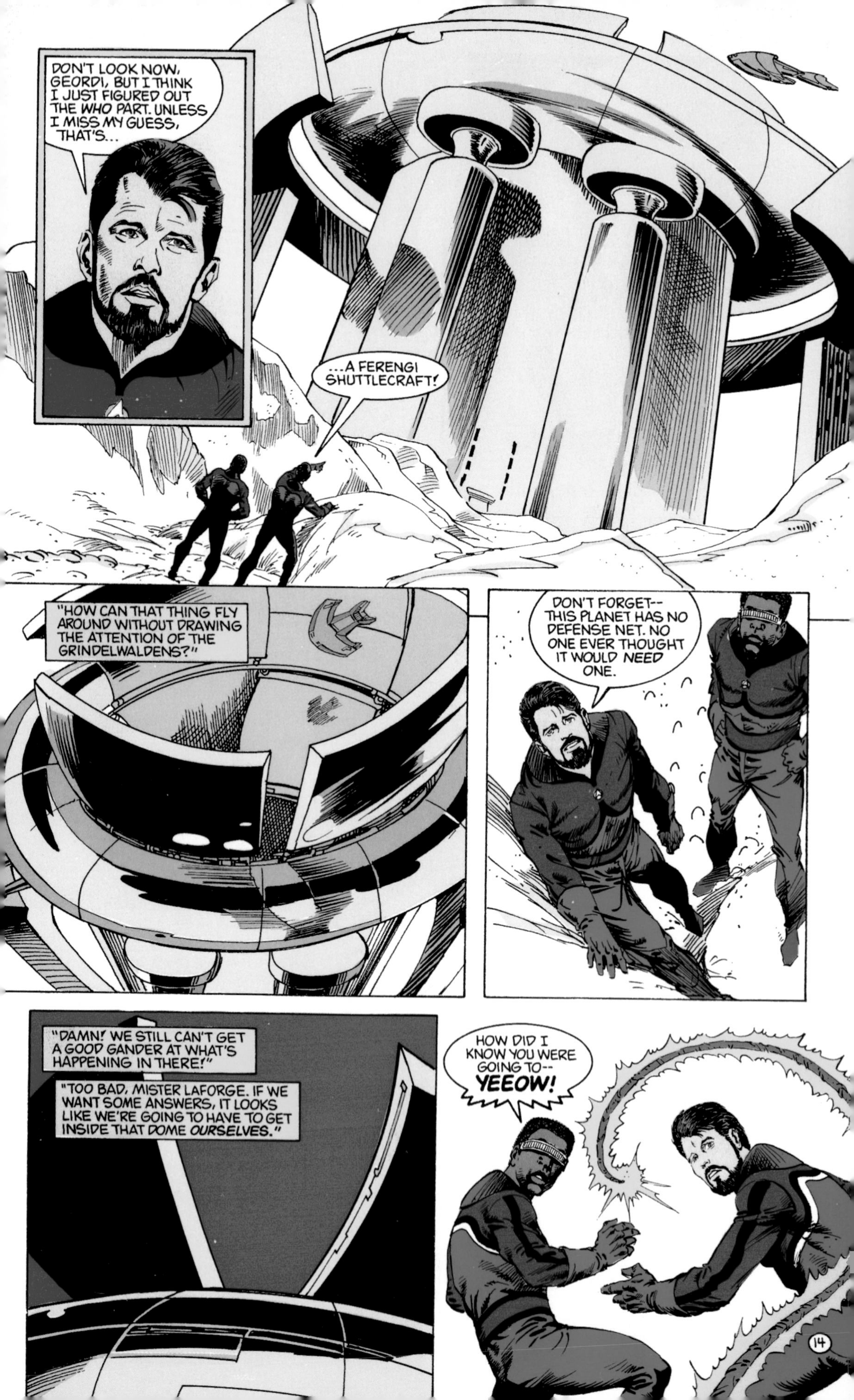

DON'T LOOK NOW, GEORDI, BUT I THINK I JUST FIGURED OUT THE *WHO* PART. UNLESS I MISS MY GUESS, THAT'S...
...A FERENGI SHUTTLECRAFT!
"HOW CAN THAT THING FLY AROUND WITHOUT DRAWING THE ATTENTION OF THE GRINDELWALDENS?"
DON'T FORGET-- THIS PLANET HAS NO DEFENSE NET. NO ONE EVER THOUGHT IT WOULD *NEED* ONE.
"DAMN! WE STILL CAN'T GET A GOOD GANDER AT WHAT'S HAPPENING IN THERE!"
"TOO BAD, MISTER LAFORGE. IF WE WANT SOME ANSWERS, IT LOOKS LIKE WE'RE GOING TO HAVE TO GET INSIDE THAT DOME *OURSELVES*."
HOW DID I KNOW YOU WERE GOING TO-- **YEEOW!**

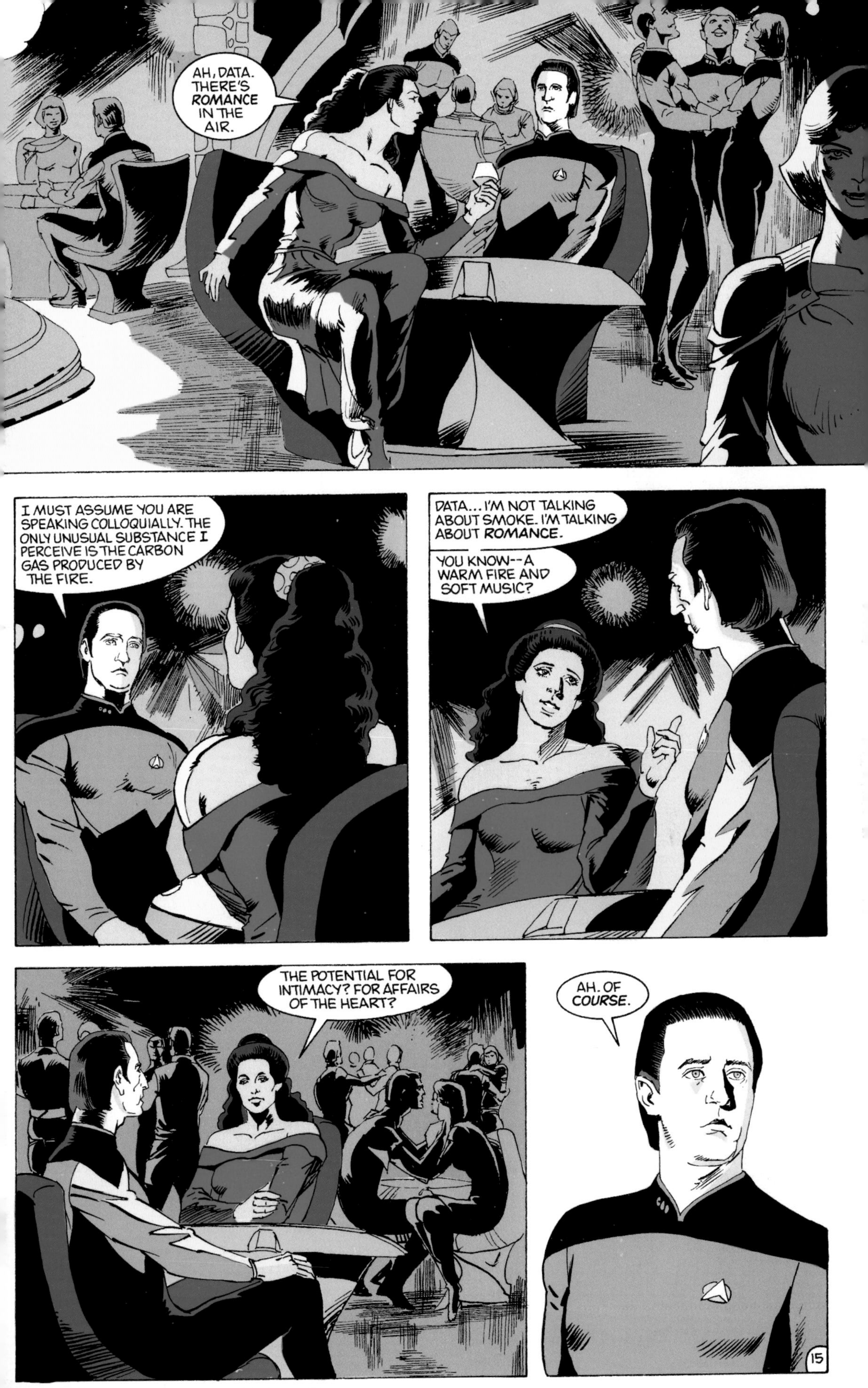
AH, DATA. THERE'S ROMANCE IN THE AIR.
I MUST ASSUME YOU ARE SPEAKING COLLOQUIALLY. THE ONLY UNUSUAL SUBSTANCE I PERCEIVE IS THE CARBON GAS PRODUCED BY THE FIRE.
DATA... I'M NOT TALKING ABOUT SMOKE. I'M TALKING ABOUT ROMANCE.
YOU KNOW--A WARM FIRE AND SOFT MUSIC?
THE POTENTIAL FOR INTIMACY? FOR AFFAIRS OF THE HEART?
AH. OF COURSE.
15

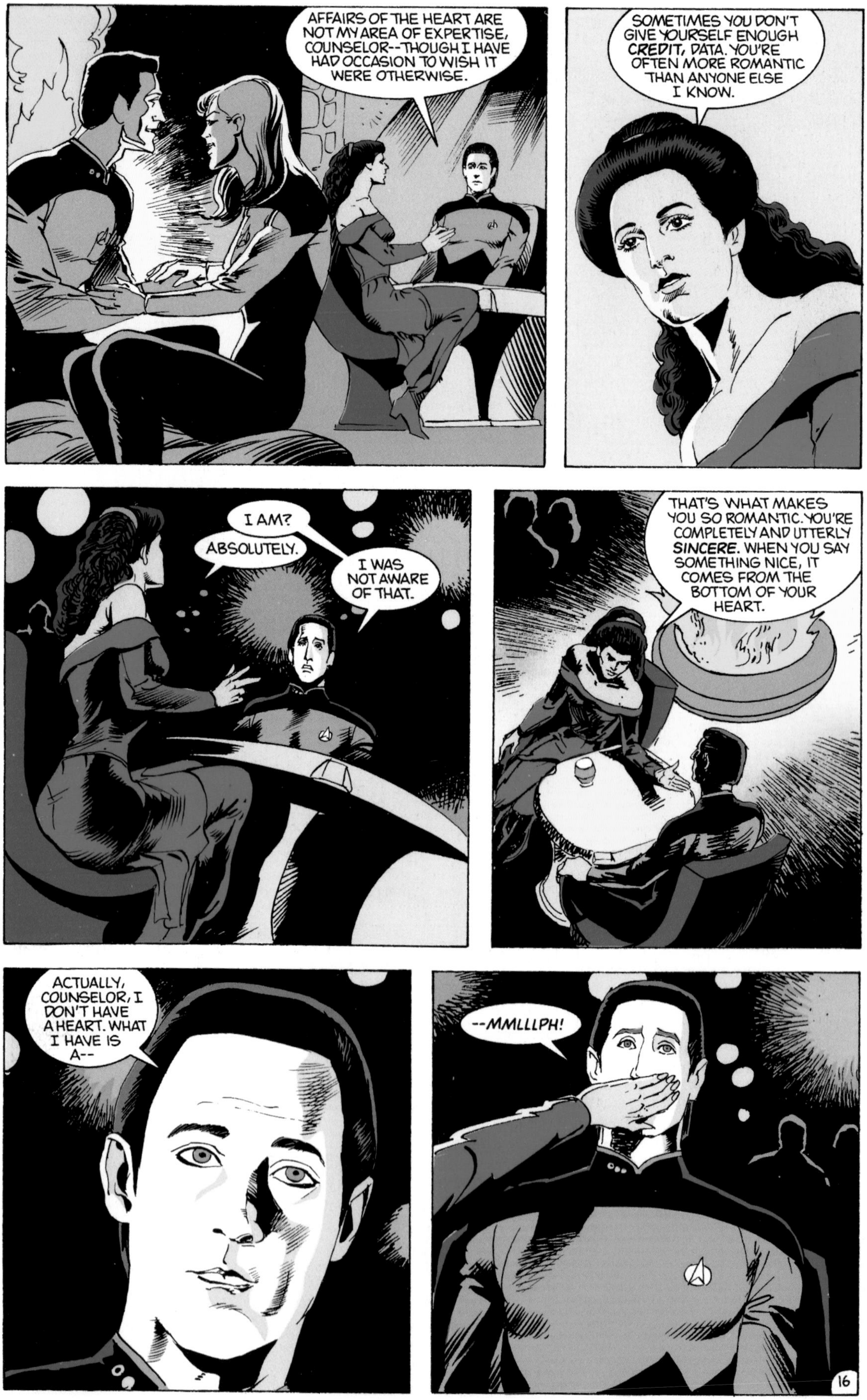
AFFAIRS OF THE HEART ARE NOT MY AREA OF EXPERTISE, COUNSELOR--THOUGH I HAVE HAD OCCASION TO WISH IT WERE OTHERWISE.
SOMETIMES YOU DON'T GIVE YOURSELF ENOUGH CREDIT, DATA. YOU'RE OFTEN MORE ROMANTIC THAN ANYONE ELSE I KNOW.
I AM?
ABSOLUTELY.
I WAS NOT AWARE OF THAT.
THAT'S WHAT MAKES YOU SO ROMANTIC. YOU'RE COMPLETELY AND UTTERLY SINCERE. WHEN YOU SAY SOMETHING NICE, IT COMES FROM THE BOTTOM OF YOUR HEART.
ACTUALLY, COUNSELOR, I DON'T HAVE A HEART. WHAT I HAVE IS A--
--MMLLLPH!
16

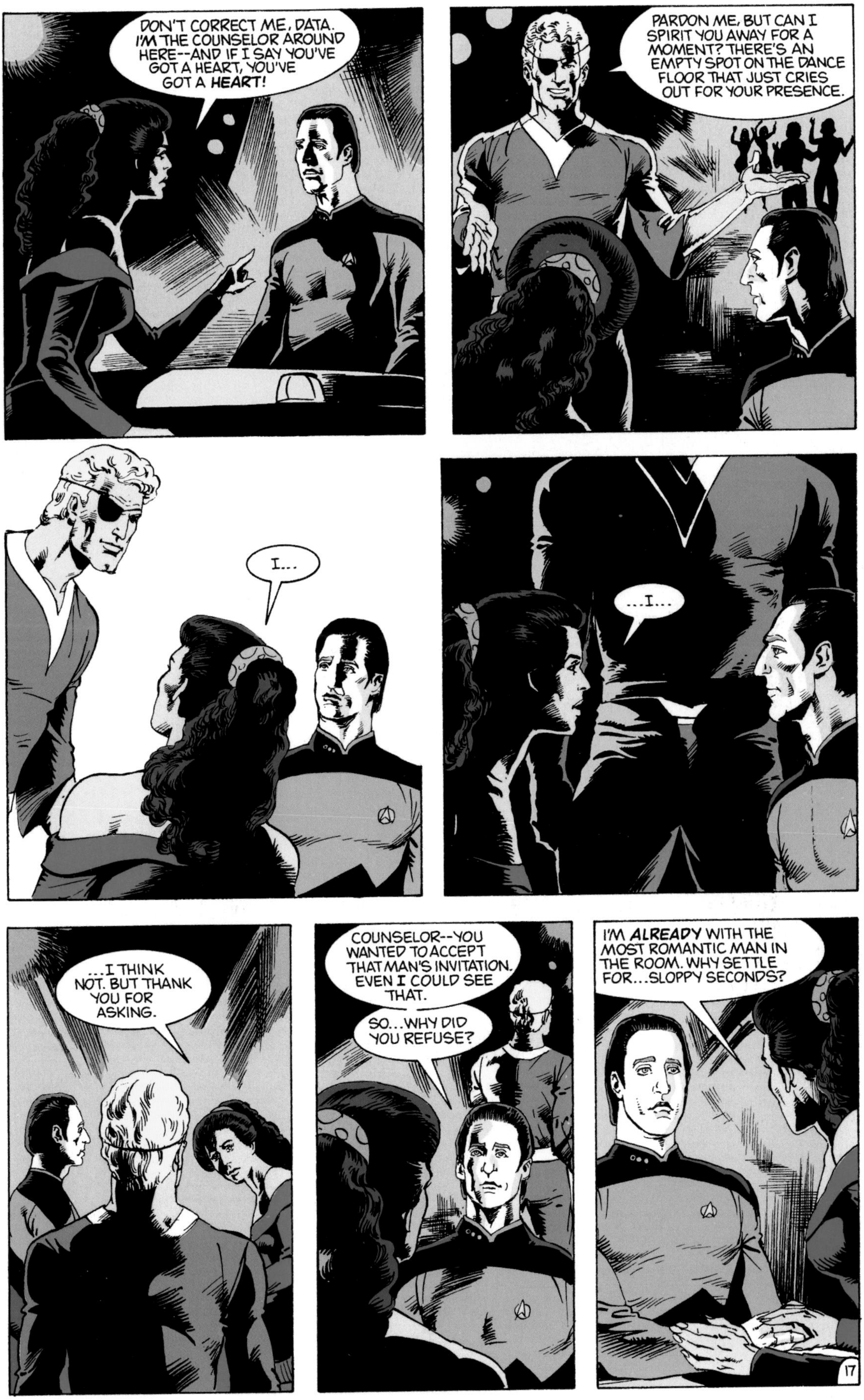
DON'T CORRECT ME, DATA. I'M THE COUNSELOR AROUND HERE--AND IF I SAY YOU'VE GOT A HEART, YOU'VE GOT A **HEART**!
PARDON ME, BUT CAN I SPIRIT YOU AWAY FOR A MOMENT? THERE'S AN EMPTY SPOT ON THE DANCE FLOOR THAT JUST CRIES OUT FOR YOUR PRESENCE.
I...
...I...
...I THINK NOT. BUT THANK YOU FOR ASKING.
COUNSELOR--YOU WANTED TO ACCEPT THAT MAN'S INVITATION. EVEN I COULD SEE THAT.
SO...WHY DID YOU REFUSE?
I'M **ALREADY** WITH THE MOST ROMANTIC MAN IN THE ROOM. WHY SETTLE FOR...SLOPPY SECONDS?
17

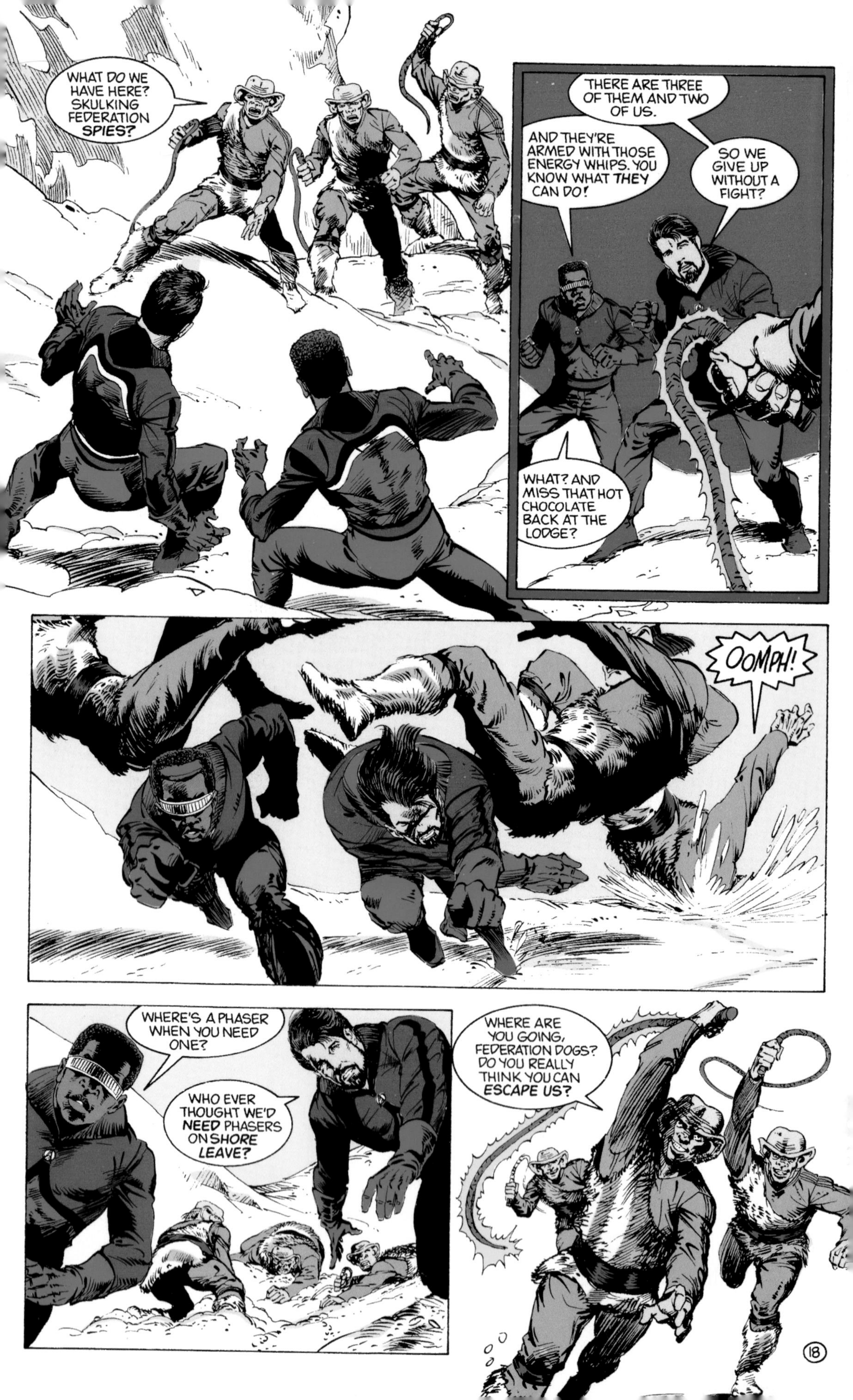
WHAT DO WE HAVE HERE? SKULKING FEDERATION SPIES?
THERE ARE THREE OF THEM AND TWO OF US.
AND THEY'RE ARMED WITH THOSE ENERGY WHIPS. YOU KNOW WHAT THEY CAN DO!
SO WE GIVE UP WITHOUT A FIGHT?
WHAT? AND MISS THAT HOT CHOCOLATE BACK AT THE LODGE?
OOMPH!
WHERE'S A PHASER WHEN YOU NEED ONE?
WHO EVER THOUGHT WE'D NEED PHASERS ON SHORE LEAVE?
WHERE ARE YOU GOING, FEDERATION DOGS? DO YOU REALLY THINK YOU CAN ESCAPE US?
18

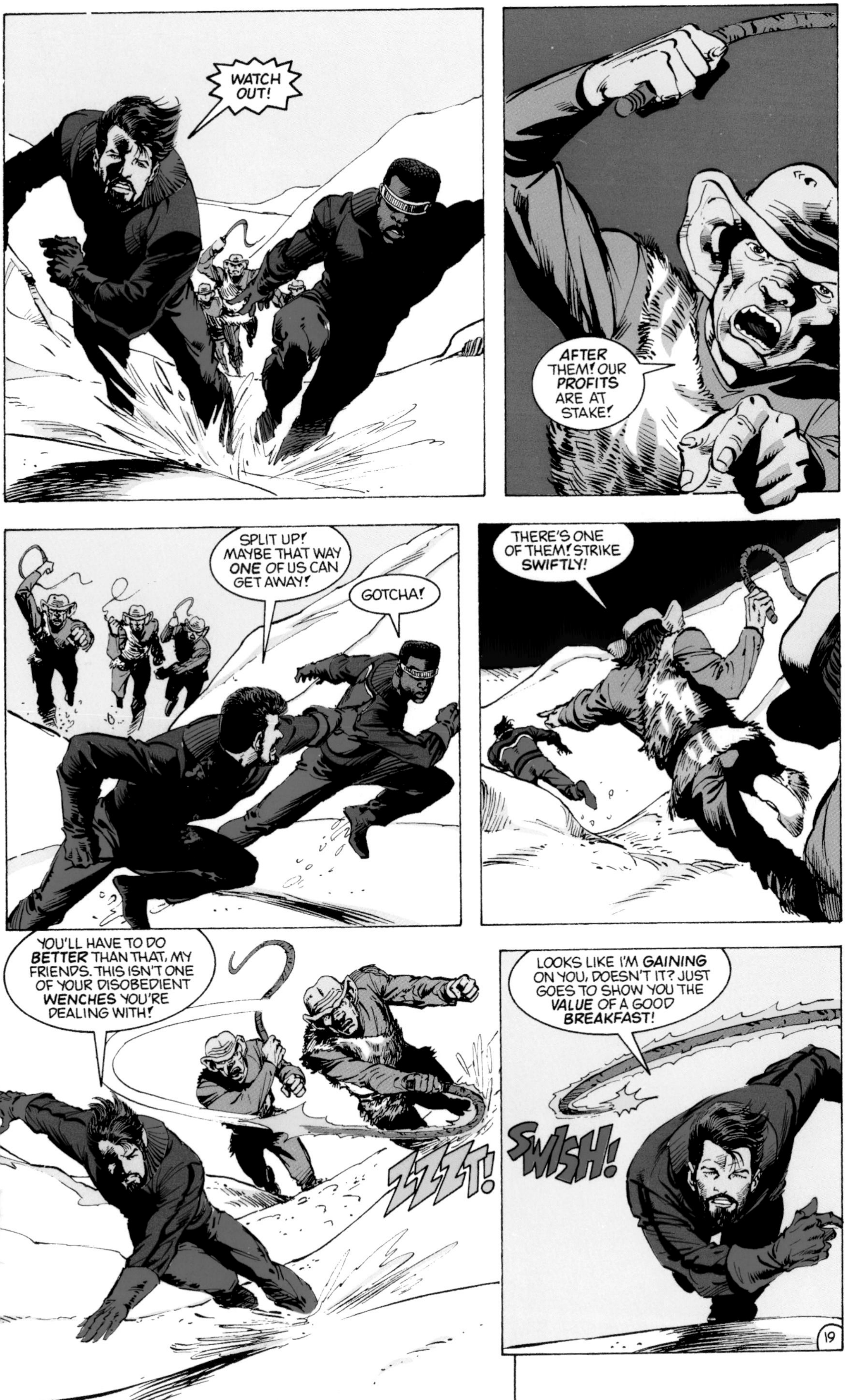
WATCH OUT!
AFTER THEM! OUR PROFITS ARE AT STAKE!
SPLIT UP! MAYBE THAT WAY ONE OF US CAN GET AWAY!
GOTCHA!
THERE'S ONE OF THEM! STRIKE SWIFTLY!
YOU'LL HAVE TO DO BETTER THAN THAT, MY FRIENDS. THIS ISN'T ONE OF YOUR DISOBEDIENT WENCHES YOU'RE DEALING WITH!
ZZZT!
SWISH!
LOOKS LIKE I'M GAINING ON YOU, DOESN'T IT? JUST GOES TO SHOW YOU THE VALUE OF A GOOD BREAKFAST!

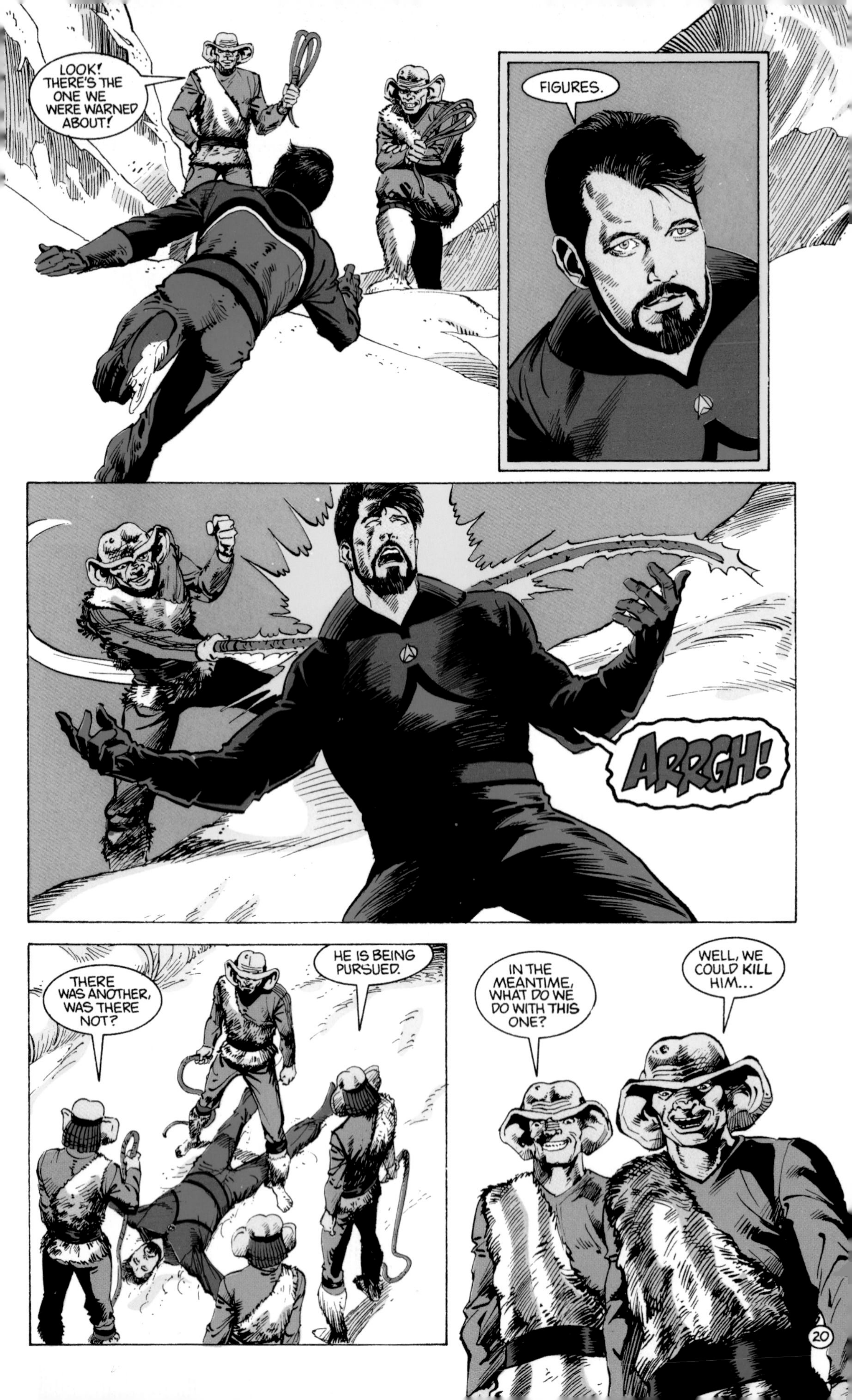
LOOK! THERE'S THE ONE WE WERE WARNED ABOUT!
FIGURES.
ARRGH!
THERE WAS ANOTHER, WAS THERE NOT?
HE IS BEING PURSUED.
IN THE MEANTIME, WHAT DO WE DO WITH THIS ONE?
WELL, WE COULD **KILL** HIM...
20

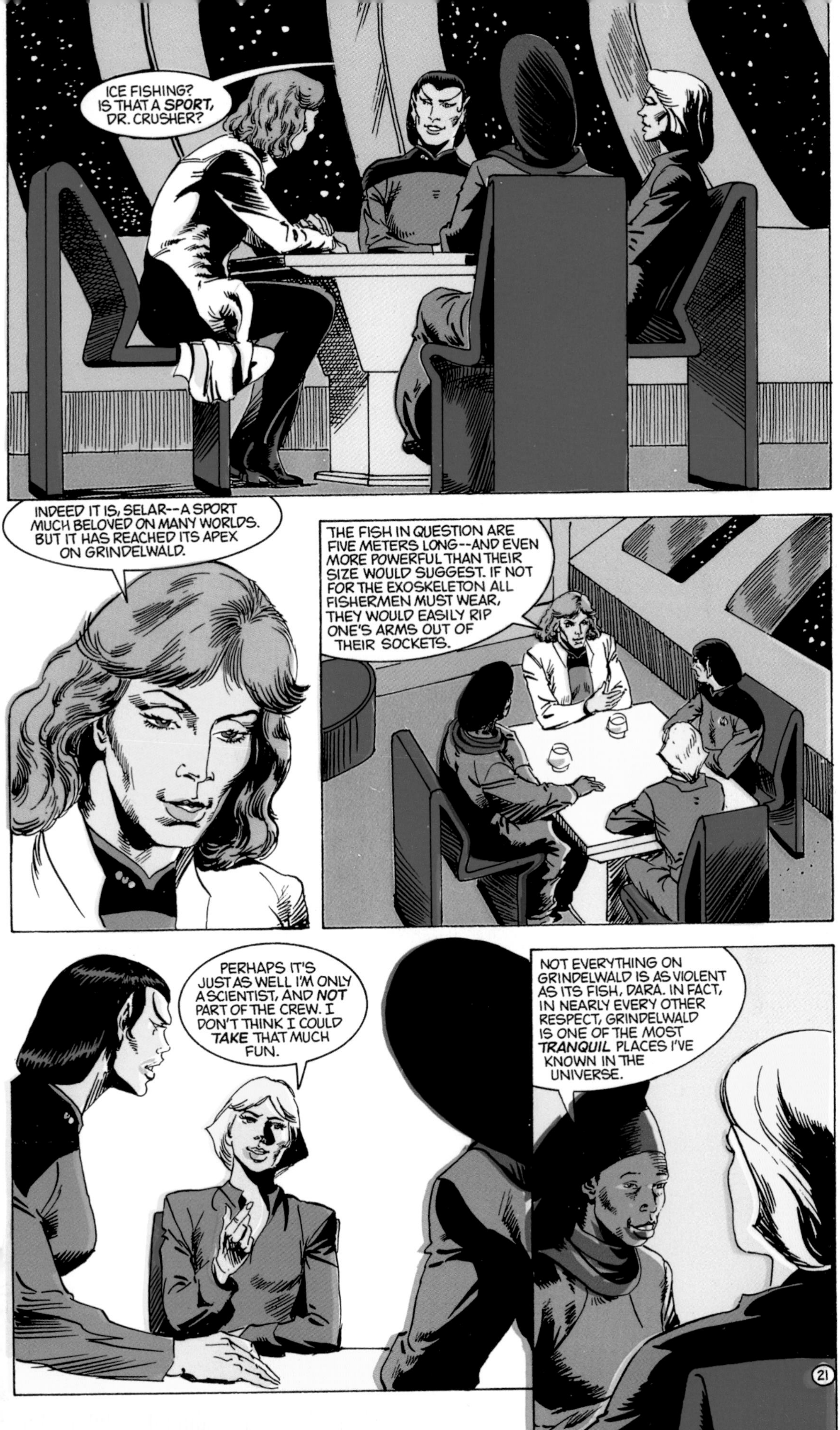

ICE FISHING? IS THAT A SPORT, DR. CRUSHER?
INDEED IT IS, SELAR--A SPORT MUCH BELOVED ON MANY WORLDS. BUT IT HAS REACHED ITS APEX ON GRINDELWALD.
THE FISH IN QUESTION ARE FIVE METERS LONG--AND EVEN MORE POWERFUL THAN THEIR SIZE WOULD SUGGEST. IF NOT FOR THE EXOSKELETON ALL FISHERMEN MUST WEAR, THEY WOULD EASILY RIP ONE'S ARMS OUT OF THEIR SOCKETS.
PERHAPS IT'S JUST AS WELL I'M ONLY A SCIENTIST, AND NOT PART OF THE CREW. I DON'T THINK I COULD TAKE THAT MUCH FUN.
NOT EVERYTHING ON GRINDELWALD IS AS VIOLENT AS ITS FISH, DARA. IN FACT, IN NEARLY EVERY OTHER RESPECT, GRINDELWALD IS ONE OF THE MOST TRANQUIL PLACES I'VE KNOWN IN THE UNIVERSE.

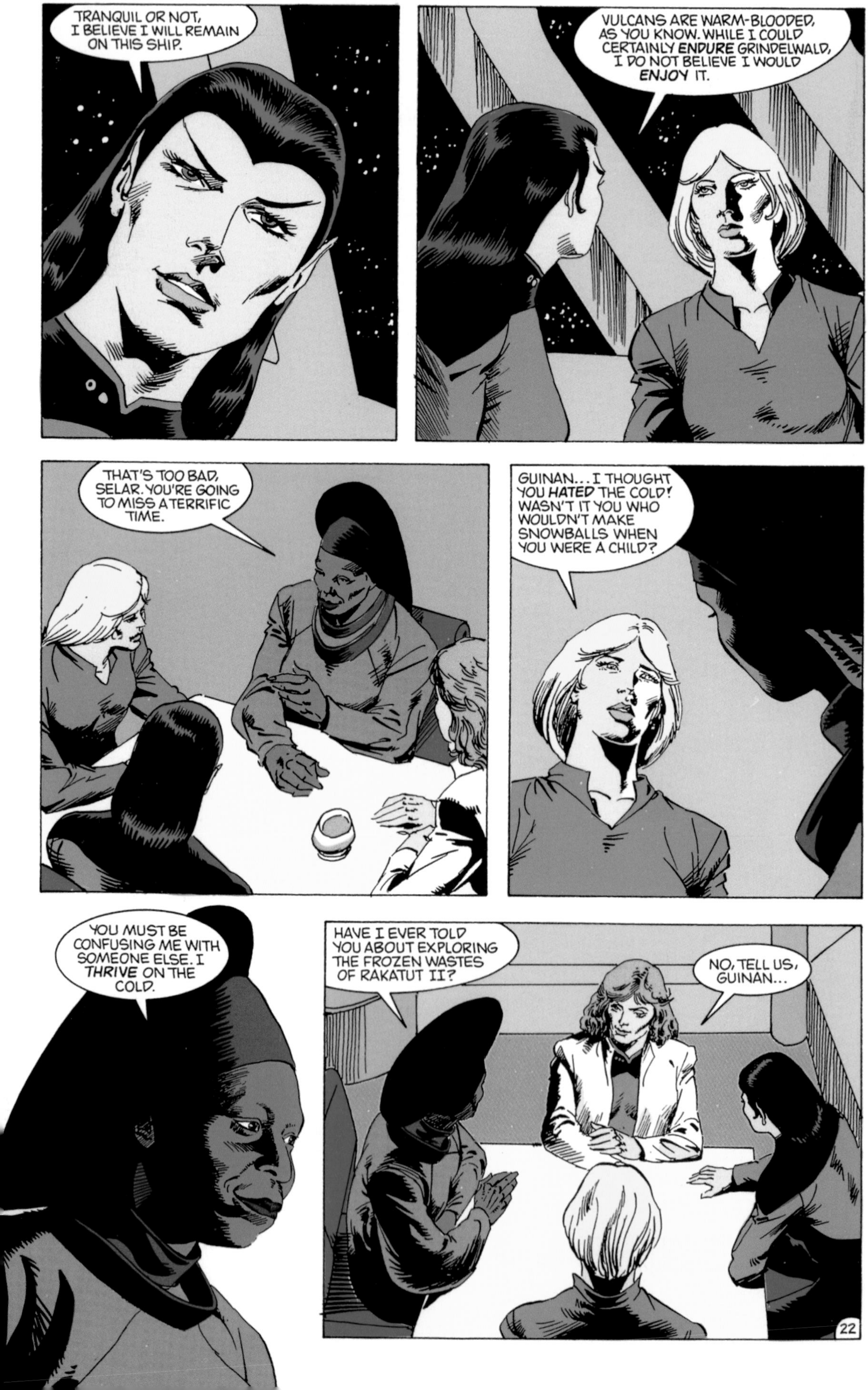
TRANQUIL OR NOT, I BELIEVE I WILL REMAIN ON THIS SHIP.
VULCANS ARE WARM-BLOODED, AS YOU KNOW. WHILE I COULD CERTAINLY **ENDURE** GRINDELWALD, I DO NOT BELIEVE I WOULD **ENJOY** IT.
THAT'S TOO BAD, SELAR. YOU'RE GOING TO MISS A TERRIFIC TIME.
GUINAN... I THOUGHT YOU **HATED** THE COLD! WASN'T IT YOU WHO WOULDN'T MAKE SNOWBALLS WHEN YOU WERE A CHILD?
YOU MUST BE CONFUSING ME WITH SOMEONE ELSE. I **THRIVE** ON THE COLD.
HAVE I EVER TOLD YOU ABOUT EXPLORING THE FROZEN WASTES OF RAKATUT II?
NO, TELL US, GUINAN...
22

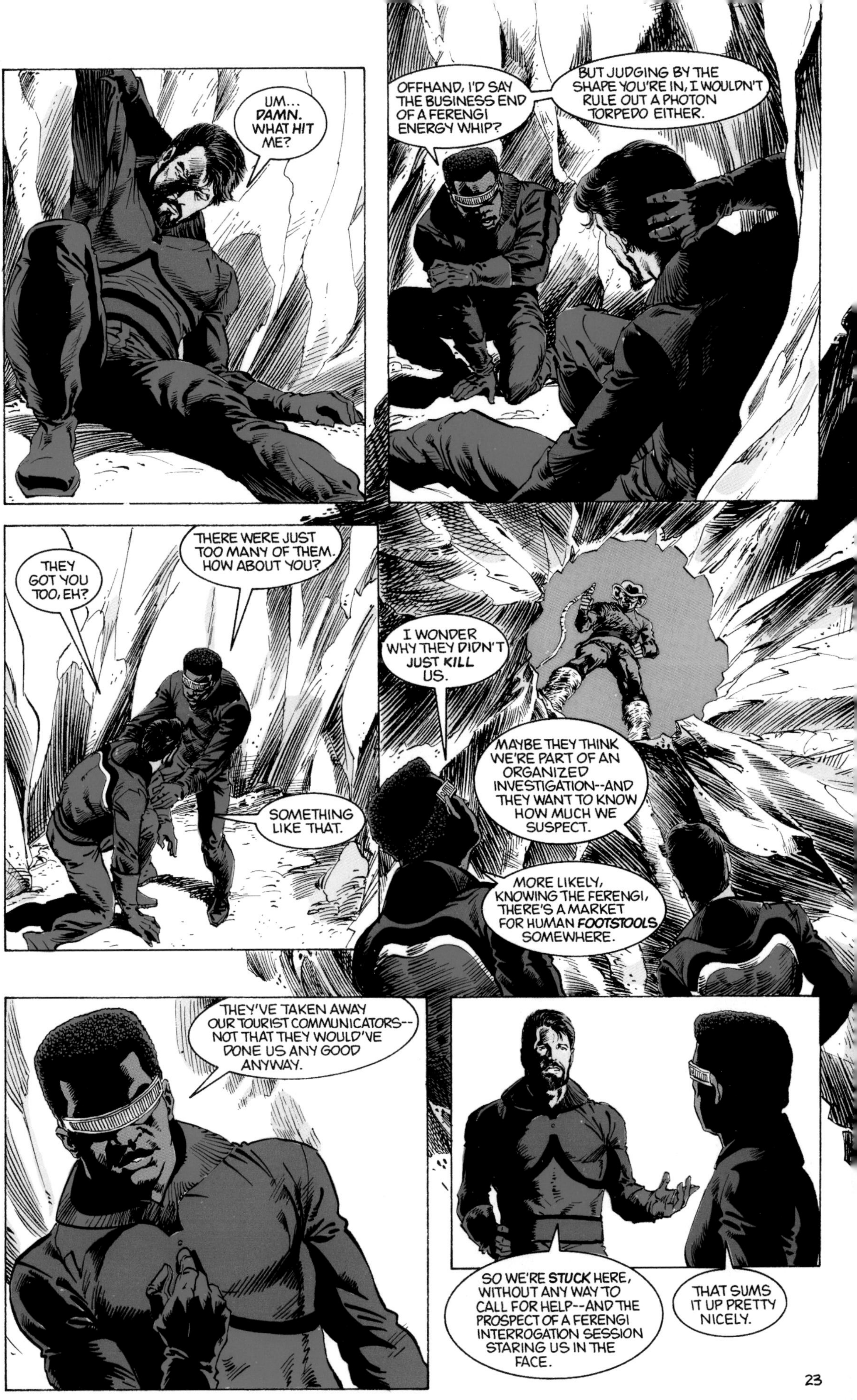
UM... DAMN. WHAT HIT ME?
OFFHAND, I'D SAY THE BUSINESS END OF A FERENGI ENERGY WHIP?
BUT JUDGING BY THE SHAPE YOU'RE IN, I WOULDN'T RULE OUT A PHOTON TORPEDO EITHER.
THEY GOT YOU TOO, EH?
THERE WERE JUST TOO MANY OF THEM. HOW ABOUT YOU?
SOMETHING LIKE THAT.
I WONDER WHY THEY DIDN'T JUST KILL US.
MAYBE THEY THINK WE'RE PART OF AN ORGANIZED INVESTIGATION--AND THEY WANT TO KNOW HOW MUCH WE SUSPECT.
MORE LIKELY, KNOWING THE FERENGI, THERE'S A MARKET FOR HUMAN FOOTSTOOLS SOMEWHERE.
THEY'VE TAKEN AWAY OUR TOURIST COMMUNICATORS--NOT THAT THEY WOULD'VE DONE US ANY GOOD ANYWAY.
SO WE'RE STUCK HERE, WITHOUT ANY WAY TO CALL FOR HELP--AND THE PROSPECT OF A FERENGI INTERROGATION SESSION STARING US IN THE FACE.
THAT SUMS IT UP PRETTY NICELY.

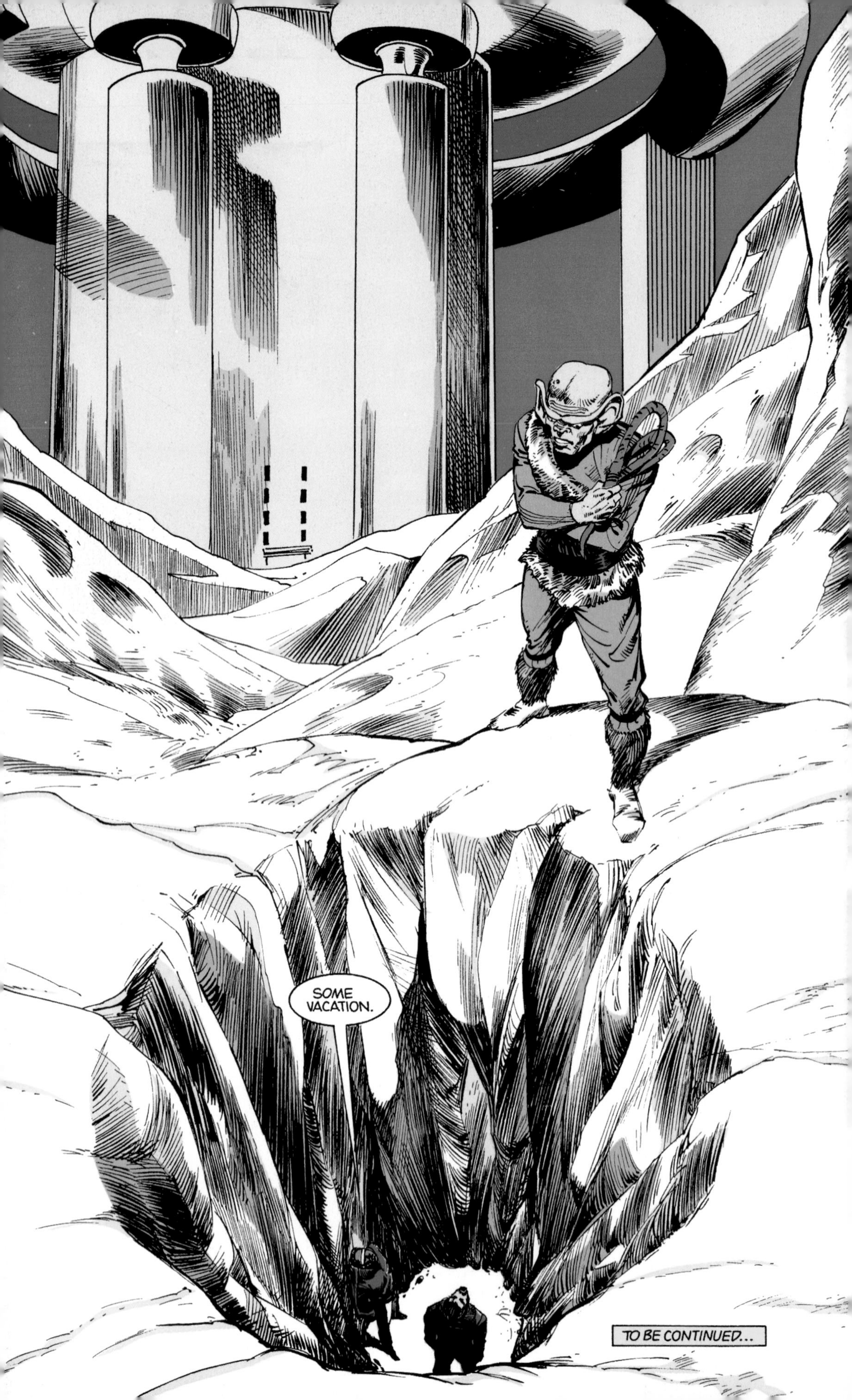
SOME VACATION.
TO BE CONTINUED...

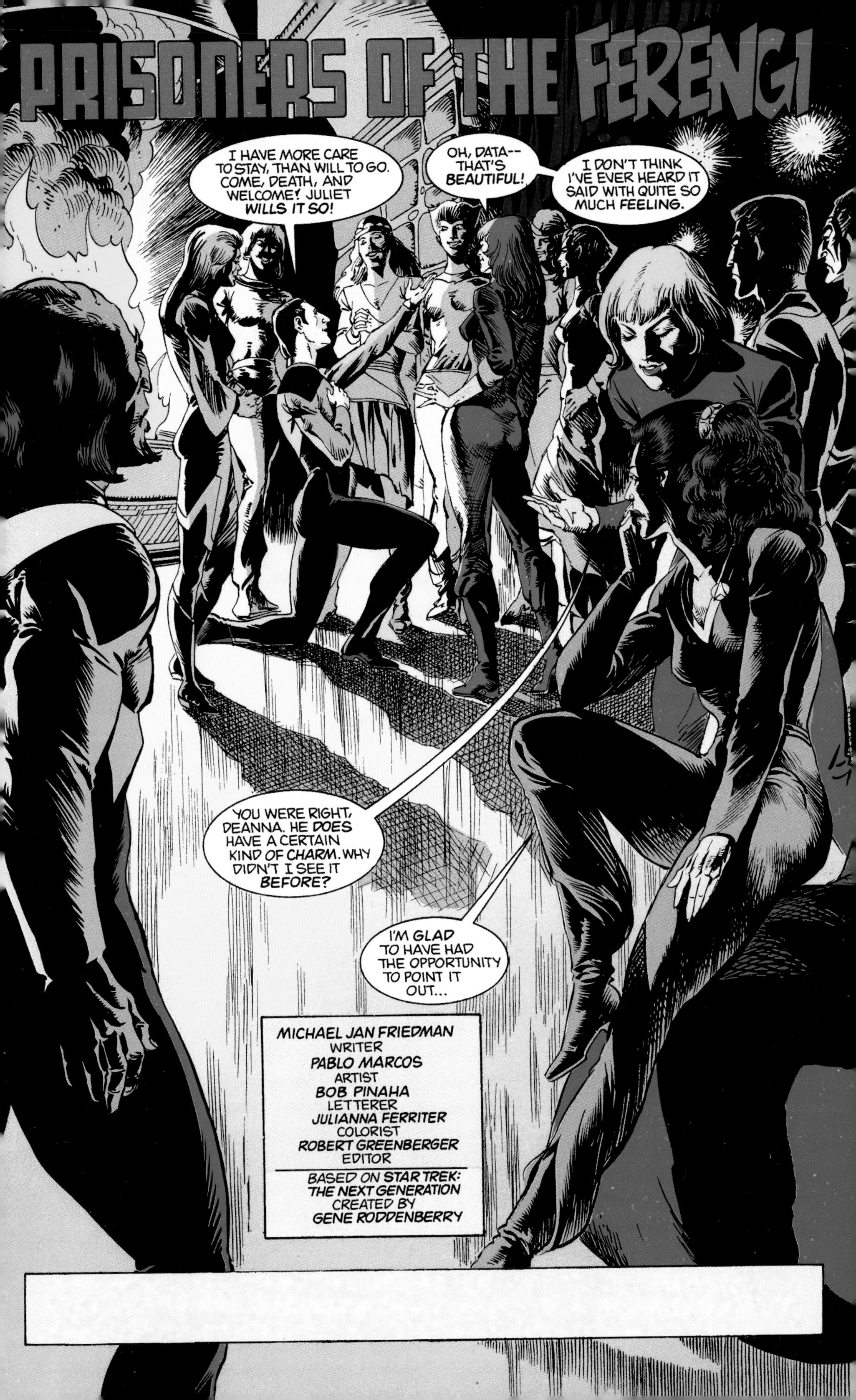
PRISONERS OF THE FERENGI
I HAVE MORE CARE TO STAY, THAN WILL TO GO. COME, DEATH, AND WELCOME! JULIET WILLS IT SO!
OH, DATA-- THAT'S BEAUTIFUL!
I DON'T THINK I'VE EVER HEARD IT SAID WITH QUITE SO MUCH FEELING.
YOU WERE RIGHT, DEANNA. HE DOES HAVE A CERTAIN KIND OF CHARM. WHY DIDN'T I SEE IT BEFORE?
I'M GLAD TO HAVE HAD THE OPPORTUNITY TO POINT IT OUT...
MICHAEL JAN FRIEDMAN WRITER
PABLO MARCOS ARTIST
BOB PINAHA LETTERER
JULIANNA FERRITER COLORIST
ROBERT GREENBERGER EDITOR
BASED ON STAR TREK: THE NEXT GENERATION CREATED BY GENE RODDENBERRY

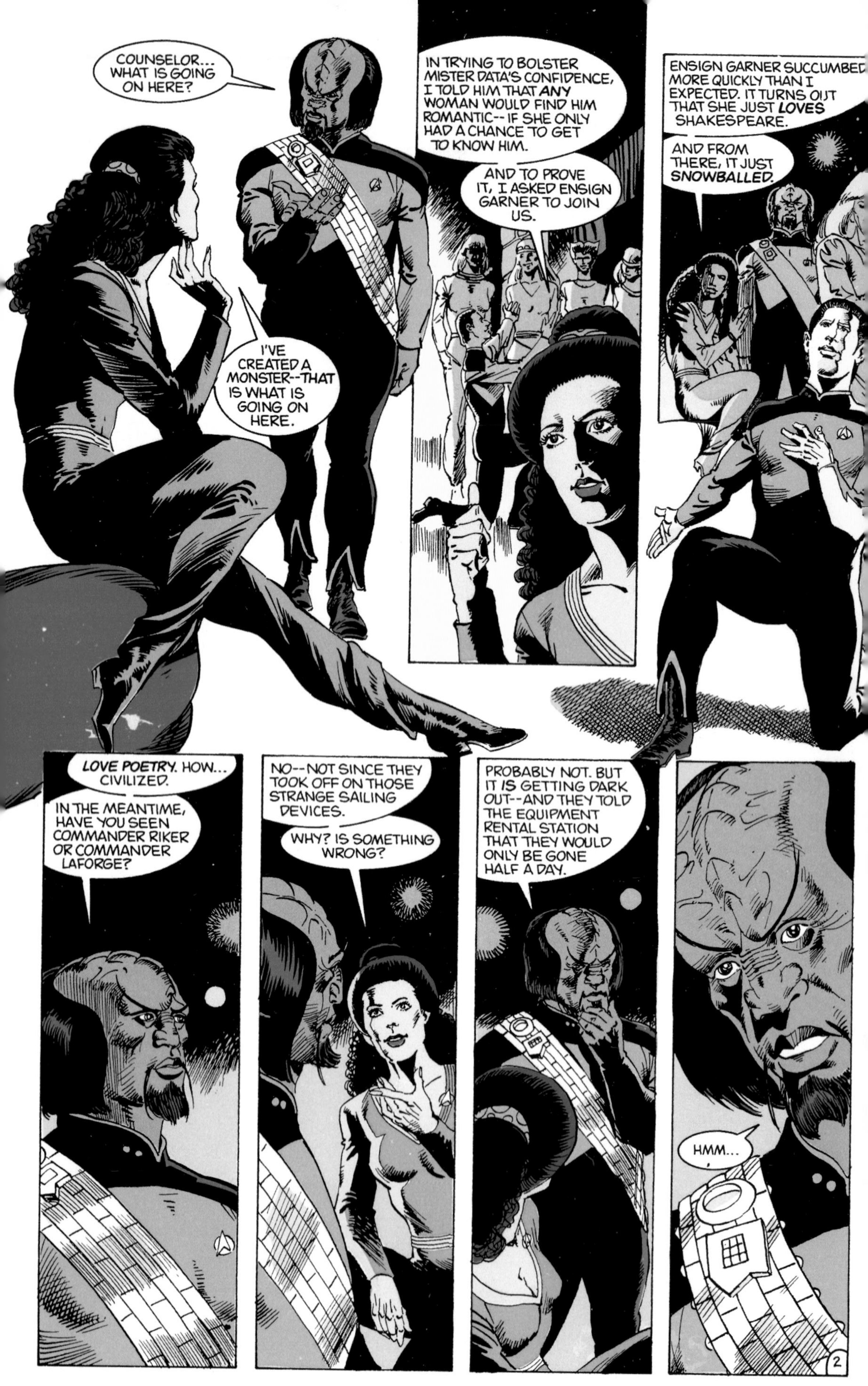
COUNSELOR... WHAT IS GOING ON HERE?
I'VE CREATED A MONSTER--THAT IS WHAT IS GOING ON HERE.
IN TRYING TO BOLSTER MISTER DATA'S CONFIDENCE, I TOLD HIM THAT ANY WOMAN WOULD FIND HIM ROMANTIC-- IF SHE ONLY HAD A CHANCE TO GET TO KNOW HIM.
AND TO PROVE IT, I ASKED ENSIGN GARNER TO JOIN US.
ENSIGN GARNER SUCCUMBED MORE QUICKLY THAN I EXPECTED. IT TURNS OUT THAT SHE JUST LOVES SHAKESPEARE.
AND FROM THERE, IT JUST SNOWBALLED.
LOVE POETRY. HOW... CIVILIZED.
IN THE MEANTIME, HAVE YOU SEEN COMMANDER RIKER OR COMMANDER LAFORGE?
NO--NOT SINCE THEY TOOK OFF ON THOSE STRANGE SAILING DEVICES.
WHY? IS SOMETHING WRONG?
PROBABLY NOT. BUT IT IS GETTING DARK OUT--AND THEY TOLD THE EQUIPMENT RENTAL STATION THAT THEY WOULD ONLY BE GONE HALF A DAY.
HMM...

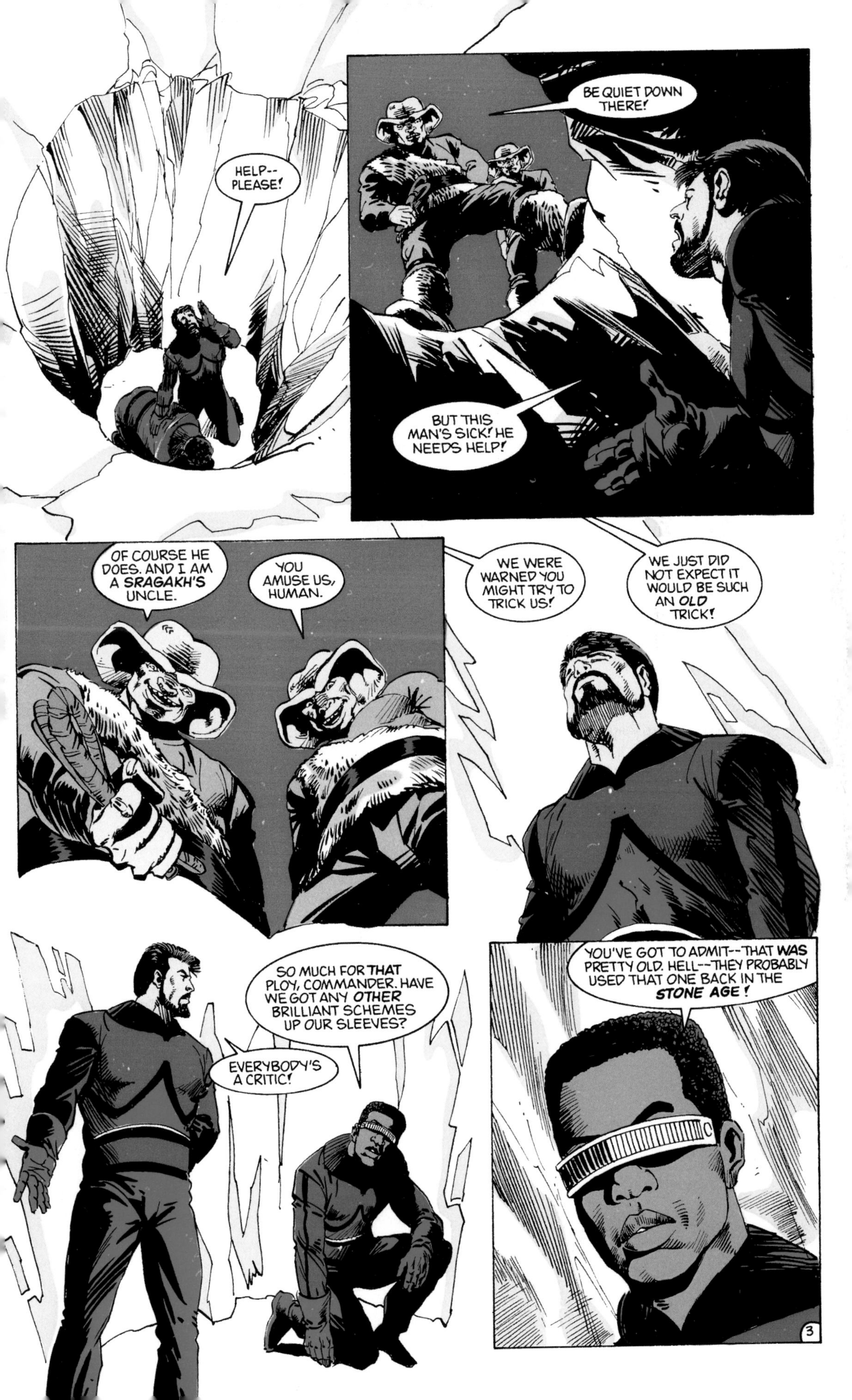
HELP-- PLEASE!
BE QUIET DOWN THERE!
BUT THIS MAN'S SICK! HE NEEDS HELP!
OF COURSE HE DOES. AND I AM A SRAGAKH'S UNCLE.
YOU AMUSE US, HUMAN.
WE WERE WARNED YOU MIGHT TRY TO TRICK US!
WE JUST DID NOT EXPECT IT WOULD BE SUCH AN OLD TRICK!
SO MUCH FOR THAT PLOY, COMMANDER. HAVE WE GOT ANY OTHER BRILLIANT SCHEMES UP OUR SLEEVES?
EVERYBODY'S A CRITIC!
YOU'VE GOT TO ADMIT--THAT WAS PRETTY OLD. HELL--THEY PROBABLY USED THAT ONE BACK IN THE STONE AGE!
3

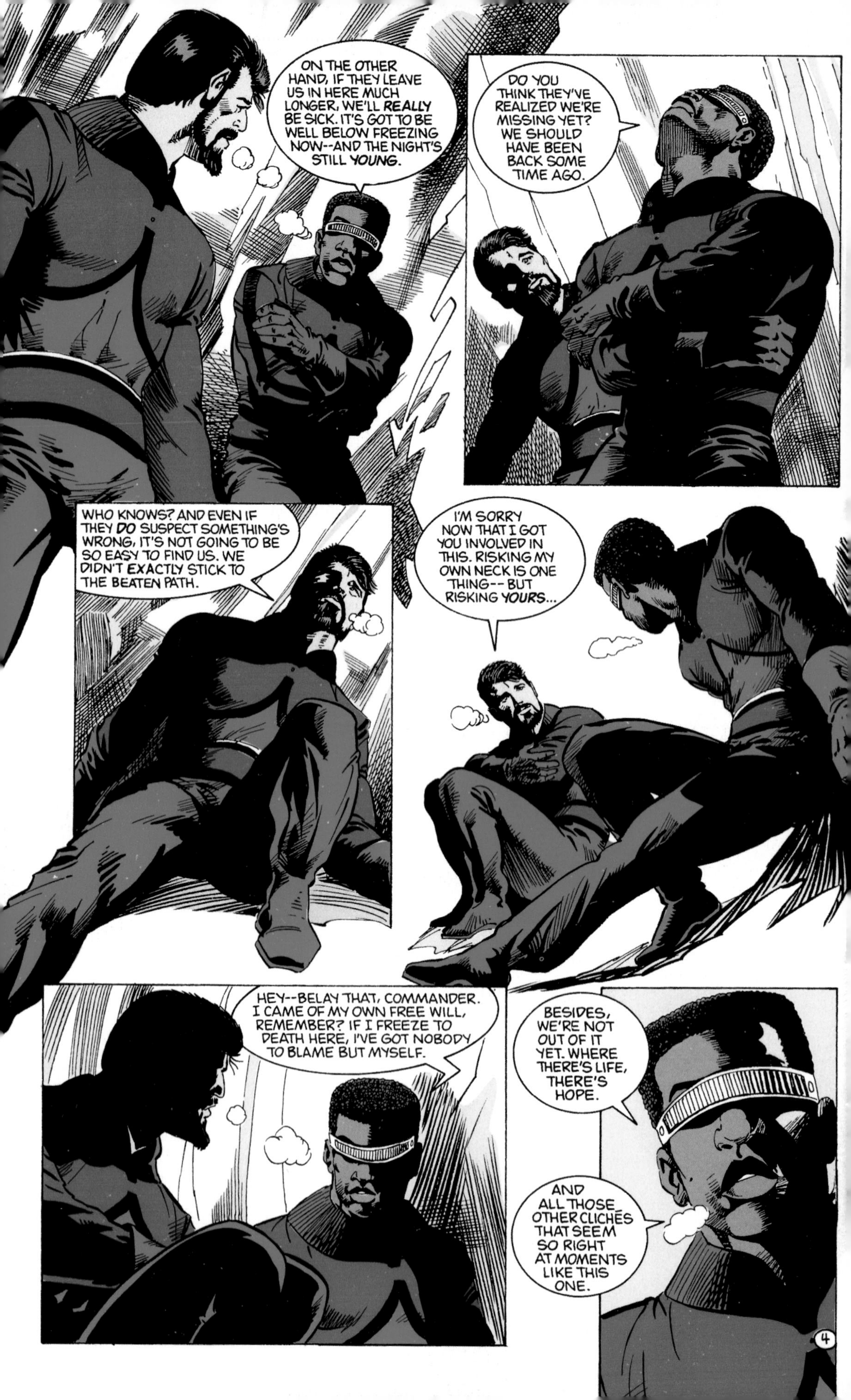

ON THE OTHER HAND, IF THEY LEAVE US IN HERE MUCH LONGER, WE'LL REALLY BE SICK. IT'S GOT TO BE WELL BELOW FREEZING NOW--AND THE NIGHT'S STILL YOUNG.
DO YOU THINK THEY'VE REALIZED WE'RE MISSING YET? WE SHOULD HAVE BEEN BACK SOME TIME AGO.
WHO KNOWS? AND EVEN IF THEY DO SUSPECT SOMETHING'S WRONG, IT'S NOT GOING TO BE SO EASY TO FIND US. WE DIDN'T EXACTLY STICK TO THE BEATEN PATH.
I'M SORRY NOW THAT I GOT YOU INVOLVED IN THIS. RISKING MY OWN NECK IS ONE THING-- BUT RISKING YOURS...
HEY--BELAY THAT, COMMANDER. I CAME OF MY OWN FREE WILL, REMEMBER? IF I FREEZE TO DEATH HERE, I'VE GOT NOBODY TO BLAME BUT MYSELF.
BESIDES, WE'RE NOT OUT OF IT YET. WHERE THERE'S LIFE, THERE'S HOPE.
AND ALL THOSE OTHER CLICHÉS THAT SEEM SO RIGHT AT MOMENTS LIKE THIS ONE.

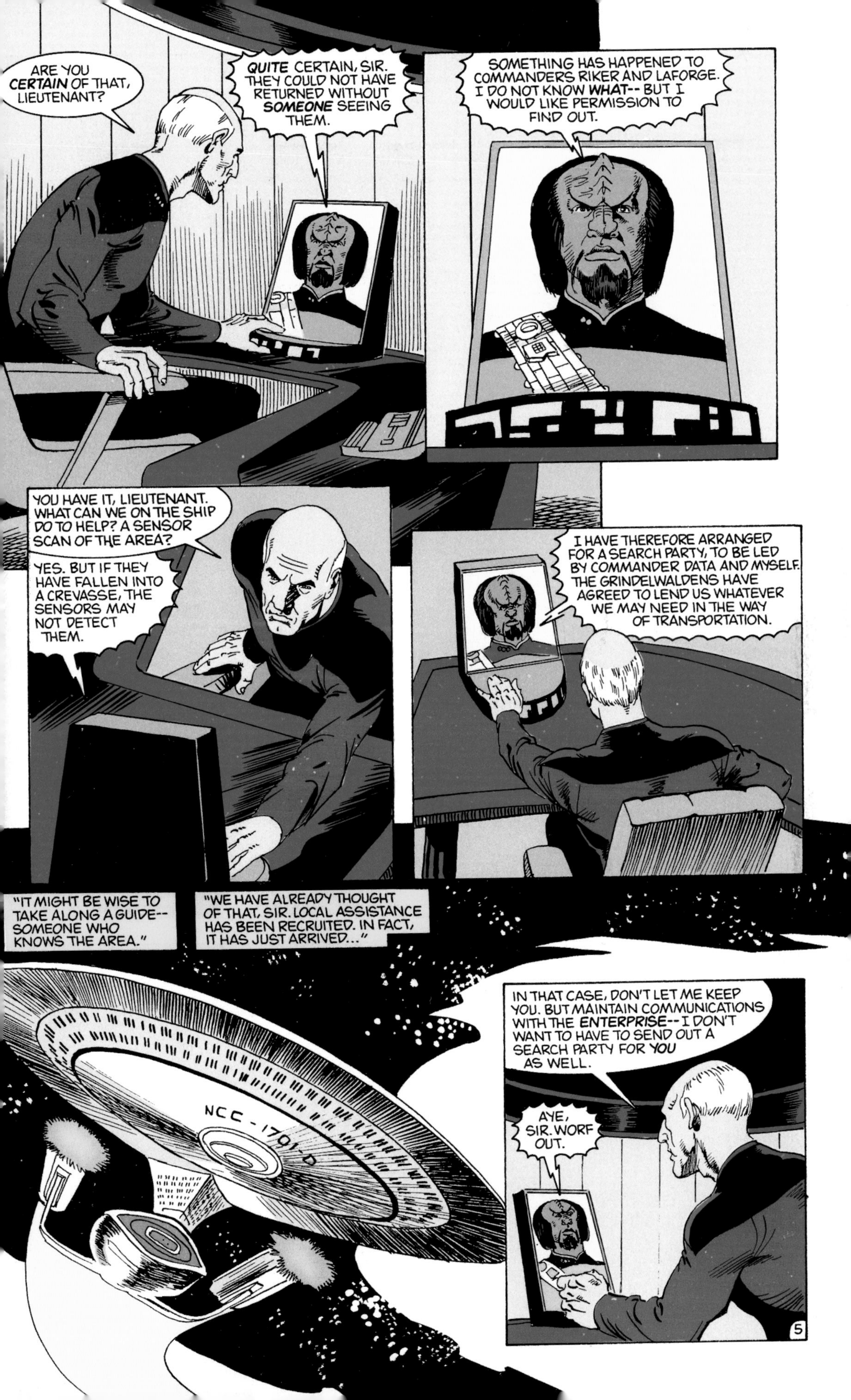
ARE YOU CERTAIN OF THAT, LIEUTENANT?
QUITE CERTAIN, SIR. THEY COULD NOT HAVE RETURNED WITHOUT SOMEONE SEEING THEM.
SOMETHING HAS HAPPENED TO COMMANDERS RIKER AND LAFORGE. I DO NOT KNOW WHAT-- BUT I WOULD LIKE PERMISSION TO FIND OUT.
YOU HAVE IT, LIEUTENANT. WHAT CAN WE ON THE SHIP DO TO HELP? A SENSOR SCAN OF THE AREA?
YES. BUT IF THEY HAVE FALLEN INTO A CREVASSE, THE SENSORS MAY NOT DETECT THEM.
I HAVE THEREFORE ARRANGED FOR A SEARCH PARTY, TO BE LED BY COMMANDER DATA AND MYSELF. THE GRINDELWALDENS HAVE AGREED TO LEND US WHATEVER WE MAY NEED IN THE WAY OF TRANSPORTATION.
"IT MIGHT BE WISE TO TAKE ALONG A GUIDE-- SOMEONE WHO KNOWS THE AREA."
"WE HAVE ALREADY THOUGHT OF THAT, SIR. LOCAL ASSISTANCE HAS BEEN RECRUITED. IN FACT, IT HAS JUST ARRIVED..."
NCC-1701-D
IN THAT CASE, DON'T LET ME KEEP YOU. BUT MAINTAIN COMMUNICATIONS WITH THE ENTERPRISE-- I DON'T WANT TO HAVE TO SEND OUT A SEARCH PARTY FOR YOU AS WELL.
AYE, SIR. WORF OUT.

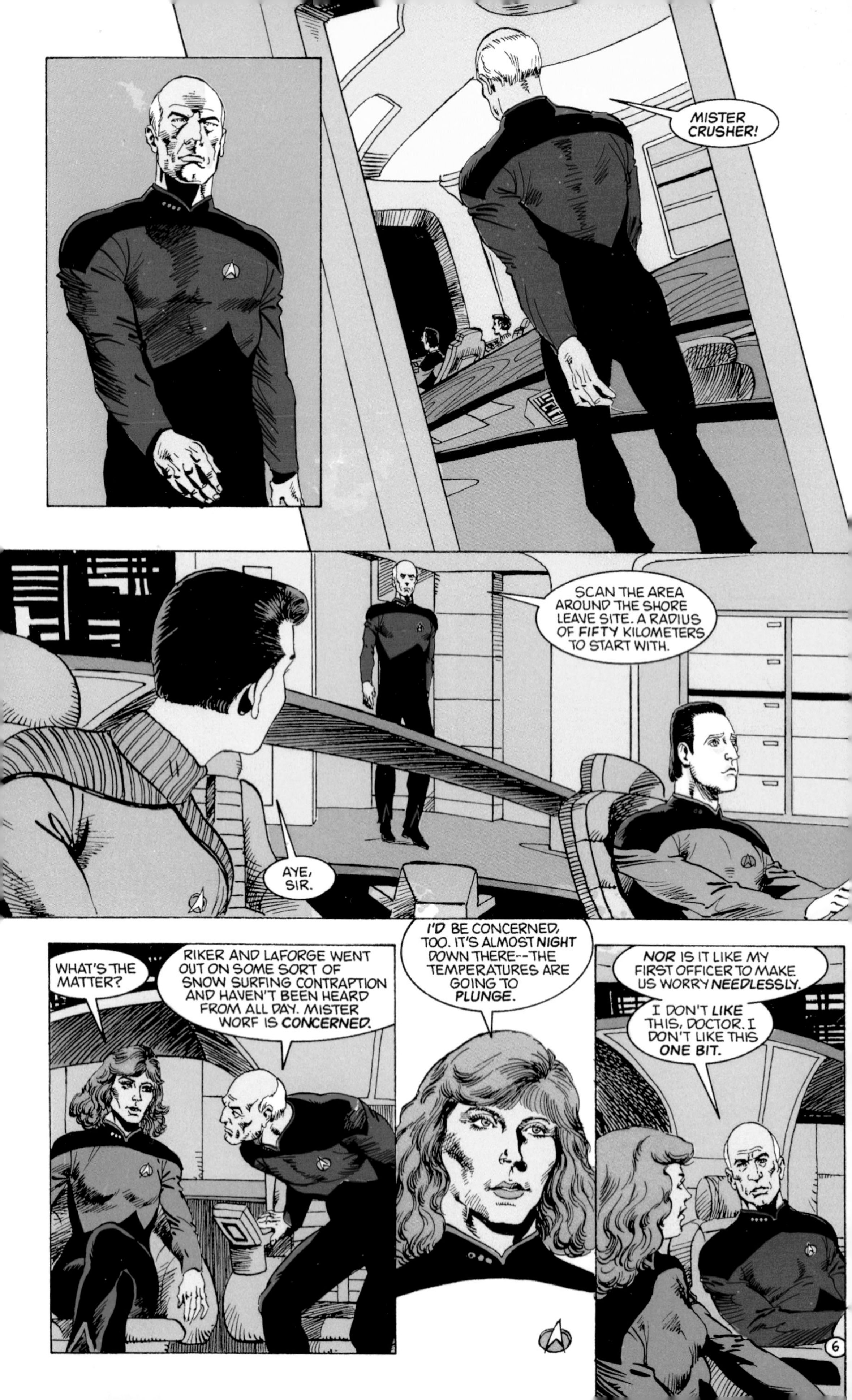
MISTER CRUSHER!
SCAN THE AREA AROUND THE SHORE LEAVE SITE. A RADIUS OF FIFTY KILOMETERS TO START WITH.
AYE, SIR.
WHAT'S THE MATTER?
RIKER AND LAFORGE WENT OUT ON SOME SORT OF SNOW SURFING CONTRAPTION AND HAVEN'T BEEN HEARD FROM ALL DAY. MISTER WORF IS CONCERNED.
I'D BE CONCERNED, TOO. IT'S ALMOST NIGHT DOWN THERE--THE TEMPERATURES ARE GOING TO PLUNGE.
NOR IS IT LIKE MY FIRST OFFICER TO MAKE US WORRY NEEDLESSLY.
I DON'T LIKE THIS, DOCTOR. I DON'T LIKE THIS ONE BIT.
6

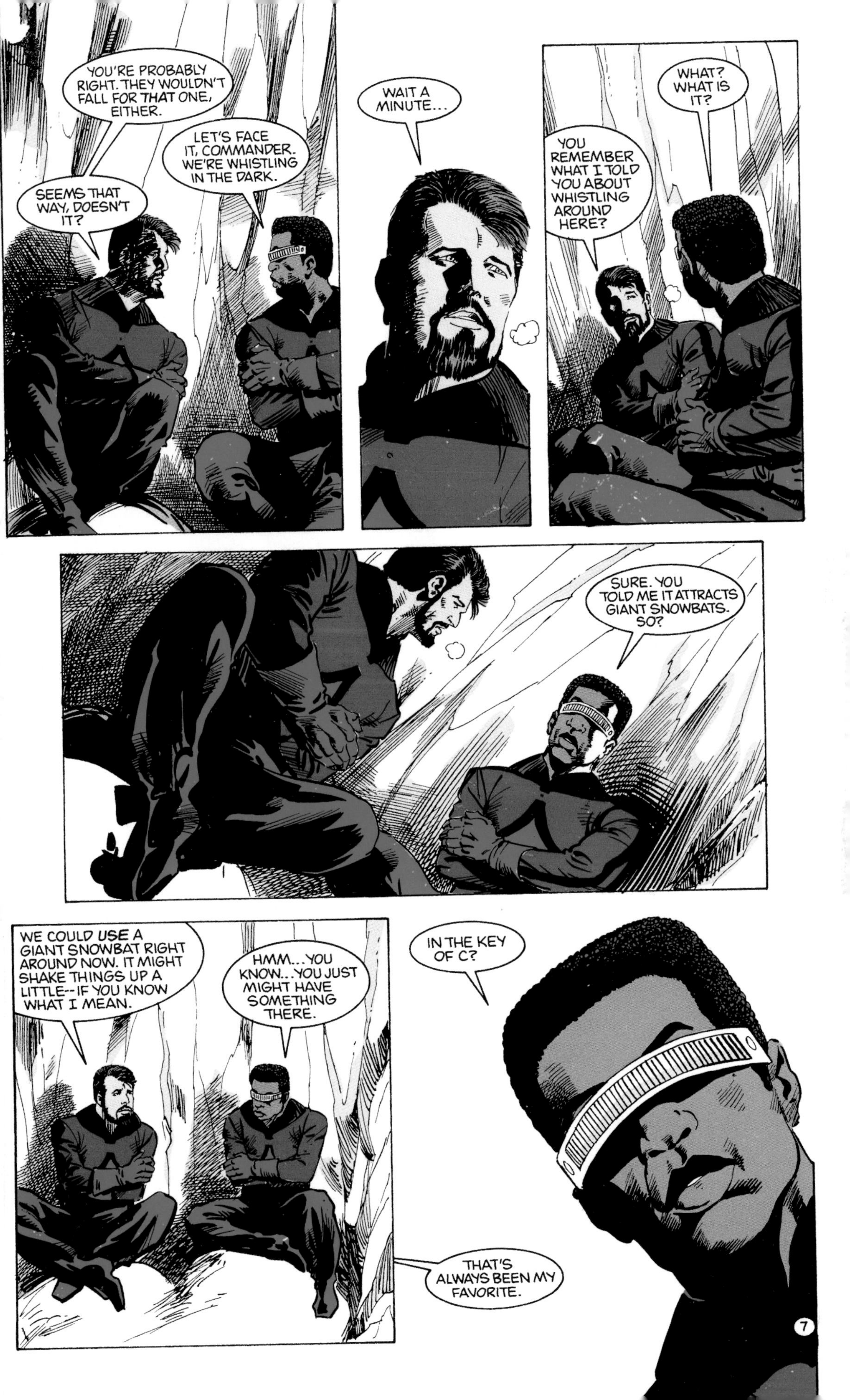

YOU'RE PROBABLY RIGHT. THEY WOULDN'T FALL FOR THAT ONE, EITHER.
LET'S FACE IT, COMMANDER. WE'RE WHISTLING IN THE DARK.
SEEMS THAT WAY, DOESN'T IT?
WAIT A MINUTE...
WHAT? WHAT IS IT?
YOU REMEMBER WHAT I TOLD YOU ABOUT WHISTLING AROUND HERE?
SURE. YOU TOLD ME IT ATTRACTS GIANT SNOWBATS. SO?
WE COULD USE A GIANT SNOWBAT RIGHT AROUND NOW. IT MIGHT SHAKE THINGS UP A LITTLE--IF YOU KNOW WHAT I MEAN.
HMM... YOU KNOW... YOU JUST MIGHT HAVE SOMETHING THERE.
IN THE KEY OF C?
THAT'S ALWAYS BEEN MY FAVORITE.

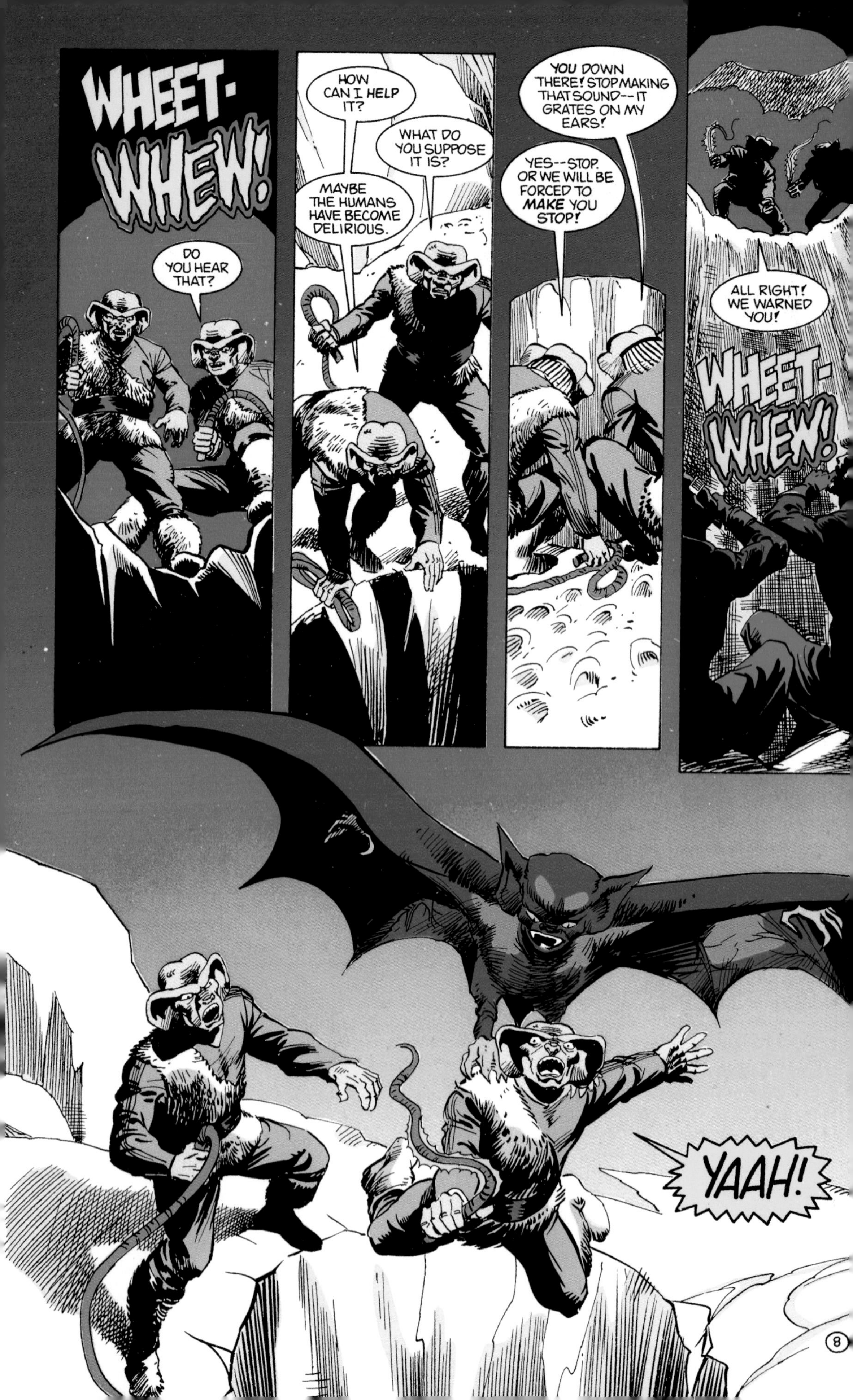
WHEET-WHEW!
DO YOU HEAR THAT?
HOW CAN I HELP IT?
WHAT DO YOU SUPPOSE IT IS?
MAYBE THE HUMANS HAVE BECOME DELIRIOUS.
YOU DOWN THERE! STOP MAKING THAT SOUND-- IT GRATES ON MY EARS!
YES--STOP. OR WE WILL BE FORCED TO MAKE YOU STOP!
ALL RIGHT! WE WARNED YOU!
WHEET-WHEW!
YAAH!

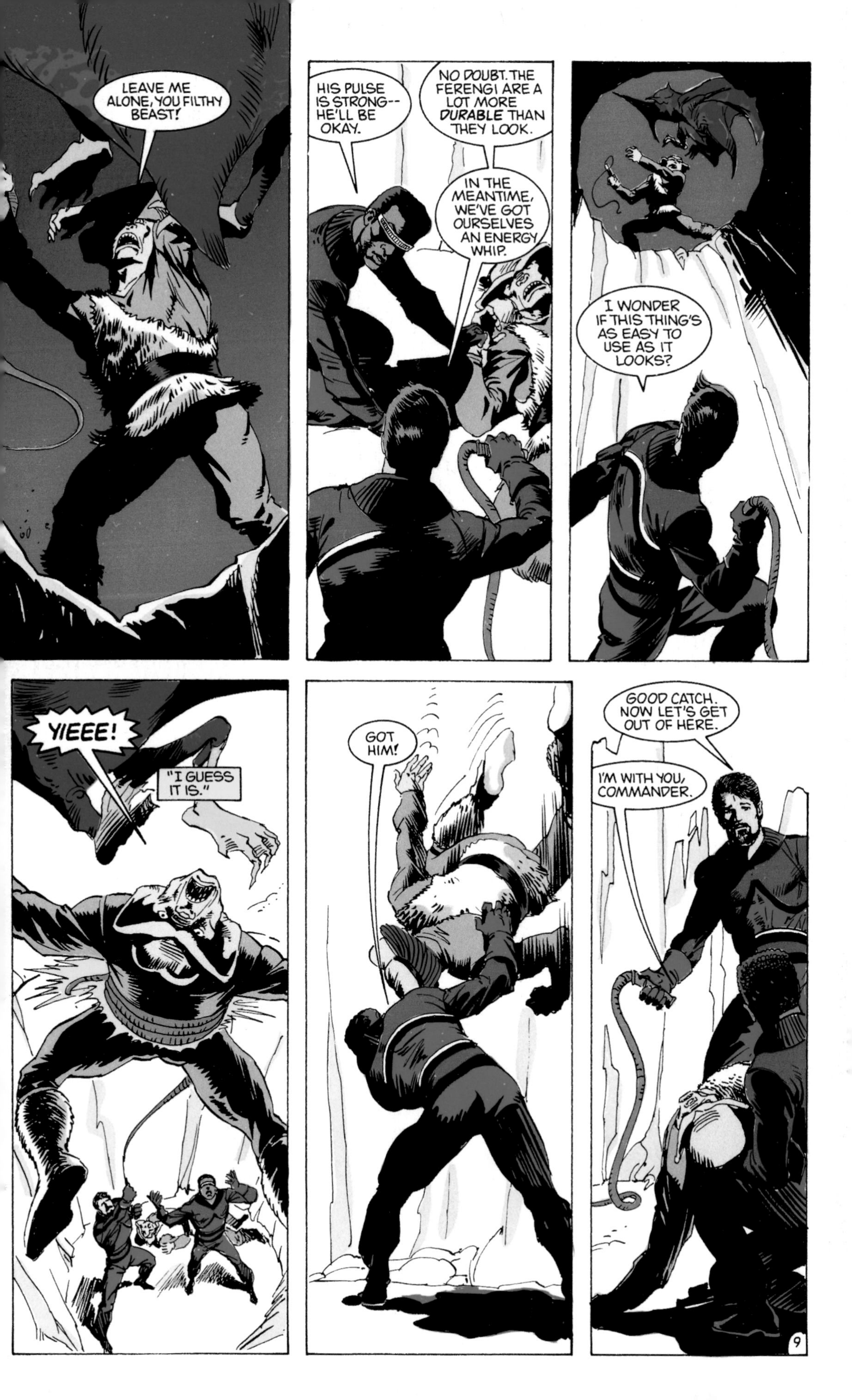
LEAVE ME ALONE, YOU FILTHY BEAST!
HIS PULSE IS STRONG-- HE'LL BE OKAY.
NO DOUBT. THE FERENGI ARE A LOT MORE DURABLE THAN THEY LOOK.
IN THE MEANTIME, WE'VE GOT OURSELVES AN ENERGY WHIP.
I WONDER IF THIS THING'S AS EASY TO USE AS IT LOOKS?
YIEEE!
"I GUESS IT IS."
GOT HIM!
GOOD CATCH. NOW LET'S GET OUT OF HERE.
I'M WITH YOU, COMMANDER.
9

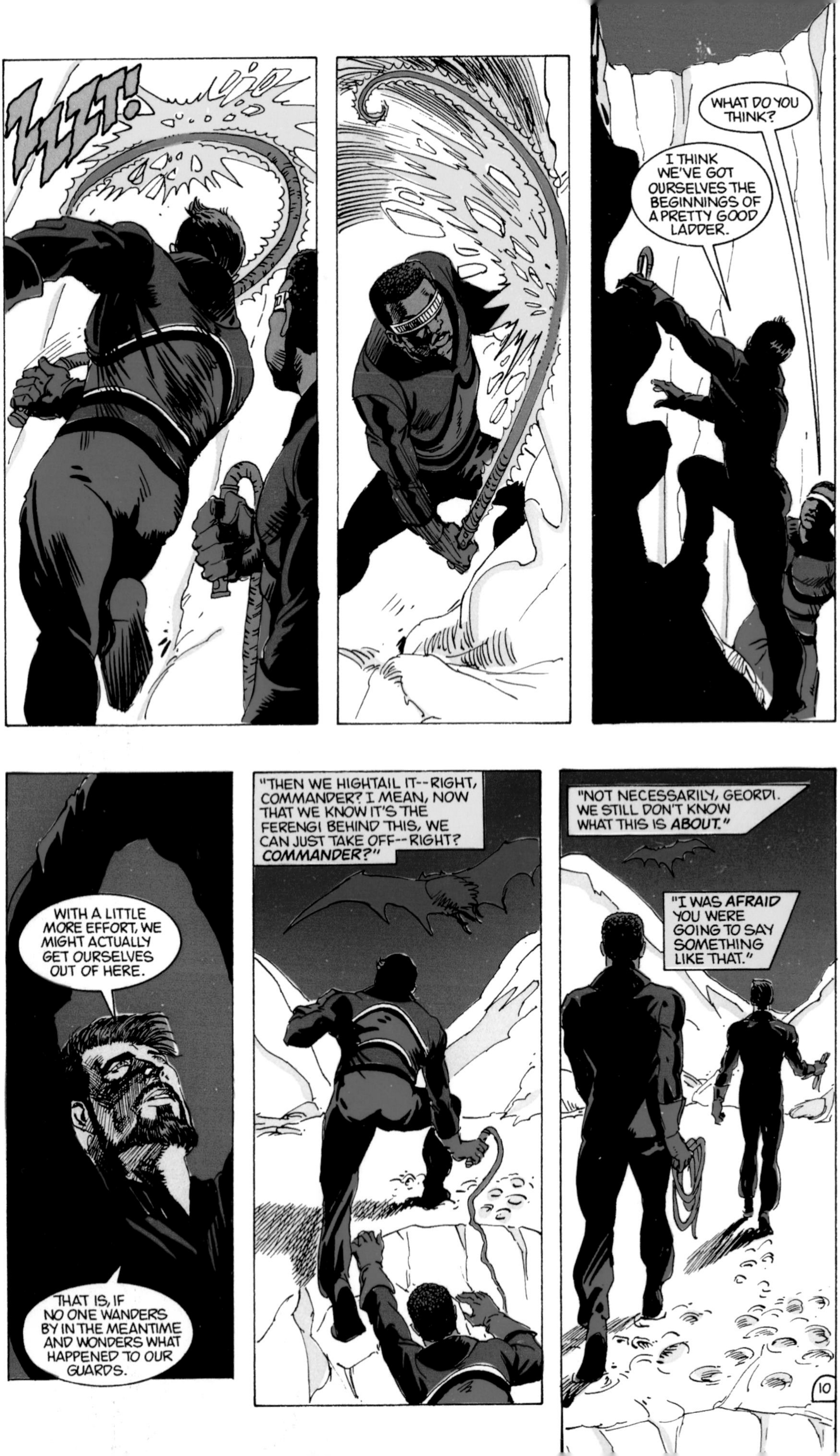
ZZZT!
WHAT DO YOU THINK?
I THINK WE'VE GOT OURSELVES THE BEGINNINGS OF A PRETTY GOOD LADDER.
WITH A LITTLE MORE EFFORT, WE MIGHT ACTUALLY GET OURSELVES OUT OF HERE.
THAT IS, IF NO ONE WANDERS BY IN THE MEANTIME AND WONDERS WHAT HAPPENED TO OUR GUARDS.
"THEN WE HIGHTAIL IT--RIGHT, COMMANDER? I MEAN, NOW THAT WE KNOW IT'S THE FERENGI BEHIND THIS, WE CAN JUST TAKE OFF--RIGHT? COMMANDER?"
"NOT NECESSARILY, GEORDI. WE STILL DON'T KNOW WHAT THIS IS ABOUT."
"I WAS AFRAID YOU WERE GOING TO SAY SOMETHING LIKE THAT."
10

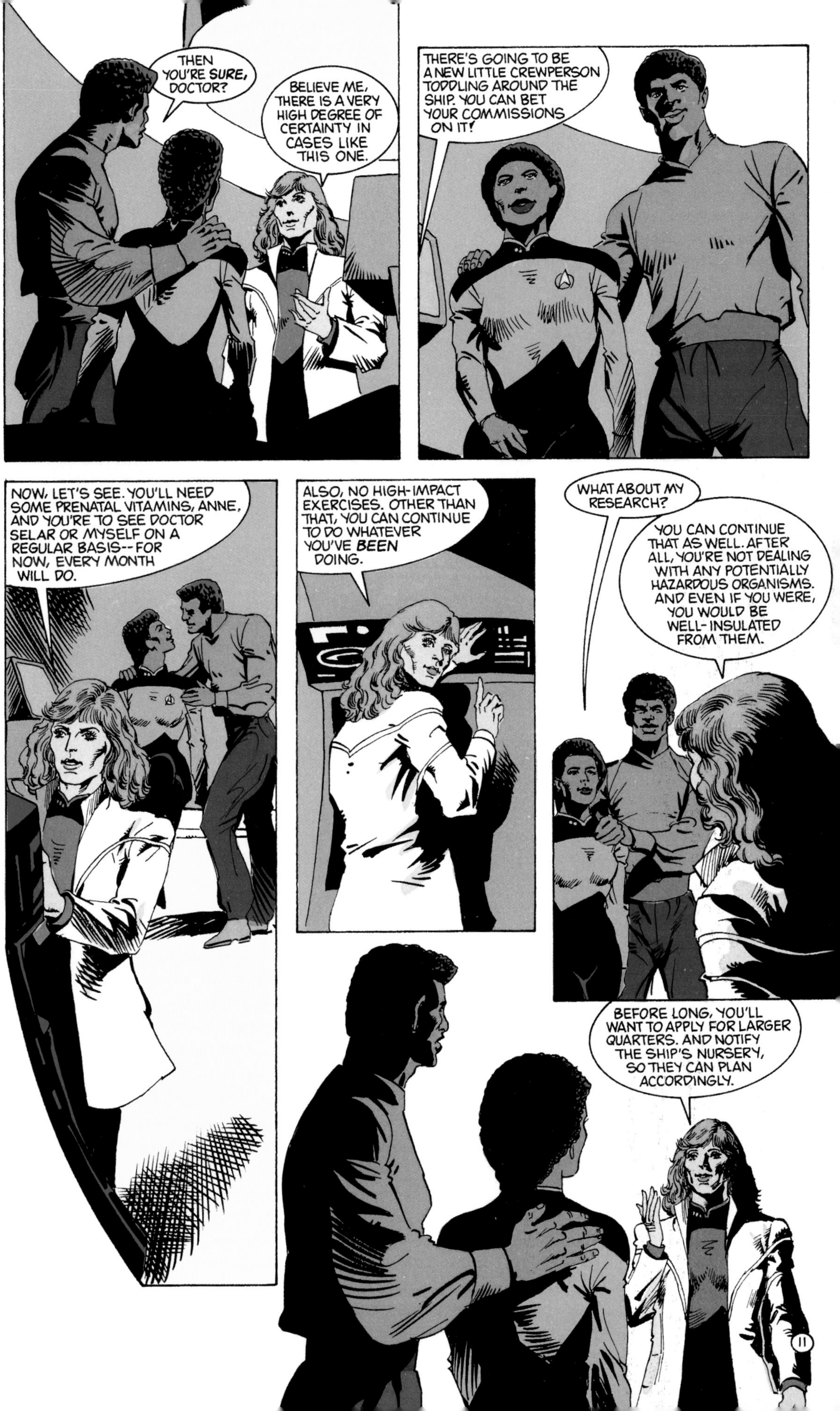
THEN YOU'RE SURE, DOCTOR?
BELIEVE ME, THERE IS A VERY HIGH DEGREE OF CERTAINTY IN CASES LIKE THIS ONE.
THERE'S GOING TO BE A NEW LITTLE CREWPERSON TODDLING AROUND THE SHIP. YOU CAN BET YOUR COMMISSIONS ON IT!
NOW, LET'S SEE. YOU'LL NEED SOME PRENATAL VITAMINS, ANNE, AND YOU'RE TO SEE DOCTOR SELAR OR MYSELF ON A REGULAR BASIS--FOR NOW, EVERY MONTH WILL DO.
ALSO, NO HIGH-IMPACT EXERCISES. OTHER THAN THAT, YOU CAN CONTINUE TO DO WHATEVER YOU'VE BEEN DOING.
WHAT ABOUT MY RESEARCH?
YOU CAN CONTINUE THAT AS WELL. AFTER ALL, YOU'RE NOT DEALING WITH ANY POTENTIALLY HAZARDOUS ORGANISMS. AND EVEN IF YOU WERE, YOU WOULD BE WELL-INSULATED FROM THEM.
BEFORE LONG, YOU'LL WANT TO APPLY FOR LARGER QUARTERS. AND NOTIFY THE SHIP'S NURSERY, SO THEY CAN PLAN ACCORDINGLY.

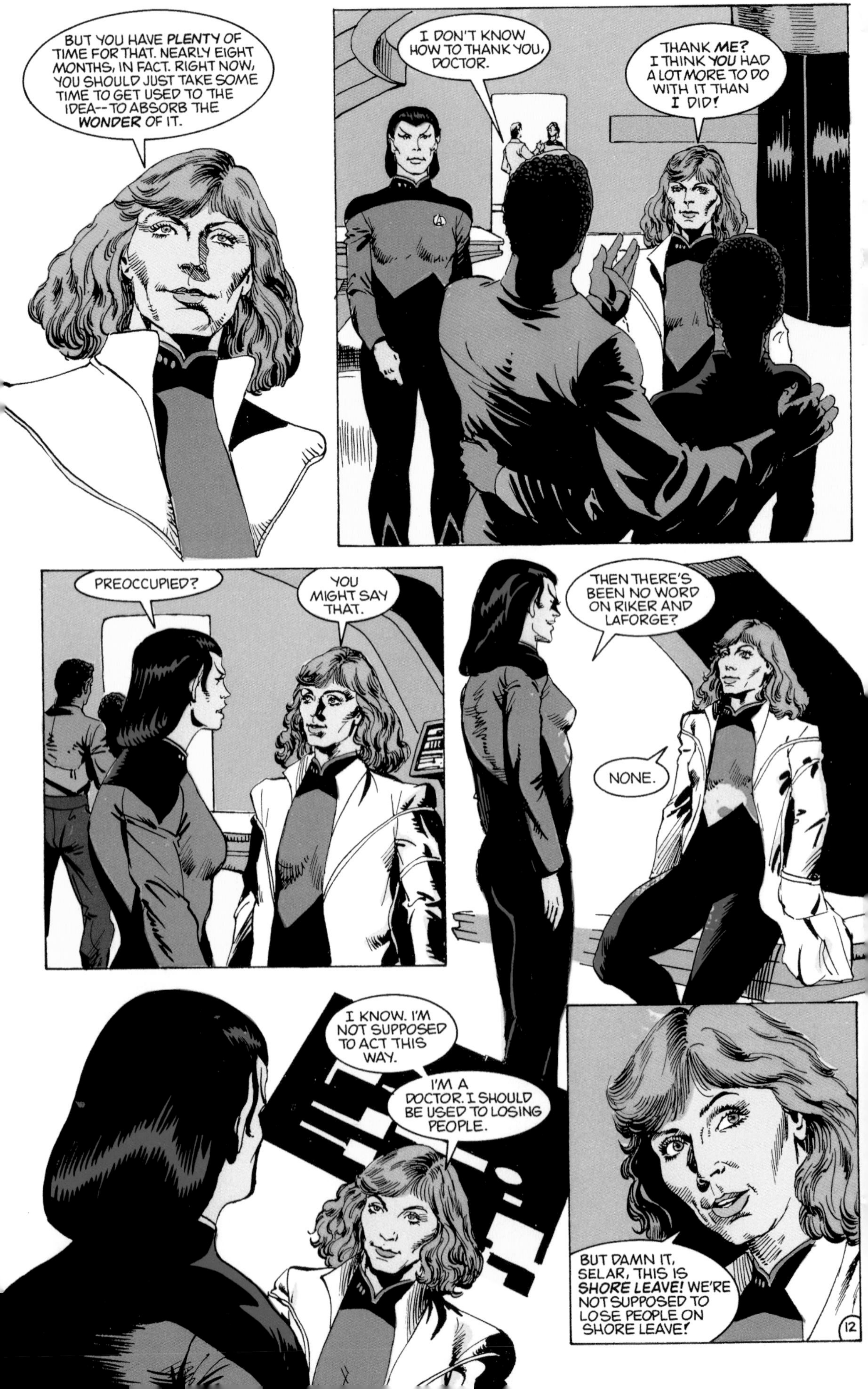
BUT YOU HAVE PLENTY OF TIME FOR THAT. NEARLY EIGHT MONTHS, IN FACT. RIGHT NOW, YOU SHOULD JUST TAKE SOME TIME TO GET USED TO THE IDEA--TO ABSORB THE WONDER OF IT.
I DON'T KNOW HOW TO THANK YOU, DOCTOR.
THANK ME? I THINK YOU HAD A LOT MORE TO DO WITH IT THAN I DID!
PREOCCUPIED?
YOU MIGHT SAY THAT.
THEN THERE'S BEEN NO WORD ON RIKER AND LAFORGE?
NONE.
I KNOW. I'M NOT SUPPOSED TO ACT THIS WAY.
I'M A DOCTOR. I SHOULD BE USED TO LOSING PEOPLE.
BUT DAMN IT, SELAR, THIS IS SHORE LEAVE! WE'RE NOT SUPPOSED TO LOSE PEOPLE ON SHORE LEAVE!

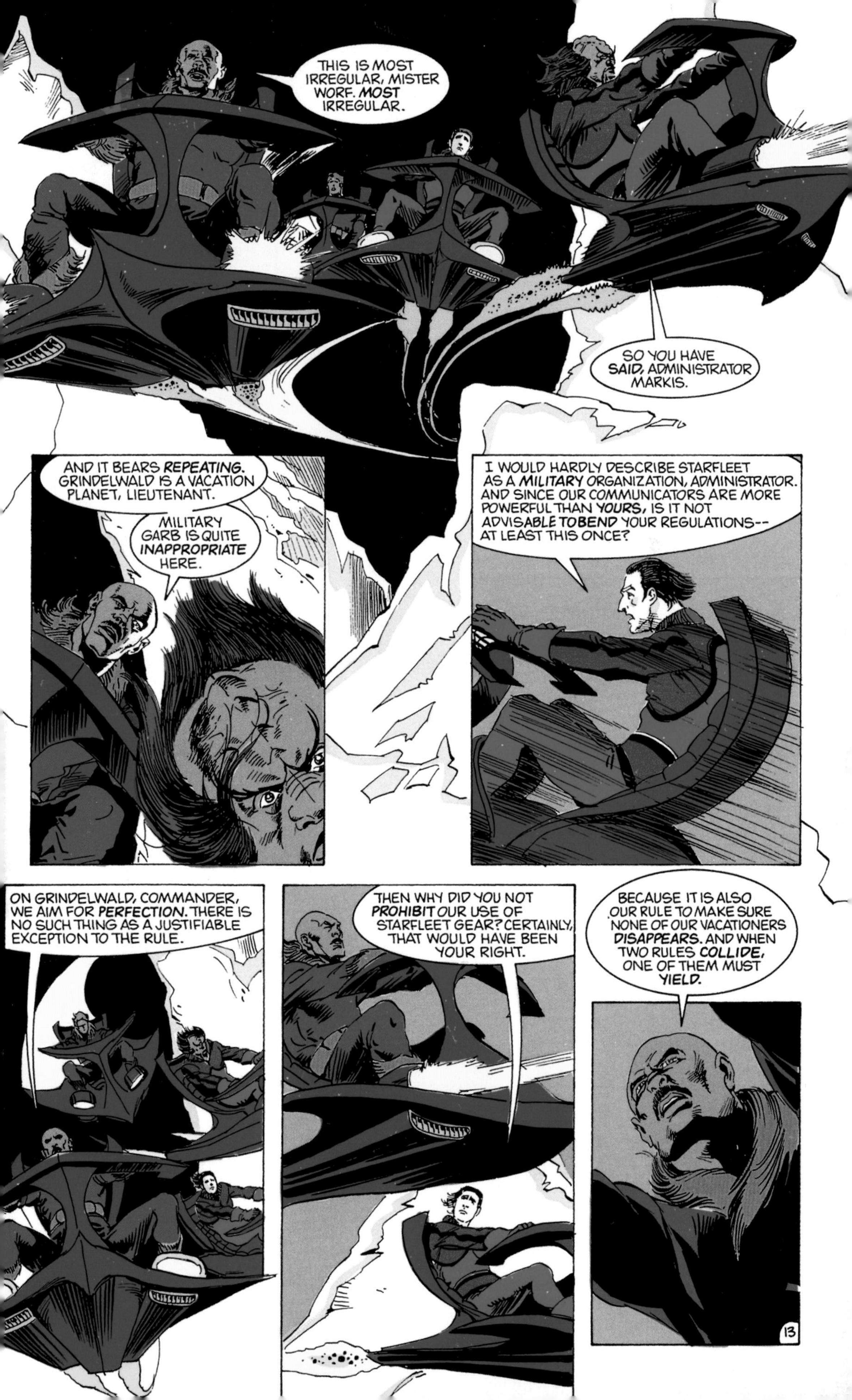
THIS IS MOST IRREGULAR, MISTER WORF. MOST IRREGULAR.
SO YOU HAVE SAID, ADMINISTRATOR MARKIS.
AND IT BEARS REPEATING. GRINDELWALD IS A VACATION PLANET, LIEUTENANT.
MILITARY GARB IS QUITE INAPPROPRIATE HERE.
I WOULD HARDLY DESCRIBE STARFLEET AS A MILITARY ORGANIZATION, ADMINISTRATOR. AND SINCE OUR COMMUNICATORS ARE MORE POWERFUL THAN YOURS, IS IT NOT ADVISABLE TOBEND YOUR REGULATIONS-- AT LEAST THIS ONCE?
ON GRINDELWALD, COMMANDER, WE AIM FOR PERFECTION. THERE IS NO SUCH THING AS A JUSTIFIABLE EXCEPTION TO THE RULE.
THEN WHY DID YOU NOT PROHIBIT OUR USE OF STARFLEET GEAR? CERTAINLY, THAT WOULD HAVE BEEN YOUR RIGHT.
BECAUSE IT IS ALSO OUR RULE TO MAKE SURE NONE OF OUR VACATIONERS DISAPPEARS. AND WHEN TWO RULES COLLIDE, ONE OF THEM MUST YIELD.
13

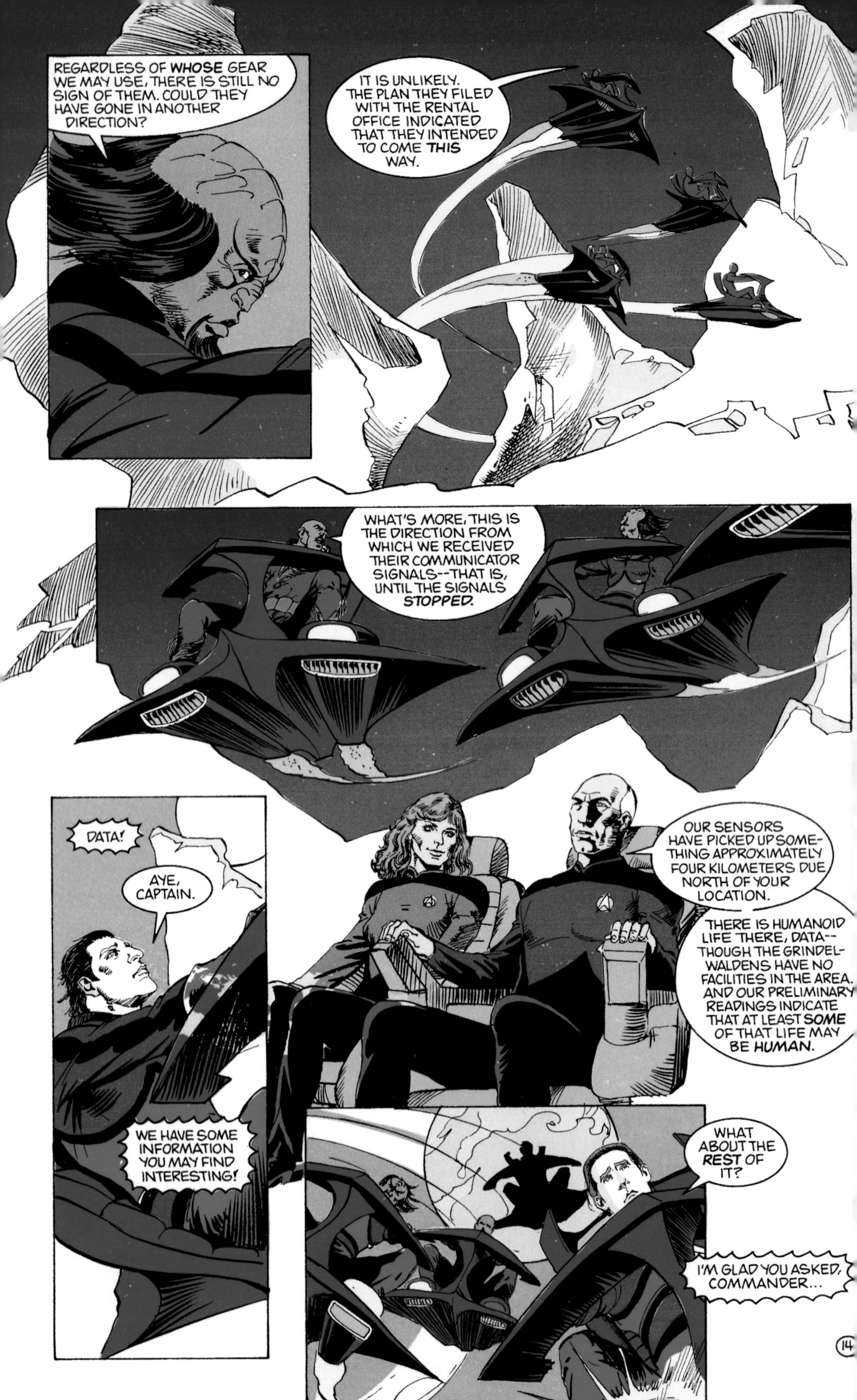
REGARDLESS OF WHOSE GEAR WE MAY USE, THERE IS STILL NO SIGN OF THEM. COULD THEY HAVE GONE IN ANOTHER DIRECTION?
IT IS UNLIKELY. THE PLAN THEY FILED WITH THE RENTAL OFFICE INDICATED THAT THEY INTENDED TO COME THIS WAY.
WHAT'S MORE, THIS IS THE DIRECTION FROM WHICH WE RECEIVED THEIR COMMUNICATOR SIGNALS--THAT IS, UNTIL THE SIGNALS STOPPED.
DATA!
AYE, CAPTAIN.
OUR SENSORS HAVE PICKED UP SOMETHING APPROXIMATELY FOUR KILOMETERS DUE NORTH OF YOUR LOCATION.
THERE IS HUMANOID LIFE THERE, DATA--THOUGH THE GRINDELWALDENS HAVE NO FACILITIES IN THE AREA. AND OUR PRELIMINARY READINGS INDICATE THAT AT LEAST SOME OF THAT LIFE MAY BE HUMAN.
WE HAVE SOME INFORMATION YOU MAY FIND INTERESTING!
WHAT ABOUT THE REST OF IT?
I'M GLAD YOU ASKED, COMMANDER...

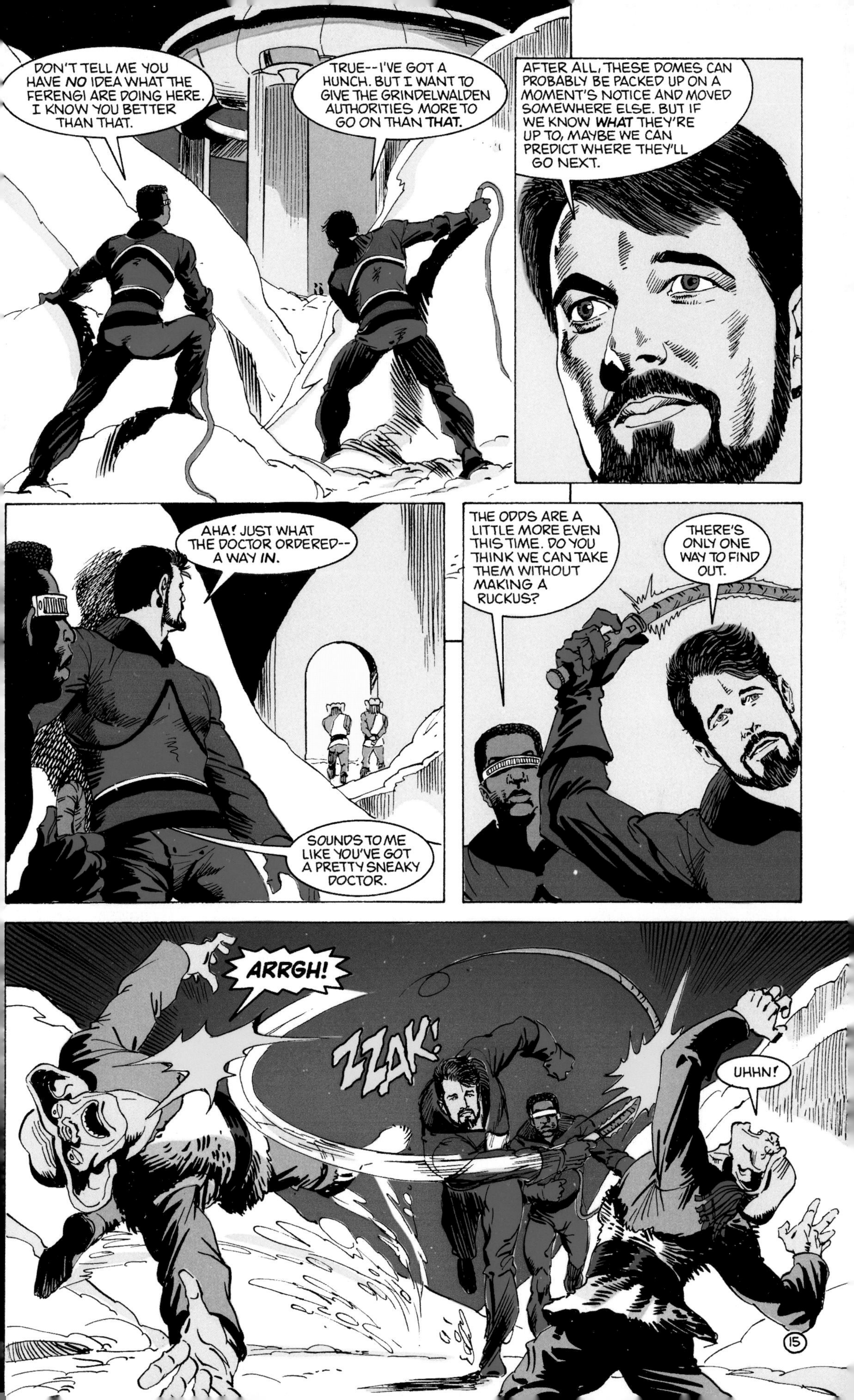
DON'T TELL ME YOU HAVE NO IDEA WHAT THE FERENGI ARE DOING HERE. I KNOW YOU BETTER THAN THAT.
TRUE--I'VE GOT A HUNCH. BUT I WANT TO GIVE THE GRINDELWALDEN AUTHORITIES MORE TO GO ON THAN THAT.
AFTER ALL, THESE DOMES CAN PROBABLY BE PACKED UP ON A MOMENT'S NOTICE AND MOVED SOMEWHERE ELSE. BUT IF WE KNOW WHAT THEY'RE UP TO, MAYBE WE CAN PREDICT WHERE THEY'LL GO NEXT.
AHA! JUST WHAT THE DOCTOR ORDERED-- A WAY IN.
SOUNDS TO ME LIKE YOU'VE GOT A PRETTY SNEAKY DOCTOR.
THE ODDS ARE A LITTLE MORE EVEN THIS TIME. DO YOU THINK WE CAN TAKE THEM WITHOUT MAKING A RUCKUS?
THERE'S ONLY ONE WAY TO FIND OUT.
ARRGH!
ZZAK!
UHHN!

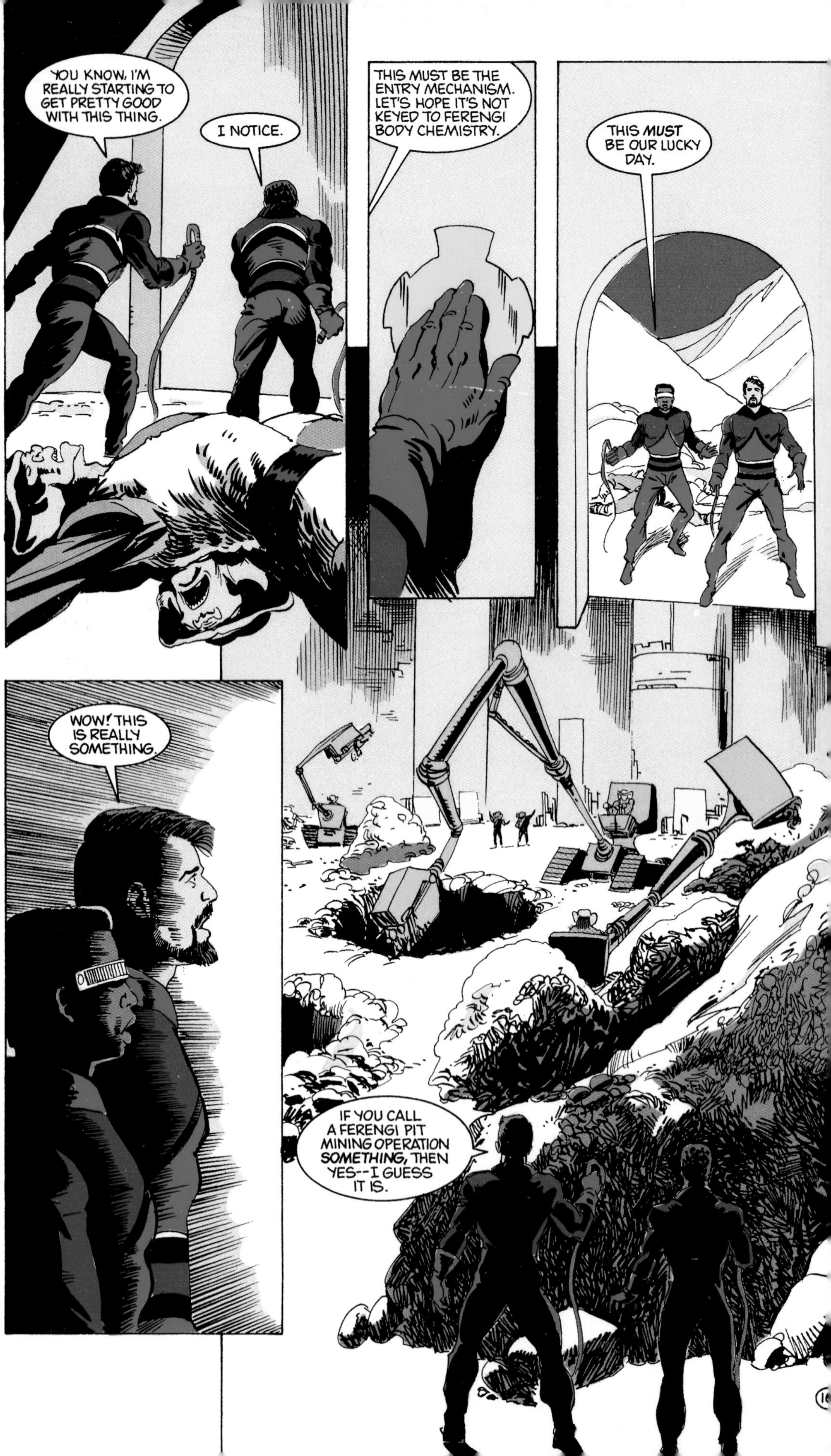
YOU KNOW, I'M REALLY STARTING TO GET PRETTY GOOD WITH THIS THING.
I NOTICE.
THIS MUST BE THE ENTRY MECHANISM. LET'S HOPE IT'S NOT KEYED TO FERENGI BODY CHEMISTRY.
THIS *MUST* BE OUR LUCKY DAY.
WOW! THIS IS REALLY SOMETHING.
IF YOU CALL A FERENGI PIT MINING OPERATION *SOMETHING*, THEN YES--I GUESS IT IS.

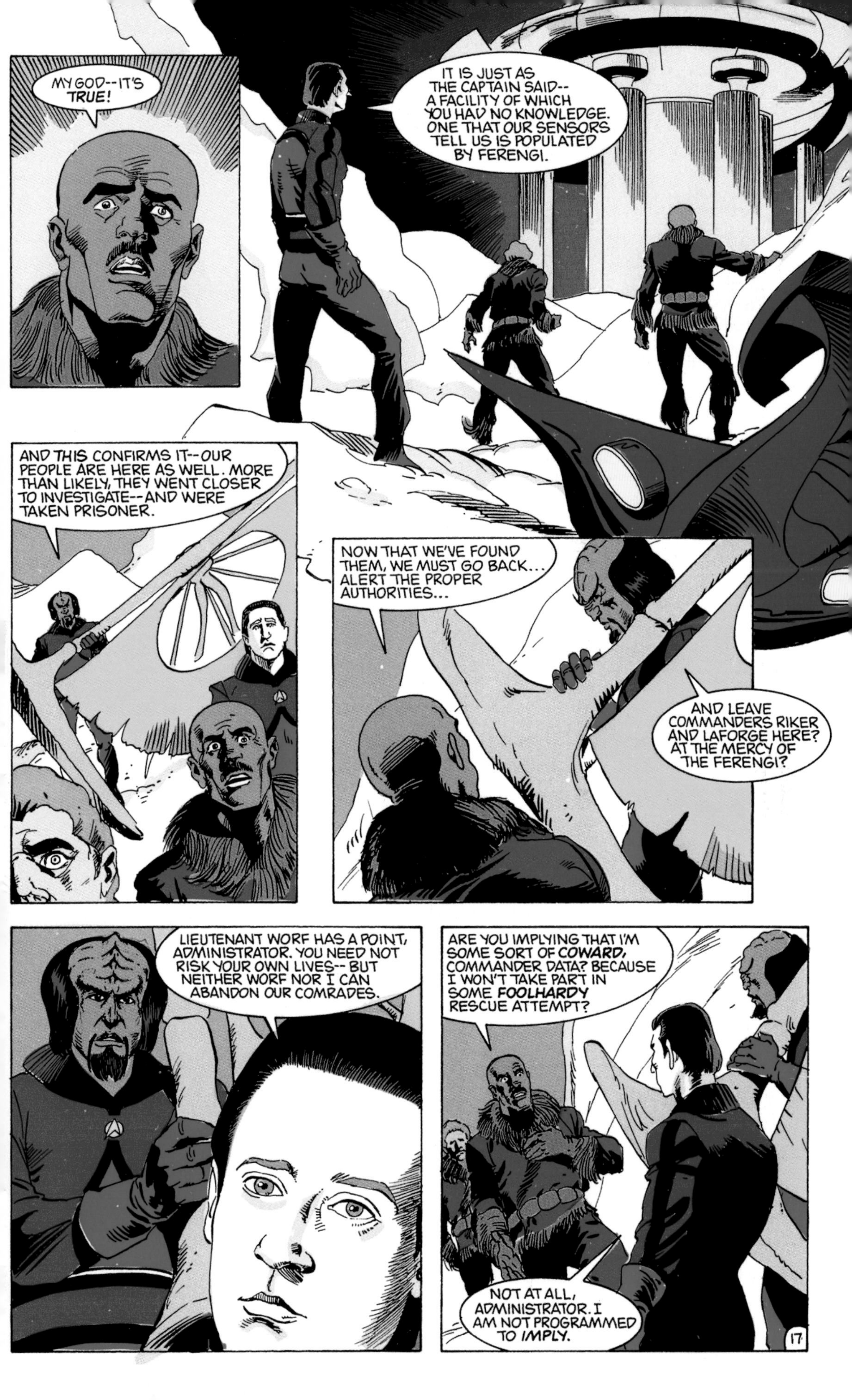
MY GOD--IT'S TRUE!
IT IS JUST AS THE CAPTAIN SAID-- A FACILITY OF WHICH YOU HAD NO KNOWLEDGE. ONE THAT OUR SENSORS TELL US IS POPULATED BY FERENGI.
AND THIS CONFIRMS IT--OUR PEOPLE ARE HERE AS WELL. MORE THAN LIKELY, THEY WENT CLOSER TO INVESTIGATE--AND WERE TAKEN PRISONER.
NOW THAT WE'VE FOUND THEM, WE MUST GO BACK... ALERT THE PROPER AUTHORITIES...
AND LEAVE COMMANDERS RIKER AND LAFORGE HERE? AT THE MERCY OF THE FERENGI?
LIEUTENANT WORF HAS A POINT, ADMINISTRATOR. YOU NEED NOT RISK YOUR OWN LIVES-- BUT NEITHER WORF NOR I CAN ABANDON OUR COMRADES.
ARE YOU IMPLYING THAT I'M SOME SORT OF COWARD, COMMANDER DATA? BECAUSE I WON'T TAKE PART IN SOME FOOLHARDY RESCUE ATTEMPT?
NOT AT ALL, ADMINISTRATOR. I AM NOT PROGRAMMED TO IMPLY.
17

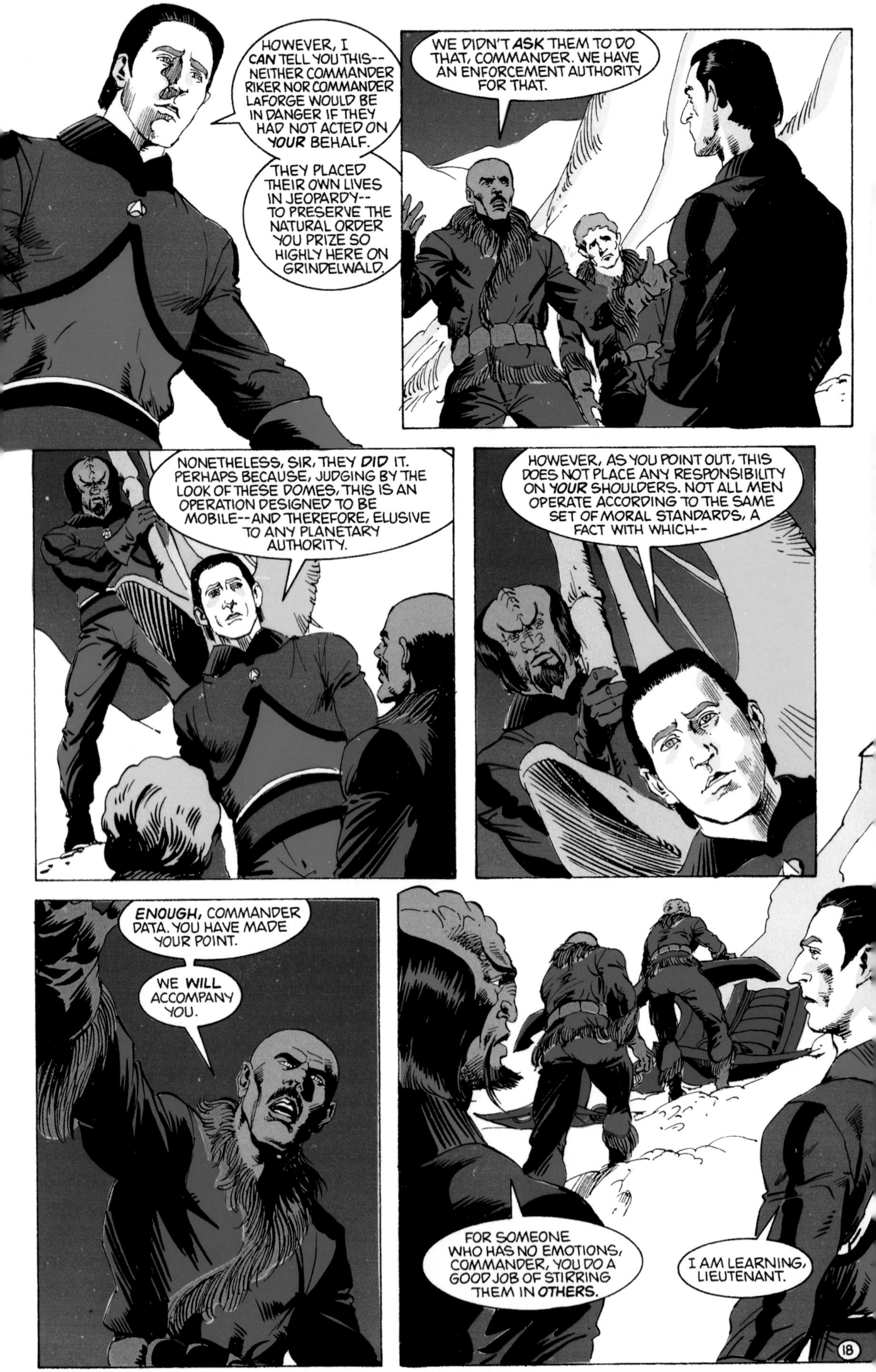
HOWEVER, I CAN TELL YOU THIS-- NEITHER COMMANDER RIKER NOR COMMANDER LAFORGE WOULD BE IN DANGER IF THEY HAD NOT ACTED ON YOUR BEHALF.
THEY PLACED THEIR OWN LIVES IN JEOPARDY-- TO PRESERVE THE NATURAL ORDER YOU PRIZE SO HIGHLY HERE ON GRINDELWALD.
WE DIDN'T ASK THEM TO DO THAT, COMMANDER. WE HAVE AN ENFORCEMENT AUTHORITY FOR THAT.
NONETHELESS, SIR, THEY DID IT. PERHAPS BECAUSE, JUDGING BY THE LOOK OF THESE DOMES, THIS IS AN OPERATION DESIGNED TO BE MOBILE--AND THEREFORE, ELUSIVE TO ANY PLANETARY AUTHORITY.
HOWEVER, AS YOU POINT OUT, THIS DOES NOT PLACE ANY RESPONSIBILITY ON YOUR SHOULDERS. NOT ALL MEN OPERATE ACCORDING TO THE SAME SET OF MORAL STANDARDS, A FACT WITH WHICH--
ENOUGH, COMMANDER DATA. YOU HAVE MADE YOUR POINT.
WE WILL ACCOMPANY YOU.
FOR SOMEONE WHO HAS NO EMOTIONS, COMMANDER, YOU DO A GOOD JOB OF STIRRING THEM IN OTHERS.
I AM LEARNING, LIEUTENANT.
18

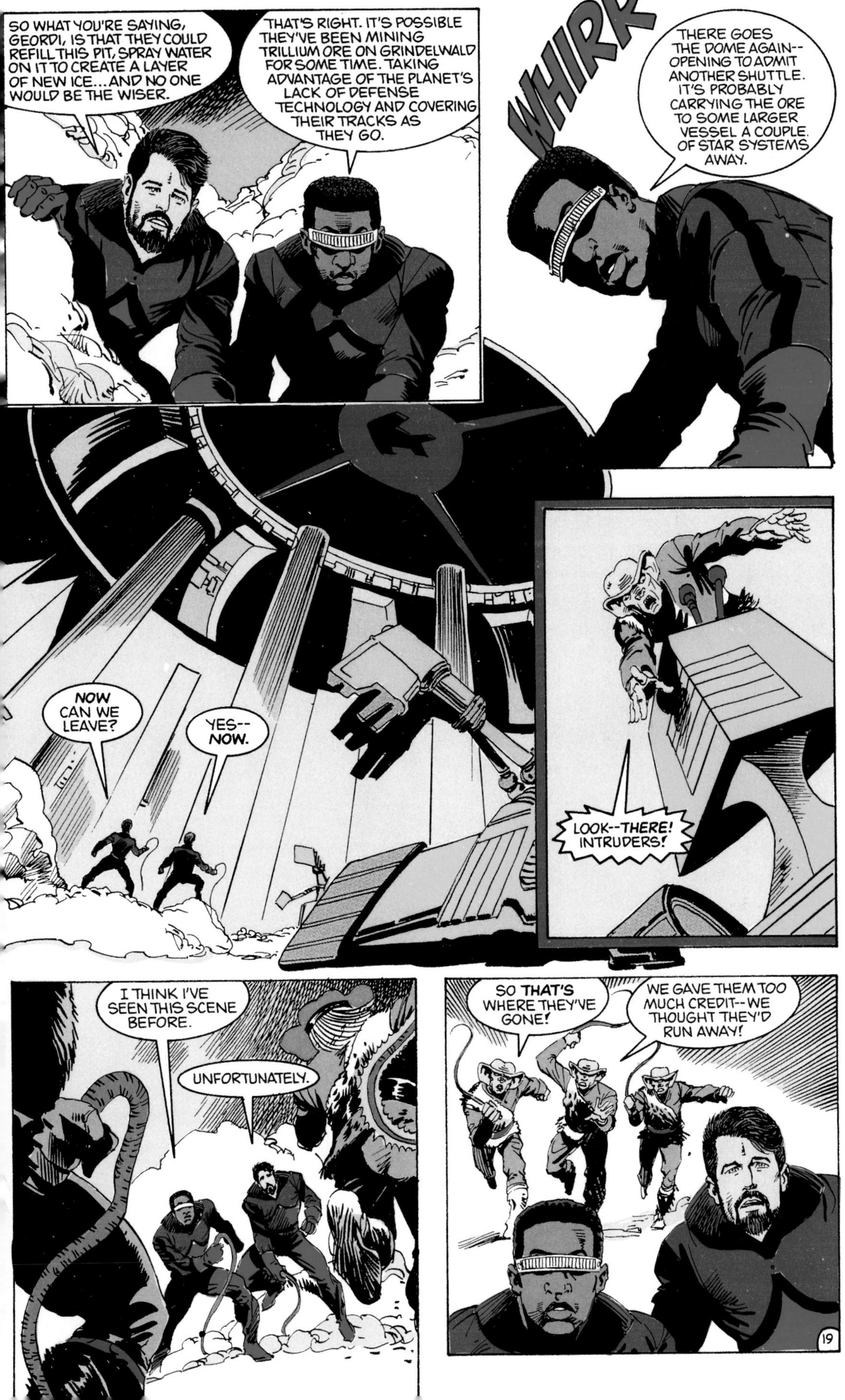
SO WHAT YOU'RE SAYING, GEORDI, IS THAT THEY COULD REFILL THIS PIT, SPRAY WATER ON IT TO CREATE A LAYER OF NEW ICE... AND NO ONE WOULD BE THE WISER.
THAT'S RIGHT. IT'S POSSIBLE THEY'VE BEEN MINING TRILLIUM ORE ON GRINDELWALD FOR SOME TIME. TAKING ADVANTAGE OF THE PLANET'S LACK OF DEFENSE TECHNOLOGY AND COVERING THEIR TRACKS AS THEY GO.
WHIRR
THERE GOES THE DOME AGAIN-- OPENING TO ADMIT ANOTHER SHUTTLE. IT'S PROBABLY CARRYING THE ORE TO SOME LARGER VESSEL A COUPLE OF STAR SYSTEMS AWAY.
NOW CAN WE LEAVE?
YES-- NOW.
LOOK--THERE! INTRUDERS!
I THINK I'VE SEEN THIS SCENE BEFORE.
UNFORTUNATELY.
SO THAT'S WHERE THEY'VE GONE!
WE GAVE THEM TOO MUCH CREDIT--WE THOUGHT THEY'D RUN AWAY!
19

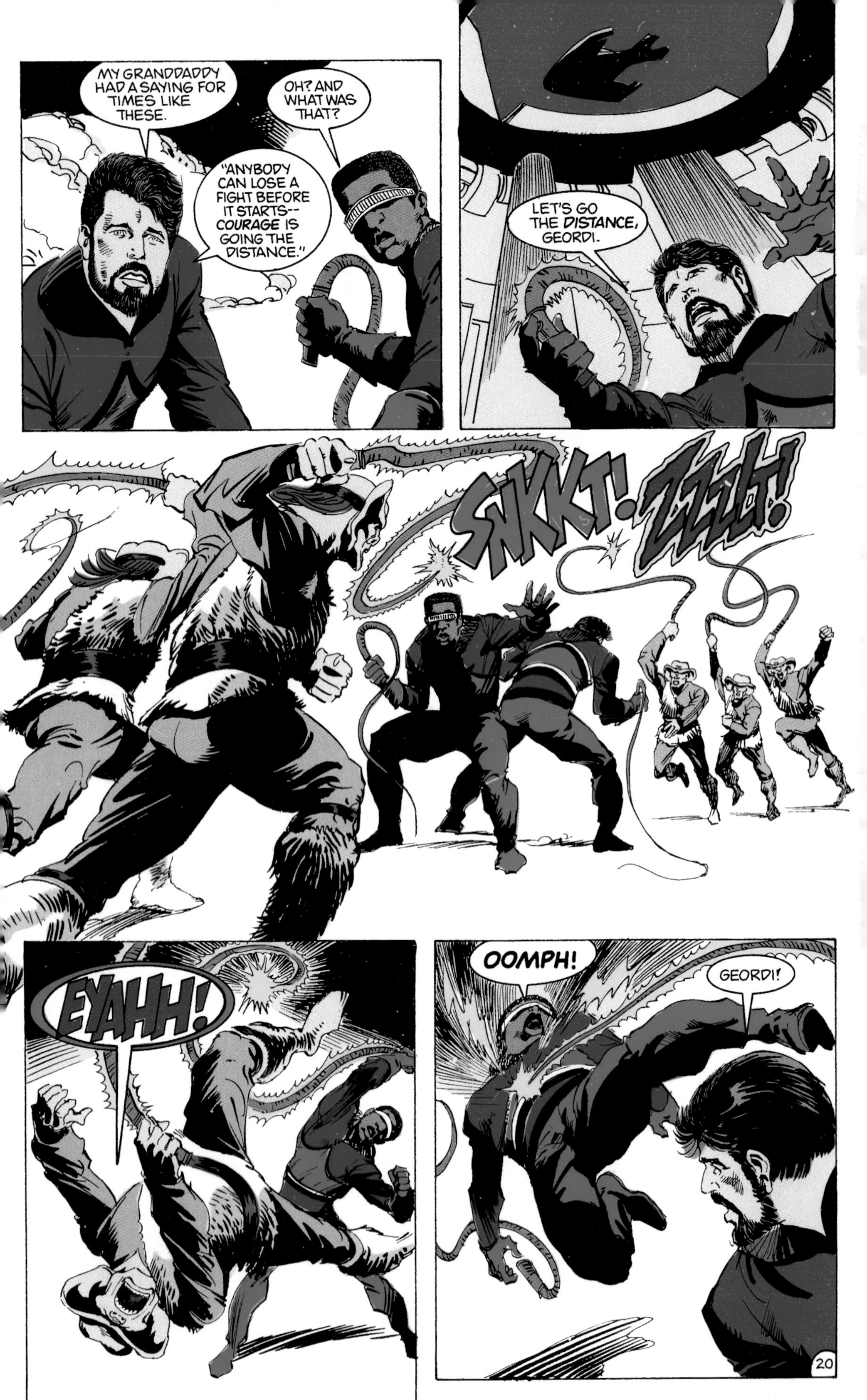
MY GRANDDADDY HAD A SAYING FOR TIMES LIKE THESE.
OH? AND WHAT WAS THAT?
"ANYBODY CAN LOSE A FIGHT BEFORE IT STARTS-- COURAGE IS GOING THE DISTANCE."
LET'S GO THE DISTANCE, GEORDI.
SNKKT!
ZZZLT!
EYAHH!
OOMPH!
GEORDI!
20

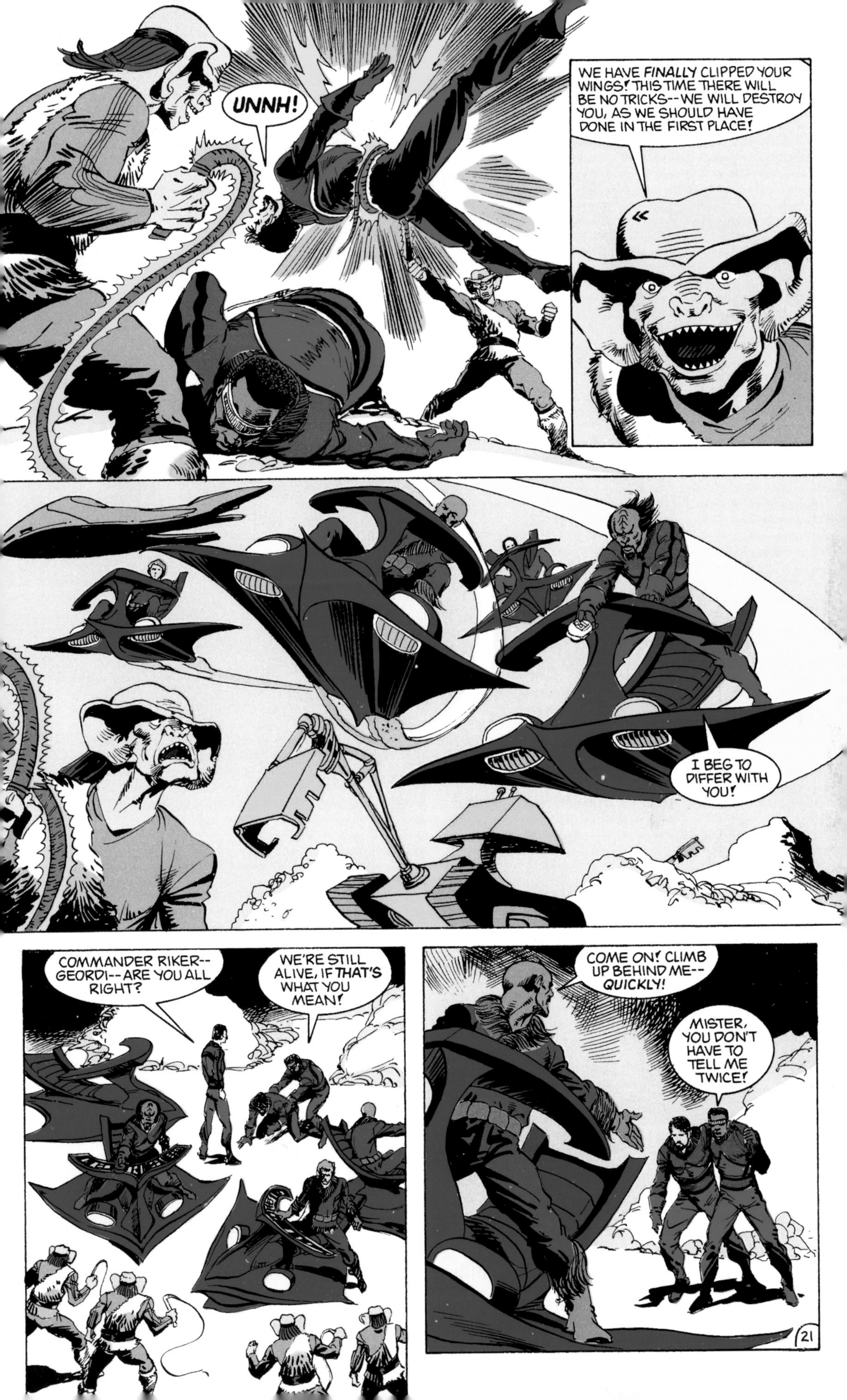
UNNH!
WE HAVE FINALLY CLIPPED YOUR WINGS! THIS TIME THERE WILL BE NO TRICKS--WE WILL DESTROY YOU, AS WE SHOULD HAVE DONE IN THE FIRST PLACE!
I BEG TO DIFFER WITH YOU!
COMMANDER RIKER-- GEORDI--ARE YOU ALL RIGHT?
WE'RE STILL ALIVE, IF THAT'S WHAT YOU MEAN!
COME ON! CLIMB UP BEHIND ME-- QUICKLY!
MISTER, YOU DON'T HAVE TO TELL ME TWICE!

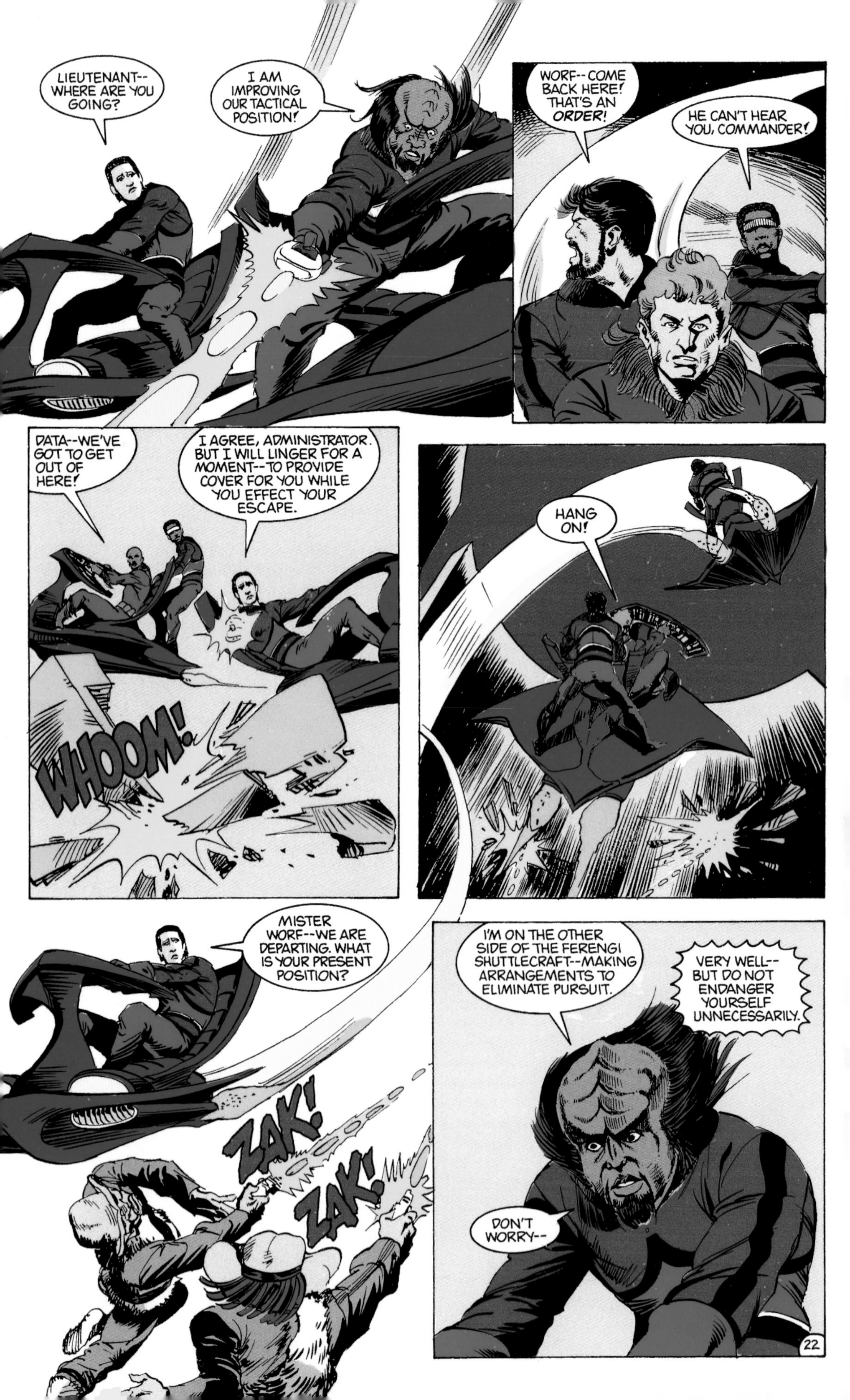
LIEUTENANT-- WHERE ARE YOU GOING?
I AM IMPROVING OUR TACTICAL POSITION!
WORF-- COME BACK HERE! THAT'S AN ORDER!
HE CAN'T HEAR YOU, COMMANDER!
DATA--WE'VE GOT TO GET OUT OF HERE!
I AGREE, ADMINISTRATOR. BUT I WILL LINGER FOR A MOMENT--TO PROVIDE COVER FOR YOU WHILE YOU EFFECT YOUR ESCAPE.
WHOOM!
HANG ON!
MISTER WORF--WE ARE DEPARTING. WHAT IS YOUR PRESENT POSITION?
ZAK!
ZAK!
I'M ON THE OTHER SIDE OF THE FERENGI SHUTTLECRAFT--MAKING ARRANGEMENTS TO ELIMINATE PURSUIT.
VERY WELL-- BUT DO NOT ENDANGER YOURSELF UNNECESSARILY.
DON'T WORRY--

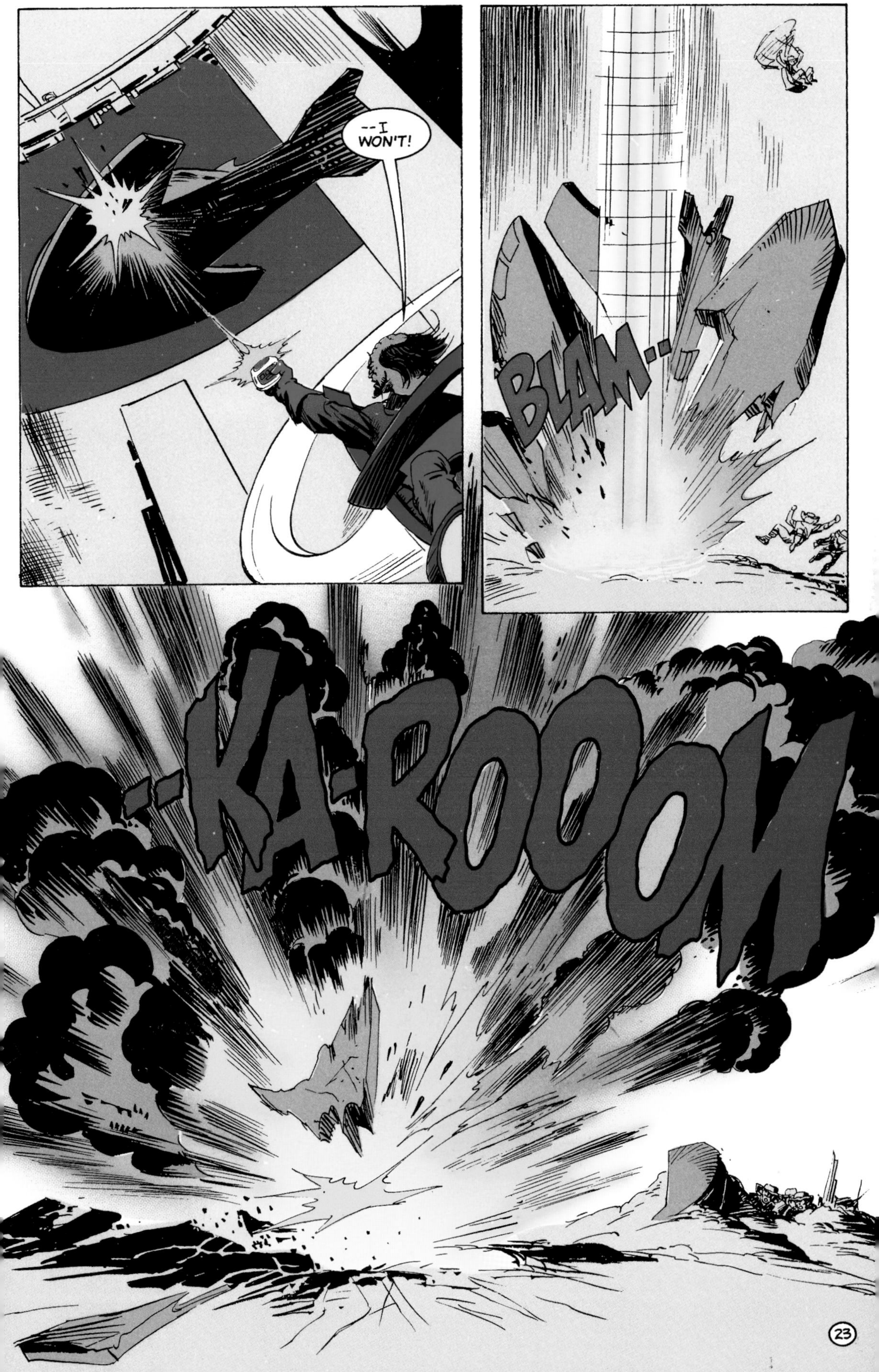
--I WON'T!
BLAM--
--KA-ROOOM

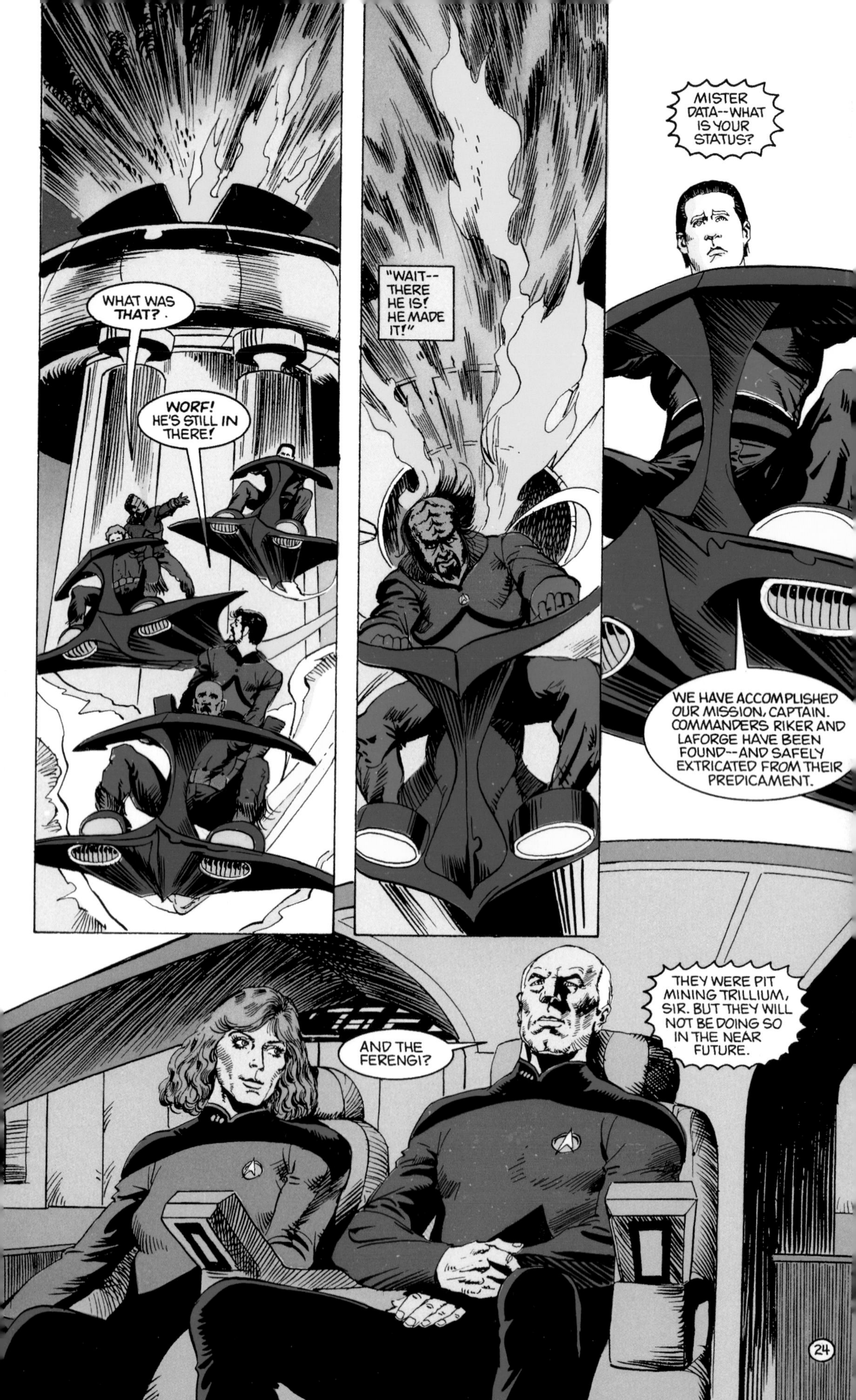
WHAT WAS THAT?
WORF! HE'S STILL IN THERE!
"WAIT-- THERE HE IS! HE MADE IT!"
MISTER DATA--WHAT IS YOUR STATUS?
WE HAVE ACCOMPLISHED OUR MISSION, CAPTAIN. COMMANDERS RIKER AND LAFORGE HAVE BEEN FOUND--AND SAFELY EXTRICATED FROM THEIR PREDICAMENT.
AND THE FERENGI?
THEY WERE PIT MINING TRILLIUM, SIR. BUT THEY WILL NOT BE DOING SO IN THE NEAR FUTURE.

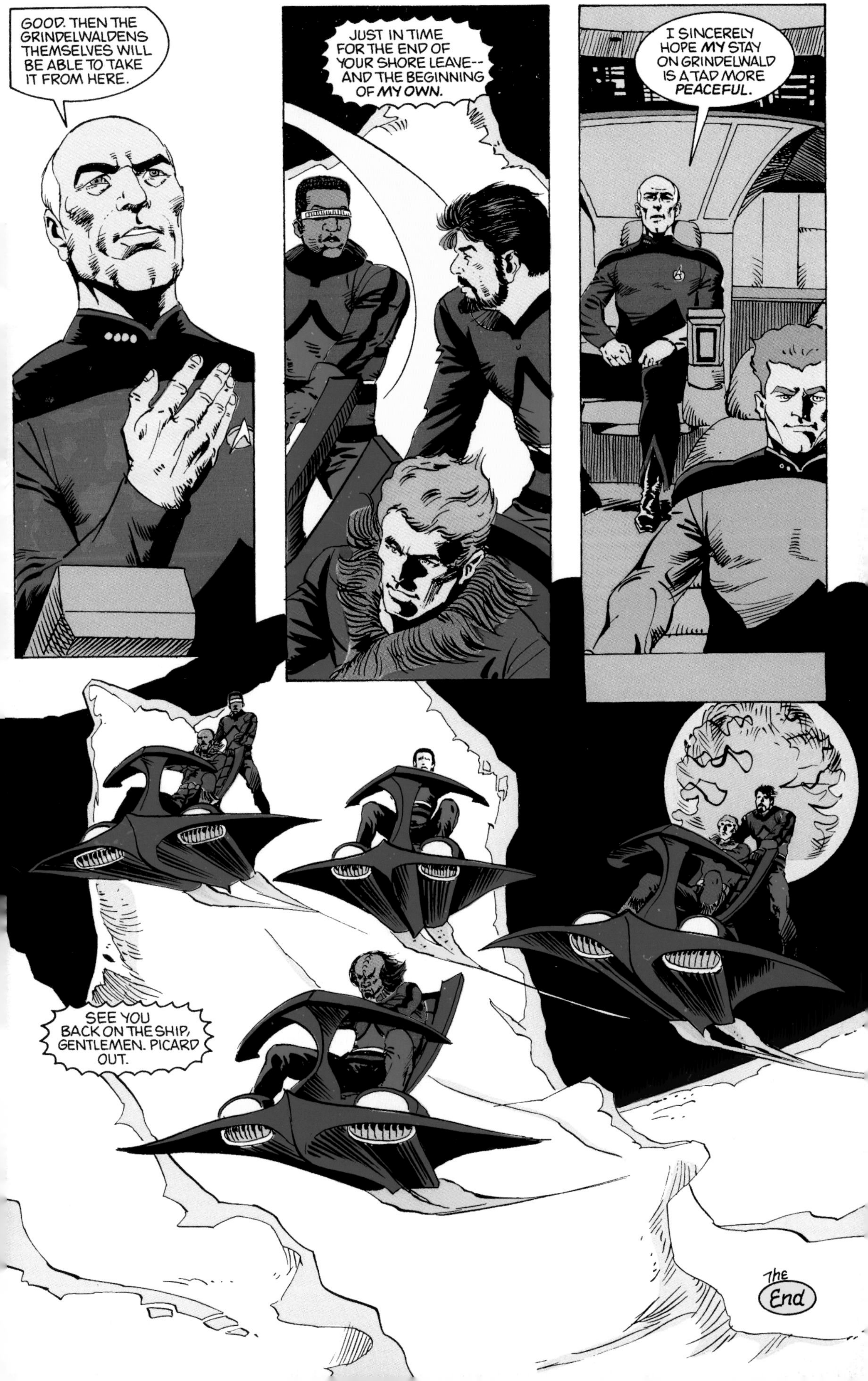
GOOD. THEN THE GRINDELWALDENS THEMSELVES WILL BE ABLE TO TAKE IT FROM HERE.
JUST IN TIME FOR THE END OF YOUR SHORE LEAVE-- AND THE BEGINNING OF MY OWN.
I SINCERELY HOPE MY STAY ON GRINDELWALD IS A TAD MORE PEACEFUL.
SEE YOU BACK ON THE SHIP, GENTLEMEN. PICARD OUT.
The End

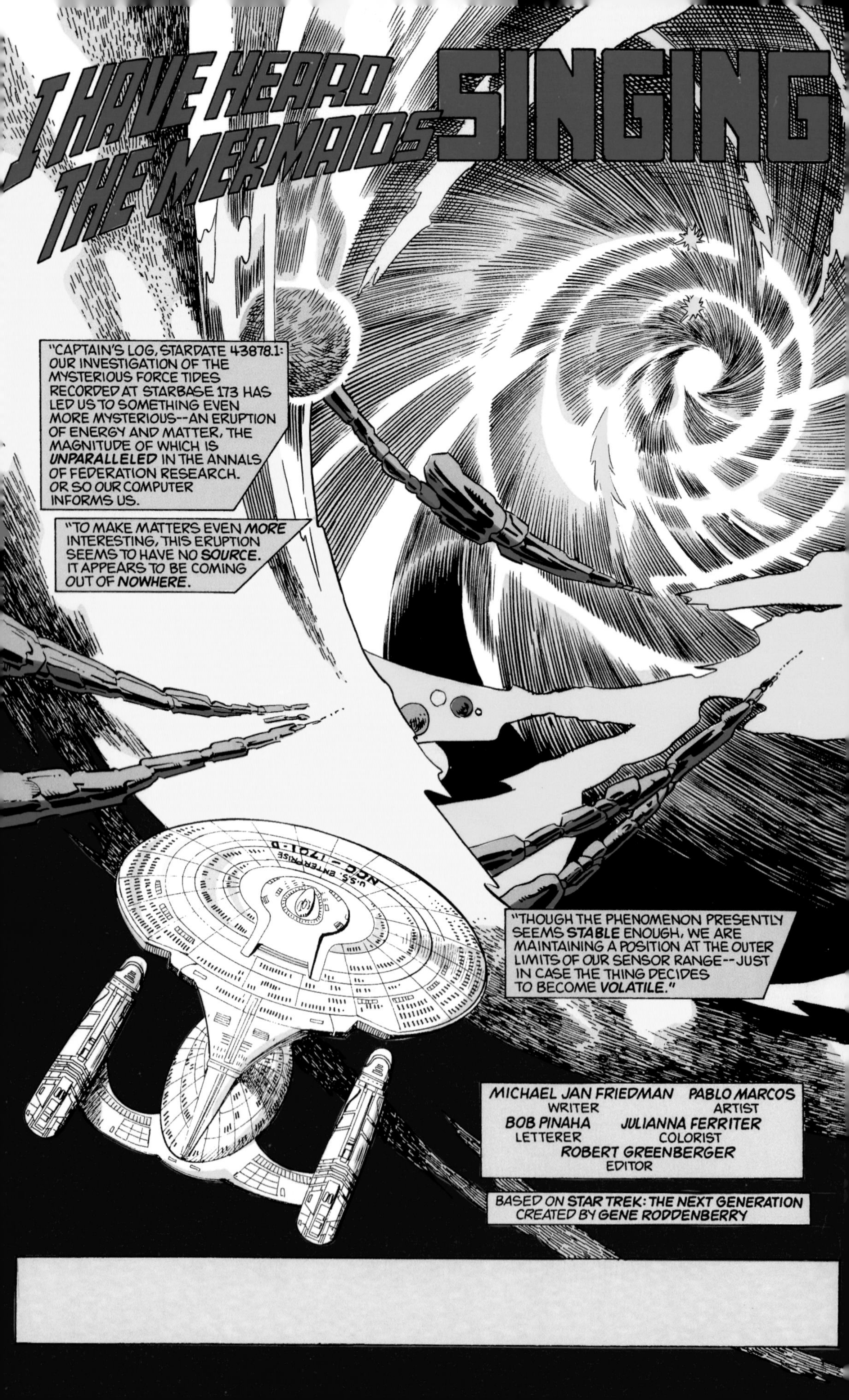
I HAVE HEARD THE MERMAIDS SINGING
"CAPTAIN'S LOG, STARDATE 43878.1: OUR INVESTIGATION OF THE MYSTERIOUS FORCE TIDES RECORDED AT STARBASE 173 HAS LED US TO SOMETHING EVEN MORE MYSTERIOUS--AN ERUPTION OF ENERGY AND MATTER, THE MAGNITUDE OF WHICH IS UNPARALLELED IN THE ANNALS OF FEDERATION RESEARCH. OR SO OUR COMPUTER INFORMS US.
"TO MAKE MATTERS EVEN MORE INTERESTING, THIS ERUPTION SEEMS TO HAVE NO SOURCE. IT APPEARS TO BE COMING OUT OF NOWHERE.
U.S.S. ENTERPRISE NCC-1701-D
"THOUGH THE PHENOMENON PRESENTLY SEEMS STABLE ENOUGH, WE ARE MAINTAINING A POSITION AT THE OUTER LIMITS OF OUR SENSOR RANGE--JUST IN CASE THE THING DECIDES TO BECOME VOLATILE."
MICHAEL JAN FRIEDMAN WRITER
PABLO MARCOS ARTIST
BOB PINAHA LETTERER
JULIANNA FERRITER COLORIST
ROBERT GREENBERGER EDITOR
BASED ON STAR TREK: THE NEXT GENERATION CREATED BY GENE RODDENBERRY

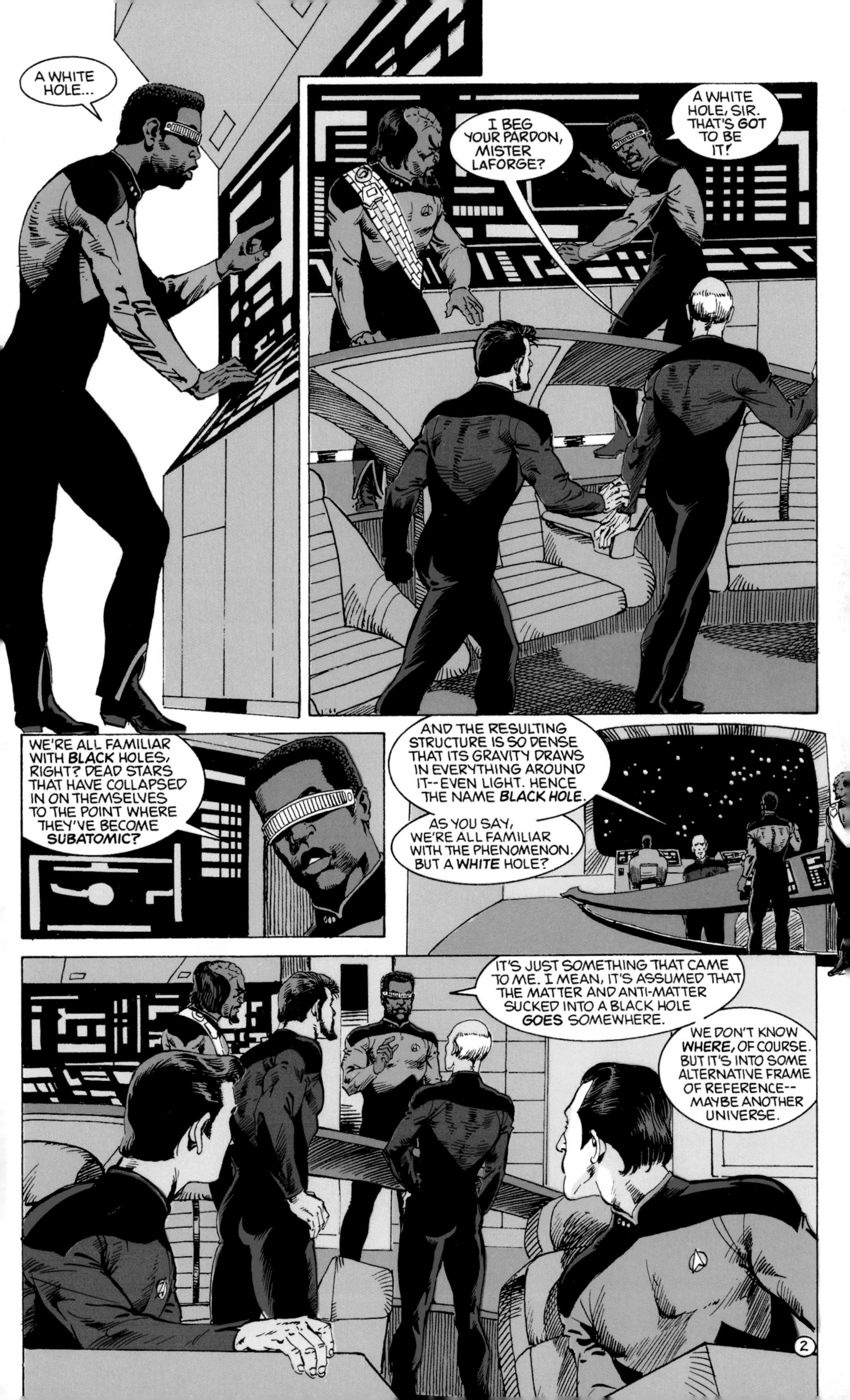
A WHITE HOLE...
I BEG YOUR PARDON, MISTER LAFORGE?
A WHITE HOLE, SIR. THAT'S GOT TO BE IT!
WE'RE ALL FAMILIAR WITH BLACK HOLES, RIGHT? DEAD STARS THAT HAVE COLLAPSED IN ON THEMSELVES TO THE POINT WHERE THEY'VE BECOME SUBATOMIC?
AND THE RESULTING STRUCTURE IS SO DENSE THAT ITS GRAVITY DRAWS IN EVERYTHING AROUND IT--EVEN LIGHT. HENCE THE NAME BLACK HOLE.
AS YOU SAY, WE'RE ALL FAMILIAR WITH THE PHENOMENON. BUT A WHITE HOLE?
IT'S JUST SOMETHING THAT CAME TO ME. I MEAN, IT'S ASSUMED THAT THE MATTER AND ANTI-MATTER SUCKED INTO A BLACK HOLE GOES SOMEWHERE.
WE DON'T KNOW WHERE, OF COURSE. BUT IT'S INTO SOME ALTERNATIVE FRAME OF REFERENCE--MAYBE ANOTHER UNIVERSE.
2

IMAGINE YOURSELF IN THAT OTHER FRAME OF REFERENCE-- LOOKING AT THE BACK END OF A BLACK HOLE.

WOULDN'T IT LOOK SOMETHING...

...LIKE *THAT?*

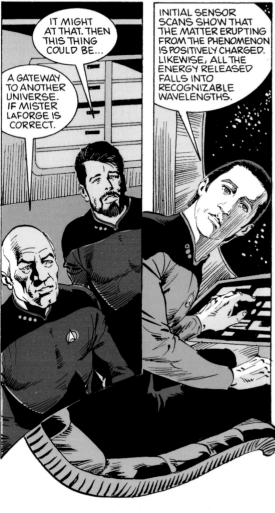

IT MIGHT AT THAT. THEN THIS THING COULD BE...

A GATEWAY TO ANOTHER UNIVERSE. IF MISTER LAFORGE IS CORRECT.

INITIAL SENSOR SCANS SHOW THAT THE MATTER ERUPTING FROM THE PHENOMENON IS POSITIVELY CHARGED. LIKEWISE, ALL THE ENERGY RELEASED FALLS INTO RECOGNIZABLE WAVELENGTHS.

SO IT ALL COMES FROM SOMEWHERE ELSE IN *OUR* UNIVERSE-- AND NOT SOME OTHER ONE. IS THAT WHAT YOU'RE SAYING, DATA?

NOT EXACTLY, SIR. ONE CANNOT RULE OUT COMMANDER LAFORGE'S CONCLUSIONS BASED ON THIS EVIDENCE ALONE.

3

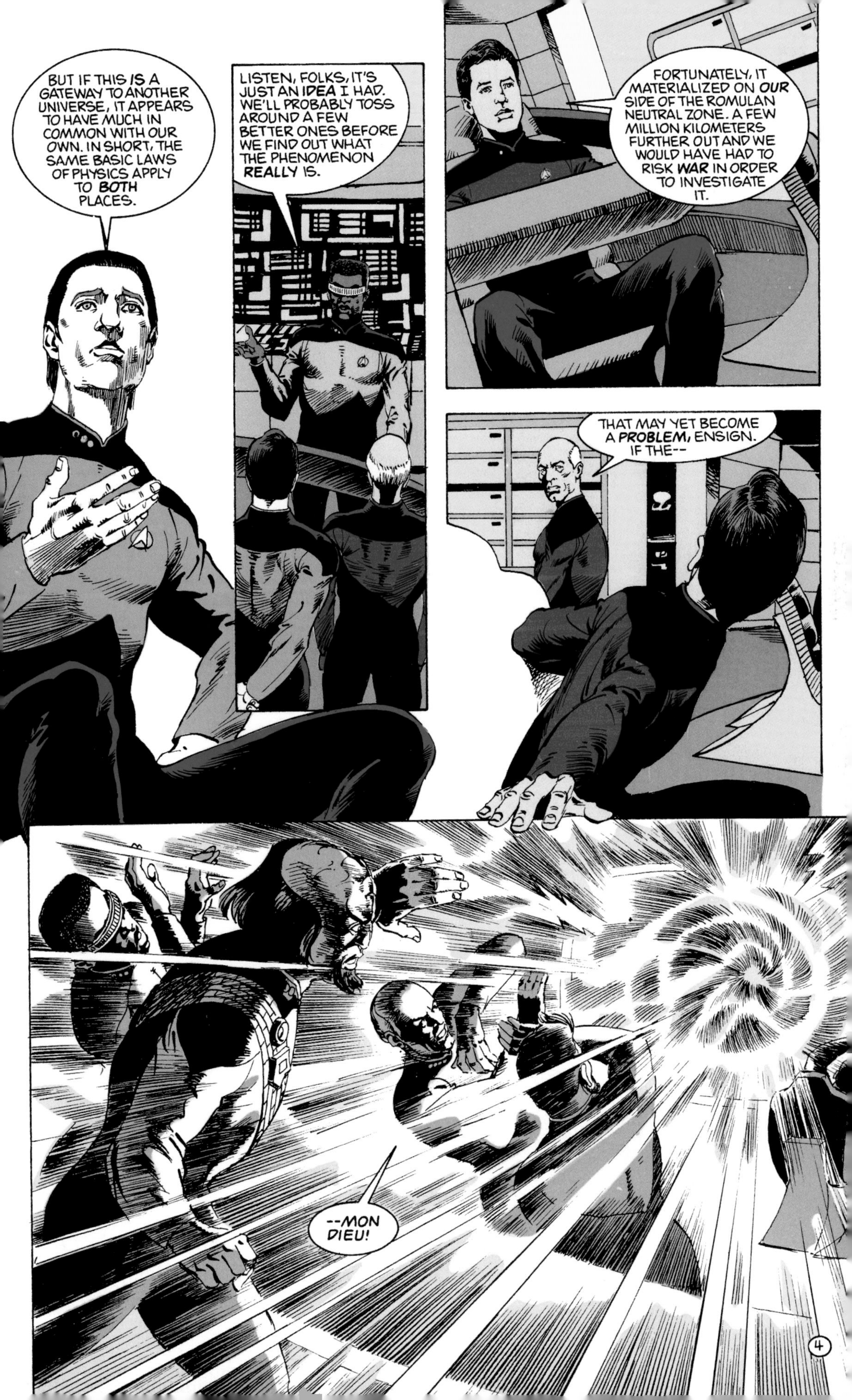
BUT IF THIS IS A GATEWAY TO ANOTHER UNIVERSE, IT APPEARS TO HAVE MUCH IN COMMON WITH OUR OWN. IN SHORT, THE SAME BASIC LAWS OF PHYSICS APPLY TO BOTH PLACES.
LISTEN, FOLKS, IT'S JUST AN IDEA I HAD. WE'LL PROBABLY TOSS AROUND A FEW BETTER ONES BEFORE WE FIND OUT WHAT THE PHENOMENON REALLY IS.
FORTUNATELY, IT MATERIALIZED ON OUR SIDE OF THE ROMULAN NEUTRAL ZONE. A FEW MILLION KILOMETERS FURTHER OUT AND WE WOULD HAVE HAD TO RISK WAR IN ORDER TO INVESTIGATE IT.
THAT MAY YET BECOME A PROBLEM, ENSIGN. IF THE--
--MON DIEU!
4

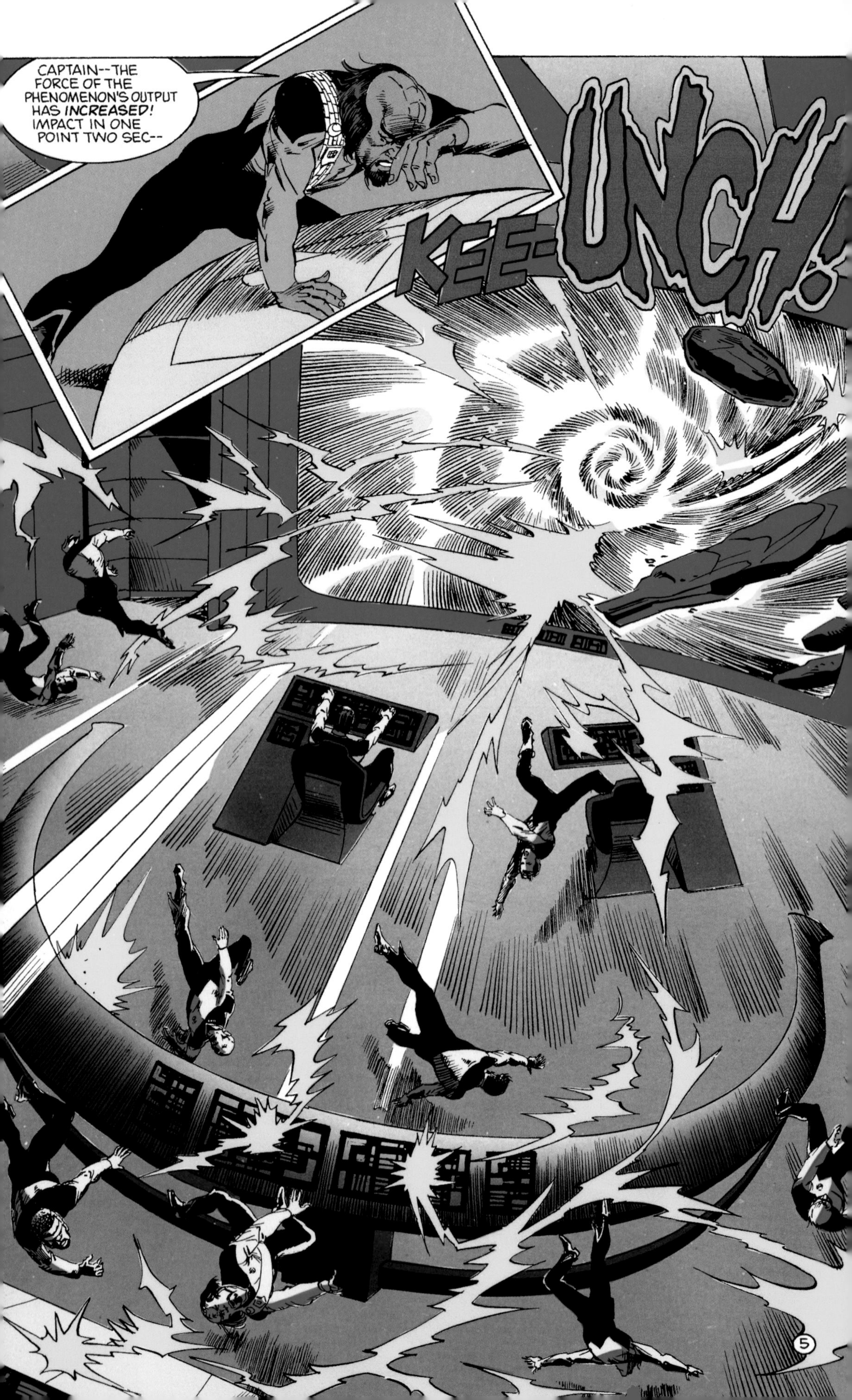

CAPTAIN--THE FORCE OF THE PHENOMENON'S OUTPUT HAS INCREASED! IMPACT IN ONE POINT TWO SEC--
KEE-UNCH!

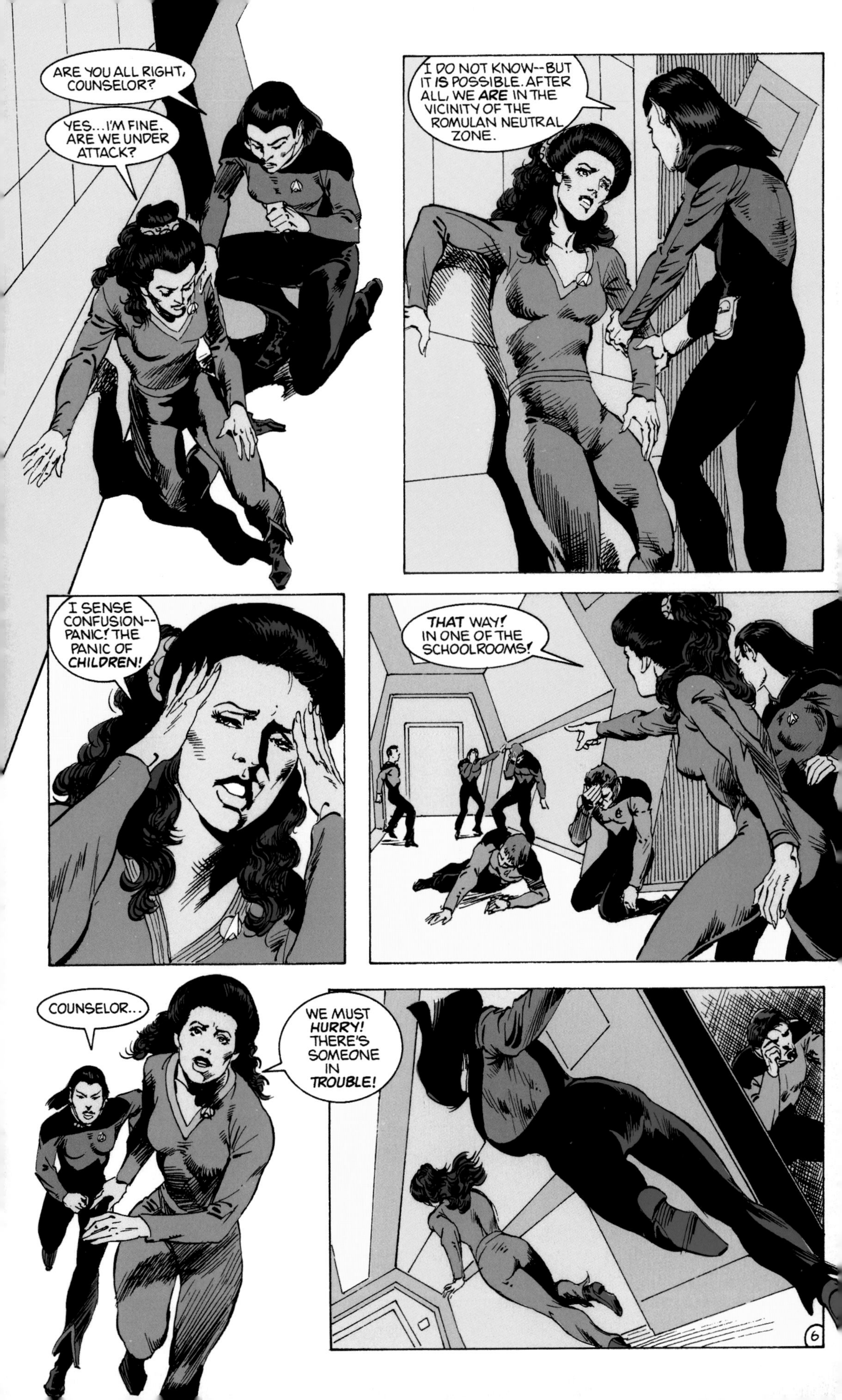
ARE YOU ALL RIGHT, COUNSELOR?
YES...I'M FINE. ARE WE UNDER ATTACK?
I DO NOT KNOW--BUT IT IS POSSIBLE. AFTER ALL, WE ARE IN THE VICINITY OF THE ROMULAN NEUTRAL ZONE.
I SENSE CONFUSION--PANIC! THE PANIC OF CHILDREN!
THAT WAY! IN ONE OF THE SCHOOLROOMS!
COUNSELOR...
WE MUST HURRY! THERE'S SOMEONE IN TROUBLE!
6

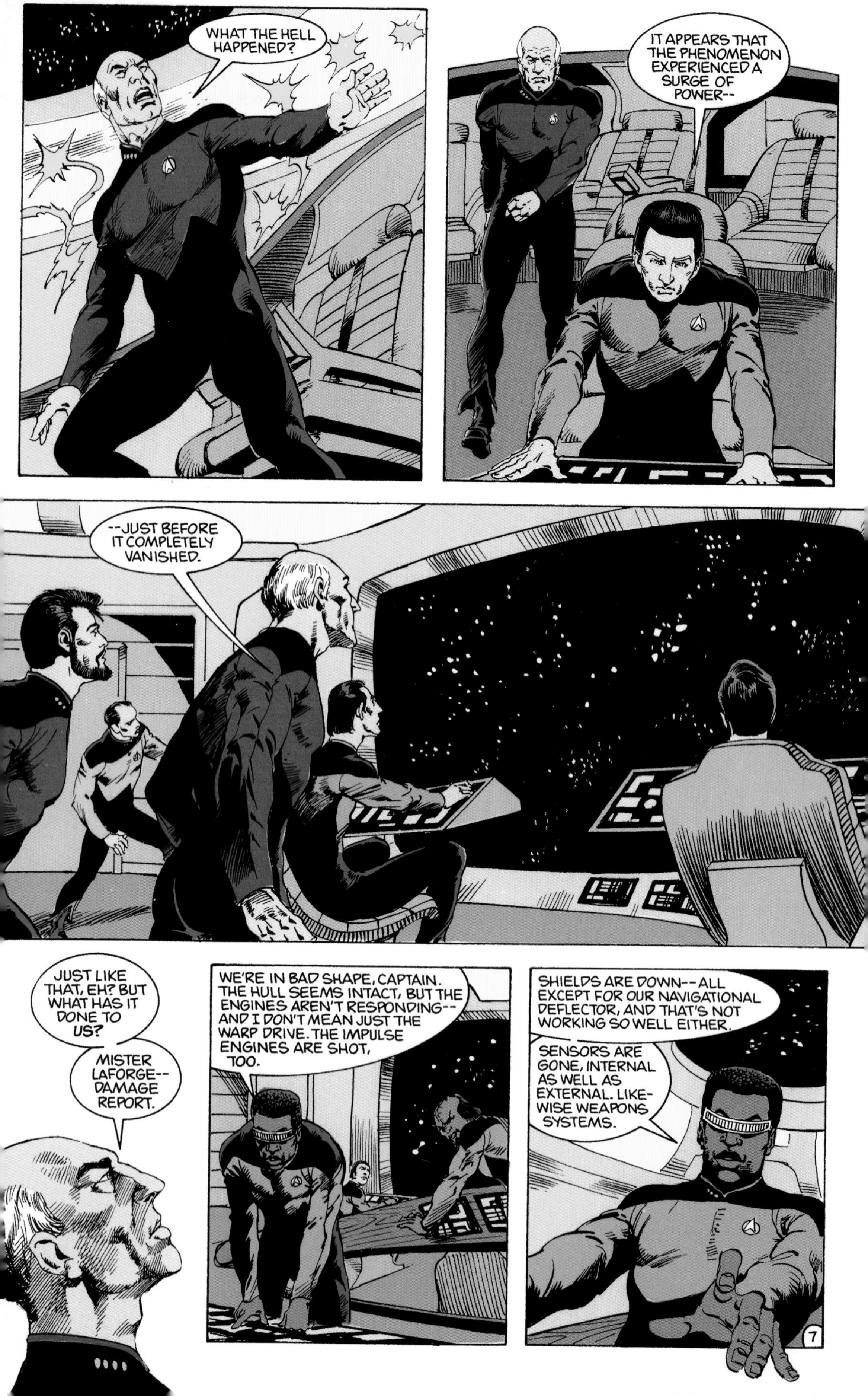
WHAT THE HELL HAPPENED?
IT APPEARS THAT THE PHENOMENON EXPERIENCED A SURGE OF POWER--
--JUST BEFORE IT COMPLETELY VANISHED.
JUST LIKE THAT, EH? BUT WHAT HAS IT DONE TO US?
MISTER LAFORGE-- DAMAGE REPORT.
WE'RE IN BAD SHAPE, CAPTAIN. THE HULL SEEMS INTACT, BUT THE ENGINES AREN'T RESPONDING-- AND I DON'T MEAN JUST THE WARP DRIVE. THE IMPULSE ENGINES ARE SHOT, TOO.
SHIELDS ARE DOWN-- ALL EXCEPT FOR OUR NAVIGATIONAL DEFLECTOR, AND THAT'S NOT WORKING SO WELL EITHER.
SENSORS ARE GONE, INTERNAL AS WELL AS EXTERNAL. LIKE-WISE WEAPONS SYSTEMS.
7

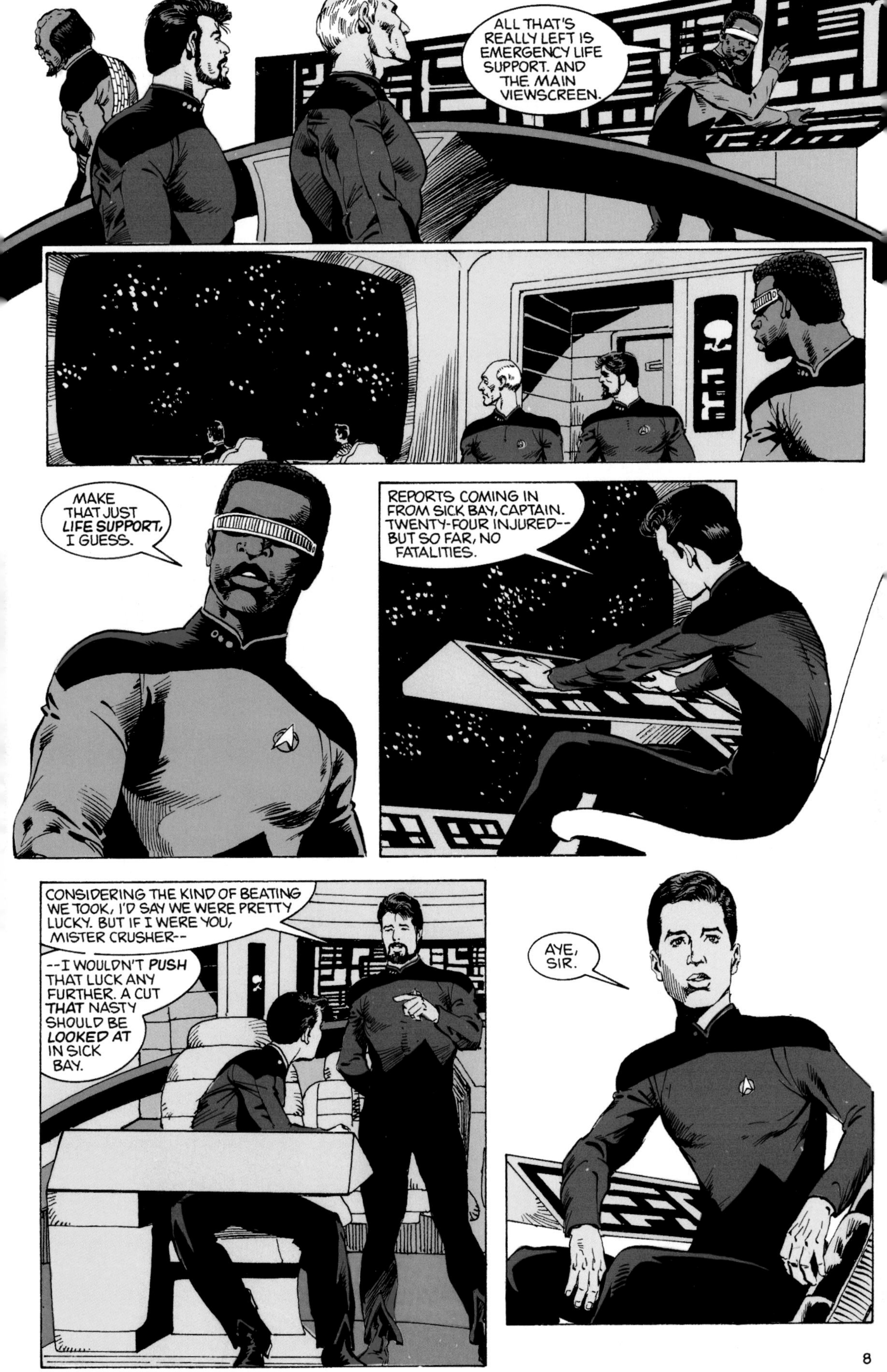
ALL THAT'S REALLY LEFT IS EMERGENCY LIFE SUPPORT. AND THE MAIN VIEWSCREEN.
MAKE THAT JUST LIFE SUPPORT, I GUESS.
REPORTS COMING IN FROM SICK BAY, CAPTAIN. TWENTY-FOUR INJURED-- BUT SO FAR, NO FATALITIES.
CONSIDERING THE KIND OF BEATING WE TOOK, I'D SAY WE WERE PRETTY LUCKY. BUT IF I WERE YOU, MISTER CRUSHER--
--I WOULDN'T PUSH THAT LUCK ANY FURTHER. A CUT THAT NASTY SHOULD BE LOOKED AT IN SICK BAY.
AYE, SIR.

MISTER LAFORGE-- WE CAN'T ALLOW OURSELVES TO DRIFT *BLINDLY*. PARTICULARLY WHEN WE'RE SO CLOSE TO THE *NEUTRAL ZONE*.

I HEAR YOU, CAPTAIN. I'VE ALREADY GOT PEOPLE WORKING ON THE SHIELDS AND THE EXTERNAL SENSOR SYSTEMS.

OF COURSE, THE ENGINES ARE GOING TO BE A LITTLE TRICKIER. I'M GOING TO WANT TO OVERSEE THAT SORT OF THING MYSELF.

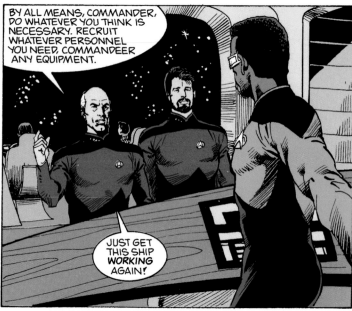

BY ALL MEANS, COMMANDER, DO WHATEVER YOU THINK IS NECESSARY. RECRUIT WHATEVER PERSONNEL YOU NEED, COMMANDEER ANY EQUIPMENT.

JUST GET THIS SHIP *WORKING* AGAIN!

ON MY WAY, SIR.

DECK FORTY-- AND STEP ON IT.

COMMANDER... YOU NEED ALL THE HELP YOU CAN GET, DON'T YOU?

9

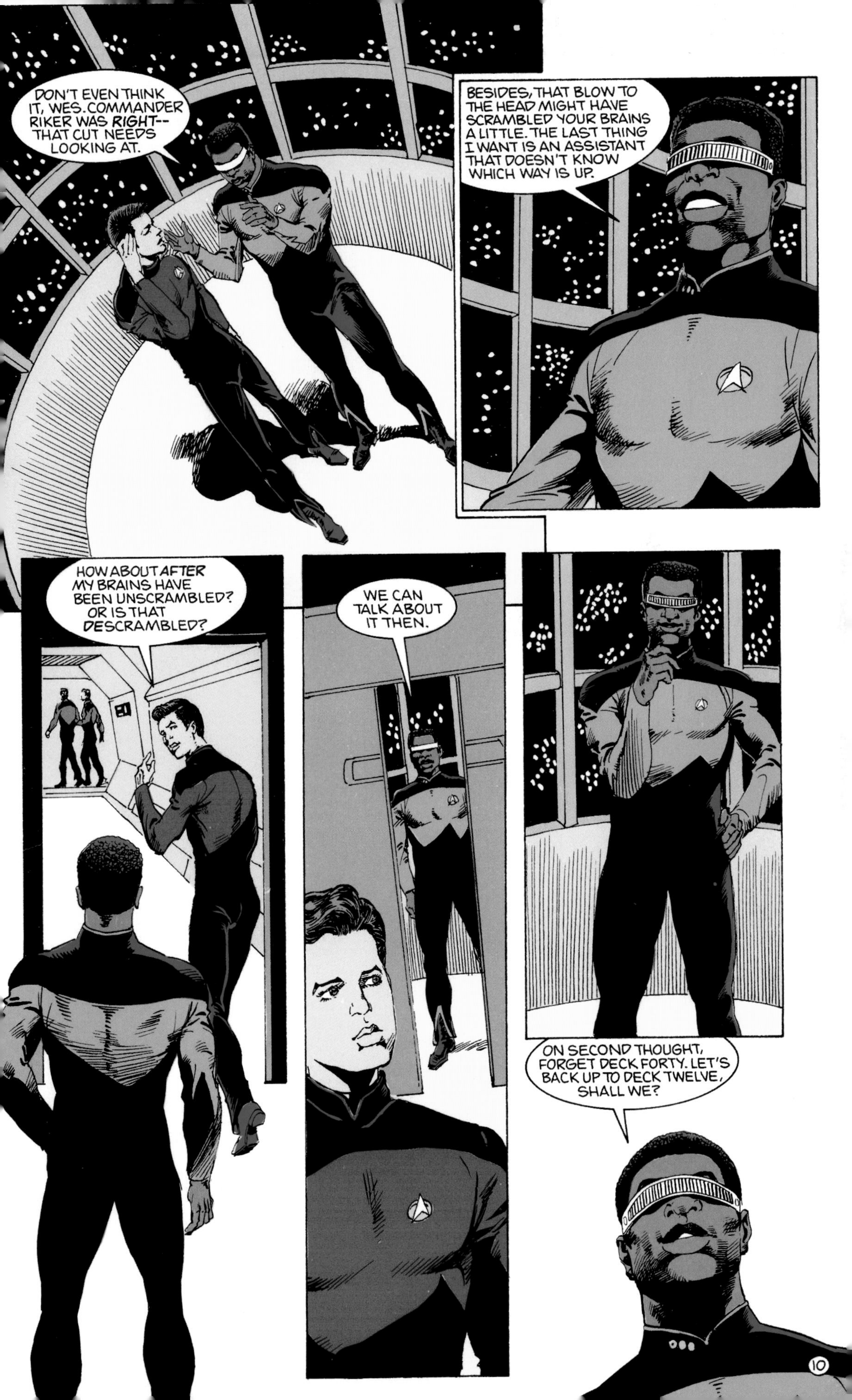
DON'T EVEN THINK IT, WES. COMMANDER RIKER WAS RIGHT-- THAT CUT NEEDS LOOKING AT.
BESIDES, THAT BLOW TO THE HEAD MIGHT HAVE SCRAMBLED YOUR BRAINS A LITTLE. THE LAST THING I WANT IS AN ASSISTANT THAT DOESN'T KNOW WHICH WAY IS UP.
HOW ABOUT AFTER MY BRAINS HAVE BEEN UNSCRAMBLED? OR IS THAT DESCRAMBLED?
WE CAN TALK ABOUT IT THEN.
ON SECOND THOUGHT, FORGET DECK FORTY. LET'S BACK UP TO DECK TWELVE, SHALL WE?
10

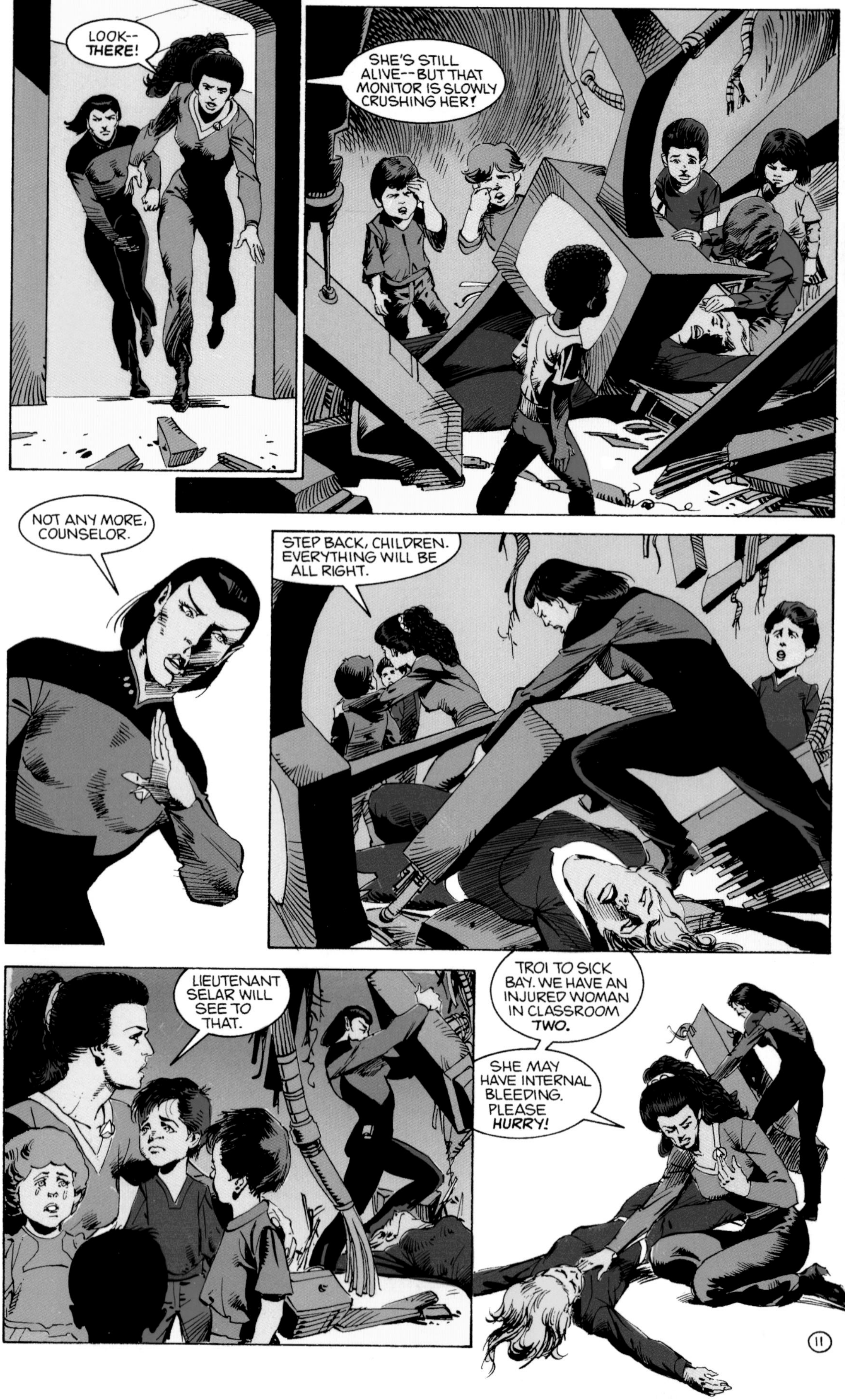
LOOK-- THERE!
SHE'S STILL ALIVE--BUT THAT MONITOR IS SLOWLY CRUSHING HER!
NOT ANY MORE, COUNSELOR.
STEP BACK, CHILDREN. EVERYTHING WILL BE ALL RIGHT.
LIEUTENANT SELAR WILL SEE TO THAT.
TROI TO SICK BAY. WE HAVE AN INJURED WOMAN IN CLASSROOM **TWO.**
SHE MAY HAVE INTERNAL BLEEDING. PLEASE **HURRY!**

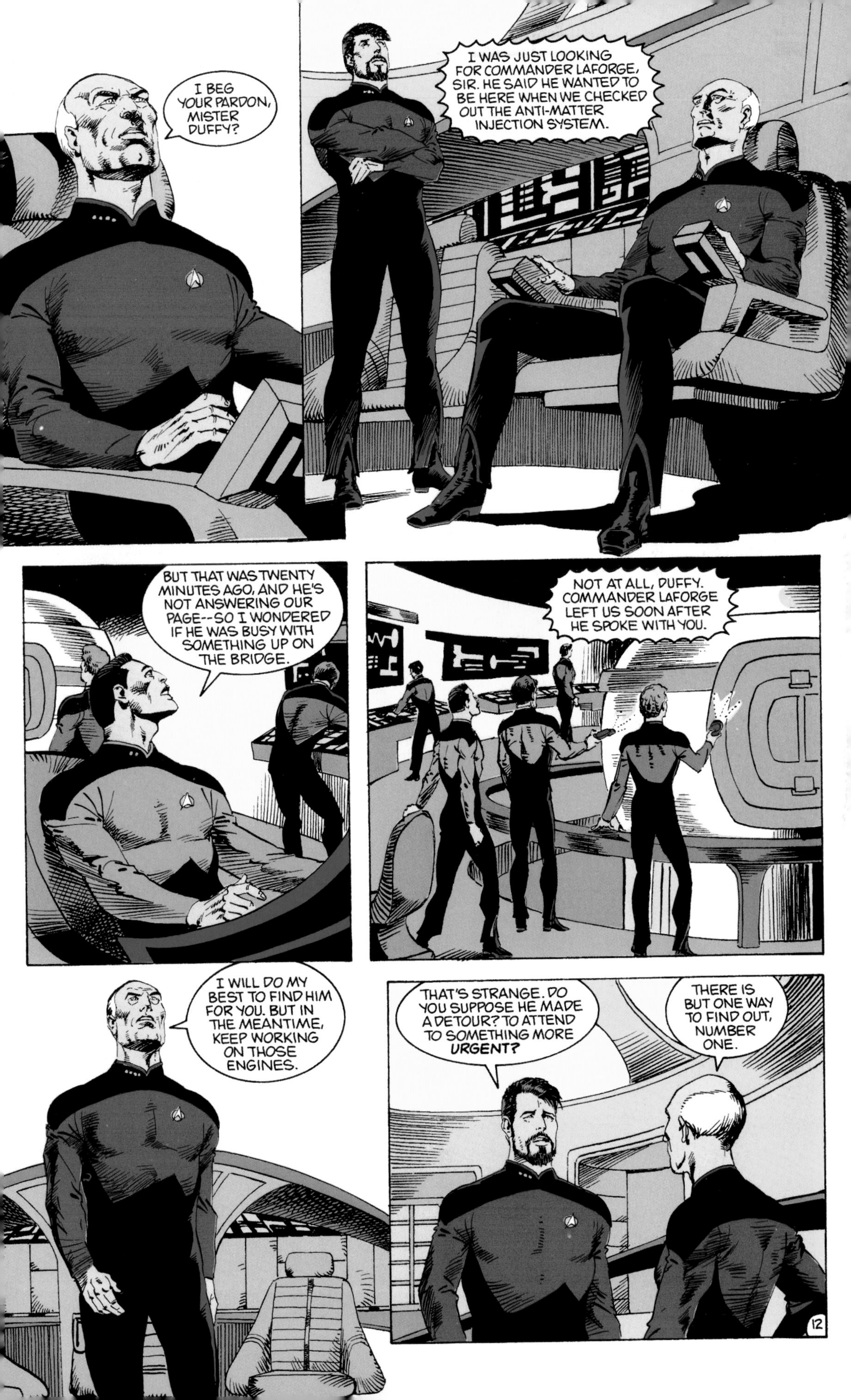
I BEG YOUR PARDON, MISTER DUFFY?
I WAS JUST LOOKING FOR COMMANDER LAFORGE, SIR. HE SAID HE WANTED TO BE HERE WHEN WE CHECKED OUT THE ANTI-MATTER INJECTION SYSTEM.
BUT THAT WAS TWENTY MINUTES AGO, AND HE'S NOT ANSWERING OUR PAGE--SO I WONDERED IF HE WAS BUSY WITH SOMETHING UP ON THE BRIDGE.
NOT AT ALL, DUFFY. COMMANDER LAFORGE LEFT US SOON AFTER HE SPOKE WITH YOU.
I WILL DO MY BEST TO FIND HIM FOR YOU. BUT IN THE MEANTIME, KEEP WORKING ON THOSE ENGINES.
THAT'S STRANGE. DO YOU SUPPOSE HE MADE A DETOUR? TO ATTEND TO SOMETHING MORE **URGENT?**
THERE IS BUT ONE WAY TO FIND OUT, NUMBER ONE.
12

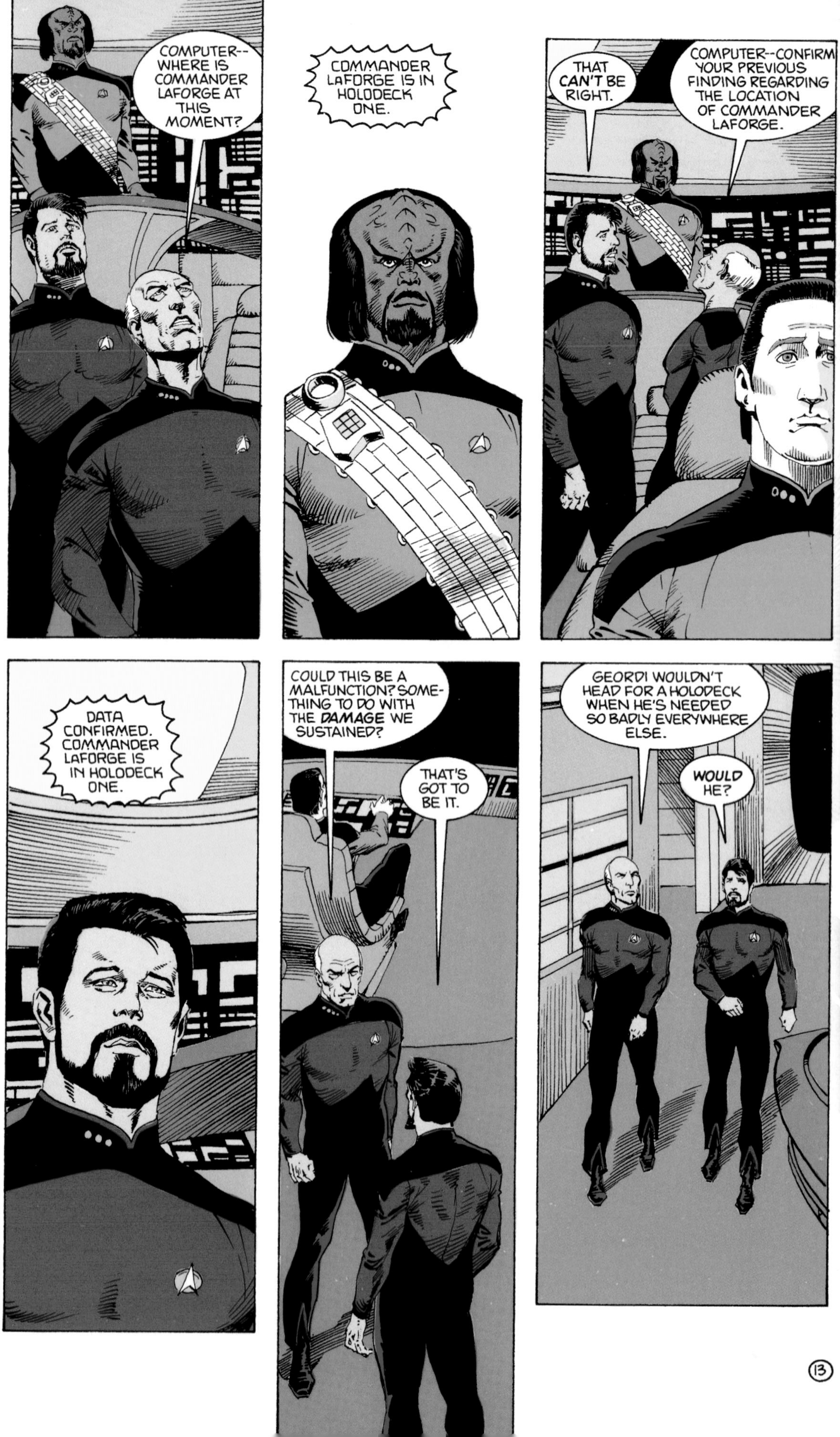
COMPUTER--WHERE IS COMMANDER LAFORGE AT THIS MOMENT?
COMMANDER LAFORGE IS IN HOLODECK ONE.
THAT **CAN'T** BE RIGHT.
COMPUTER--CONFIRM YOUR PREVIOUS FINDING REGARDING THE LOCATION OF COMMANDER LAFORGE.
DATA CONFIRMED. COMMANDER LAFORGE IS IN HOLODECK ONE.
COULD THIS BE A MALFUNCTION? SOMETHING TO DO WITH THE ***DAMAGE*** WE SUSTAINED?
THAT'S GOT TO BE IT.
GEORDI WOULDN'T HEAD FOR A HOLODECK WHEN HE'S NEEDED SO BADLY EVERYWHERE ELSE.
WOULD HE?

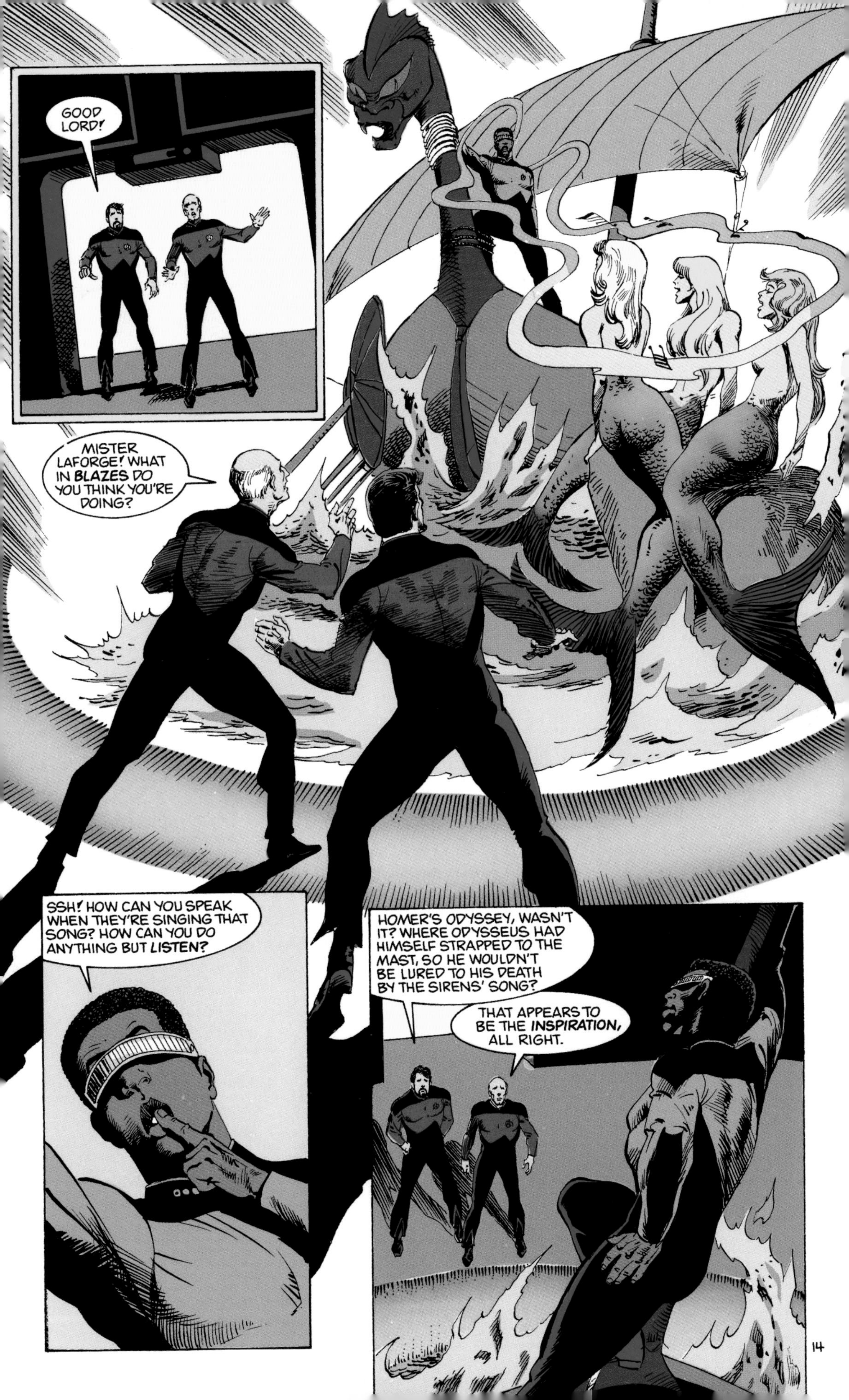

GOOD LORD!
MISTER LAFORGE! WHAT IN **BLAZES** DO YOU THINK YOU'RE DOING?
SSH! HOW CAN YOU SPEAK WHEN THEY'RE SINGING THAT SONG? HOW CAN YOU DO ANYTHING BUT **LISTEN**?
HOMER'S ODYSSEY, WASN'T IT? WHERE ODYSSEUS HAD HIMSELF STRAPPED TO THE MAST, SO HE WOULDN'T BE LURED TO HIS DEATH BY THE SIRENS' SONG?
THAT APPEARS TO BE THE ***INSPIRATION***, ALL RIGHT.

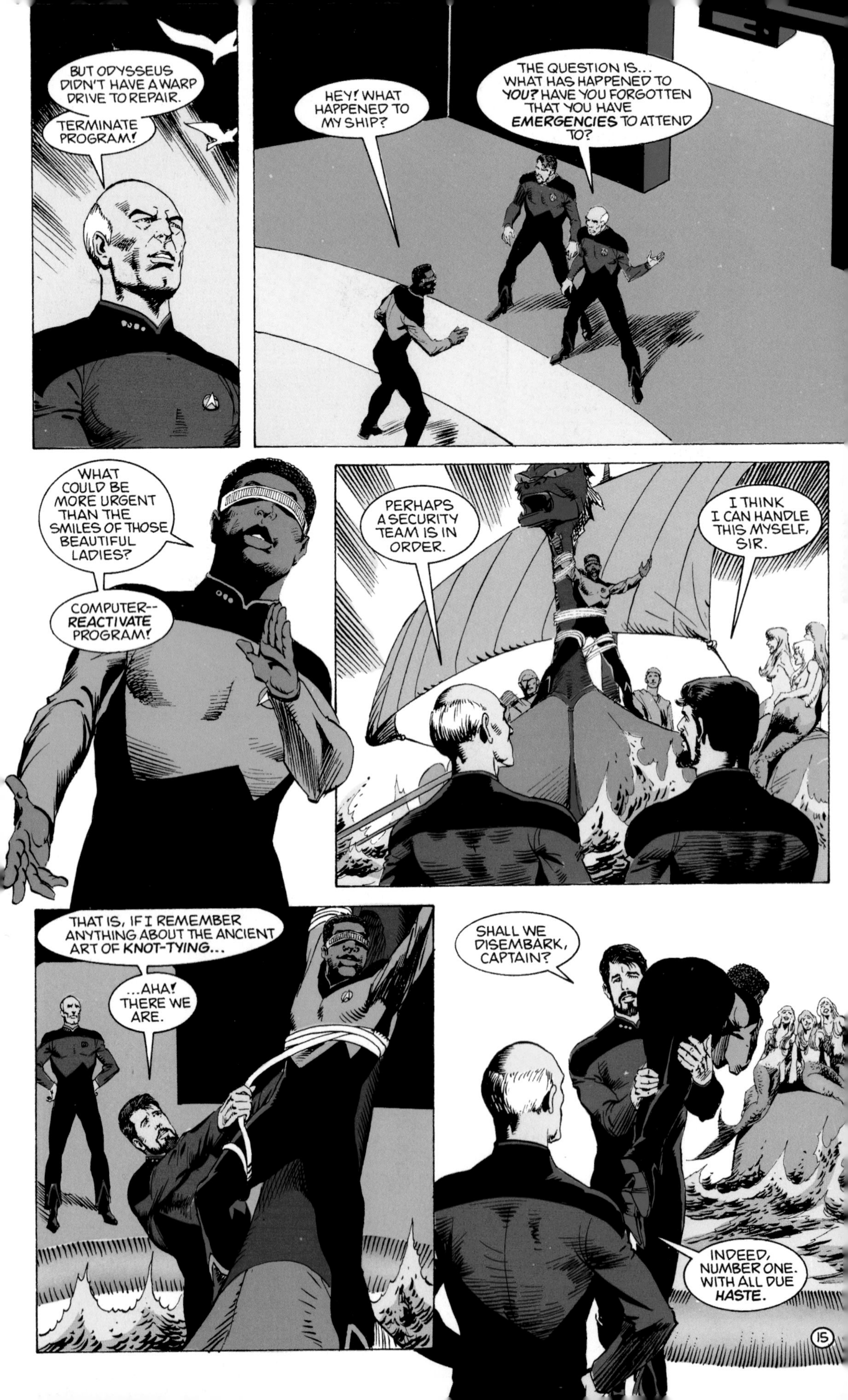
BUT ODYSSEUS DIDN'T HAVE A WARP DRIVE TO REPAIR.
TERMINATE PROGRAM!
HEY! WHAT HAPPENED TO MY SHIP?
THE QUESTION IS... WHAT HAS HAPPENED TO YOU? HAVE YOU FORGOTTEN THAT YOU HAVE EMERGENCIES TO ATTEND TO?
WHAT COULD BE MORE URGENT THAN THE SMILES OF THOSE BEAUTIFUL LADIES?
COMPUTER-- REACTIVATE PROGRAM!
PERHAPS A SECURITY TEAM IS IN ORDER.
I THINK I CAN HANDLE THIS MYSELF, SIR.
THAT IS, IF I REMEMBER ANYTHING ABOUT THE ANCIENT ART OF KNOT-TYING...
...AHA! THERE WE ARE.
SHALL WE DISEMBARK, CAPTAIN?
INDEED, NUMBER ONE. WITH ALL DUE HASTE.
15

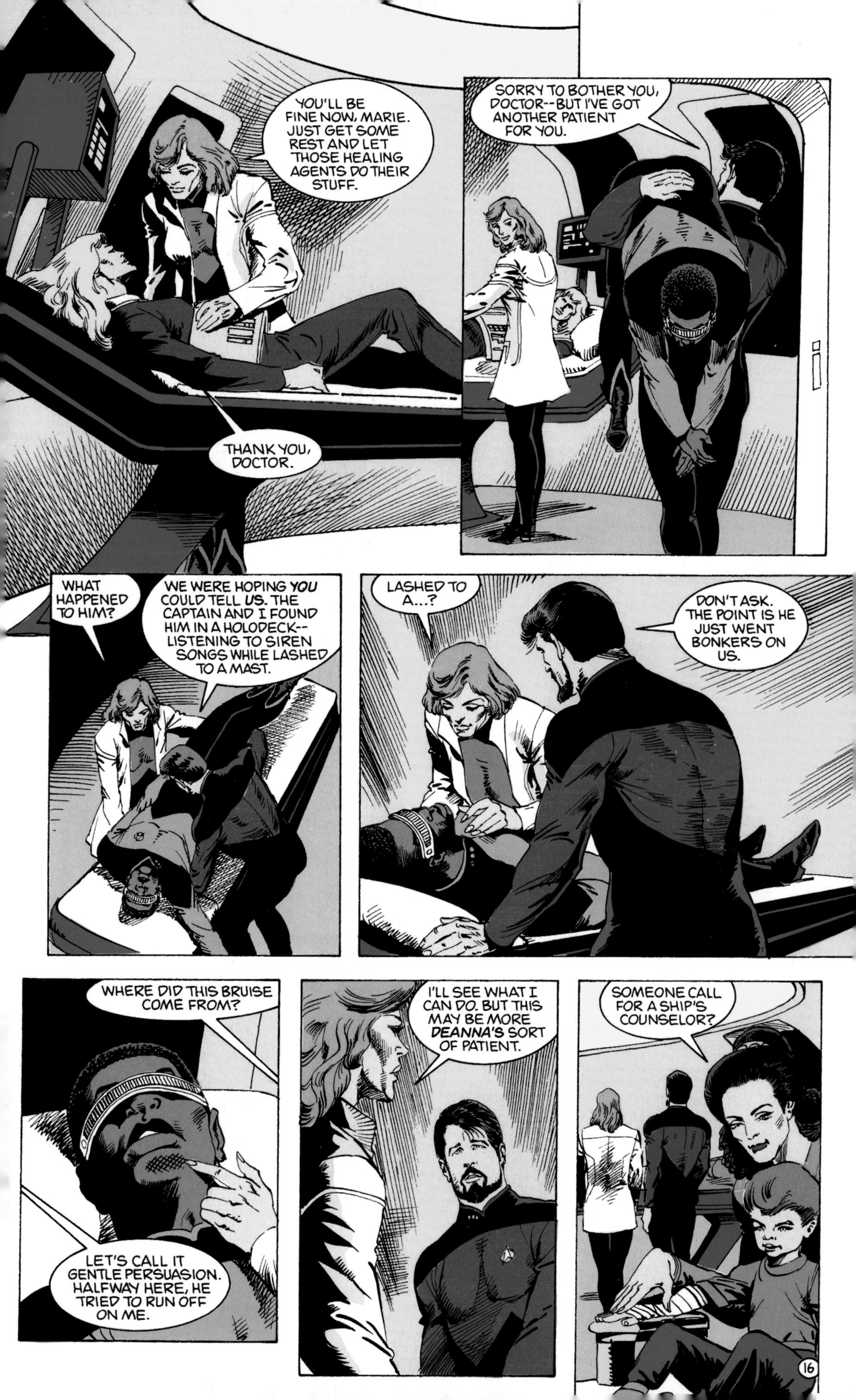
YOU'LL BE FINE NOW, MARIE. JUST GET SOME REST AND LET THOSE HEALING AGENTS DO THEIR STUFF.
THANK YOU, DOCTOR.
SORRY TO BOTHER YOU, DOCTOR--BUT I'VE GOT ANOTHER PATIENT FOR YOU.
WHAT HAPPENED TO HIM?
WE WERE HOPING YOU COULD TELL US. THE CAPTAIN AND I FOUND HIM IN A HOLODECK--LISTENING TO SIREN SONGS WHILE LASHED TO A MAST.
LASHED TO A...?
DON'T ASK. THE POINT IS HE JUST WENT BONKERS ON US.
WHERE DID THIS BRUISE COME FROM?
LET'S CALL IT GENTLE PERSUASION. HALFWAY HERE, HE TRIED TO RUN OFF ON ME.
I'LL SEE WHAT I CAN DO. BUT THIS MAY BE MORE DEANNA'S SORT OF PATIENT.
SOMEONE CALL FOR A SHIP'S COUNSELOR?
16

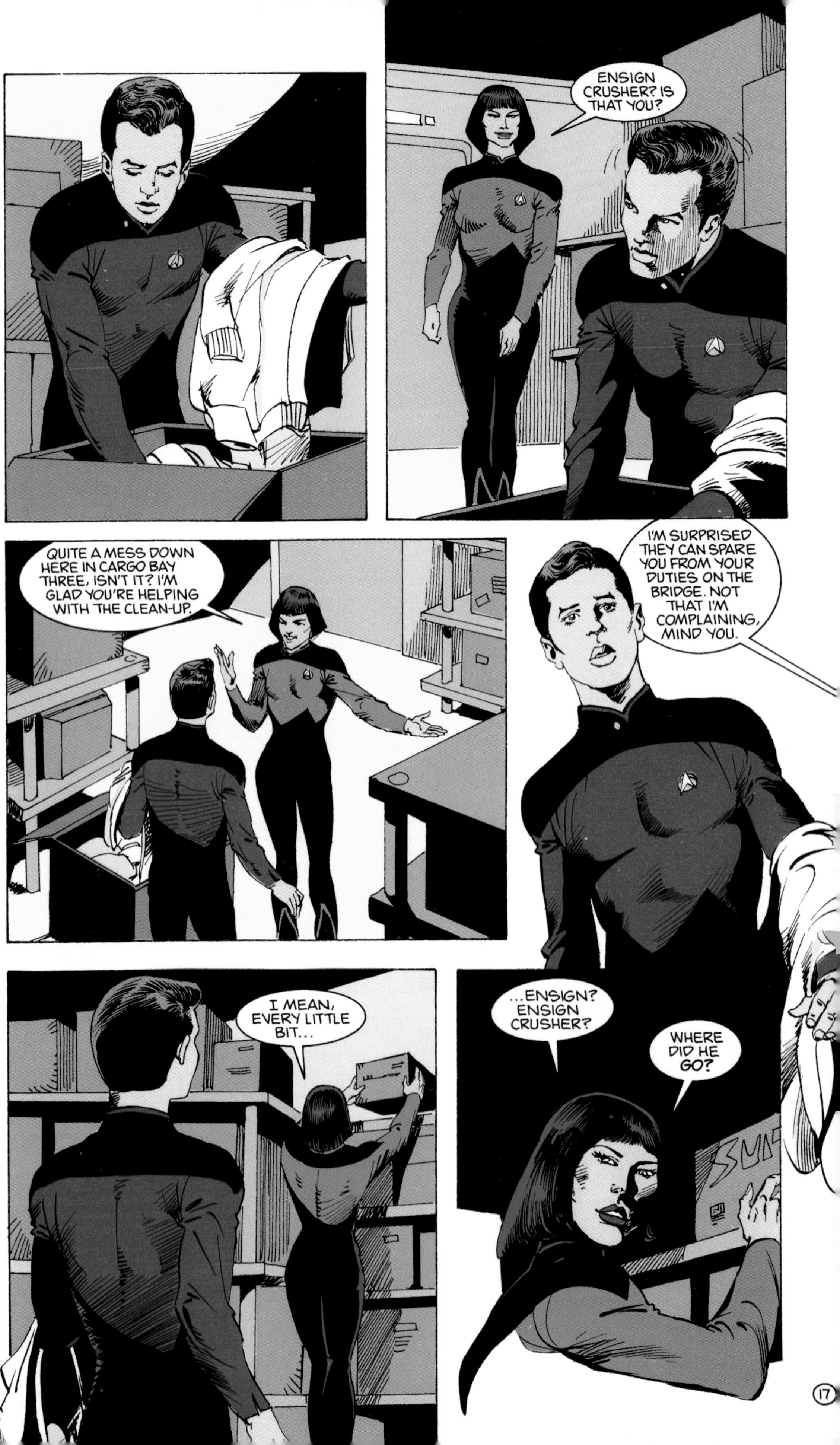
ENSIGN CRUSHER? IS THAT YOU?
QUITE A MESS DOWN HERE IN CARGO BAY THREE, ISN'T IT? I'M GLAD YOU'RE HELPING WITH THE CLEAN-UP.
I'M SURPRISED THEY CAN SPARE YOU FROM YOUR DUTIES ON THE BRIDGE. NOT THAT I'M COMPLAINING, MIND YOU.
I MEAN, EVERY LITTLE BIT...
...ENSIGN? ENSIGN CRUSHER?
WHERE DID HE GO?

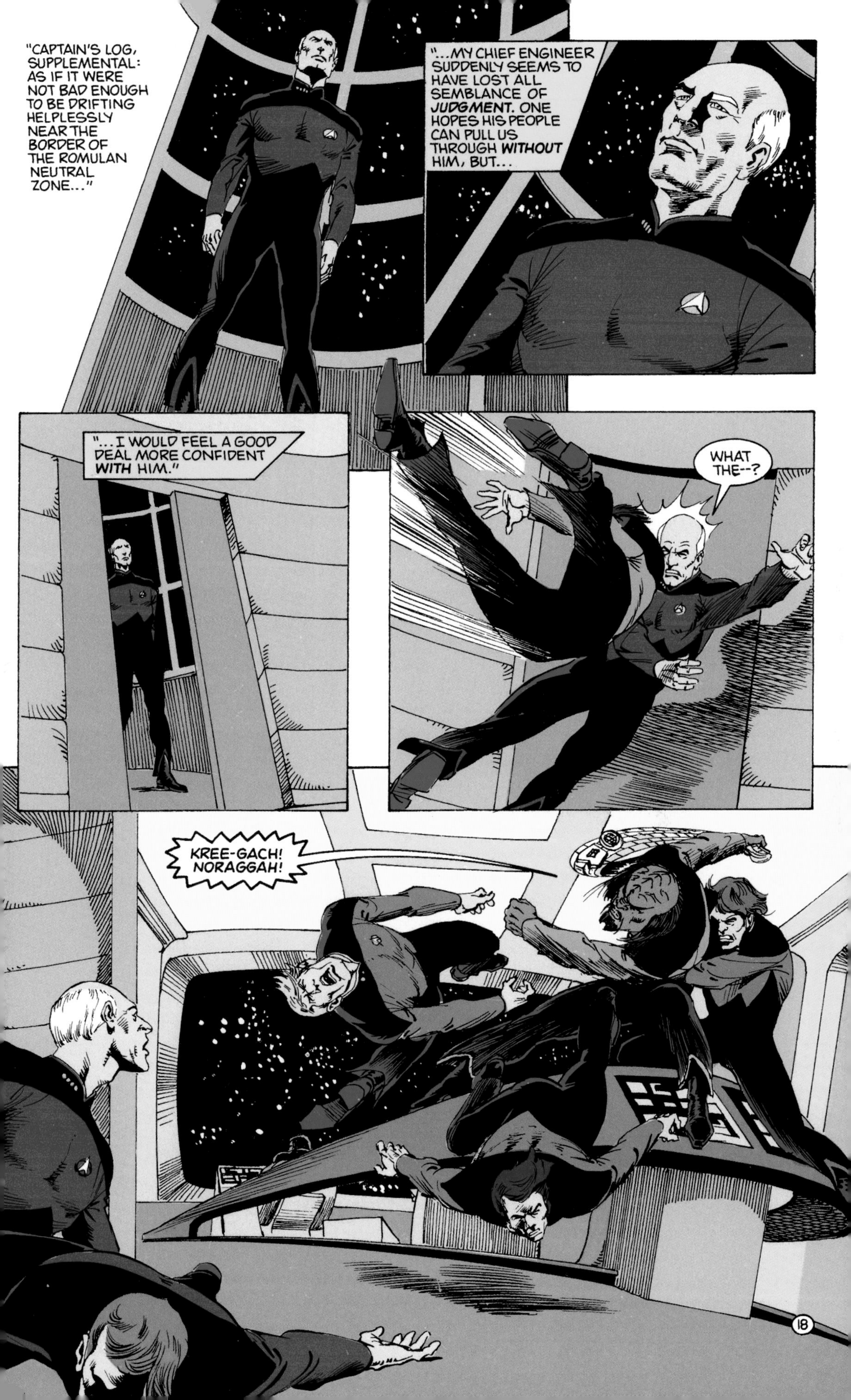
"CAPTAIN'S LOG, SUPPLEMENTAL: AS IF IT WERE NOT BAD ENOUGH TO BE DRIFTING HELPLESSLY NEAR THE BORDER OF THE ROMULAN NEUTRAL ZONE..."
"...MY CHIEF ENGINEER SUDDENLY SEEMS TO HAVE LOST ALL SEMBLANCE OF JUDGMENT. ONE HOPES HIS PEOPLE CAN PULL US THROUGH WITHOUT HIM, BUT...
"...I WOULD FEEL A GOOD DEAL MORE CONFIDENT WITH HIM."
WHAT THE--?
KREE-GACH! NORAGGAH!

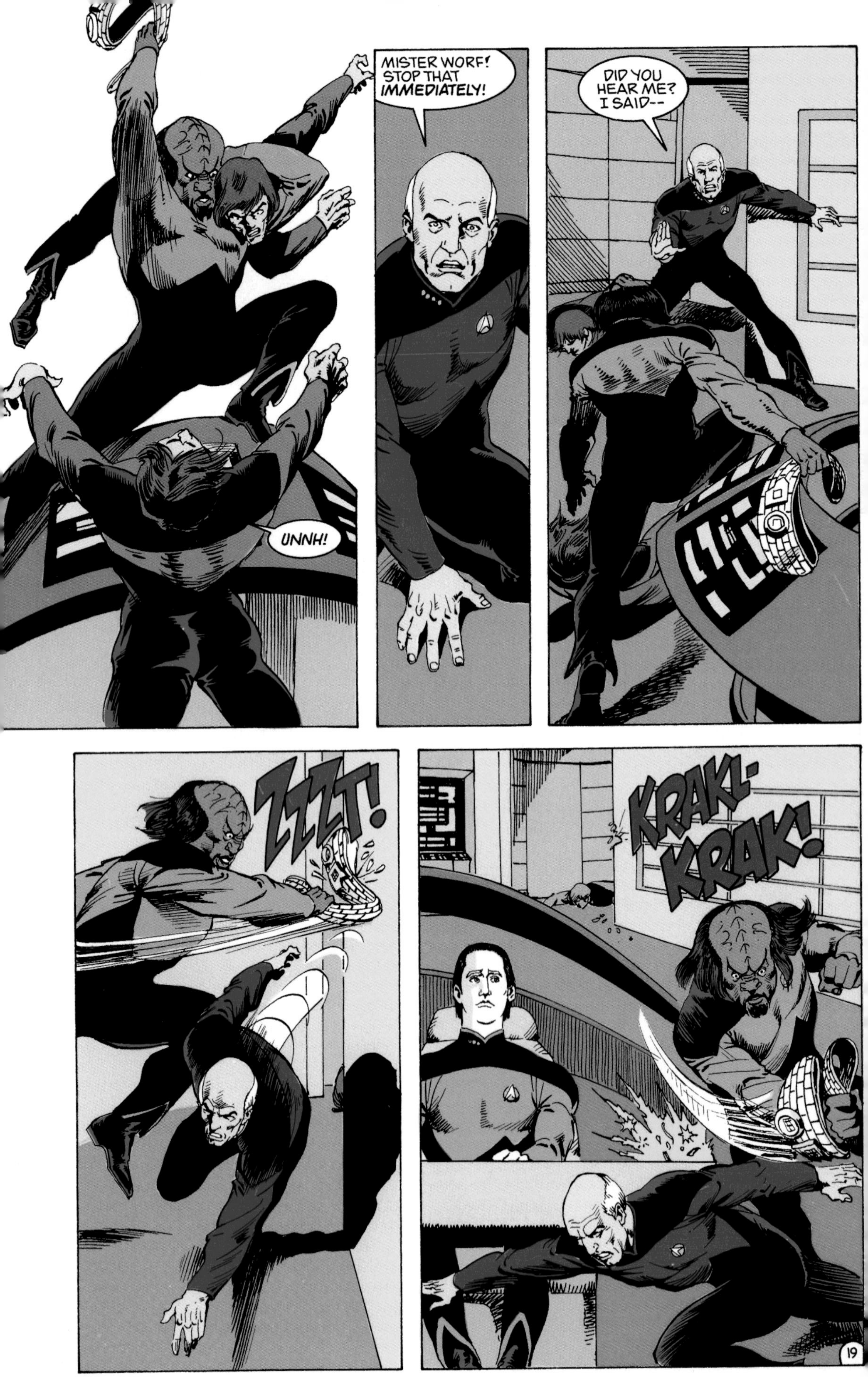
UNNH!
MISTER WORF! STOP THAT IMMEDIATELY!
DID YOU HEAR ME? I SAID--
ZZZT!
KRAKL-KRAK!
19

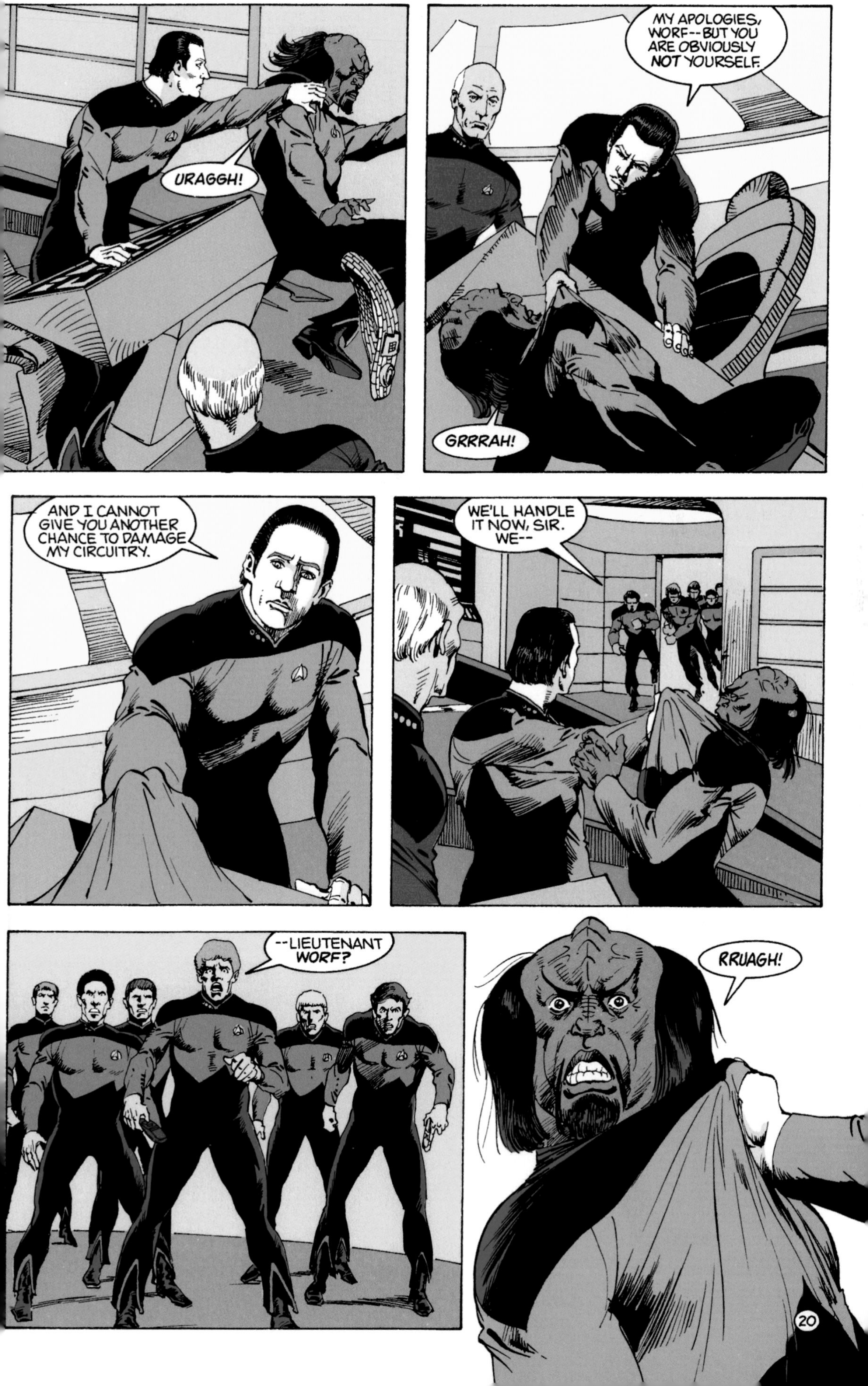
URAGGH!
MY APOLOGIES, WORF--BUT YOU ARE OBVIOUSLY NOT YOURSELF.
GRRRAH!
AND I CANNOT GIVE YOU ANOTHER CHANCE TO DAMAGE MY CIRCUITRY.
WE'LL HANDLE IT NOW, SIR. WE--
--LIEUTENANT WORF?
RRUAGH!

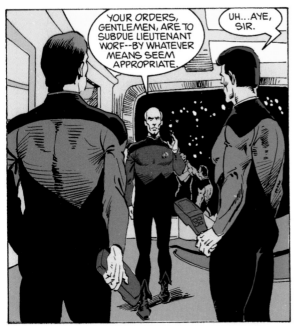

YOUR ORDERS, GENTLEMEN, ARE TO SUBDUE LIEUTENANT WORF--BY WHATEVER MEANS SEEM APPROPRIATE.

UH...AYE, SIR.

DATA--YOU MAY PUT LIEUTENANT WORF DOWN NOW. *CAREFULLY.*

AS YOU WISH, CAPTAIN.

KREEGAH...

...*KRAGHLAT!*

GOT HIM, CAPTAIN. I... THINK.

THEN TAKE HIM TO SICK BAY.

㉑

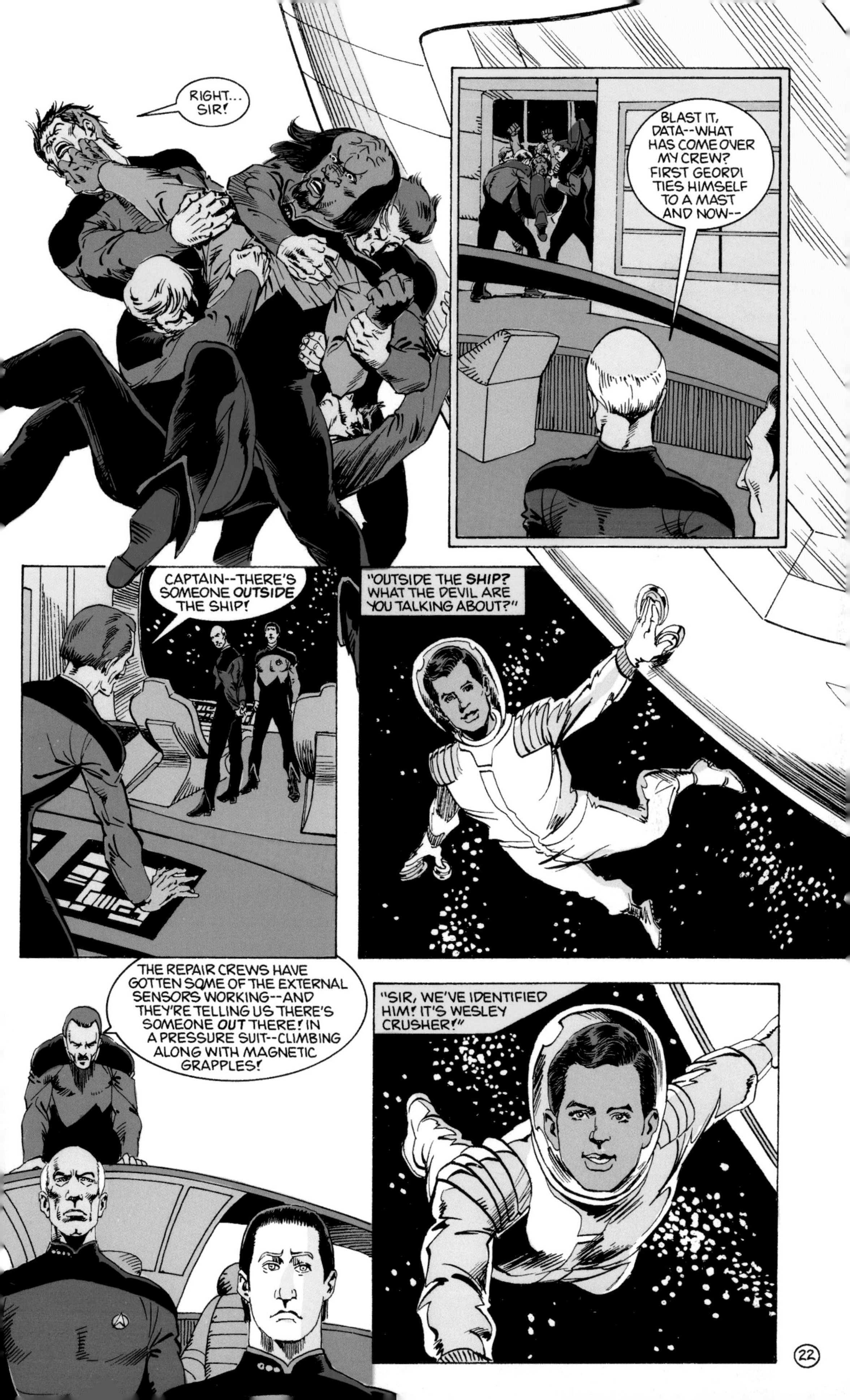
RIGHT... SIR!
BLAST IT, DATA--WHAT HAS COME OVER MY CREW? FIRST GEORDI TIES HIMSELF TO A MAST AND NOW--
CAPTAIN--THERE'S SOMEONE OUTSIDE THE SHIP!
"OUTSIDE THE SHIP? WHAT THE DEVIL ARE YOU TALKING ABOUT?"
THE REPAIR CREWS HAVE GOTTEN SOME OF THE EXTERNAL SENSORS WORKING--AND THEY'RE TELLING US THERE'S SOMEONE OUT THERE! IN A PRESSURE SUIT--CLIMBING ALONG WITH MAGNETIC GRAPPLES!
"SIR, WE'VE IDENTIFIED HIM! IT'S WESLEY CRUSHER!"

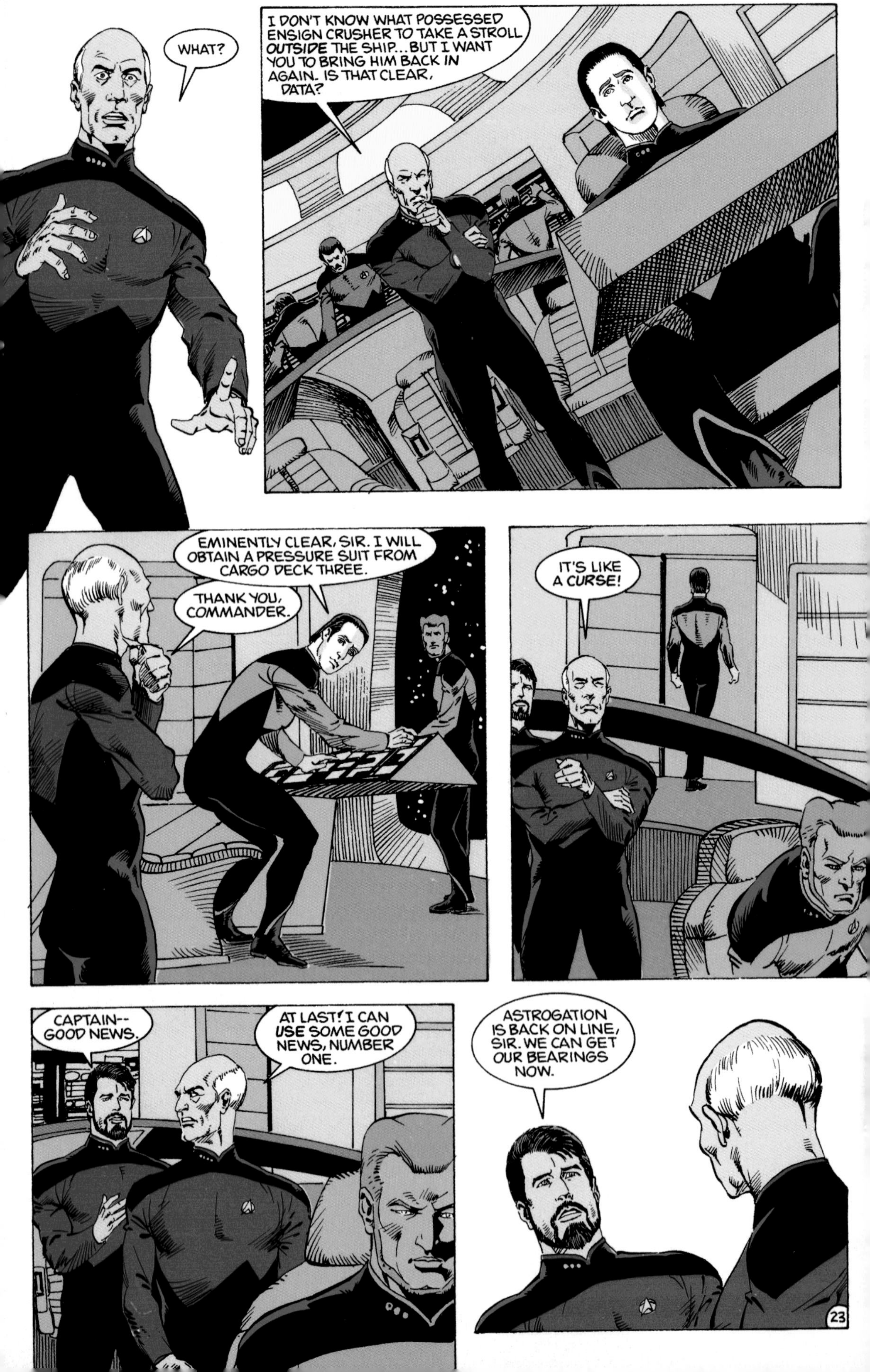
WHAT?
I DON'T KNOW WHAT POSSESSED ENSIGN CRUSHER TO TAKE A STROLL OUTSIDE THE SHIP... BUT I WANT YOU TO BRING HIM BACK IN AGAIN. IS THAT CLEAR, DATA?
EMINENTLY CLEAR, SIR. I WILL OBTAIN A PRESSURE SUIT FROM CARGO DECK THREE.
THANK YOU, COMMANDER.
IT'S LIKE A CURSE!
CAPTAIN-- GOOD NEWS.
AT LAST! I CAN USE SOME GOOD NEWS, NUMBER ONE.
ASTROGATION IS BACK ON LINE, SIR. WE CAN GET OUR BEARINGS NOW.
23

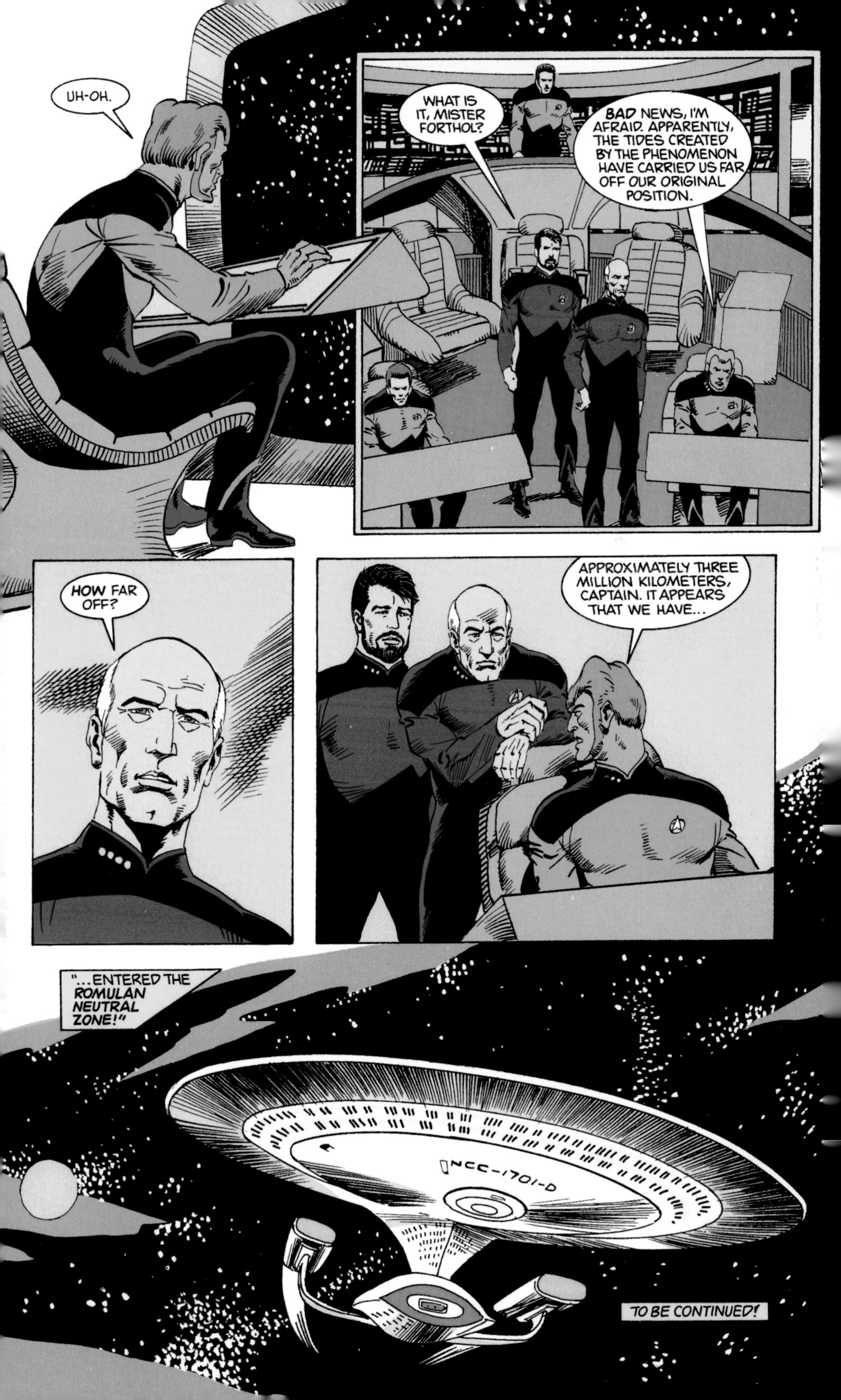
UH-OH.
WHAT IS IT, MISTER FORTHOL?
BAD NEWS, I'M AFRAID. APPARENTLY, THE TIDES CREATED BY THE PHENOMENON HAVE CARRIED US FAR OFF OUR ORIGINAL POSITION.
HOW FAR OFF?
APPROXIMATELY THREE MILLION KILOMETERS, CAPTAIN. IT APPEARS THAT WE HAVE...
"...ENTERED THE ROMULAN NEUTRAL ZONE!"
NCC-1701-D
TO BE CONTINUED!

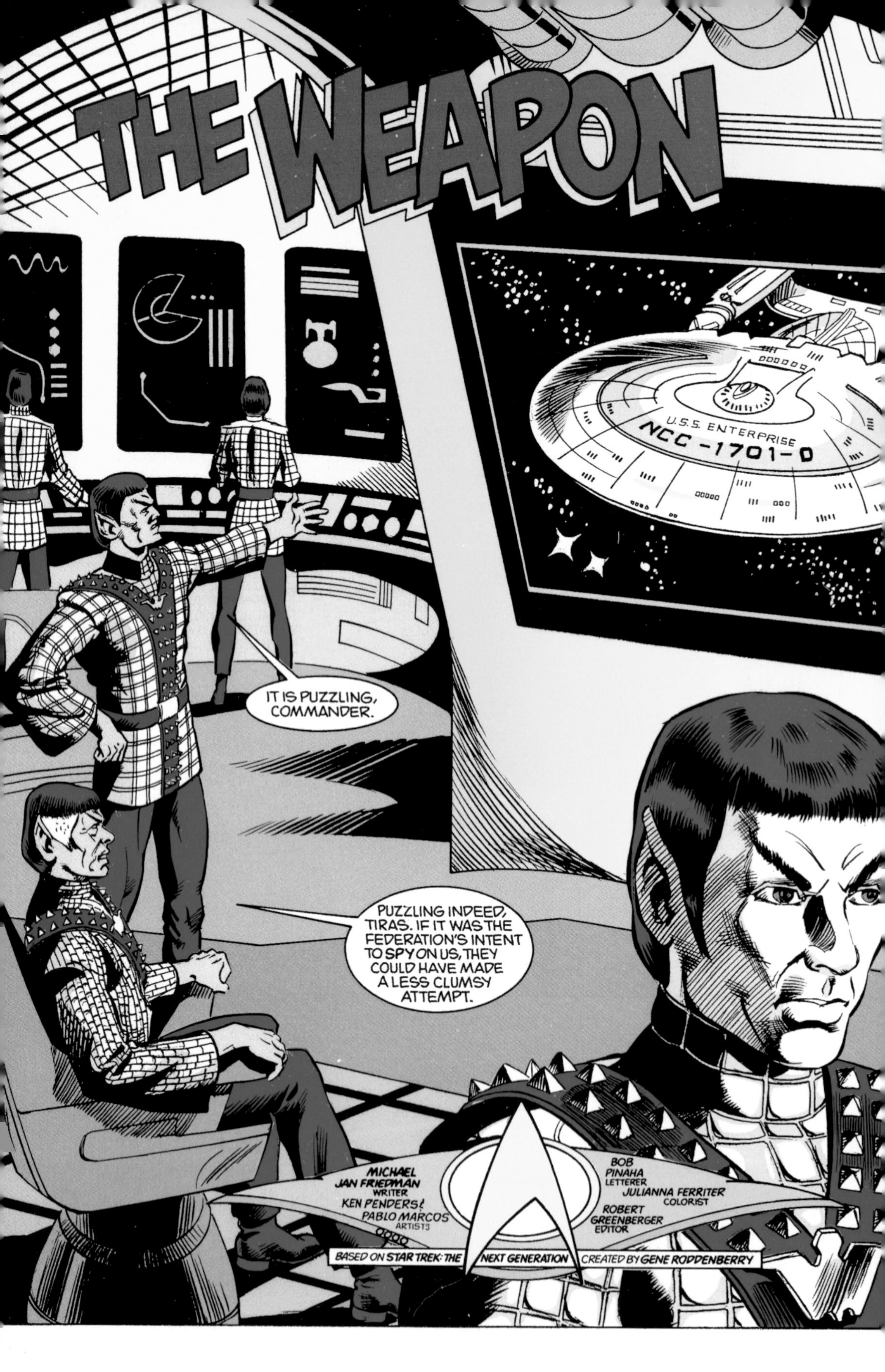
THE WEAPON
U.S.S. ENTERPRISE
NCC-1701-D
IT IS PUZZLING, COMMANDER.
PUZZLING INDEED, TIRAS. IF IT WAS THE FEDERATION'S INTENT TO SPY ON US, THEY COULD HAVE MADE A LESS CLUMSY ATTEMPT.
MICHAEL JAN FRIEDMAN WRITER
KEN PENDERS & PABLO MARCOS ARTISTS
BOB PINAHA LETTERER
JULIANNA FERRITER COLORIST
ROBERT GREENBERGER EDITOR
BASED ON STAR TREK: THE NEXT GENERATION CREATED BY GENE RODDENBERRY

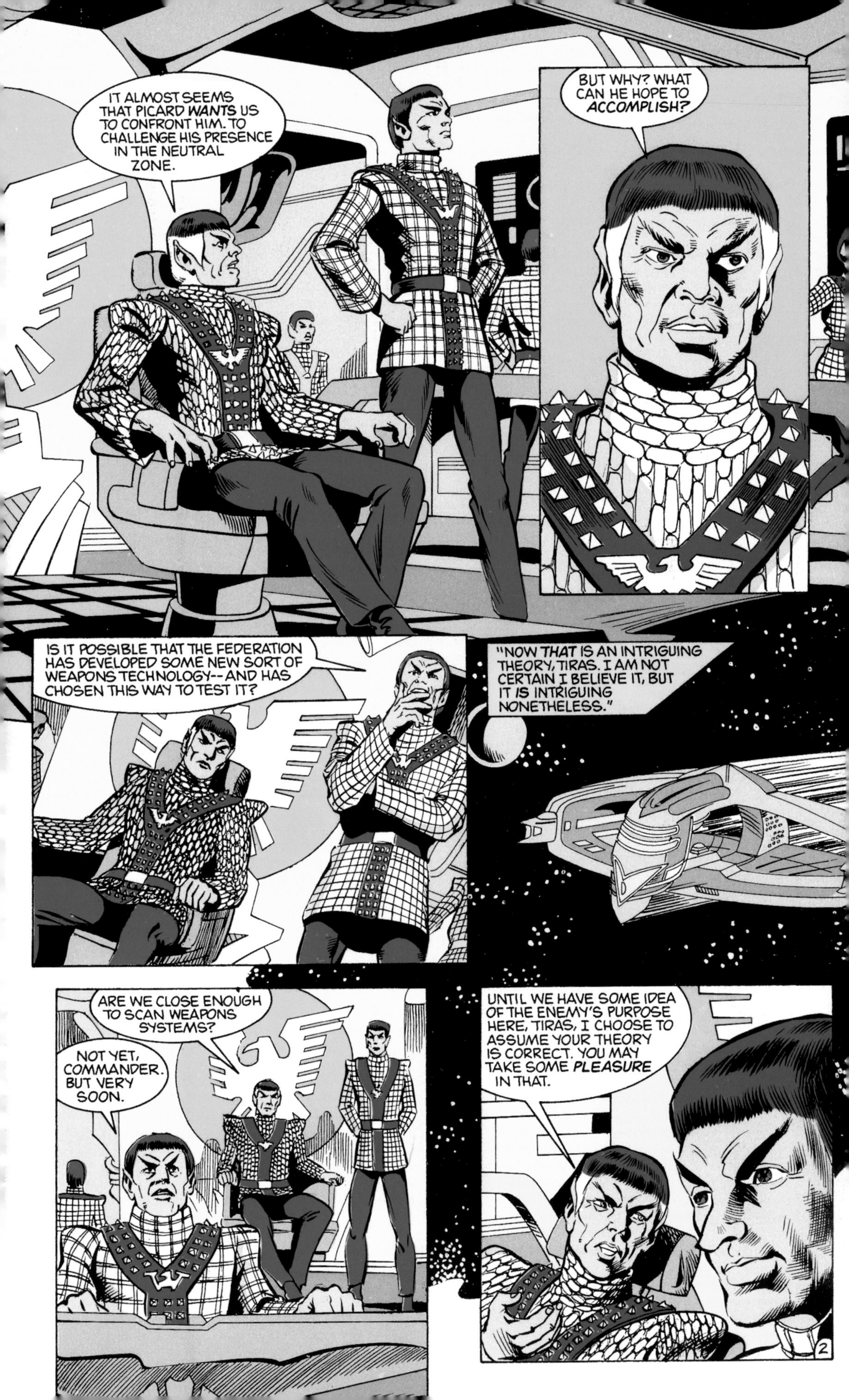

IT ALMOST SEEMS THAT PICARD WANTS US TO CONFRONT HIM. TO CHALLENGE HIS PRESENCE IN THE NEUTRAL ZONE.
BUT WHY? WHAT CAN HE HOPE TO ACCOMPLISH?
IS IT POSSIBLE THAT THE FEDERATION HAS DEVELOPED SOME NEW SORT OF WEAPONS TECHNOLOGY--AND HAS CHOSEN THIS WAY TO TEST IT?
"NOW THAT IS AN INTRIGUING THEORY, TIRAS. I AM NOT CERTAIN I BELIEVE IT, BUT IT IS INTRIGUING NONETHELESS."
ARE WE CLOSE ENOUGH TO SCAN WEAPONS SYSTEMS?
NOT YET, COMMANDER. BUT VERY SOON.
UNTIL WE HAVE SOME IDEA OF THE ENEMY'S PURPOSE HERE, TIRAS, I CHOOSE TO ASSUME YOUR THEORY IS CORRECT. YOU MAY TAKE SOME PLEASURE IN THAT.
2

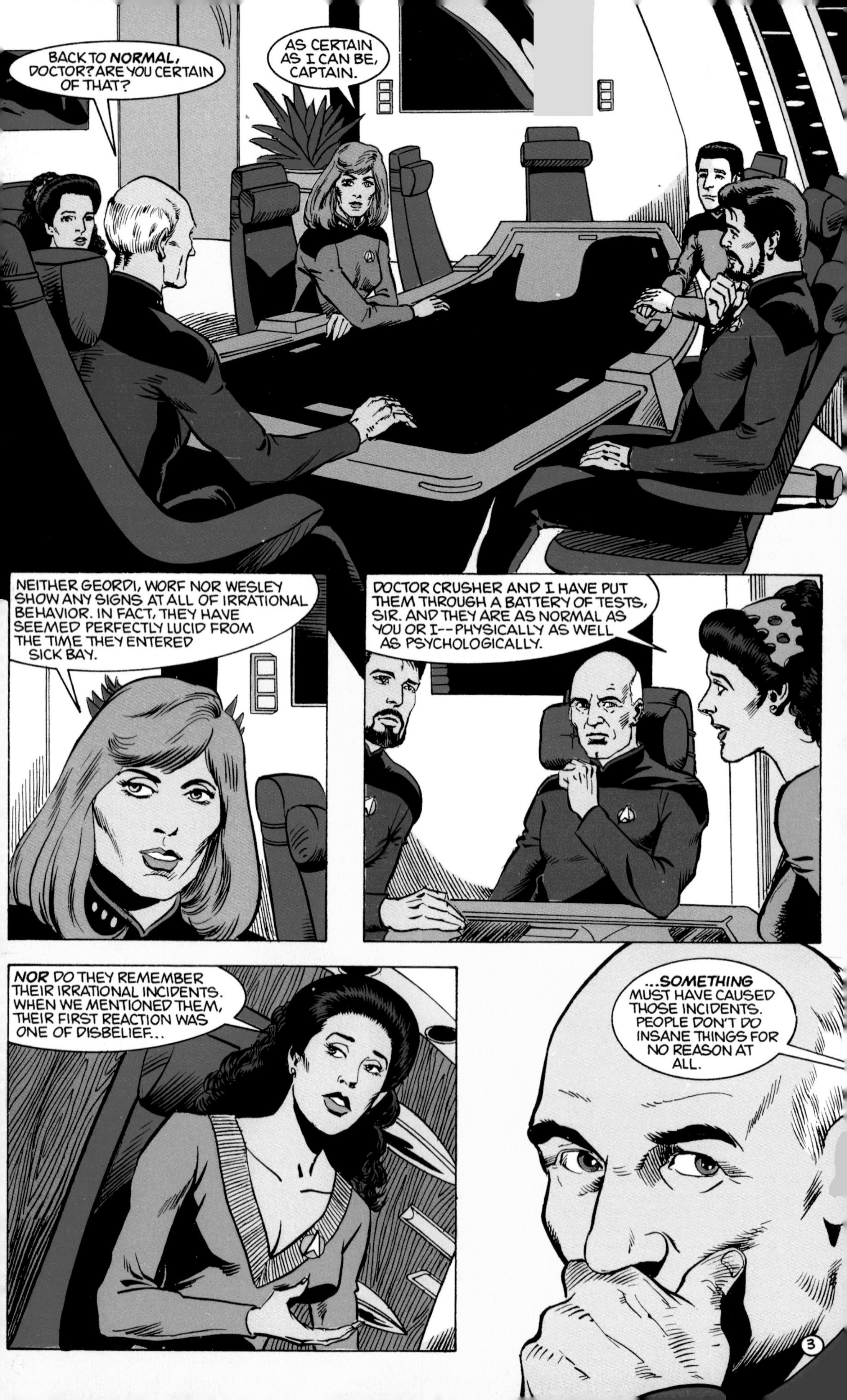
BACK TO NORMAL, DOCTOR? ARE YOU CERTAIN OF THAT?
AS CERTAIN AS I CAN BE, CAPTAIN.
NEITHER GEORDI, WORF NOR WESLEY SHOW ANY SIGNS AT ALL OF IRRATIONAL BEHAVIOR. IN FACT, THEY HAVE SEEMED PERFECTLY LUCID FROM THE TIME THEY ENTERED SICK BAY.
DOCTOR CRUSHER AND I HAVE PUT THEM THROUGH A BATTERY OF TESTS, SIR. AND THEY ARE AS NORMAL AS YOU OR I--PHYSICALLY AS WELL AS PSYCHOLOGICALLY.
NOR DO THEY REMEMBER THEIR IRRATIONAL INCIDENTS. WHEN WE MENTIONED THEM, THEIR FIRST REACTION WAS ONE OF DISBELIEF...
...SOMETHING MUST HAVE CAUSED THOSE INCIDENTS. PEOPLE DON'T DO INSANE THINGS FOR NO REASON AT ALL.
3

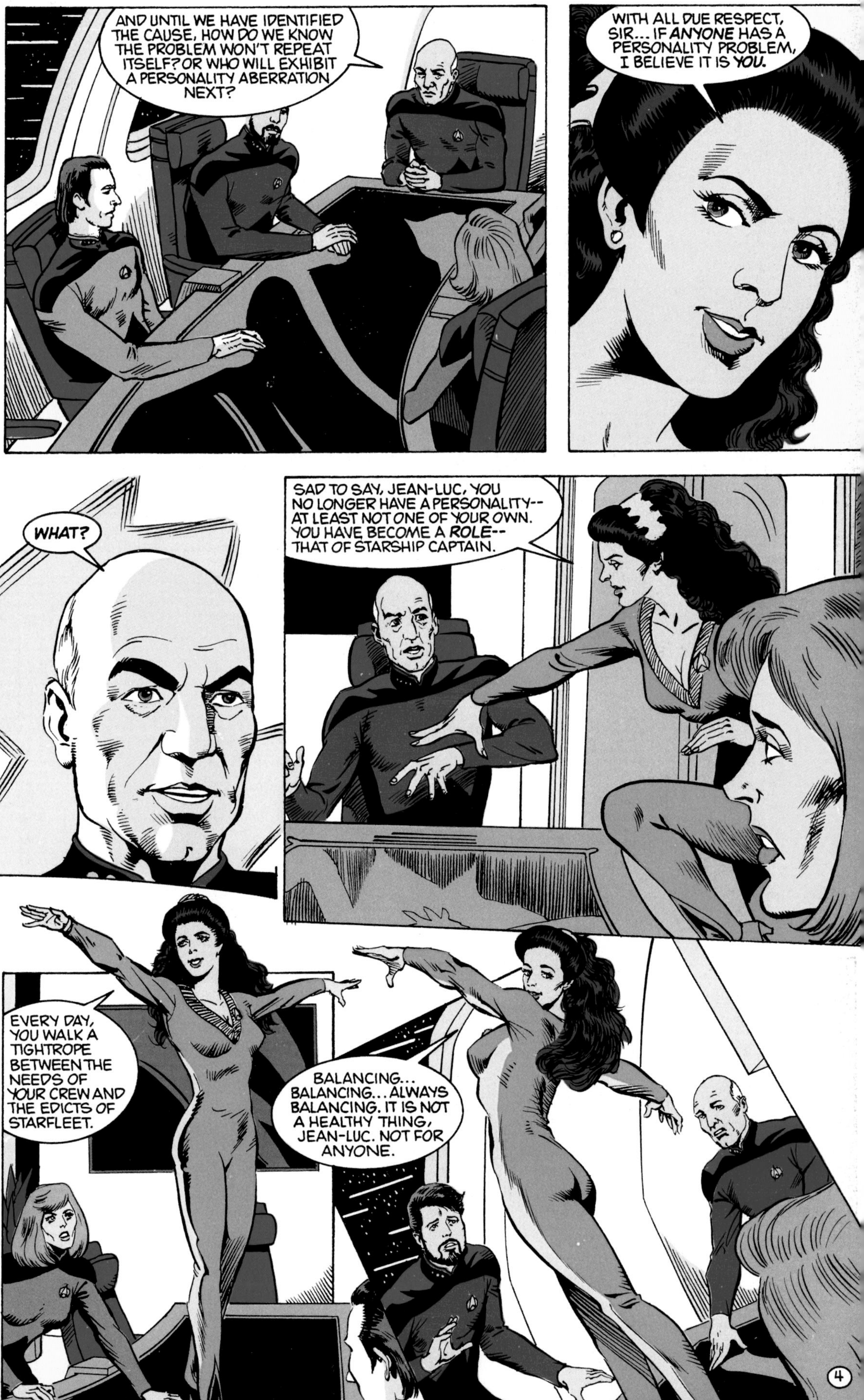
AND UNTIL WE HAVE IDENTIFIED THE CAUSE, HOW DO WE KNOW THE PROBLEM WON'T REPEAT ITSELF? OR WHO WILL EXHIBIT A PERSONALITY ABERRATION NEXT?
WITH ALL DUE RESPECT, SIR... IF ANYONE HAS A PERSONALITY PROBLEM, I BELIEVE IT IS YOU.
WHAT?
SAD TO SAY, JEAN-LUC, YOU NO LONGER HAVE A PERSONALITY-- AT LEAST NOT ONE OF YOUR OWN. YOU HAVE BECOME A ROLE-- THAT OF STARSHIP CAPTAIN.
EVERY DAY, YOU WALK A TIGHTROPE BETWEEN THE NEEDS OF YOUR CREW AND THE EDICTS OF STARFLEET.
BALANCING... BALANCING... ALWAYS BALANCING. IT IS NOT A HEALTHY THING, JEAN-LUC. NOT FOR ANYONE.

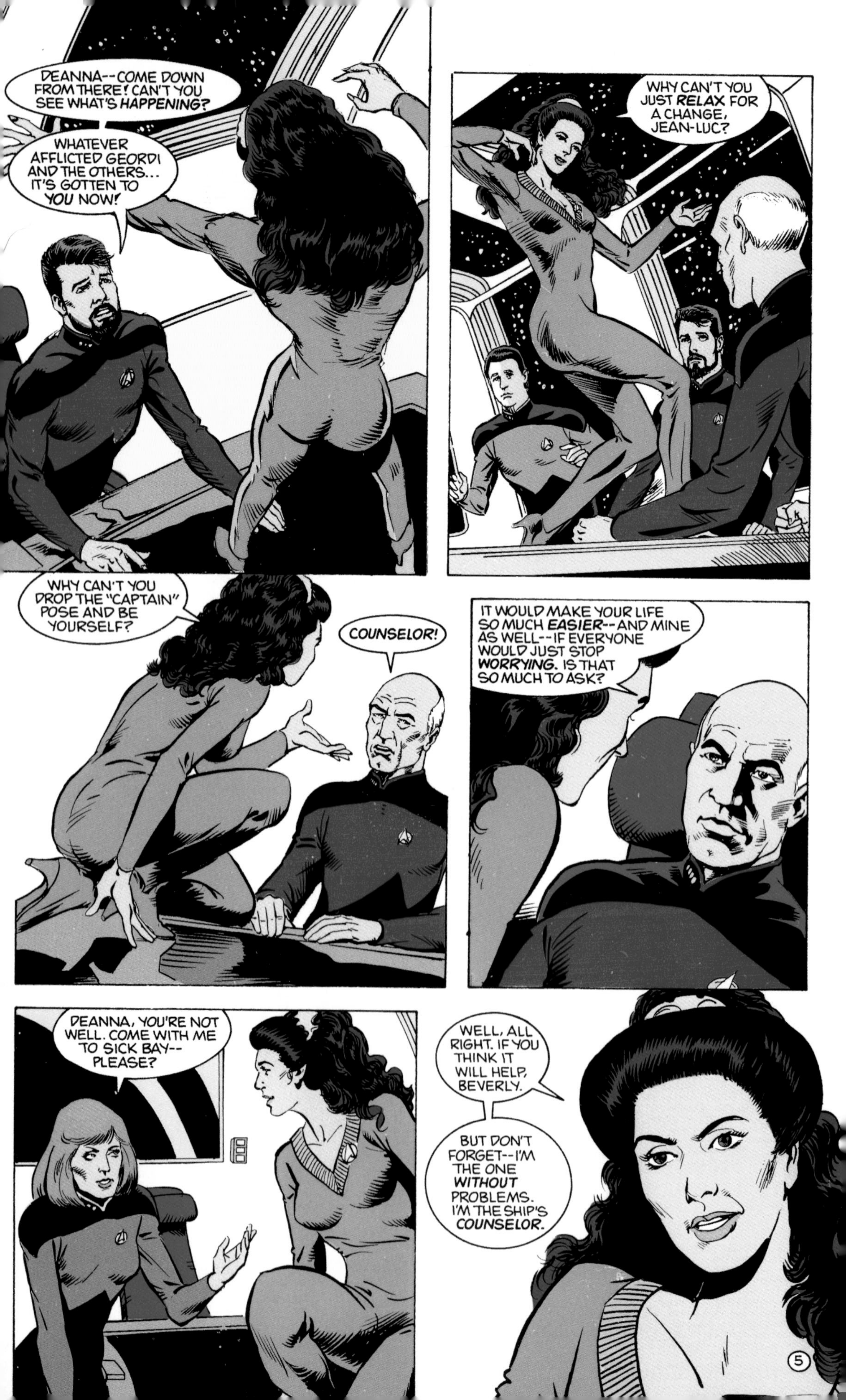

DEANNA--COME DOWN FROM THERE! CAN'T YOU SEE WHAT'S HAPPENING?
WHATEVER AFFLICTED GEORDI AND THE OTHERS... IT'S GOTTEN TO YOU NOW!
WHY CAN'T YOU JUST RELAX FOR A CHANGE, JEAN-LUC?
WHY CAN'T YOU DROP THE "CAPTAIN" POSE AND BE YOURSELF?
COUNSELOR!
IT WOULD MAKE YOUR LIFE SO MUCH EASIER--AND MINE AS WELL--IF EVERYONE WOULD JUST STOP WORRYING. IS THAT SO MUCH TO ASK?
DEANNA, YOU'RE NOT WELL. COME WITH ME TO SICK BAY--PLEASE?
WELL, ALL RIGHT. IF YOU THINK IT WILL HELP, BEVERLY.
BUT DON'T FORGET--I'M THE ONE WITHOUT PROBLEMS. I'M THE SHIP'S COUNSELOR.
5

WHATEVER THE PROBLEM MAY BE, NUMBER ONE, IT IS FAR FROM OVER. AND IF DEANNA CAN BE AFFLICTED, *NONE* OF US IS SAFE.

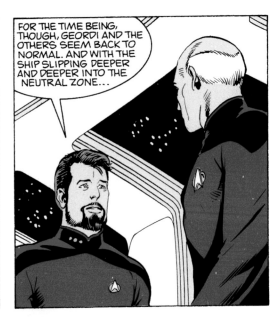

FOR THE TIME BEING, THOUGH, GEORDI AND THE OTHERS SEEM BACK TO NORMAL. AND WITH THE SHIP SLIPPING DEEPER AND DEEPER INTO THE NEUTRAL ZONE...

WE CAN USE ALL THE HELP WE CAN GET, EH? I AGREE, COMMANDER.

HAVE GEORDI, WORF AND WESLEY RELEASED FROM SICK BAY. BUT I WANT THEM WATCHED-- *CLOSELY.* THERE IS NO GUARANTEE THAT THEY WON'T BECOME IRRATIONAL AGAIN.

SIR, EVEN WITH THE ADDITIONS OF COMMANDER LAFORGE AND THE OTHERS--

I KNOW, DATA, I KNOW.

THE ODDS ARE THAT WE WILL STILL BE HELPLESS WHEN THE ROMULANS APPEAR. SOMEHOW, I WILL HAVE TO FIND A WAY TO BUY TIME FOR US.

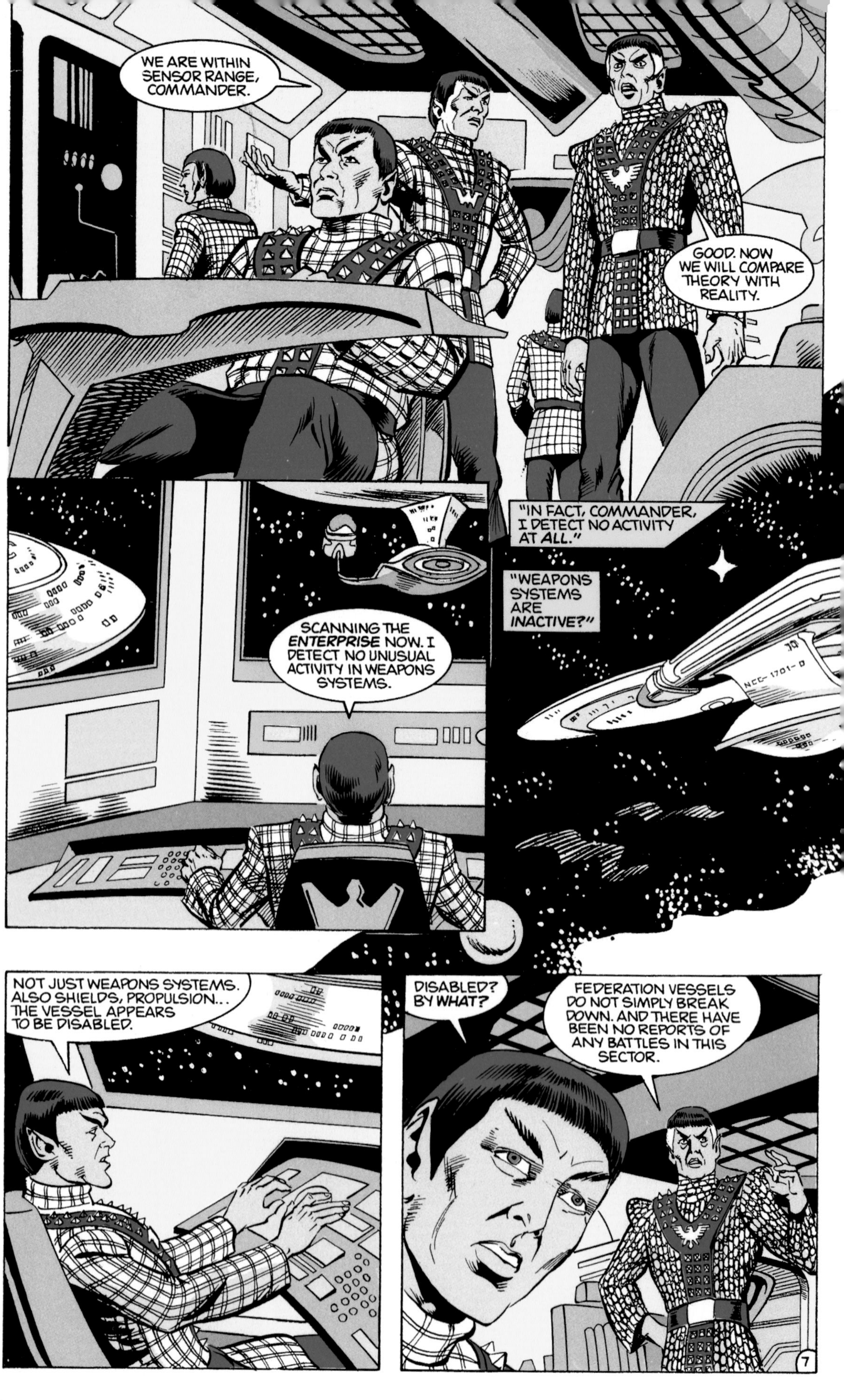
WE ARE WITHIN SENSOR RANGE, COMMANDER.
GOOD. NOW WE WILL COMPARE THEORY WITH REALITY.
SCANNING THE *ENTERPRISE* NOW. I DETECT NO UNUSUAL ACTIVITY IN WEAPONS SYSTEMS.
"IN FACT, COMMANDER, I DETECT NO ACTIVITY AT *ALL*."
"WEAPONS SYSTEMS ARE *INACTIVE*?"
NCC-1701-D
NOT JUST WEAPONS SYSTEMS. ALSO SHIELDS, PROPULSION... THE VESSEL APPEARS TO BE DISABLED.
DISABLED? BY *WHAT*?
FEDERATION VESSELS DO NOT SIMPLY BREAK DOWN. AND THERE HAVE BEEN NO REPORTS OF ANY BATTLES IN THIS SECTOR.

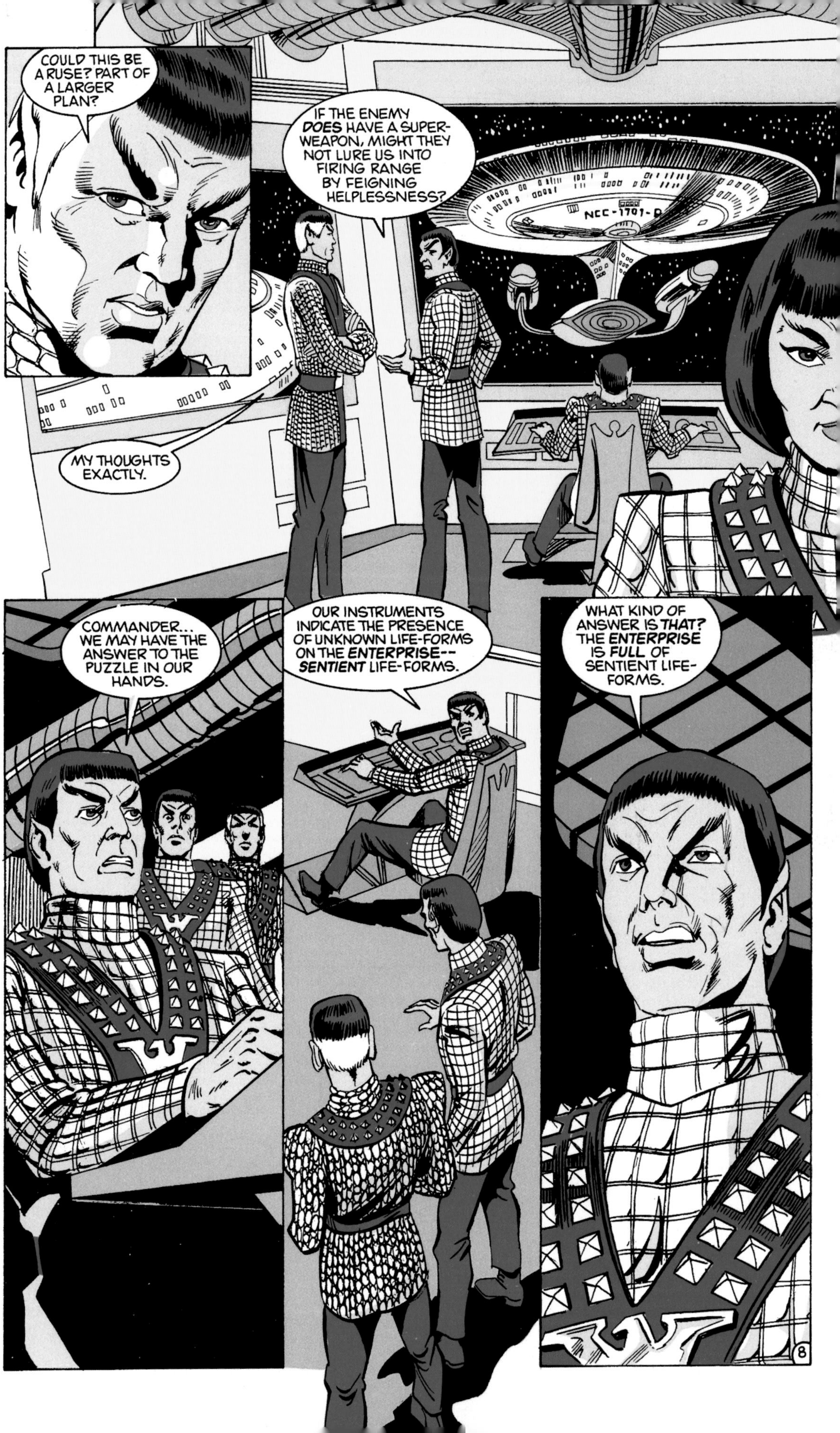
COULD THIS BE A RUSE? PART OF A LARGER PLAN?
IF THE ENEMY DOES HAVE A SUPER-WEAPON, MIGHT THEY NOT LURE US INTO FIRING RANGE BY FEIGNING HELPLESSNESS?
NCC-1701-D
MY THOUGHTS EXACTLY.
COMMANDER... WE MAY HAVE THE ANSWER TO THE PUZZLE IN OUR HANDS.
OUR INSTRUMENTS INDICATE THE PRESENCE OF UNKNOWN LIFE-FORMS ON THE ENTERPRISE-- SENTIENT LIFE-FORMS.
WHAT KIND OF ANSWER IS THAT? THE ENTERPRISE IS FULL OF SENTIENT LIFE-FORMS.
8

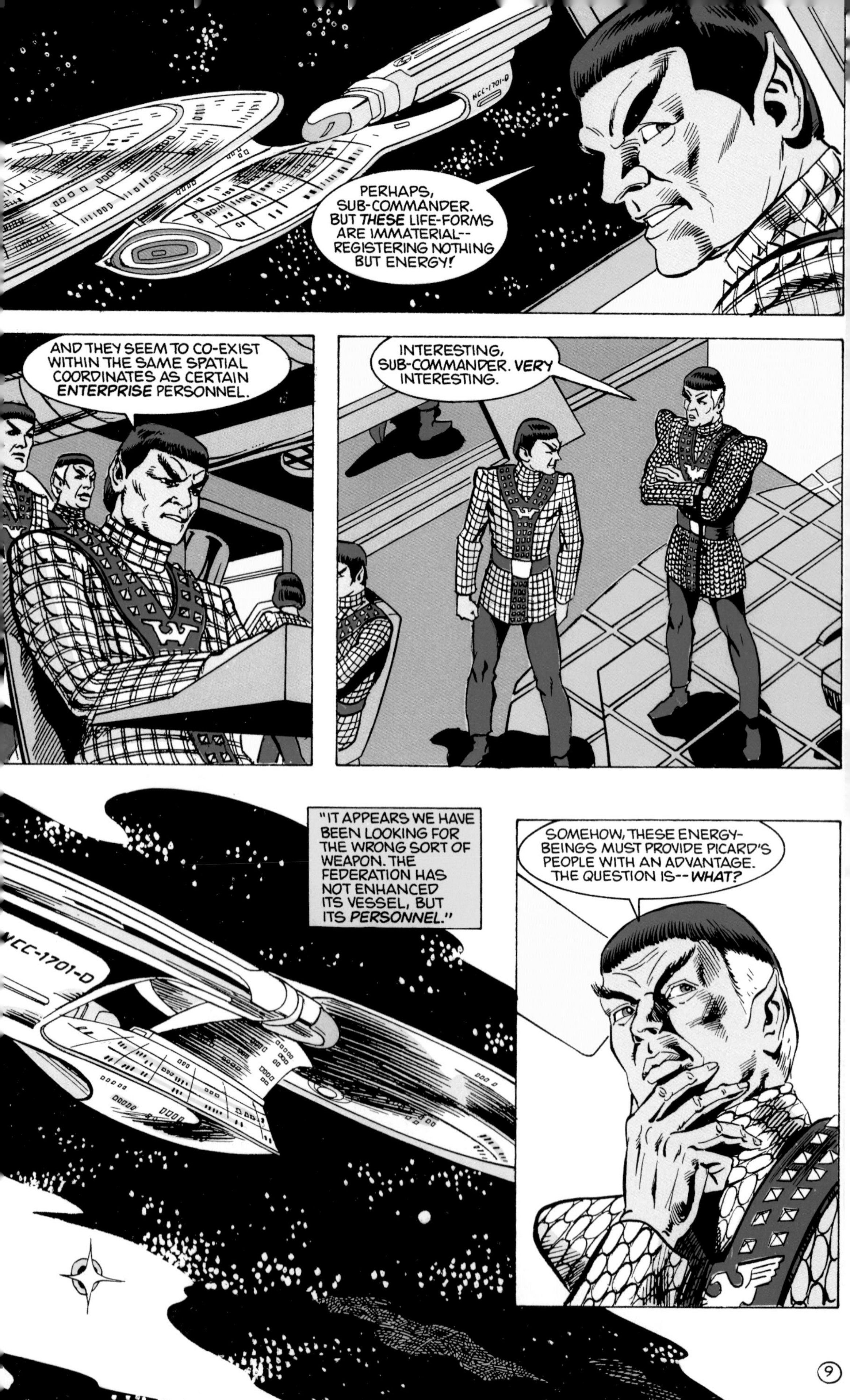
NCC-1701-D
PERHAPS, SUB-COMMANDER. BUT THESE LIFE-FORMS ARE IMMATERIAL-- REGISTERING NOTHING BUT ENERGY!
AND THEY SEEM TO CO-EXIST WITHIN THE SAME SPATIAL COORDINATES AS CERTAIN ENTERPRISE PERSONNEL.
INTERESTING, SUB-COMMANDER. VERY INTERESTING.
"IT APPEARS WE HAVE BEEN LOOKING FOR THE WRONG SORT OF WEAPON. THE FEDERATION HAS NOT ENHANCED ITS VESSEL, BUT ITS PERSONNEL."
SOMEHOW, THESE ENERGY-BEINGS MUST PROVIDE PICARD'S PEOPLE WITH AN ADVANTAGE. THE QUESTION IS-- WHAT?
NCC-1701-D

THAT'S A GOOD QUESTION, NUMBER ONE. BUT IF THERE *WERE* A WAY TO "HOTWIRE" THE FUSION REACTORS, I AM CERTAIN MISTER LAFORGE WOULD HAVE THOUGHT OF IT.

JUST A SUGGESTION, SIR. I HATE THE IDEA OF BEING SO... HELPLESS.

NO MORE THAN I, COMMANDER.

ON THE OTHER HAND, WE HAVE REASON TO HOPE. AS LONG AS OUR CHIEF ENGINEER SHOWS NO SIGNS OF A RELAPSE, THERE IS A CHANCE WE WILL ESCAPE WITH OUR SKINS.

IMAGINE SOMEONE LEAVING THIS PANEL OPEN. THAT'S NO WAY TO RUN A STARSHIP.

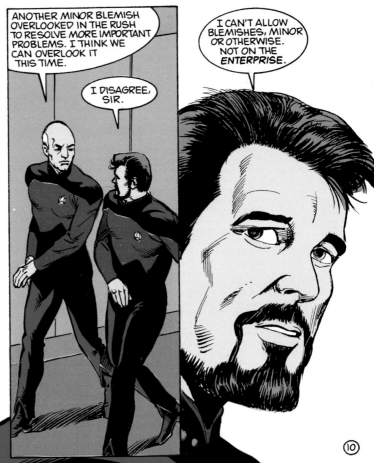

ANOTHER MINOR BLEMISH OVERLOOKED IN THE RUSH TO RESOLVE MORE IMPORTANT PROBLEMS. I THINK WE CAN OVERLOOK IT THIS TIME.

I DISAGREE, SIR.

I CAN'T ALLOW BLEMISHES, MINOR OR OTHERWISE. NOT ON THE *ENTERPRISE*.

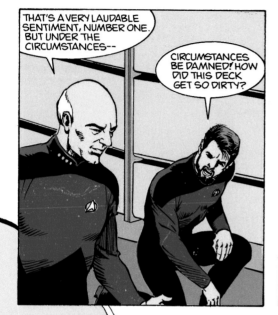

THAT'S A VERY LAUDABLE SENTIMENT, NUMBER ONE. BUT UNDER THE CIRCUMSTANCES--

CIRCUMSTANCES BE DAMNED! HOW DID THIS DECK GET SO DIRTY?

THIS WHOLE PLACE IS FILTHY! IT'S A DISGRACE!

LORD, WILL...

...NOT YOU TOO!

WHAT DO YOU CARE HOW DIRTY THIS SHIP GETS? AFTER ALL, SHE'S NOT YOUR SHIP-- NOT REALLY!

SHE'S MINE!

SECURITY-- DECK 26! ON THE DOUBLE!

CALL WHOMEVER YOU WANT-- IT WON'T MAKE A DIFFERENCE. I'M STILL THE FIRST OFFICER HERE. I'M STILL THE ONE WHO TAKES CARE OF HER!

11

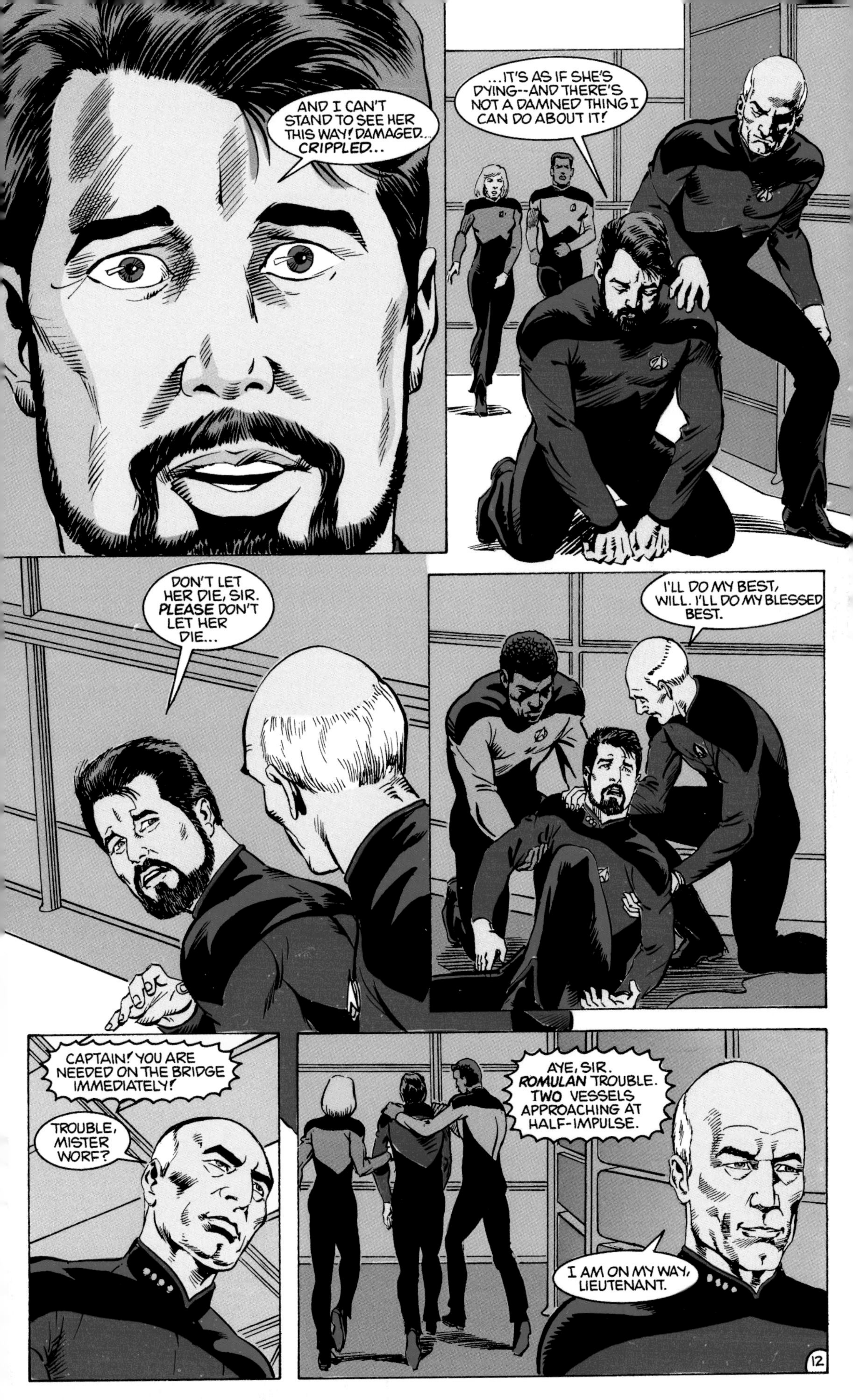
AND I CAN'T STAND TO SEE HER THIS WAY! DAMAGED... CRIPPLED...
...IT'S AS IF SHE'S DYING--AND THERE'S NOT A DAMNED THING I CAN DO ABOUT IT!
DON'T LET HER DIE, SIR. PLEASE DON'T LET HER DIE...
I'LL DO MY BEST, WILL. I'LL DO MY BLESSED BEST.
CAPTAIN! YOU ARE NEEDED ON THE BRIDGE IMMEDIATELY!
TROUBLE, MISTER WORF?
AYE, SIR. ROMULAN TROUBLE. TWO VESSELS APPROACHING AT HALF-IMPULSE.
I AM ON MY WAY, LIEUTENANT.
12

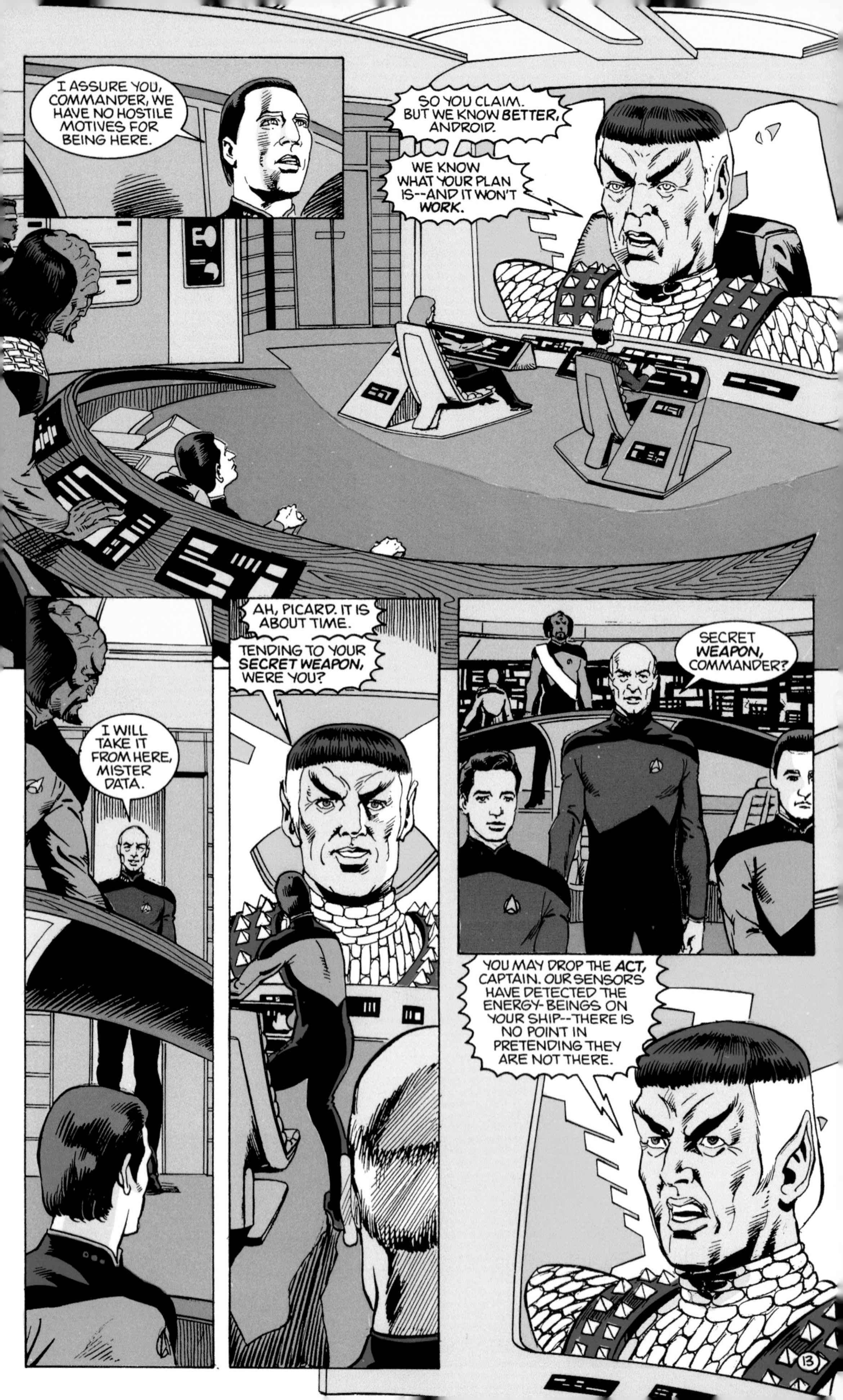

I ASSURE YOU, COMMANDER, WE HAVE NO HOSTILE MOTIVES FOR BEING HERE.
SO YOU CLAIM. BUT WE KNOW BETTER, ANDROID.
WE KNOW WHAT YOUR PLAN IS--AND IT WON'T WORK.
I WILL TAKE IT FROM HERE, MISTER DATA.
AH, PICARD. IT IS ABOUT TIME.
TENDING TO YOUR SECRET WEAPON, WERE YOU?
SECRET WEAPON, COMMANDER?
YOU MAY DROP THE ACT, CAPTAIN. OUR SENSORS HAVE DETECTED THE ENERGY-BEINGS ON YOUR SHIP--THERE IS NO POINT IN PRETENDING THEY ARE NOT THERE.
13

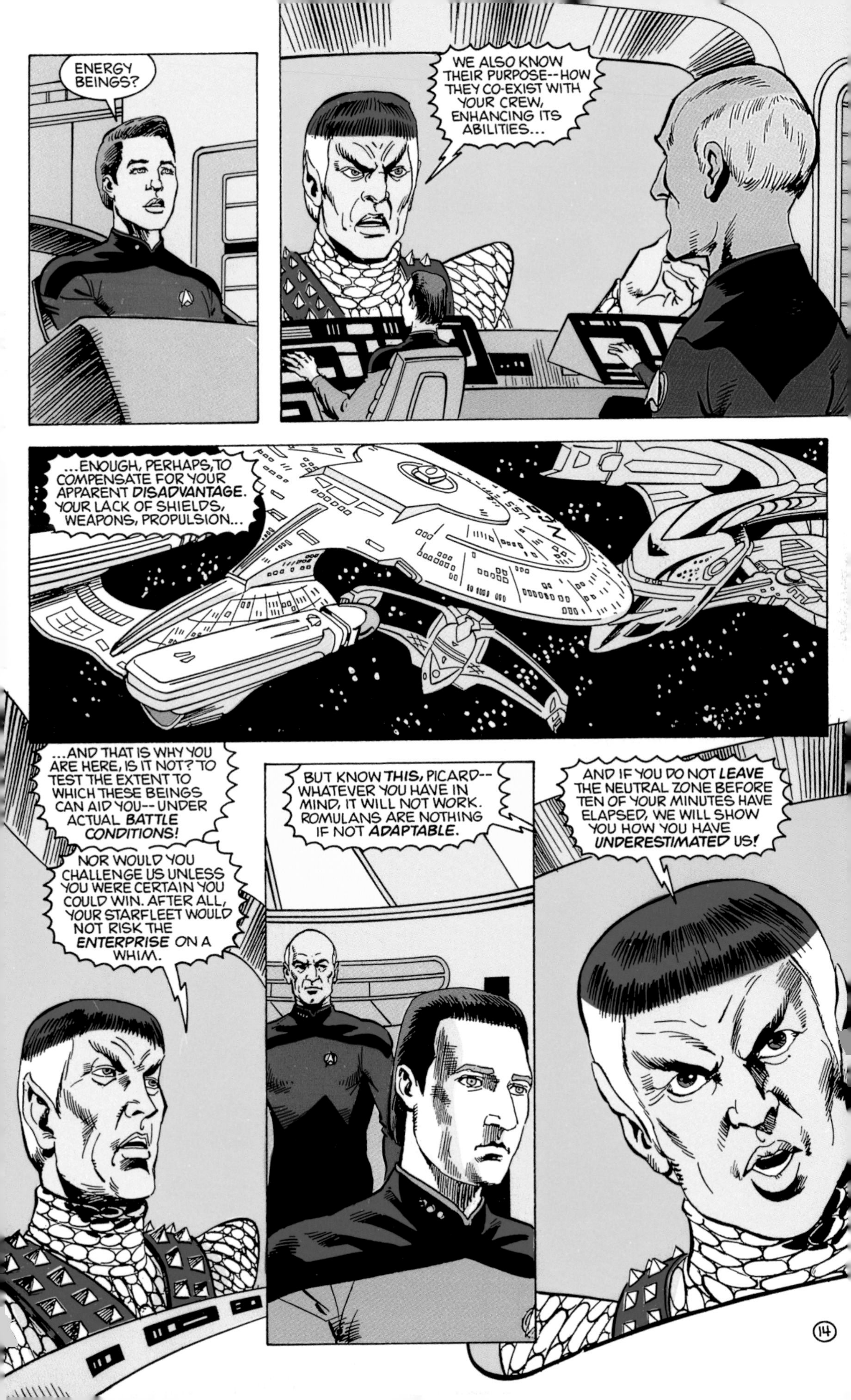
ENERGY BEINGS?
WE ALSO KNOW THEIR PURPOSE--HOW THEY CO-EXIST WITH YOUR CREW, ENHANCING ITS ABILITIES...
...ENOUGH, PERHAPS, TO COMPENSATE FOR YOUR APPARENT DISADVANTAGE. YOUR LACK OF SHIELDS, WEAPONS, PROPULSION...
...AND THAT IS WHY YOU ARE HERE, IS IT NOT? TO TEST THE EXTENT TO WHICH THESE BEINGS CAN AID YOU--UNDER ACTUAL BATTLE CONDITIONS!
NOR WOULD YOU CHALLENGE US UNLESS YOU WERE CERTAIN YOU COULD WIN. AFTER ALL, YOUR STARFLEET WOULD NOT RISK THE ENTERPRISE ON A WHIM.
BUT KNOW THIS, PICARD--WHATEVER YOU HAVE IN MIND, IT WILL NOT WORK. ROMULANS ARE NOTHING IF NOT ADAPTABLE.
AND IF YOU DO NOT LEAVE THE NEUTRAL ZONE BEFORE TEN OF YOUR MINUTES HAVE ELAPSED, WE WILL SHOW YOU HOW YOU HAVE UNDERESTIMATED US!
14

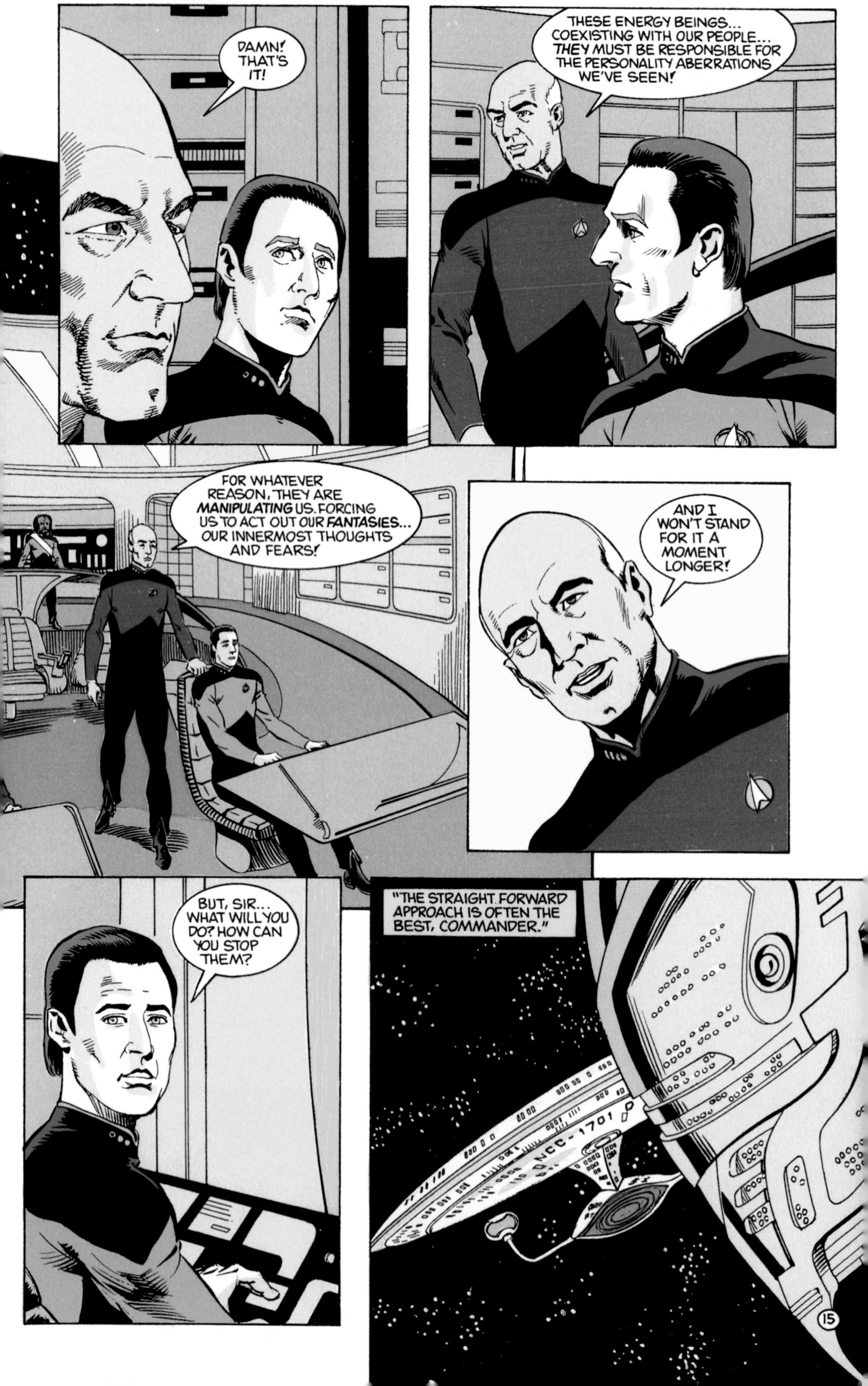
DAMN! THAT'S IT!
THESE ENERGY BEINGS... COEXISTING WITH OUR PEOPLE... THEY MUST BE RESPONSIBLE FOR THE PERSONALITY ABERRATIONS WE'VE SEEN!
FOR WHATEVER REASON, THEY ARE MANIPULATING US. FORCING US TO ACT OUT OUR FANTASIES... OUR INNERMOST THOUGHTS AND FEARS!
AND I WON'T STAND FOR IT A MOMENT LONGER!
BUT, SIR... WHAT WILL YOU DO? HOW CAN YOU STOP THEM?
"THE STRAIGHT.FORWARD APPROACH IS OFTEN THE BEST, COMMANDER."
NCC-1701 D
15

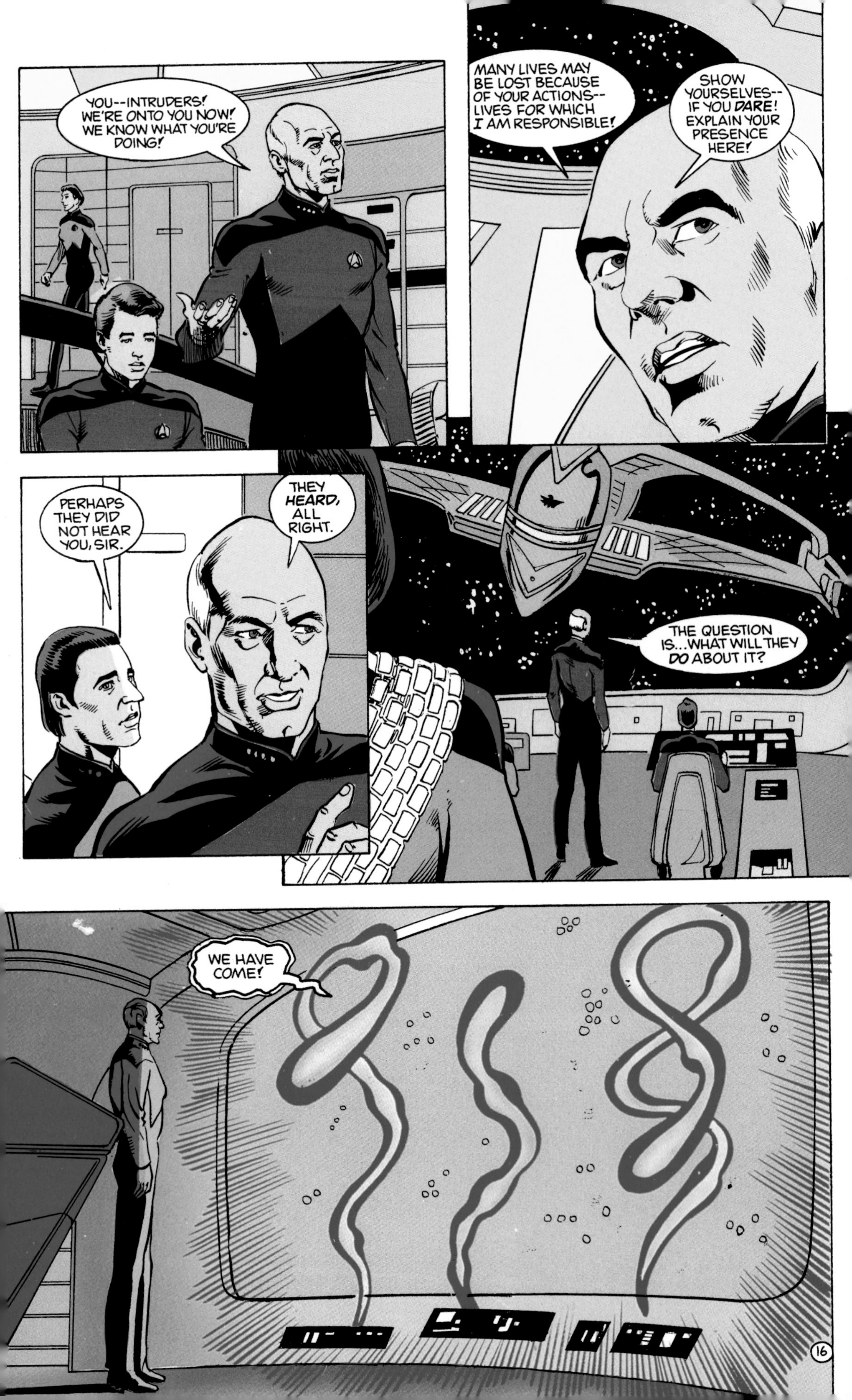
YOU--INTRUDERS! WE'RE ONTO YOU NOW! WE KNOW WHAT YOU'RE DOING!
MANY LIVES MAY BE LOST BECAUSE OF YOUR ACTIONS-- LIVES FOR WHICH I AM RESPONSIBLE!
SHOW YOURSELVES-- IF YOU DARE! EXPLAIN YOUR PRESENCE HERE!
PERHAPS THEY DID NOT HEAR YOU, SIR.
THEY HEARD, ALL RIGHT.
THE QUESTION IS...WHAT WILL THEY DO ABOUT IT?
WE HAVE COME!
16

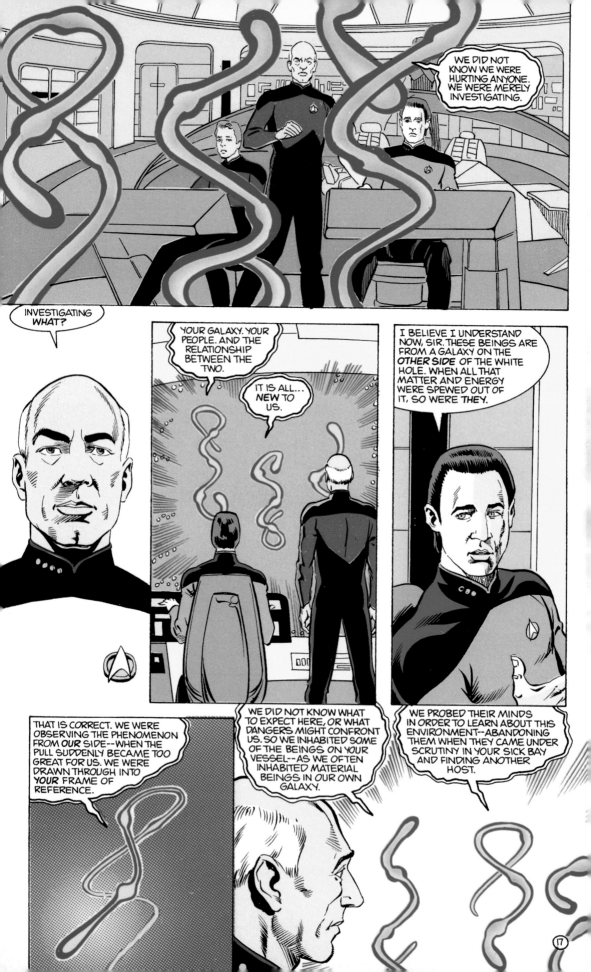

WE DID NOT KNOW WE WERE HURTING ANYONE. WE WERE MERELY INVESTIGATING.

INVESTIGATING WHAT?

YOUR GALAXY. YOUR PEOPLE. AND THE RELATIONSHIP BETWEEN THE TWO.

IT IS ALL... NEW TO US.

I BELIEVE I UNDERSTAND NOW, SIR. THESE BEINGS ARE FROM A GALAXY ON THE OTHER SIDE OF THE WHITE HOLE. WHEN ALL THAT MATTER AND ENERGY WERE SPEWED OUT OF IT, SO WERE THEY.

THAT IS CORRECT. WE WERE OBSERVING THE PHENOMENON FROM OUR SIDE--WHEN THE PULL SUDDENLY BECAME TOO GREAT FOR US. WE WERE DRAWN THROUGH INTO YOUR FRAME OF REFERENCE.

WE DID NOT KNOW WHAT TO EXPECT HERE, OR WHAT DANGERS MIGHT CONFRONT US. SO WE INHABITED SOME OF THE BEINGS ON YOUR VESSEL--AS WE OFTEN INHABITED MATERIAL BEINGS IN OUR OWN GALAXY.

WE PROBED THEIR MINDS IN ORDER TO LEARN ABOUT THIS ENVIRONMENT--ABANDONING THEM WHEN THEY CAME UNDER SCRUTINY IN YOUR SICK BAY AND FINDING ANOTHER HOST.

17

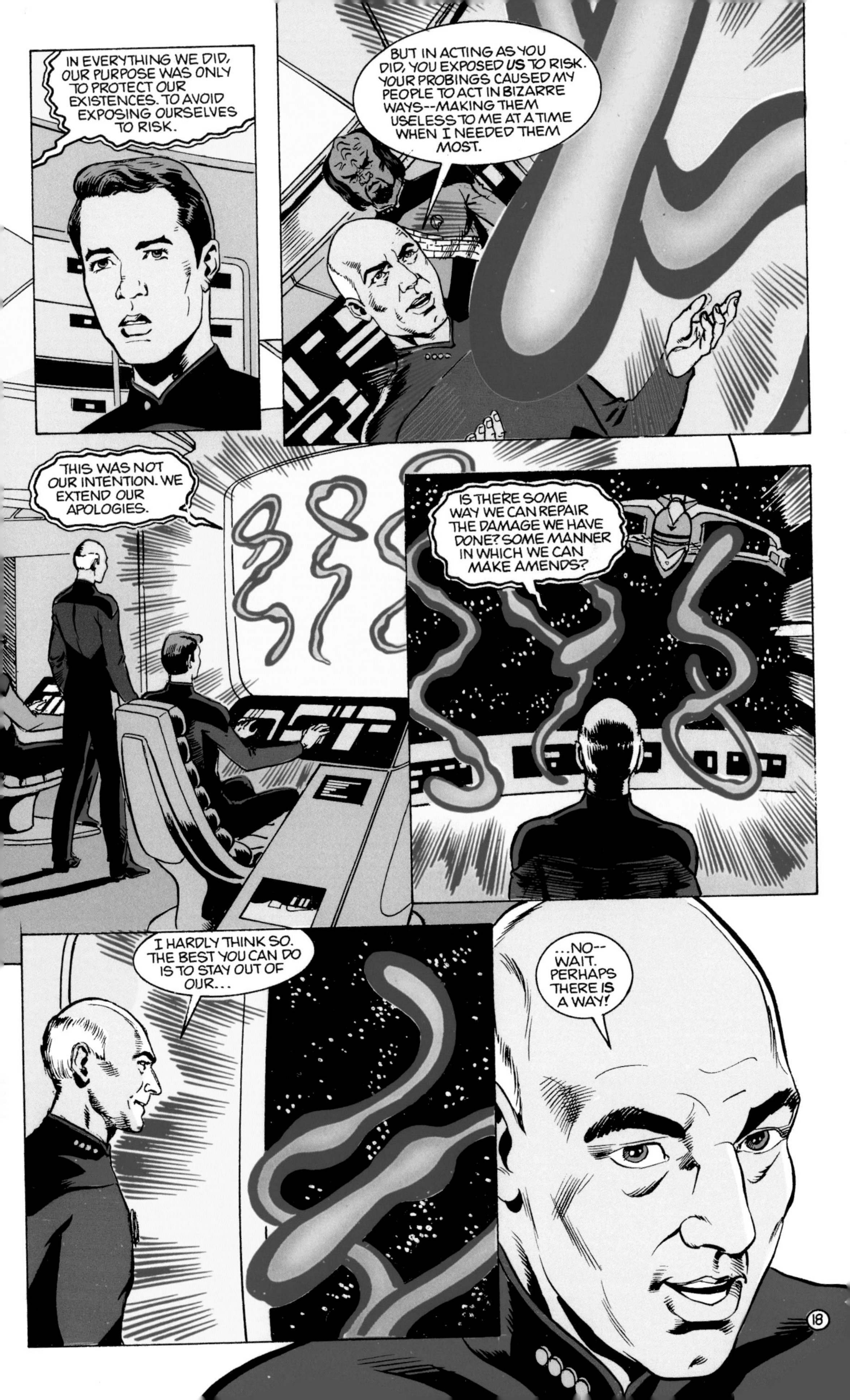

IN EVERYTHING WE DID, OUR PURPOSE WAS ONLY TO PROTECT OUR EXISTENCES. TO AVOID EXPOSING OURSELVES TO RISK.
BUT IN ACTING AS YOU DID, YOU EXPOSED US TO RISK. YOUR PROBINGS CAUSED MY PEOPLE TO ACT IN BIZARRE WAYS--MAKING THEM USELESS TO ME AT A TIME WHEN I NEEDED THEM MOST.
THIS WAS NOT OUR INTENTION. WE EXTEND OUR APOLOGIES.
IS THERE SOME WAY WE CAN REPAIR THE DAMAGE WE HAVE DONE? SOME MANNER IN WHICH WE CAN MAKE AMENDS?
I HARDLY THINK SO. THE BEST YOU CAN DO IS TO STAY OUT OF OUR...
...NO-- WAIT. PERHAPS THERE IS A WAY!

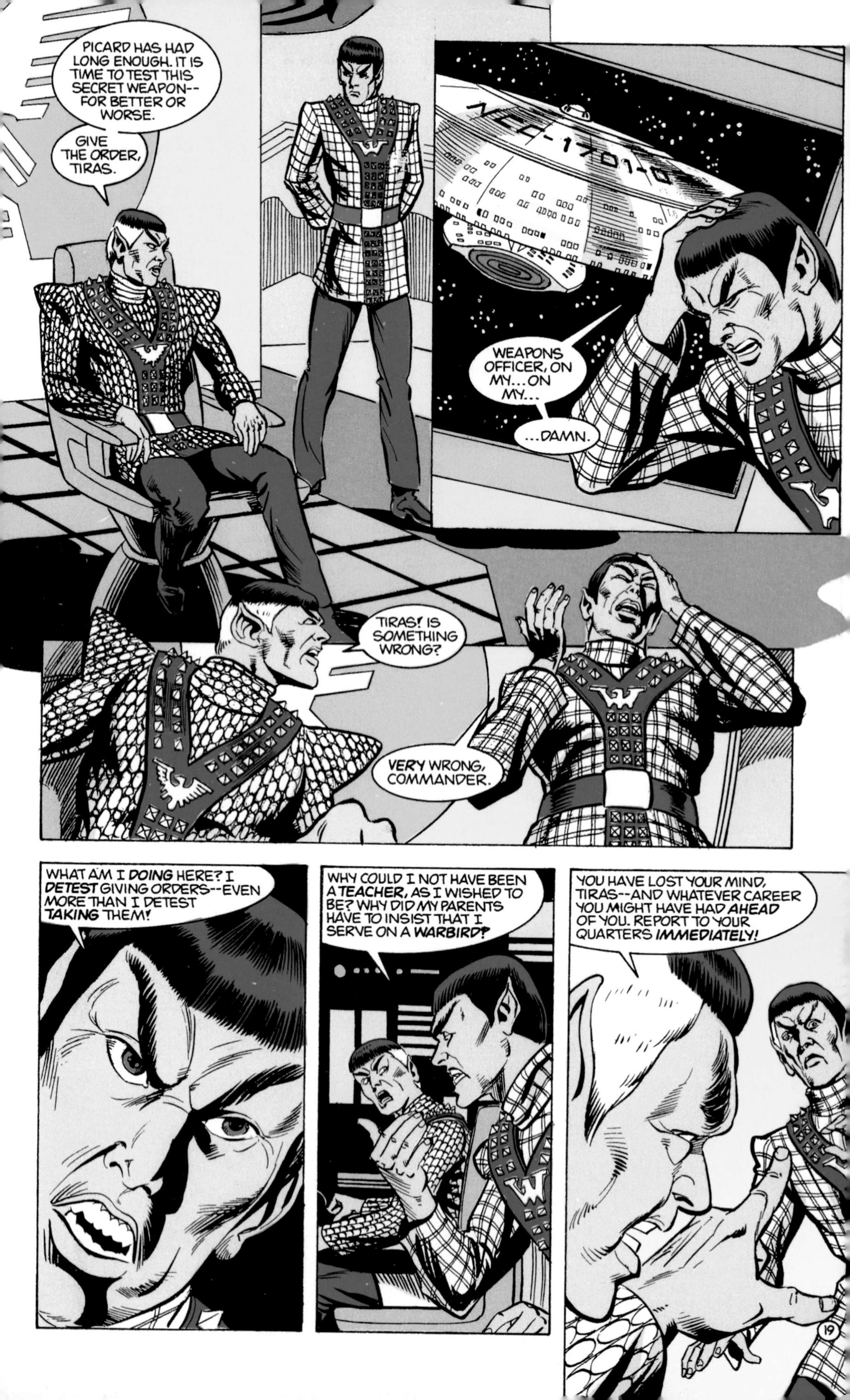
PICARD HAS HAD LONG ENOUGH. IT IS TIME TO TEST THIS SECRET WEAPON-- FOR BETTER OR WORSE.
GIVE THE ORDER, TIRAS.
NCC-1701-D
WEAPONS OFFICER, ON MY... ON MY...
...DAMN.
TIRAS! IS SOMETHING WRONG?
VERY WRONG, COMMANDER.
WHAT AM I DOING HERE? I DETEST GIVING ORDERS--EVEN MORE THAN I DETEST TAKING THEM!
WHY COULD I NOT HAVE BEEN A TEACHER, AS I WISHED TO BE? WHY DID MY PARENTS HAVE TO INSIST THAT I SERVE ON A WARBIRD?
YOU HAVE LOST YOUR MIND, TIRAS--AND WHATEVER CAREER YOU MIGHT HAVE HAD AHEAD OF YOU. REPORT TO YOUR QUARTERS IMMEDIATELY!
19

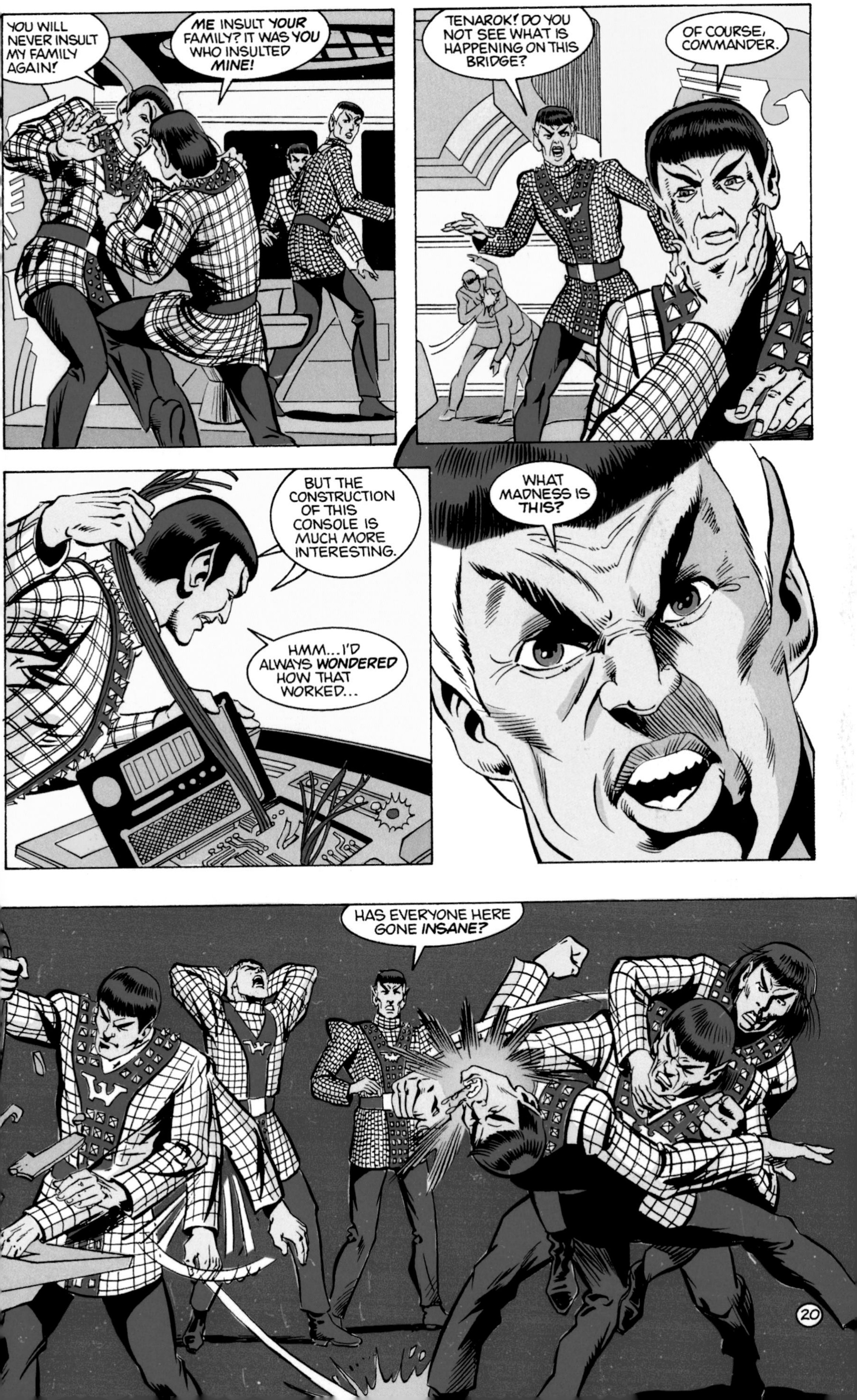

YOU WILL NEVER INSULT MY FAMILY AGAIN!
ME INSULT YOUR FAMILY? IT WAS YOU WHO INSULTED MINE!
TENAROK! DO YOU NOT SEE WHAT IS HAPPENING ON THIS BRIDGE?
OF COURSE, COMMANDER.
BUT THE CONSTRUCTION OF THIS CONSOLE IS MUCH MORE INTERESTING.
HMM...I'D ALWAYS WONDERED HOW THAT WORKED...
WHAT MADNESS IS THIS?
HAS EVERYONE HERE GONE INSANE?

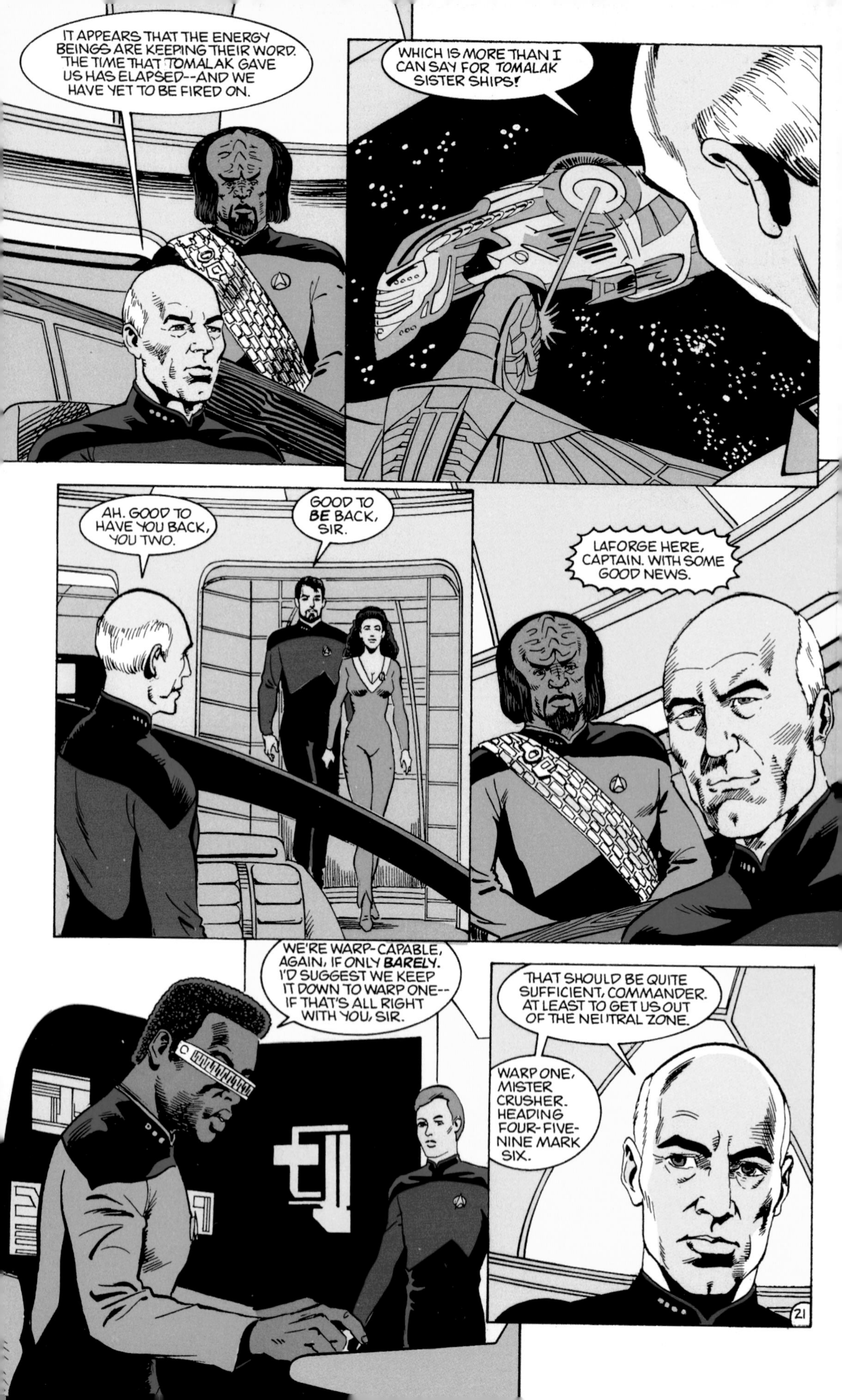
IT APPEARS THAT THE ENERGY BEINGS ARE KEEPING THEIR WORD. THE TIME THAT TOMALAK GAVE US HAS ELAPSED--AND WE HAVE YET TO BE FIRED ON.
WHICH IS MORE THAN I CAN SAY FOR TOMALAK SISTER SHIPS!
AH. GOOD TO HAVE YOU BACK, YOU TWO.
GOOD TO BE BACK, SIR.
LAFORGE HERE, CAPTAIN. WITH SOME GOOD NEWS.
WE'RE WARP-CAPABLE, AGAIN, IF ONLY BARELY. I'D SUGGEST WE KEEP IT DOWN TO WARP ONE--IF THAT'S ALL RIGHT WITH YOU, SIR.
THAT SHOULD BE QUITE SUFFICIENT, COMMANDER. AT LEAST TO GET US OUT OF THE NEUTRAL ZONE.
WARP ONE, MISTER CRUSHER. HEADING FOUR-FIVE-NINE MARK SIX.
21

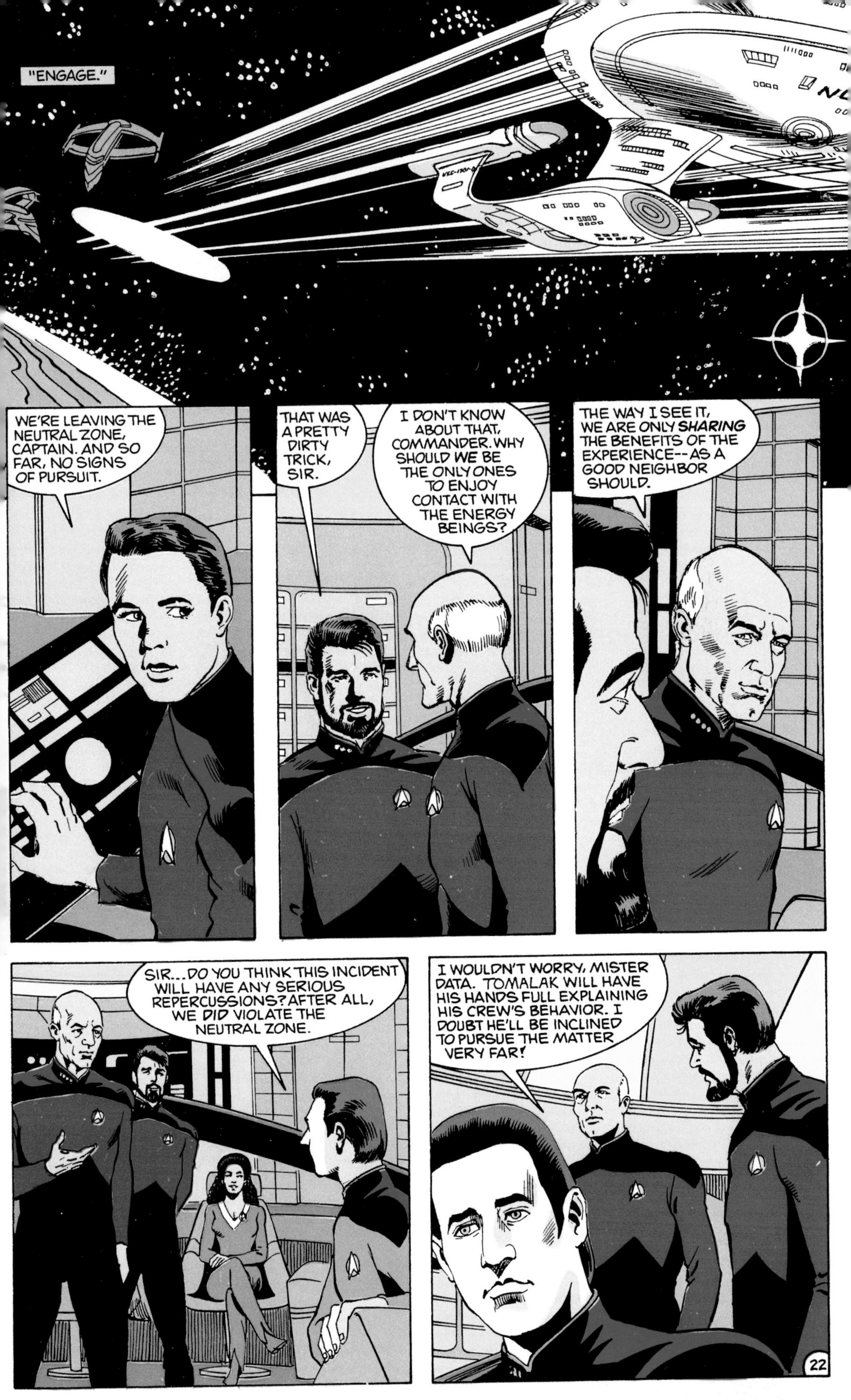
"ENGAGE."
WE'RE LEAVING THE NEUTRAL ZONE, CAPTAIN. AND SO FAR, NO SIGNS OF PURSUIT.
THAT WAS A PRETTY DIRTY TRICK, SIR.
I DON'T KNOW ABOUT THAT, COMMANDER. WHY SHOULD WE BE THE ONLY ONES TO ENJOY CONTACT WITH THE ENERGY BEINGS?
THE WAY I SEE IT, WE ARE ONLY SHARING THE BENEFITS OF THE EXPERIENCE-- AS A GOOD NEIGHBOR SHOULD.
SIR... DO YOU THINK THIS INCIDENT WILL HAVE ANY SERIOUS REPERCUSSIONS? AFTER ALL, WE DID VIOLATE THE NEUTRAL ZONE.
I WOULDN'T WORRY, MISTER DATA. TOMALAK WILL HAVE HIS HANDS FULL EXPLAINING HIS CREW'S BEHAVIOR. I DOUBT HE'LL BE INCLINED TO PURSUE THE MATTER VERY FAR!
22

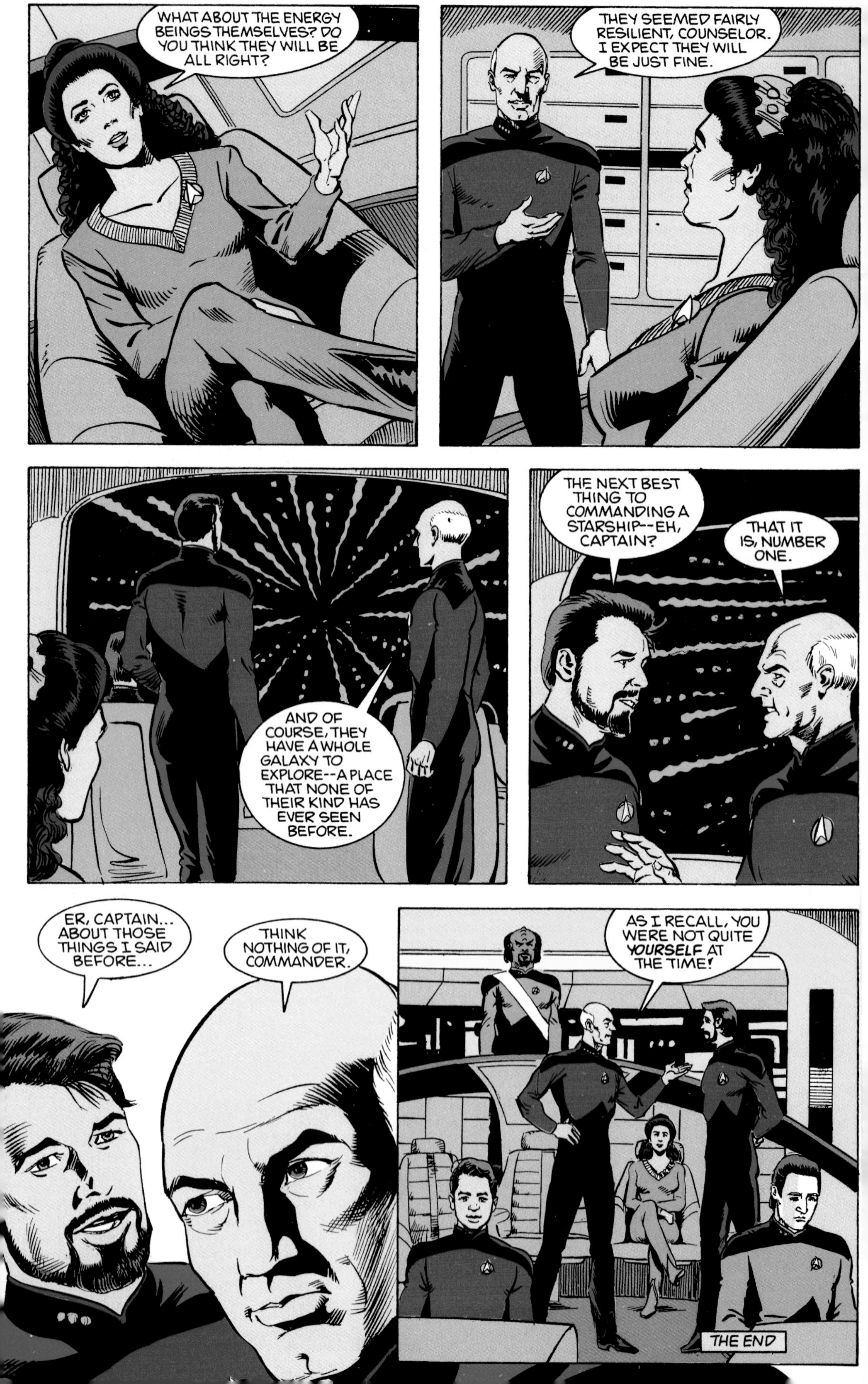
WHAT ABOUT THE ENERGY BEINGS THEMSELVES? DO YOU THINK THEY WILL BE ALL RIGHT?
THEY SEEMED FAIRLY RESILIENT, COUNSELOR. I EXPECT THEY WILL BE JUST FINE.
AND OF COURSE, THEY HAVE A WHOLE GALAXY TO EXPLORE--A PLACE THAT NONE OF THEIR KIND HAS EVER SEEN BEFORE.
THE NEXT BEST THING TO COMMANDING A STARSHIP--EH, CAPTAIN?
THAT IT IS, NUMBER ONE.
ER, CAPTAIN... ABOUT THOSE THINGS I SAID BEFORE...
THINK NOTHING OF IT, COMMANDER.
AS I RECALL, YOU WERE NOT QUITE *YOURSELF* AT THE TIME!
THE END

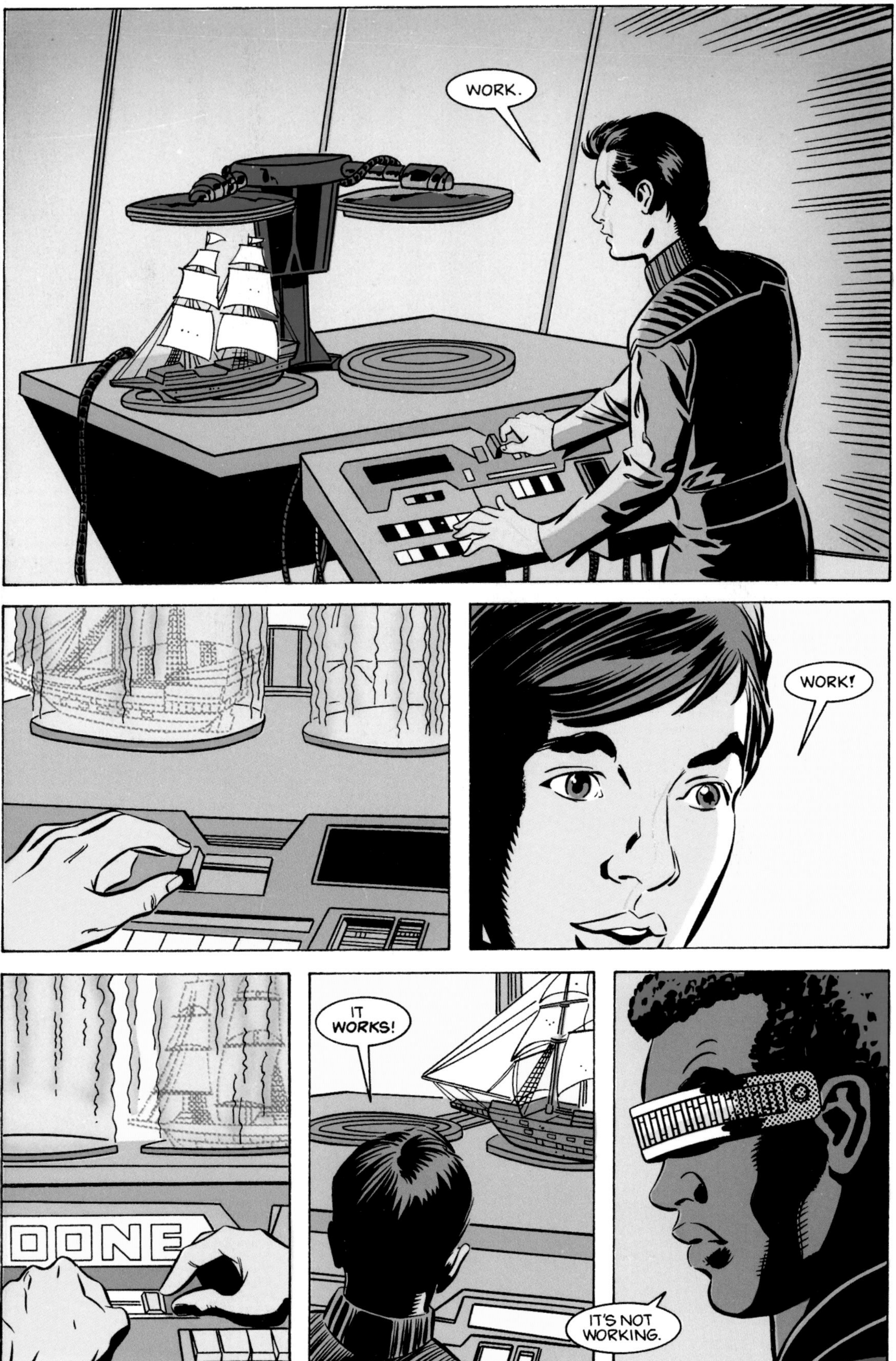
WORK.
WORK!
DONE
IT WORKS!
IT'S NOT WORKING.

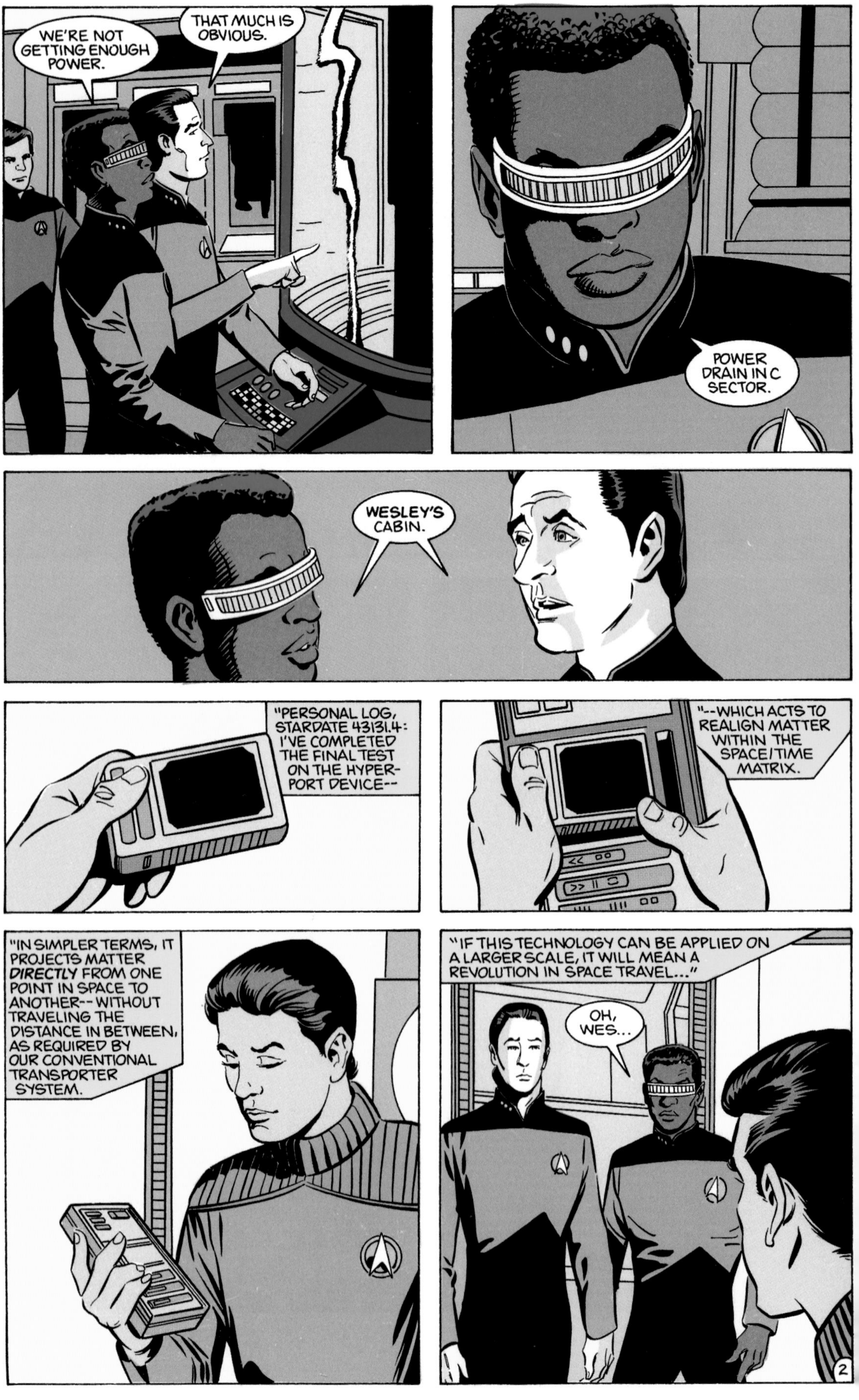
WE'RE NOT GETTING ENOUGH POWER.
THAT MUCH IS OBVIOUS.
POWER DRAIN IN C SECTOR.
WESLEY'S CABIN.
"PERSONAL LOG, STARDATE 43131.4: I'VE COMPLETED THE FINAL TEST ON THE HYPER-PORT DEVICE--
"--WHICH ACTS TO REALIGN MATTER WITHIN THE SPACE/TIME MATRIX.
"IN SIMPLER TERMS, IT PROJECTS MATTER *DIRECTLY* FROM ONE POINT IN SPACE TO ANOTHER-- WITHOUT TRAVELING THE DISTANCE IN BETWEEN, AS REQUIRED BY OUR CONVENTIONAL TRANSPORTER SYSTEM.
"IF THIS TECHNOLOGY CAN BE APPLIED ON A LARGER SCALE, IT WILL MEAN A REVOLUTION IN SPACE TRAVEL..."
OH, WES...

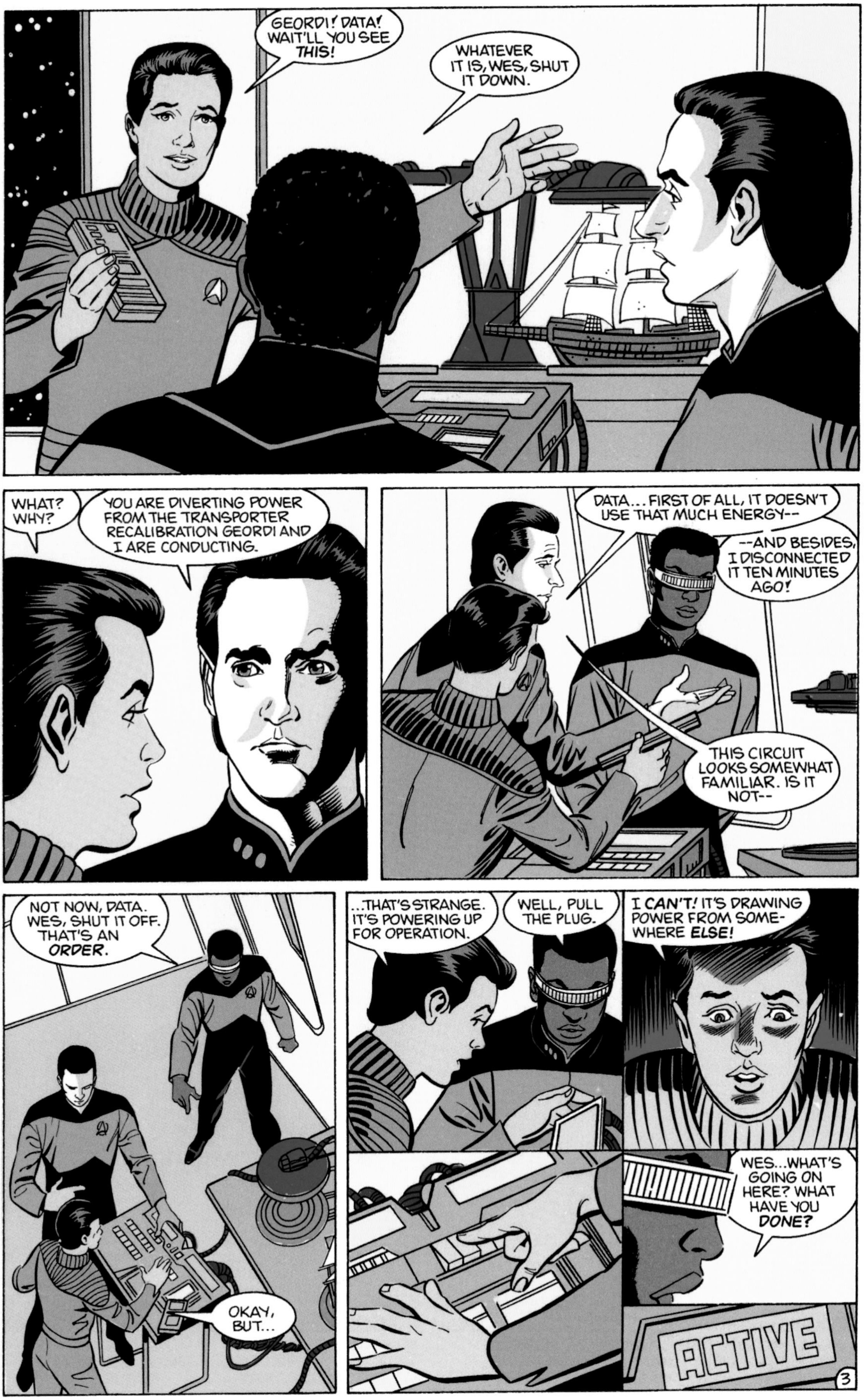

GEORDI! DATA! WAIT'LL YOU SEE THIS!
WHATEVER IT IS, WES, SHUT IT DOWN.
WHAT? WHY?
YOU ARE DIVERTING POWER FROM THE TRANSPORTER RECALIBRATION GEORDI AND I ARE CONDUCTING.
DATA... FIRST OF ALL, IT DOESN'T USE THAT MUCH ENERGY--
--AND BESIDES, I DISCONNECTED IT TEN MINUTES AGO!
THIS CIRCUIT LOOKS SOMEWHAT FAMILIAR. IS IT NOT--
NOT NOW, DATA. WES, SHUT IT OFF. THAT'S AN ORDER.
OKAY, BUT...
...THAT'S STRANGE. IT'S POWERING UP FOR OPERATION.
WELL, PULL THE PLUG.
I CAN'T! IT'S DRAWING POWER FROM SOME-WHERE ELSE!
WES... WHAT'S GOING ON HERE? WHAT HAVE YOU DONE?
ACTIVE
3

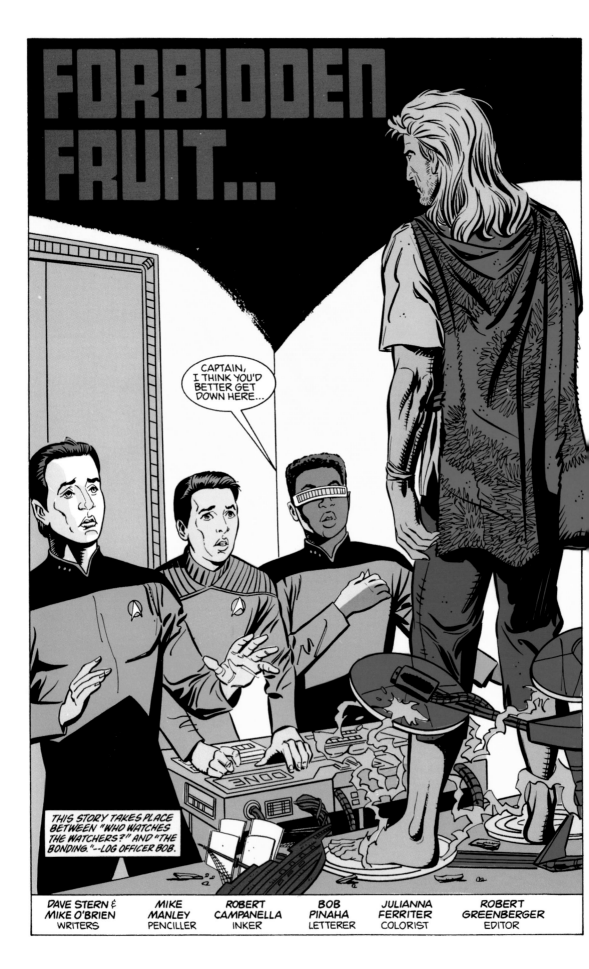

FORBIDDEN FRUIT...

CAPTAIN, I THINK YOU'D BETTER GET DOWN HERE...

THIS STORY TAKES PLACE BETWEEN "WHO WATCHES THE WATCHERS?" AND "THE BONDING."--LOG OFFICER BOB.

DAVE STERN & MIKE O'BRIEN	MIKE MANLEY	ROBERT CAMPANELLA	BOB PINAHA	JULIANNA FERRITER	ROBERT GREENBERGER
WRITERS	PENCILLER	INKER	LETTERER	COLORIST	EDITOR

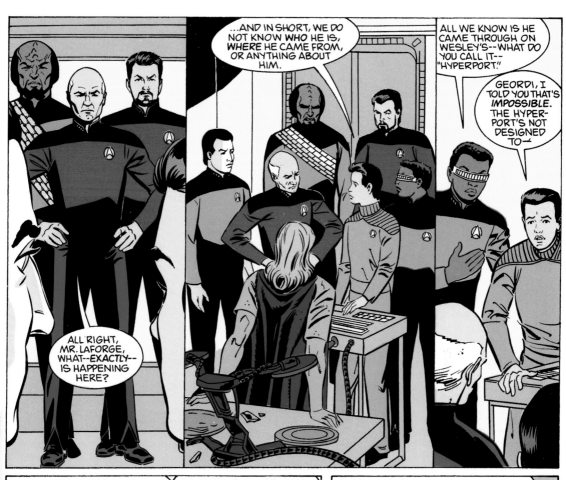

...AND IN SHORT, WE DO NOT KNOW *WHO* HE IS, *WHERE* HE CAME FROM, OR ANYTHING ABOUT HIM.

ALL WE KNOW IS HE CAME THROUGH ON WESLEY'S--WHAT DO YOU CALL IT-- "HYPERPORT."

GEORDI, I TOLD YOU THAT'S *IMPOSSIBLE.* THE HYPER-PORT'S NOT DESIGNED TO--

ALL RIGHT, MR. LAFORGE, WHAT--EXACTLY--IS HAPPENING HERE?

THAT WILL BE QUITE ENOUGH FOR THE MOMENT, MR. CRUSHER. DO YOU THINK OUR VISITOR KNOWS WHERE HE IS, OR HOW HE GOT HERE?

DOUBTFUL, SIR. HE SEEMS IGNORANT OF EVEN THE SIMPLEST TECHNOLOGY. THE VERY CONCEPT OF SPACE TRAVEL IS PROBABLY INCOMPREHENSIBLE TO HIM.

EVERYONE--CHOOSE YOUR WORDS CAREFULLY IN THE PRESENCE OF OUR... GUEST. THE PRIME DIRECTIVE IS IN FULL EFFECT.

I AM JEAN-LUC PICARD.

I AM PIERCE.

5

YOU ARE OF THE STARFLEET.

WHY--YES. YES, WE ARE OF STARFLEET.

ONE WOULD HAVE TO BE TRULY--PRIMITIVE--NOT TO KNOW OF STARFLEET AND ITS GREAT DEEDS. BUT TELL ME--WHERE AM I?

YOU'RE ABOARD THE STARSHIP ENTERPRISE. WE HAD AN ACCIDENT WITH SOME OF OUR EQUIPMENT--

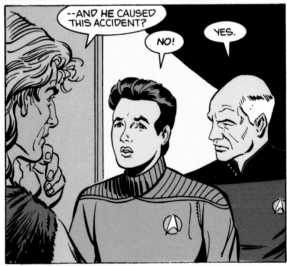

--AND HE CAUSED THIS ACCIDENT?

NO!

YES.

WHAT IS YOUR NAME?

WESLEY. WESLEY CRUSHER.

YOU SEEM...VERY YOUNG TO HAVE CAUSED SO MUCH TROUBLE.

6

LIEUTENANT WORF, PLEASE ESCORT OUR GUEST TO SICK BAY FOR AN EXAMINATION. AND FIND SOME TEMPORARY QUARTERS FOR HIM.

AYE, SIR.

AND I'D LIKE A WORD WITH YOU *ALONE*, MR. CRUSHER.

MR. DATA SAID YOUR INVENTION USES ELEMENTS OF ICONIAN TECHNOLOGY.

NOT EXACTLY, SIR. I MEAN, I JUST KIND OF BORROWED A FEW IDEAS...

ICONIAN SCIENCE IS PERHAPS THE MOST ELEGANT-- AND THE MOST *DANGEROUS*-- WE HAVE EVER ENCOUNTERED.

OUR ENGINEERS HAVE ESTABLISHED ELABORATE PRECAUTIONS CONCERNING ITS USE. WHY DIDN'T YOU FOLLOW THEM?

WELL SIR, I JUST THOUGHT--I MEAN, I DIDN'T THINK IT WOULD BE THAT BIG OF A DEAL, SIR.

NO BIG DEAL. I SEE.

YOU INVENT A DEVICE USING TECHNOLOGY WHOSE RAMIFICATIONS WE DO NOT UNDERSTAND *AT ALL*-- USE THAT DEVICE TO BRING AN ALIEN FROM GOD KNOWS WHERE ABOARD MY SHIP--

SIR, THE HYPERPORT *COULDN'T* HAVE--

--*DON'T INTERRUPT ME!*

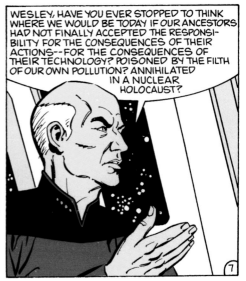

WESLEY, HAVE YOU EVER STOPPED TO THINK WHERE WE WOULD BE TODAY IF OUR ANCESTORS HAD NOT FINALLY ACCEPTED THE RESPONSIBILITY FOR THE CONSEQUENCES OF THEIR ACTIONS--FOR THE CONSEQUENCES OF THEIR TECHNOLOGY? POISONED BY THE FILTH OF OUR OWN POLLUTION? ANNIHILATED IN A NUCLEAR HOLOCAUST?

7

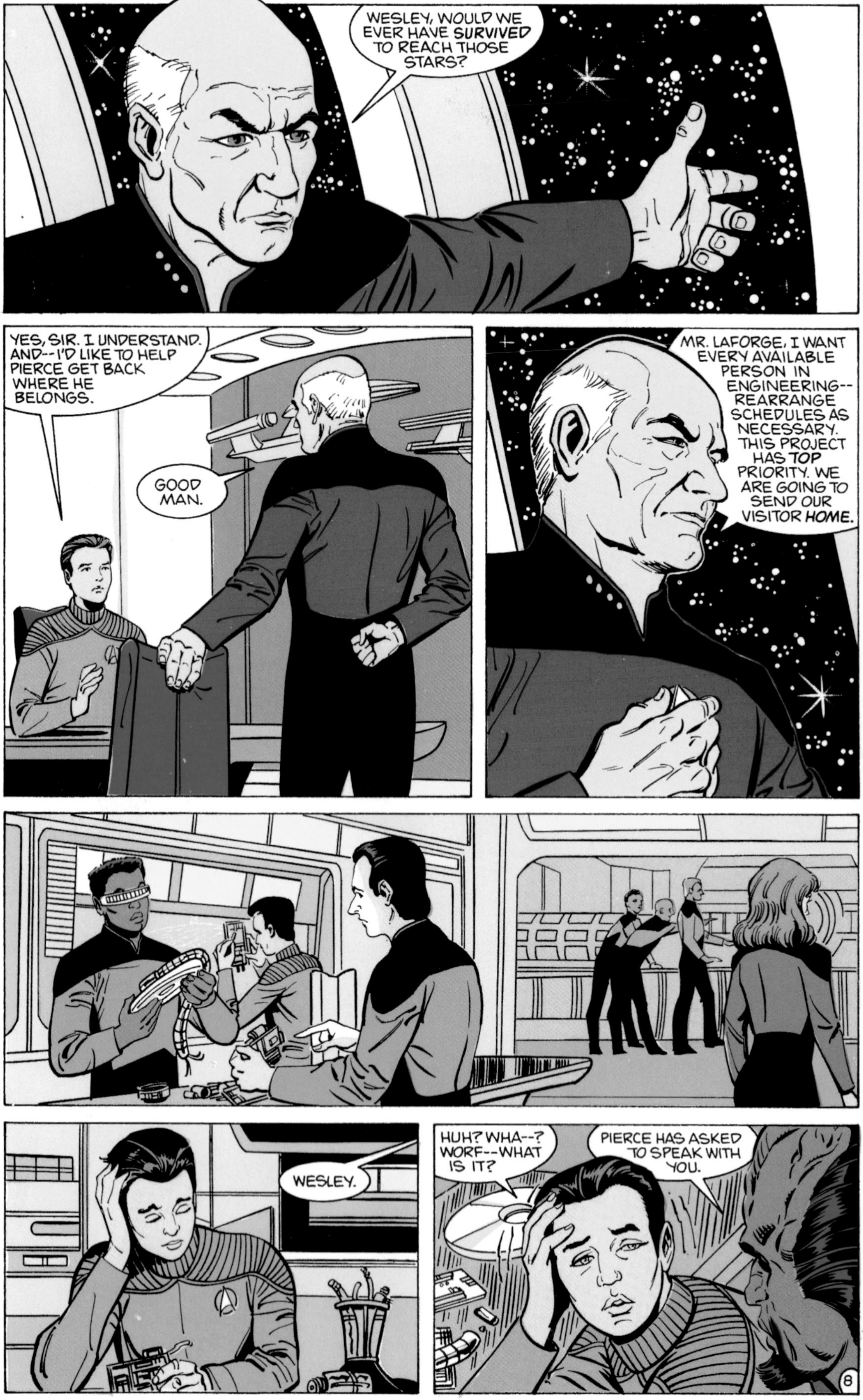
WESLEY, WOULD WE EVER HAVE SURVIVED TO REACH THOSE STARS?
YES, SIR. I UNDERSTAND. AND--I'D LIKE TO HELP PIERCE GET BACK WHERE HE BELONGS.
GOOD MAN.
MR. LAFORGE, I WANT EVERY AVAILABLE PERSON IN ENGINEERING--REARRANGE SCHEDULES AS NECESSARY. THIS PROJECT HAS TOP PRIORITY. WE ARE GOING TO SEND OUR VISITOR HOME.
WESLEY.
HUH? WHA--? WORF--WHAT IS IT?
PIERCE HAS ASKED TO SPEAK WITH YOU.
8

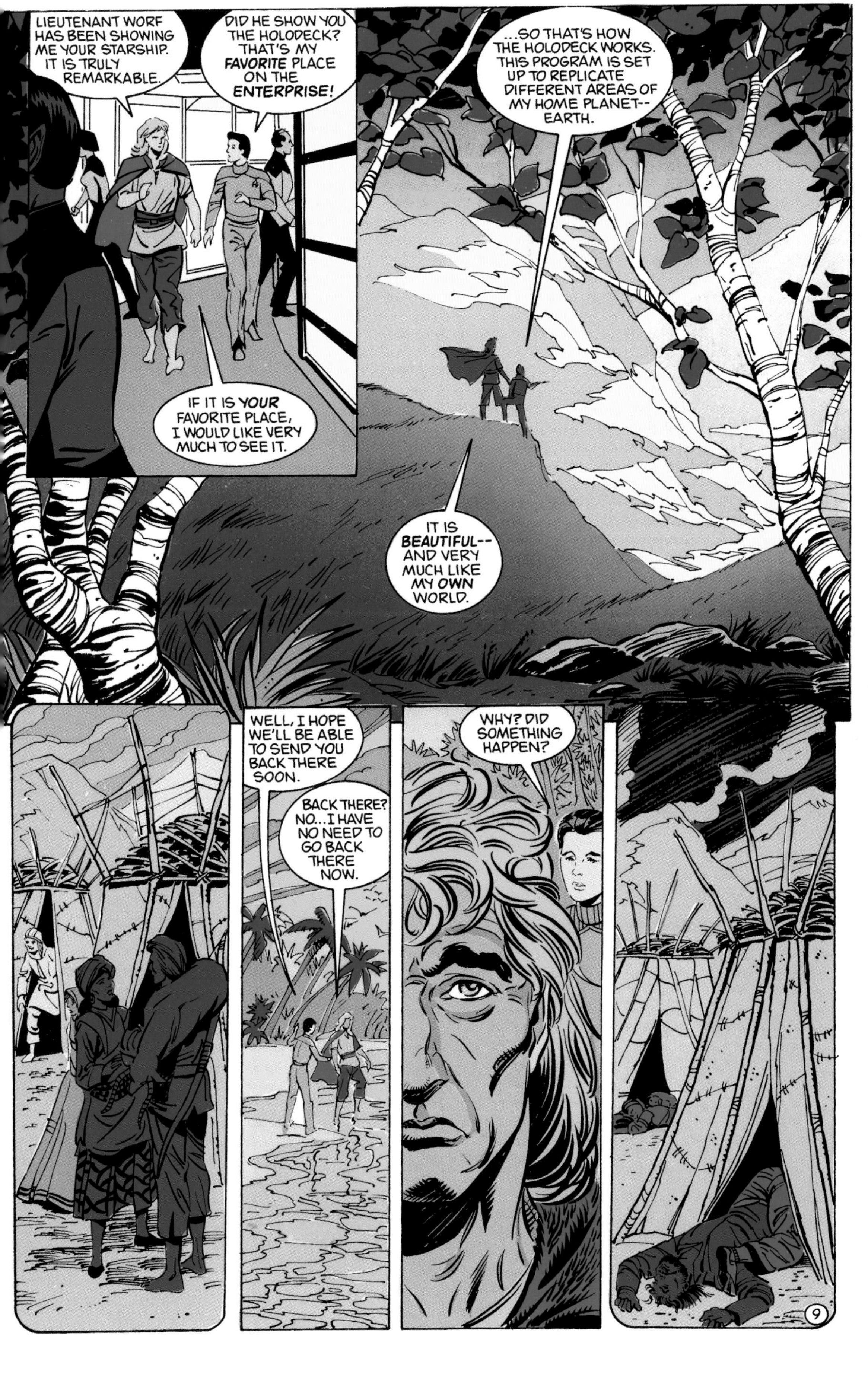

LIEUTENANT WORF HAS BEEN SHOWING ME YOUR STARSHIP. IT IS TRULY REMARKABLE.
DID HE SHOW YOU THE HOLODECK? THAT'S MY FAVORITE PLACE ON THE ENTERPRISE!
IF IT IS YOUR FAVORITE PLACE, I WOULD LIKE VERY MUCH TO SEE IT.
...SO THAT'S HOW THE HOLODECK WORKS. THIS PROGRAM IS SET UP TO REPLICATE DIFFERENT AREAS OF MY HOME PLANET--EARTH.
IT IS BEAUTIFUL--AND VERY MUCH LIKE MY OWN WORLD.
WELL, I HOPE WE'LL BE ABLE TO SEND YOU BACK THERE SOON.
BACK THERE? NO...I HAVE NO NEED TO GO BACK THERE NOW.
WHY? DID SOMETHING HAPPEN?

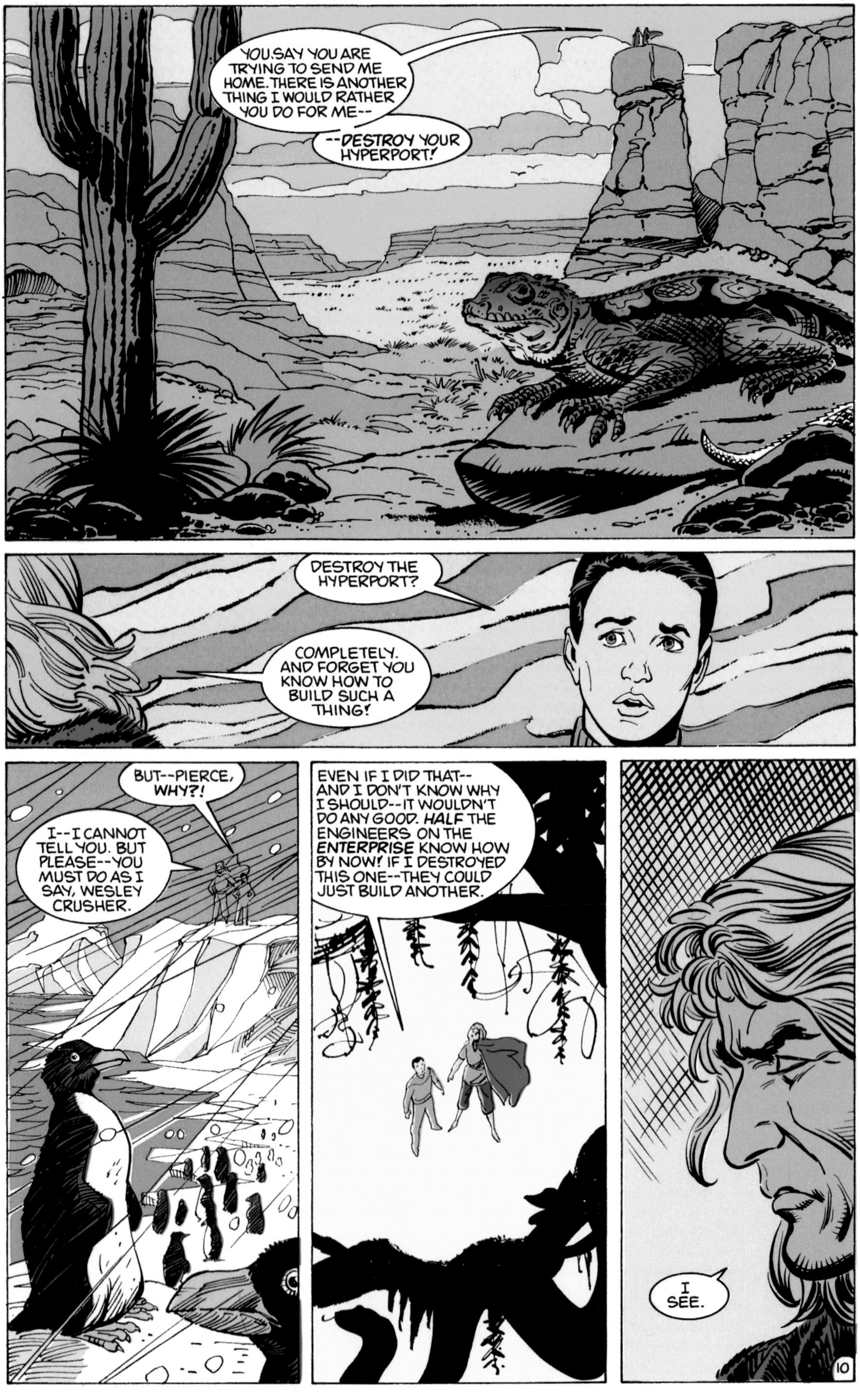
YOU SAY YOU ARE TRYING TO SEND ME HOME. THERE IS ANOTHER THING I WOULD RATHER YOU DO FOR ME--
--DESTROY YOUR HYPERPORT!
DESTROY THE HYPERPORT?
COMPLETELY. AND FORGET YOU KNOW HOW TO BUILD SUCH A THING!
BUT--PIERCE, WHY?!
I--I CANNOT TELL YOU. BUT PLEASE--YOU MUST DO AS I SAY, WESLEY CRUSHER.
EVEN IF I DID THAT-- AND I DON'T KNOW WHY I SHOULD--IT WOULDN'T DO ANY GOOD. HALF THE ENGINEERS ON THE ENTERPRISE KNOW HOW BY NOW! IF I DESTROYED THIS ONE--THEY COULD JUST BUILD ANOTHER.
I SEE.
10

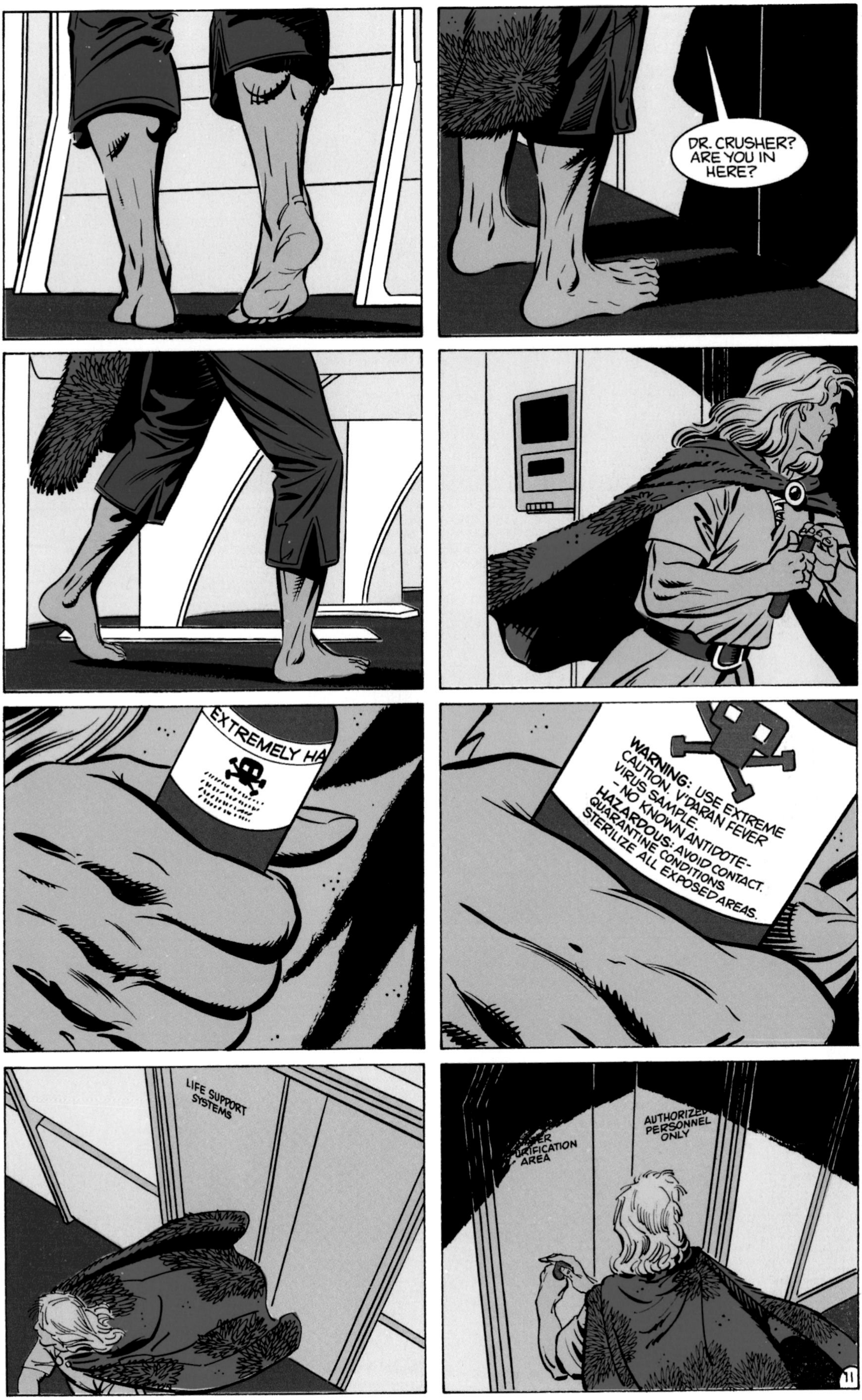
DR. CRUSHER? ARE YOU IN HERE?
EXTREMELY HA
WARNING: USE EXTREME CAUTION. V'DARAN FEVER VIRUS SAMPLE.
- NO KNOWN ANTIDOTE-
HAZARDOUS: AVOID CONTACT. QUARANTINE CONDITIONS STERILIZE ALL EXPOSED AREAS.
LIFE SUPPORT SYSTEMS
PERSONNEL ONLY
AREA

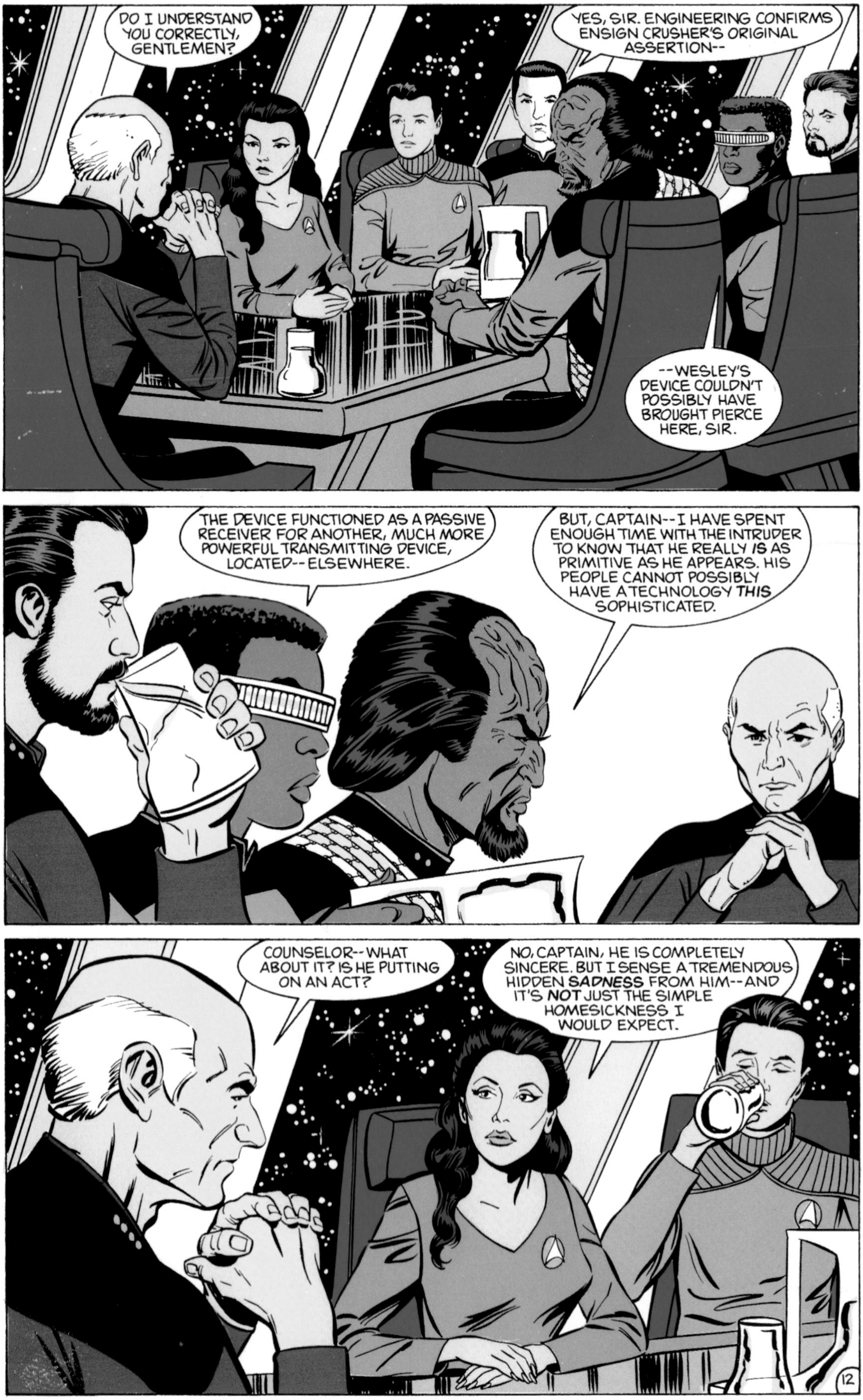
DO I UNDERSTAND YOU CORRECTLY, GENTLEMEN?
YES, SIR. ENGINEERING CONFIRMS ENSIGN CRUSHER'S ORIGINAL ASSERTION--
--WESLEY'S DEVICE COULDN'T POSSIBLY HAVE BROUGHT PIERCE HERE, SIR.
THE DEVICE FUNCTIONED AS A PASSIVE RECEIVER FOR ANOTHER, MUCH MORE POWERFUL TRANSMITTING DEVICE, LOCATED-- ELSEWHERE.
BUT, CAPTAIN--I HAVE SPENT ENOUGH TIME WITH THE INTRUDER TO KNOW THAT HE REALLY **IS** AS PRIMITIVE AS HE APPEARS. HIS PEOPLE CANNOT POSSIBLY HAVE A TECHNOLOGY **THIS** SOPHISTICATED.
COUNSELOR--WHAT ABOUT IT? IS HE PUTTING ON AN ACT?
NO, CAPTAIN, HE IS COMPLETELY SINCERE. BUT I SENSE A TREMENDOUS HIDDEN **SADNESS** FROM HIM--AND IT'S **NOT** JUST THE SIMPLE HOMESICKNESS I WOULD EXPECT.

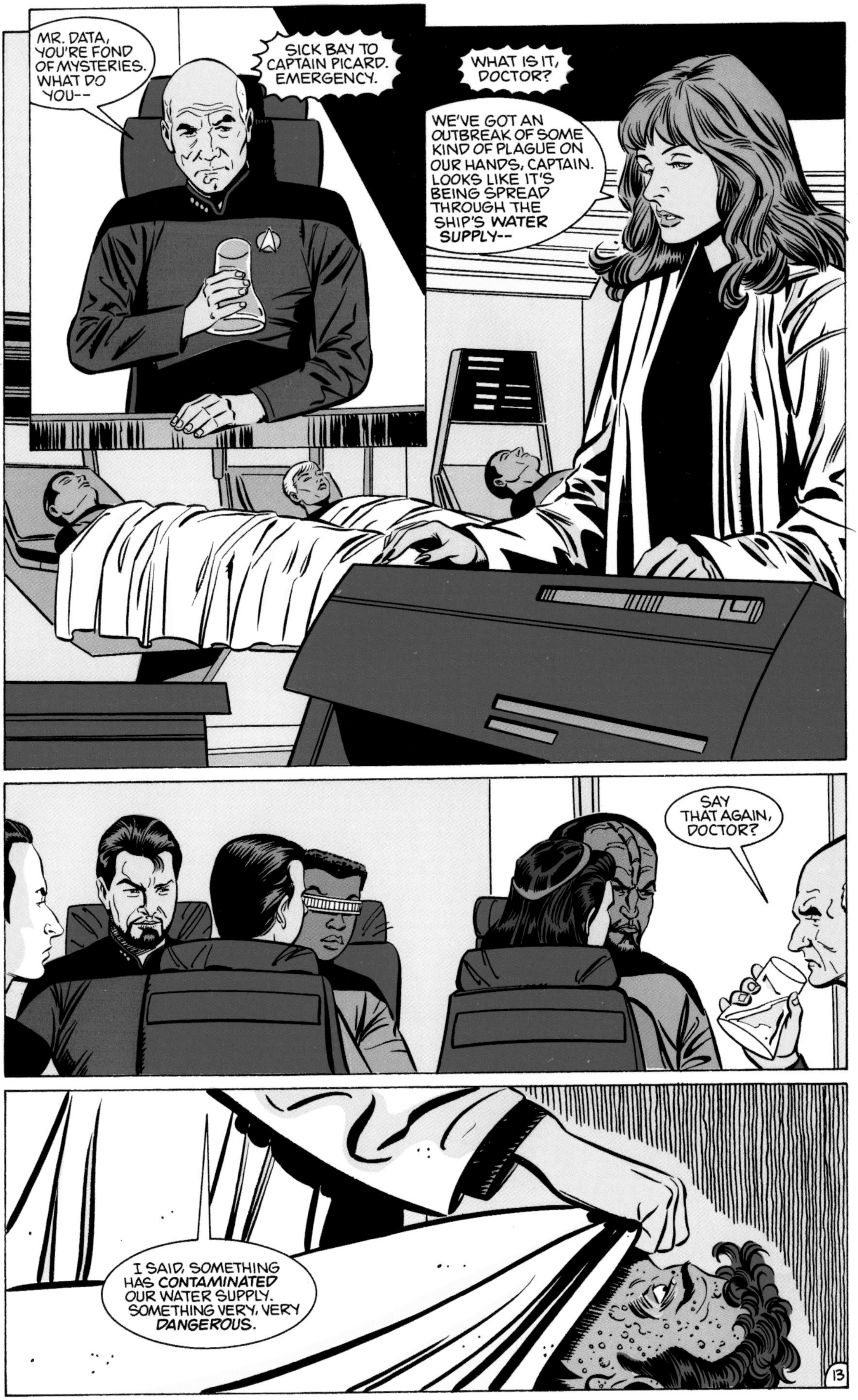
MR. DATA, YOU'RE FOND OF MYSTERIES. WHAT DO YOU--
SICK BAY TO CAPTAIN PICARD. EMERGENCY.
WHAT IS IT, DOCTOR?
WE'VE GOT AN OUTBREAK OF SOME KIND OF PLAGUE ON OUR HANDS, CAPTAIN. LOOKS LIKE IT'S BEING SPREAD THROUGH THE SHIP'S WATER SUPPLY--
SAY THAT AGAIN, DOCTOR?
I SAID, SOMETHING HAS CONTAMINATED OUR WATER SUPPLY. SOMETHING VERY, VERY DANGEROUS.

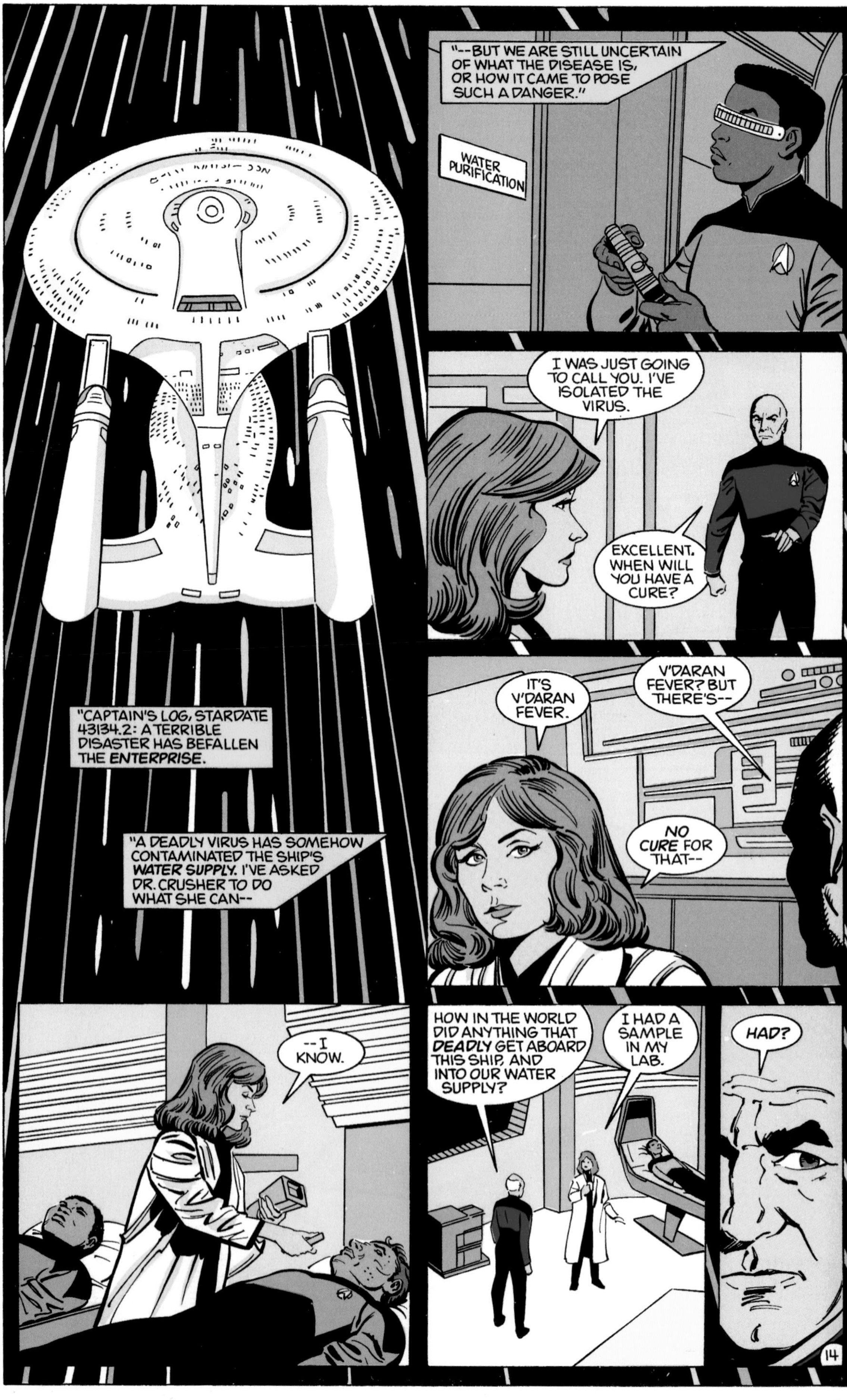
"CAPTAIN'S LOG, STARDATE 43134.2: A TERRIBLE DISASTER HAS BEFALLEN THE ENTERPRISE.
"A DEADLY VIRUS HAS SOMEHOW CONTAMINATED THE SHIP'S WATER SUPPLY. I'VE ASKED DR. CRUSHER TO DO WHAT SHE CAN--
"--BUT WE ARE STILL UNCERTAIN OF WHAT THE DISEASE IS, OR HOW IT CAME TO POSE SUCH A DANGER."
WATER PURIFICATION
I WAS JUST GOING TO CALL YOU. I'VE ISOLATED THE VIRUS.
EXCELLENT. WHEN WILL YOU HAVE A CURE?
IT'S V'DARAN FEVER.
V'DARAN FEVER? BUT THERE'S--
NO CURE FOR THAT--
--I KNOW.
HOW IN THE WORLD DID ANYTHING THAT DEADLY GET ABOARD THIS SHIP, AND INTO OUR WATER SUPPLY?
I HAD A SAMPLE IN MY LAB.
HAD?
14

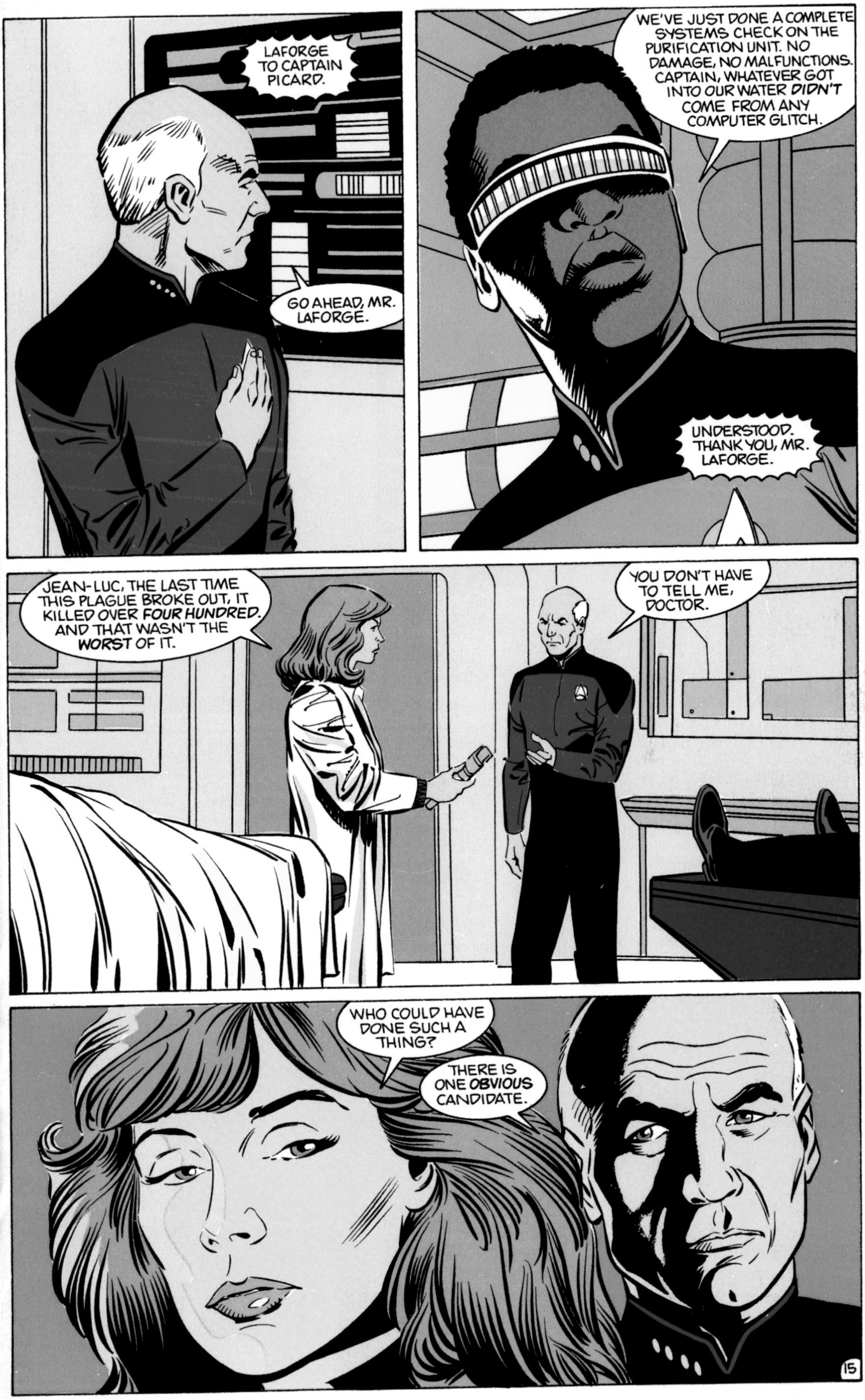
LAFORGE TO CAPTAIN PICARD.
GO AHEAD, MR. LAFORGE.
WE'VE JUST DONE A COMPLETE SYSTEMS CHECK ON THE PURIFICATION UNIT. NO DAMAGE, NO MALFUNCTIONS. CAPTAIN, WHATEVER GOT INTO OUR WATER DIDN'T COME FROM ANY COMPUTER GLITCH.
UNDERSTOOD. THANK YOU, MR. LAFORGE.
JEAN-LUC, THE LAST TIME THIS PLAGUE BROKE OUT, IT KILLED OVER FOUR HUNDRED. AND THAT WASN'T THE WORST OF IT.
YOU DON'T HAVE TO TELL ME, DOCTOR.
WHO COULD HAVE DONE SUCH A THING?
THERE IS ONE OBVIOUS CANDIDATE.
15

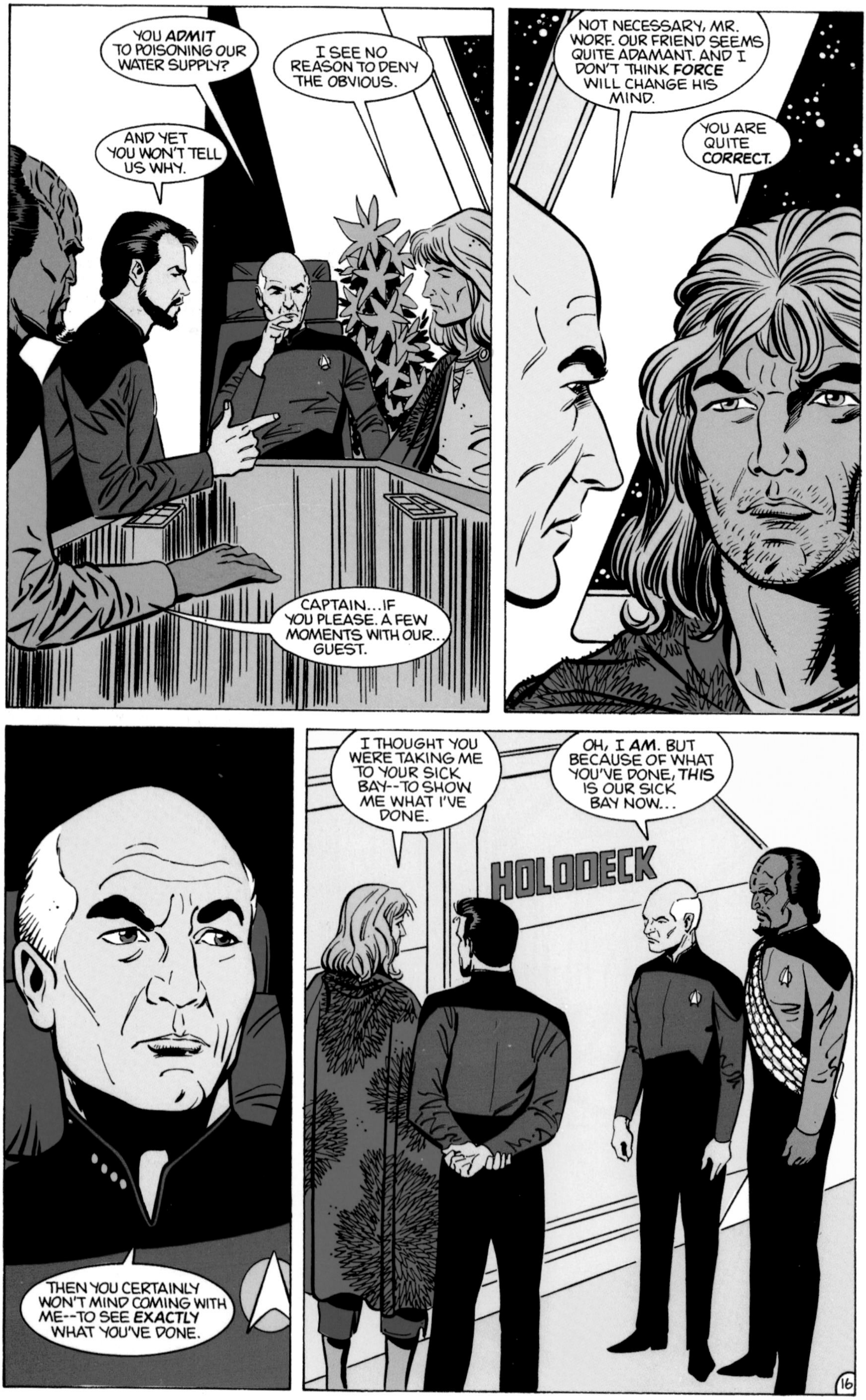

YOU ADMIT TO POISONING OUR WATER SUPPLY?
AND YET YOU WON'T TELL US WHY.
I SEE NO REASON TO DENY THE OBVIOUS.
CAPTAIN...IF YOU PLEASE. A FEW MOMENTS WITH OUR... GUEST.
NOT NECESSARY, MR. WORF. OUR FRIEND SEEMS QUITE ADAMANT. AND I DON'T THINK FORCE WILL CHANGE HIS MIND.
YOU ARE QUITE CORRECT.
THEN YOU CERTAINLY WON'T MIND COMING WITH ME--TO SEE EXACTLY WHAT YOU'VE DONE.
I THOUGHT YOU WERE TAKING ME TO YOUR SICK BAY--TO SHOW ME WHAT I'VE DONE.
OH, I AM. BUT BECAUSE OF WHAT YOU'VE DONE, THIS IS OUR SICK BAY NOW...
HOLODECK
16

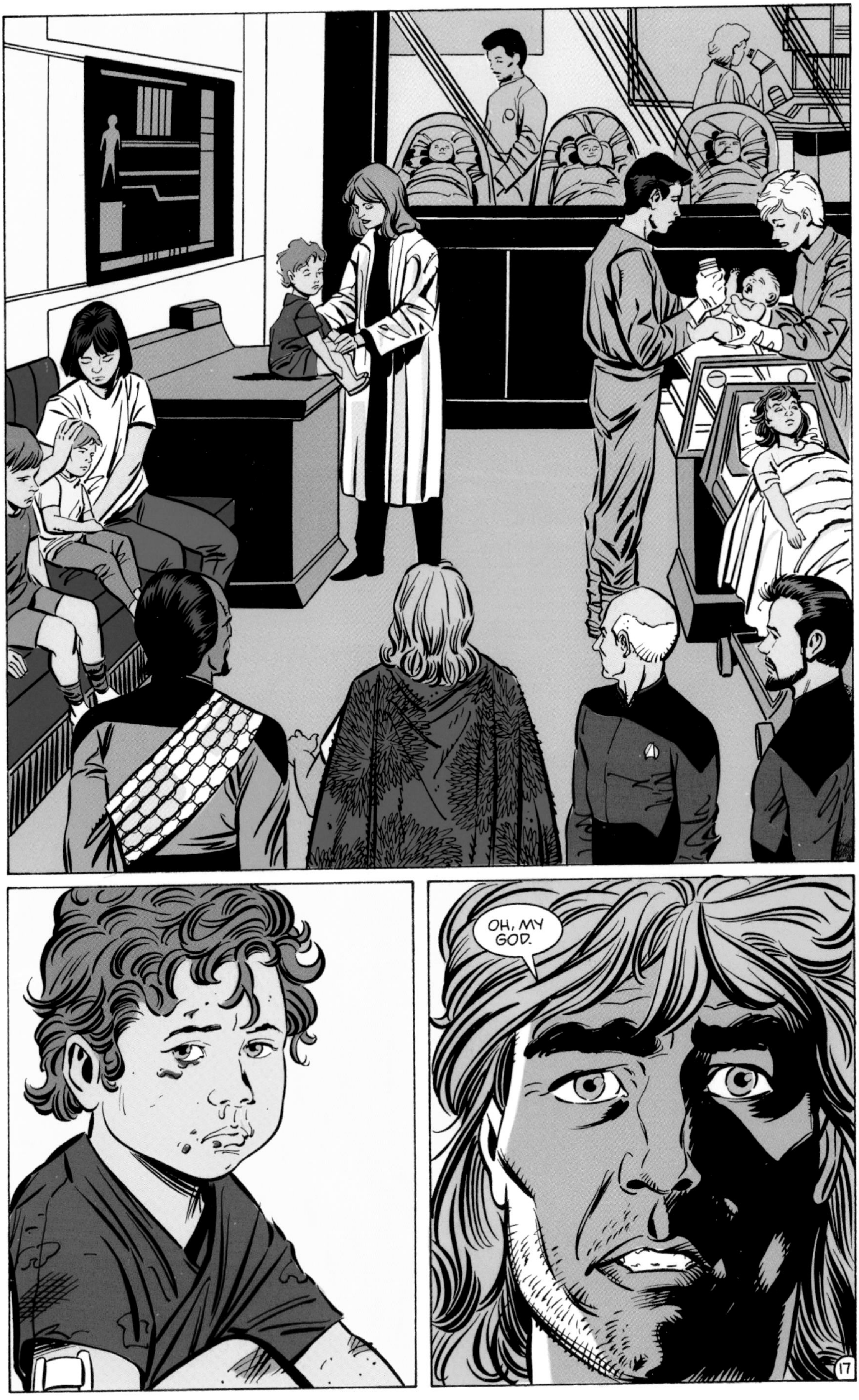
OH, MY GOD.

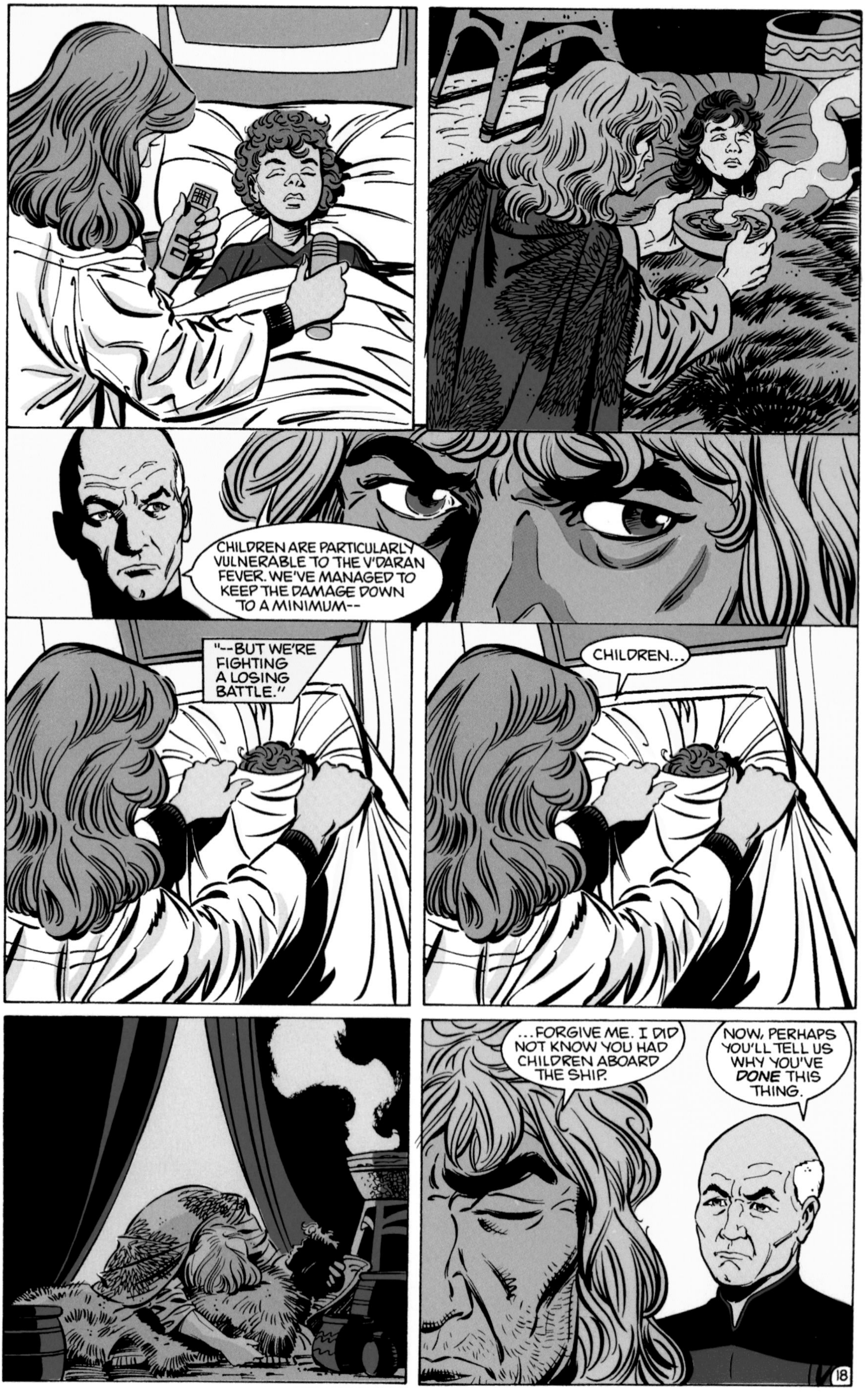
CHILDREN ARE PARTICULARLY VULNERABLE TO THE V'DARAN FEVER. WE'VE MANAGED TO KEEP THE DAMAGE DOWN TO A MINIMUM--
"--BUT WE'RE FIGHTING A LOSING BATTLE."
CHILDREN...
...FORGIVE ME. I DID NOT KNOW YOU HAD CHILDREN ABOARD THE SHIP.
NOW, PERHAPS YOU'LL TELL US WHY YOU'VE DONE THIS THING.
18

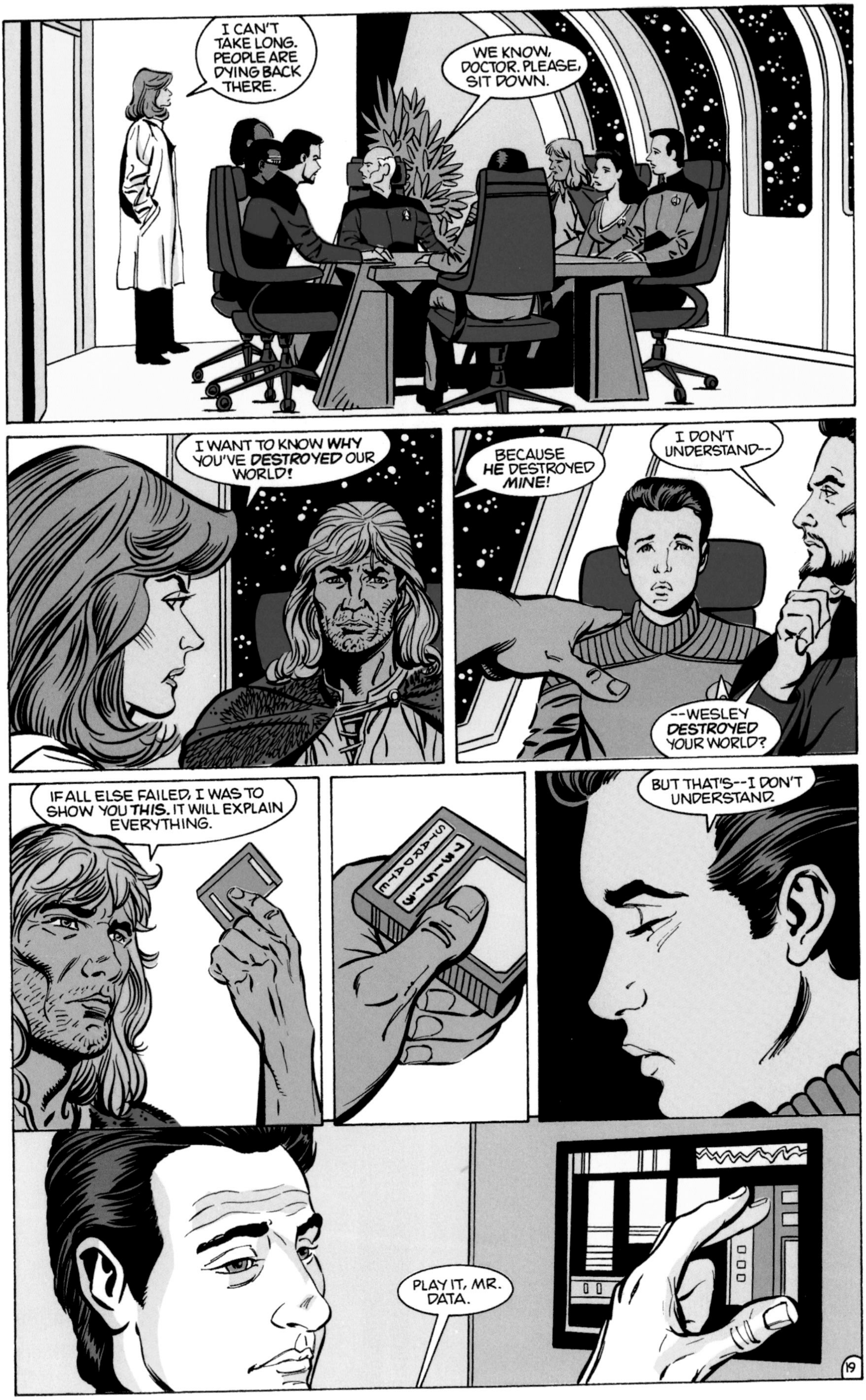
I CAN'T TAKE LONG. PEOPLE ARE DYING BACK THERE.
WE KNOW, DOCTOR. PLEASE, SIT DOWN.
I WANT TO KNOW WHY YOU'VE DESTROYED OUR WORLD!
BECAUSE HE DESTROYED MINE!
I DON'T UNDERSTAND--
--WESLEY DESTROYED YOUR WORLD?
IF ALL ELSE FAILED, I WAS TO SHOW YOU THIS. IT WILL EXPLAIN EVERYTHING.
BUT THAT'S--I DON'T UNDERSTAND.
PLAY IT, MR. DATA.
19

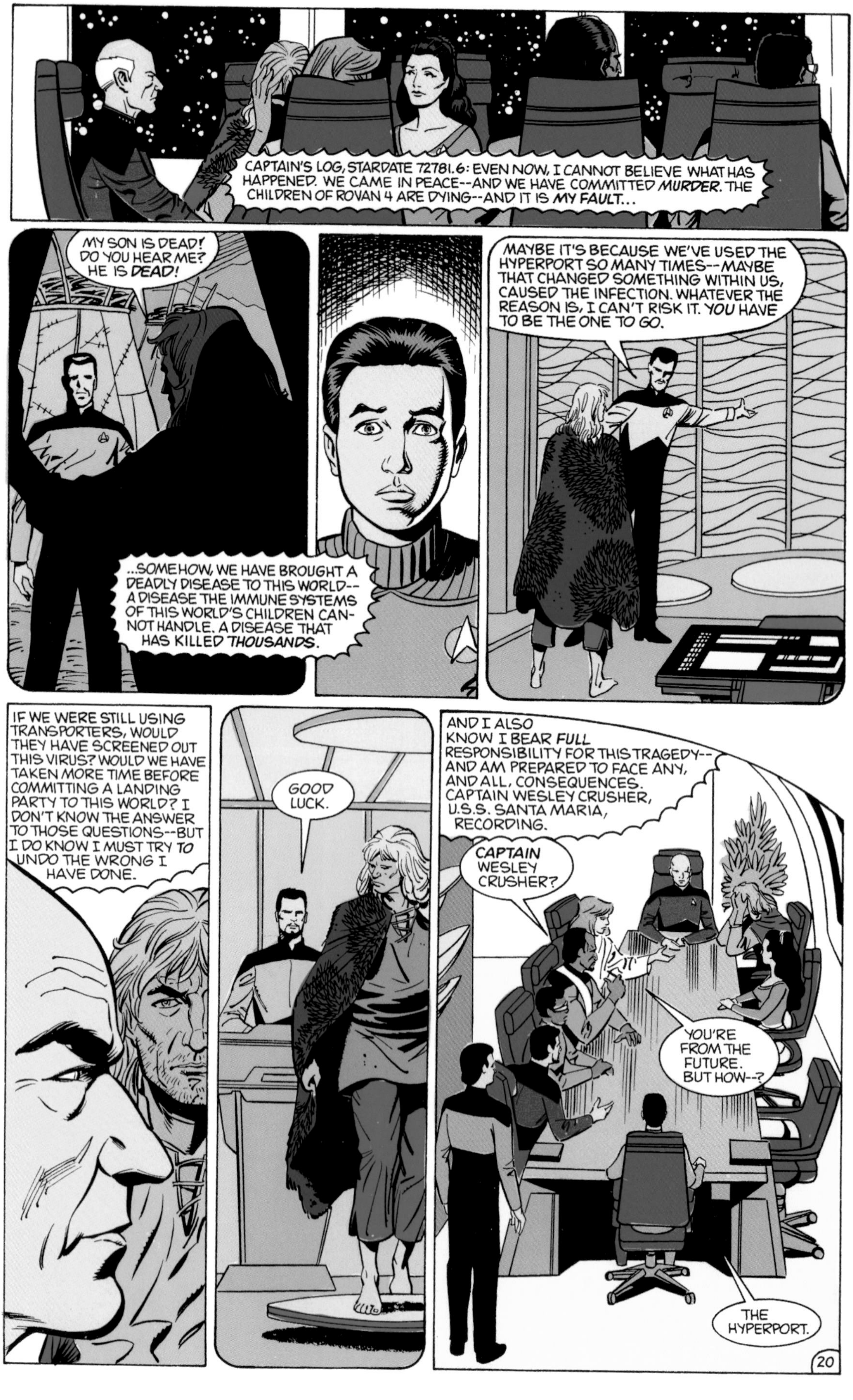
CAPTAIN'S LOG, STARDATE 72781.6: EVEN NOW, I CANNOT BELIEVE WHAT HAS HAPPENED. WE CAME IN PEACE--AND WE HAVE COMMITTED MURDER. THE CHILDREN OF ROVAN 4 ARE DYING--AND IT IS MY FAULT...
MY SON IS DEAD! DO YOU HEAR ME? HE IS DEAD!
...SOMEHOW, WE HAVE BROUGHT A DEADLY DISEASE TO THIS WORLD--A DISEASE THE IMMUNE SYSTEMS OF THIS WORLD'S CHILDREN CANNOT HANDLE. A DISEASE THAT HAS KILLED THOUSANDS.
MAYBE IT'S BECAUSE WE'VE USED THE HYPERPORT SO MANY TIMES--MAYBE THAT CHANGED SOMETHING WITHIN US, CAUSED THE INFECTION. WHATEVER THE REASON IS, I CAN'T RISK IT. YOU HAVE TO BE THE ONE TO GO.
IF WE WERE STILL USING TRANSPORTERS, WOULD THEY HAVE SCREENED OUT THIS VIRUS? WOULD WE HAVE TAKEN MORE TIME BEFORE COMMITTING A LANDING PARTY TO THIS WORLD? I DON'T KNOW THE ANSWER TO THOSE QUESTIONS--BUT I DO KNOW I MUST TRY TO UNDO THE WRONG I HAVE DONE.
GOOD LUCK.
AND I ALSO KNOW I BEAR FULL RESPONSIBILITY FOR THIS TRAGEDY--AND AM PREPARED TO FACE ANY, AND ALL, CONSEQUENCES. CAPTAIN WESLEY CRUSHER, U.S.S. SANTA MARIA, RECORDING.
CAPTAIN WESLEY CRUSHER?
YOU'RE FROM THE FUTURE. BUT HOW--?
THE HYPERPORT.

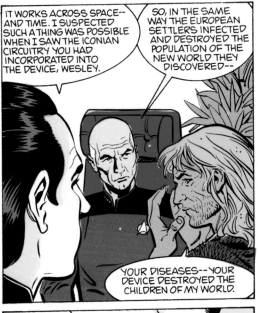

IT WORKS ACROSS SPACE-- AND TIME. I SUSPECTED SUCH A THING WAS POSSIBLE WHEN I SAW THE ICONIAN CIRCUITRY YOU HAD INCORPORATED INTO THE DEVICE, WESLEY.

SO, IN THE SAME WAY THE EUROPEAN SETTLERS INFECTED AND DESTROYED THE POPULATION OF THE NEW WORLD THEY DISCOVERED--

YOUR DISEASES-- YOUR DEVICE DESTROYED THE CHILDREN OF MY WORLD.

YOU SHOWED ME HOW TO WORK YOUR DEVICE. YOU TOLD ME TO COME BACK HERE--TO TALK TO YOU, TO CONVINCE YOU TO DESTROY YOUR DEVICE--

WHY DIDN'T YOU JUST SHOW ME THIS TAPE?

YOU TOLD ME NOT TO REVEAL THE FUTURE--TO ANY OF THOSE I WOULD MEET HERE--EVEN TO YOURSELF, UNLESS I ABSOLUTELY HAD TO. AND WHEN I DISCOVERED I HAD NOT ONLY YOU, BUT AN ENTIRE SHIP OF ENGINEERS TO CONVINCE NOT TO USE THIS TECHNOLOGY--

YOU TRIED TO MAKE SURE KNOWLEDGE OF THE HYPERPORT DIED WITH US.

I WISH I'D NEVER BUILT THIS THING.

MAYBE YOU DIDN'T.

YOU'RE SUGGESTING ONE OF US USE THE HYPERPORT NOW...?

TO GO BACK IN TIME AND STOP WESLEY!

I WILL GO. WESLEY WILL LISTEN TO ME.

21

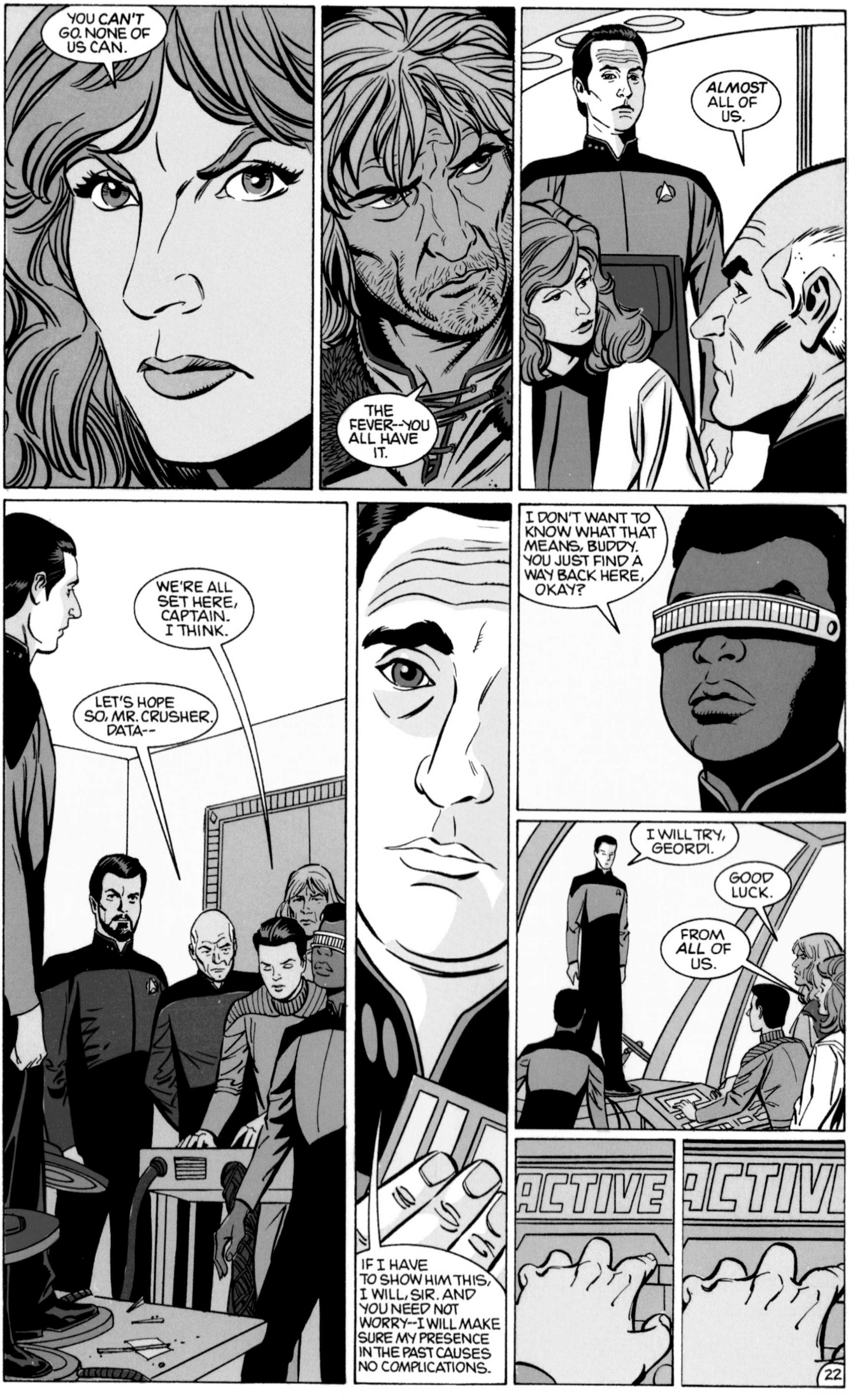
YOU CAN'T GO. NONE OF US CAN.
THE FEVER--YOU ALL HAVE IT.
ALMOST ALL OF US.
WE'RE ALL SET HERE, CAPTAIN. I THINK.
LET'S HOPE SO, MR. CRUSHER. DATA--
IF I HAVE TO SHOW HIM THIS, I WILL, SIR. AND YOU NEED NOT WORRY--I WILL MAKE SURE MY PRESENCE IN THE PAST CAUSES NO COMPLICATIONS.
I DON'T WANT TO KNOW WHAT THAT MEANS, BUDDY. YOU JUST FIND A WAY BACK HERE, OKAY?
I WILL TRY, GEORDI.
GOOD LUCK.
FROM ALL OF US.
ACTIVE
ACTIVE

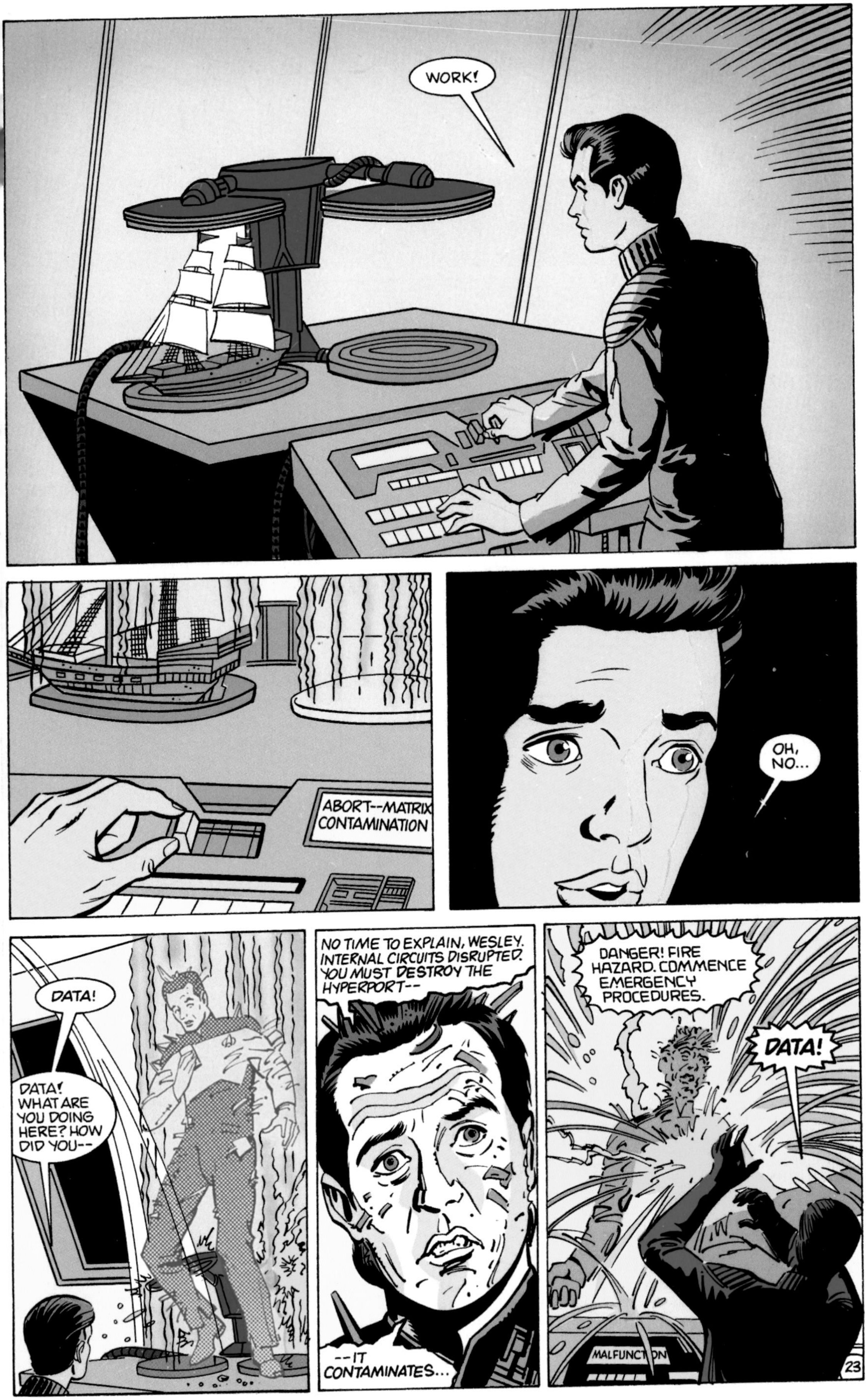
WORK!
ABORT--MATRIX CONTAMINATION
OH, NO...
DATA!
DATA! WHAT ARE YOU DOING HERE? HOW DID YOU--
NO TIME TO EXPLAIN, WESLEY. INTERNAL CIRCUITS DISRUPTED. YOU MUST DESTROY THE HYPERPORT--
--IT CONTAMINATES...
DANGER! FIRE HAZARD. COMMENCE EMERGENCY PROCEDURES.
DATA!
MALFUNCTION
23

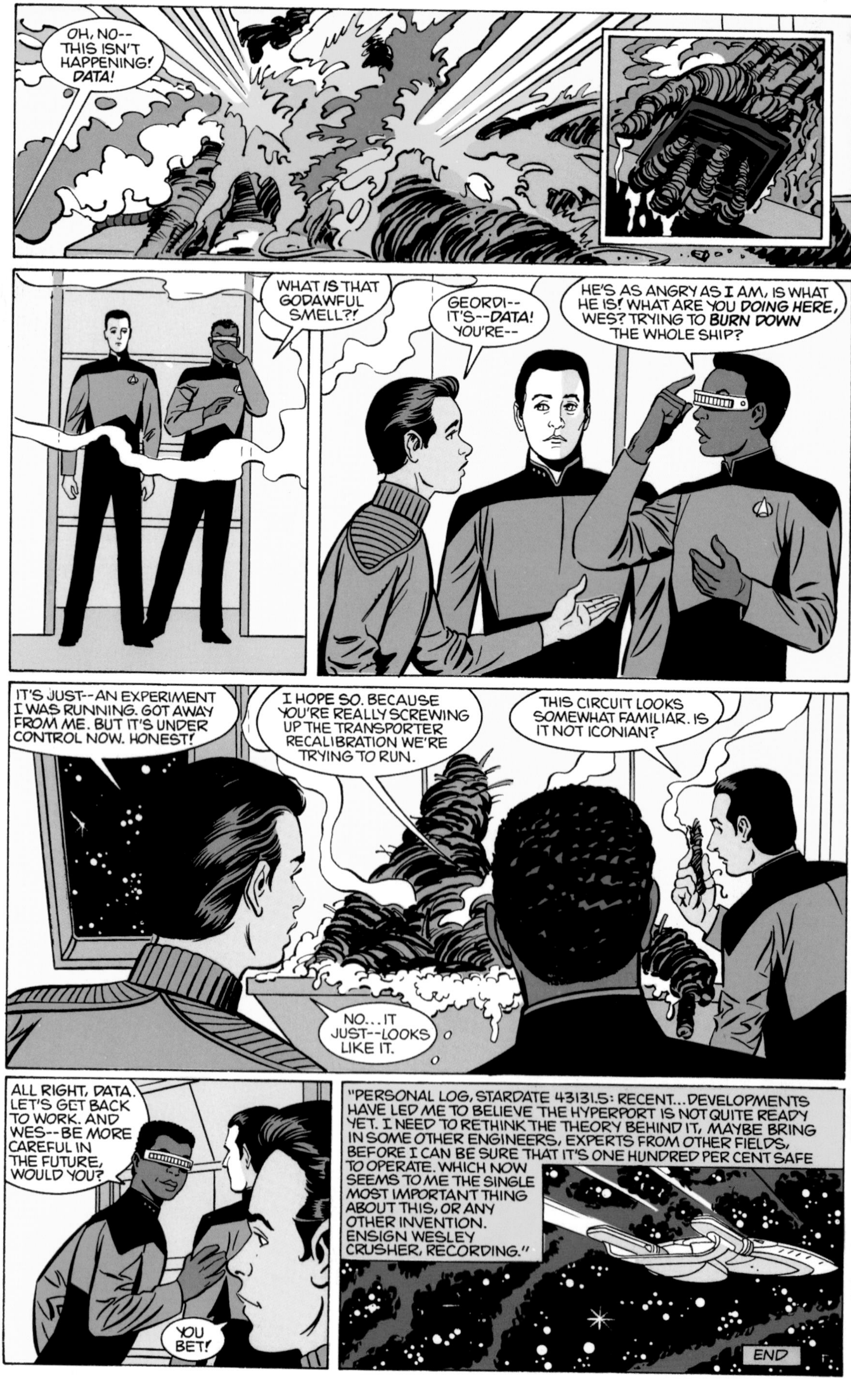
OH, NO-- THIS ISN'T HAPPENING! DATA!
WHAT IS THAT GODAWFUL SMELL?!
GEORDI-- IT'S--DATA! YOU'RE--
HE'S AS ANGRY AS I AM, IS WHAT HE IS! WHAT ARE YOU DOING HERE, WES? TRYING TO BURN DOWN THE WHOLE SHIP?
IT'S JUST--AN EXPERIMENT I WAS RUNNING. GOT AWAY FROM ME. BUT IT'S UNDER CONTROL NOW. HONEST!
I HOPE SO. BECAUSE YOU'RE REALLY SCREWING UP THE TRANSPORTER RECALIBRATION WE'RE TRYING TO RUN.
THIS CIRCUIT LOOKS SOMEWHAT FAMILIAR. IS IT NOT ICONIAN?
NO... IT JUST--LOOKS LIKE IT.
ALL RIGHT, DATA. LET'S GET BACK TO WORK. AND WES--BE MORE CAREFUL IN THE FUTURE, WOULD YOU?
YOU BET!
"PERSONAL LOG, STARDATE 43131.5: RECENT... DEVELOPMENTS HAVE LED ME TO BELIEVE THE HYPERPORT IS NOT QUITE READY YET. I NEED TO RETHINK THE THEORY BEHIND IT, MAYBE BRING IN SOME OTHER ENGINEERS, EXPERTS FROM OTHER FIELDS, BEFORE I CAN BE SURE THAT IT'S ONE HUNDRED PER CENT SAFE TO OPERATE. WHICH NOW SEEMS TO ME THE SINGLE MOST IMPORTANT THING ABOUT THIS, OR ANY OTHER INVENTION. ENSIGN WESLEY CRUSHER, RECORDING."
END

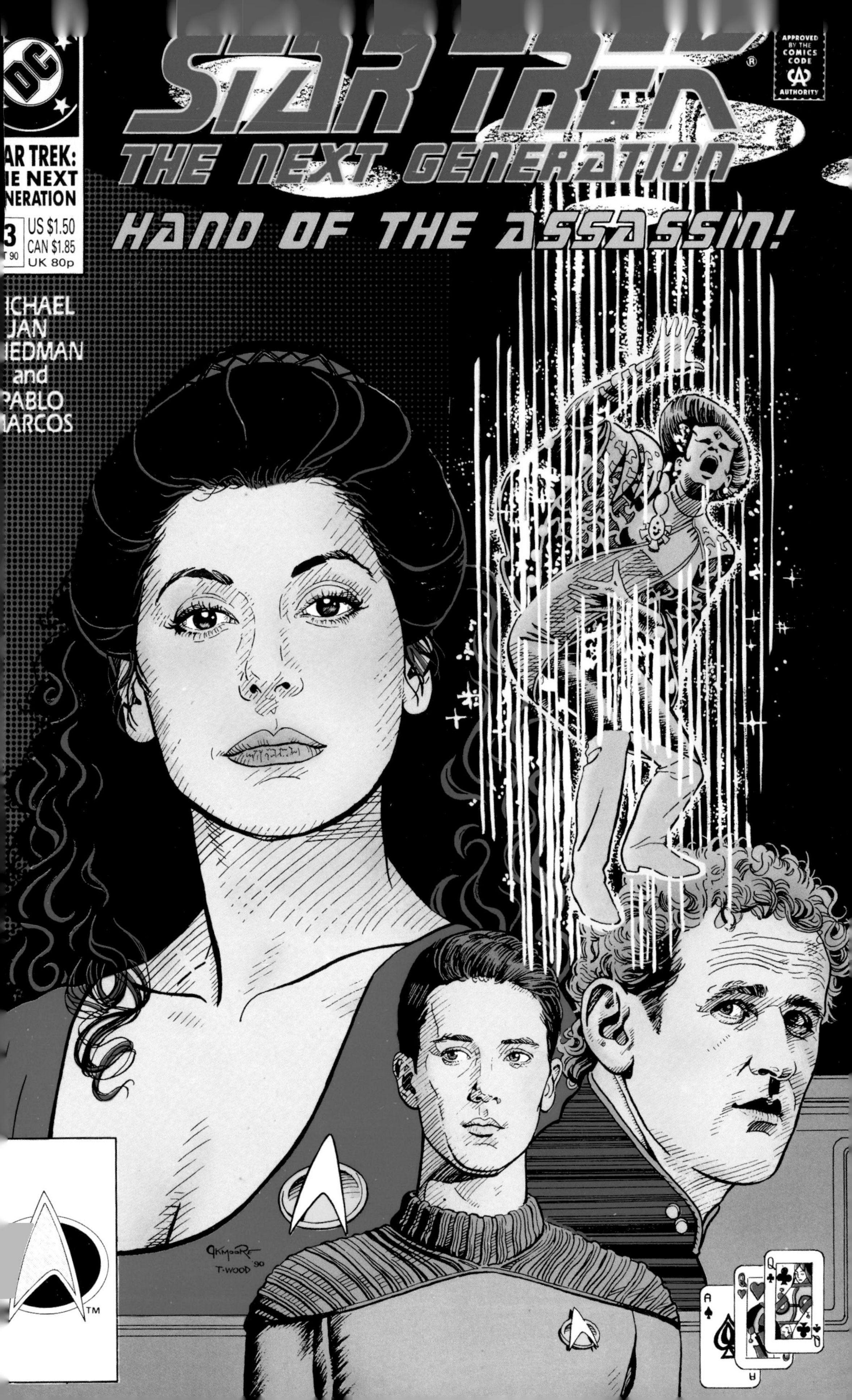

DC
STAR TREK®
THE NEXT GENERATION
HAND OF THE ASSASSIN!
APPROVED BY THE COMICS CODE AUTHORITY
AR TREK:
IE NEXT
NERATION
3
US $1.50
CAN $1.85
UK 80p
ICHAEL
JAN
IEDMAN
and
PABLO
ARCOS
T·WOOD '90
TM

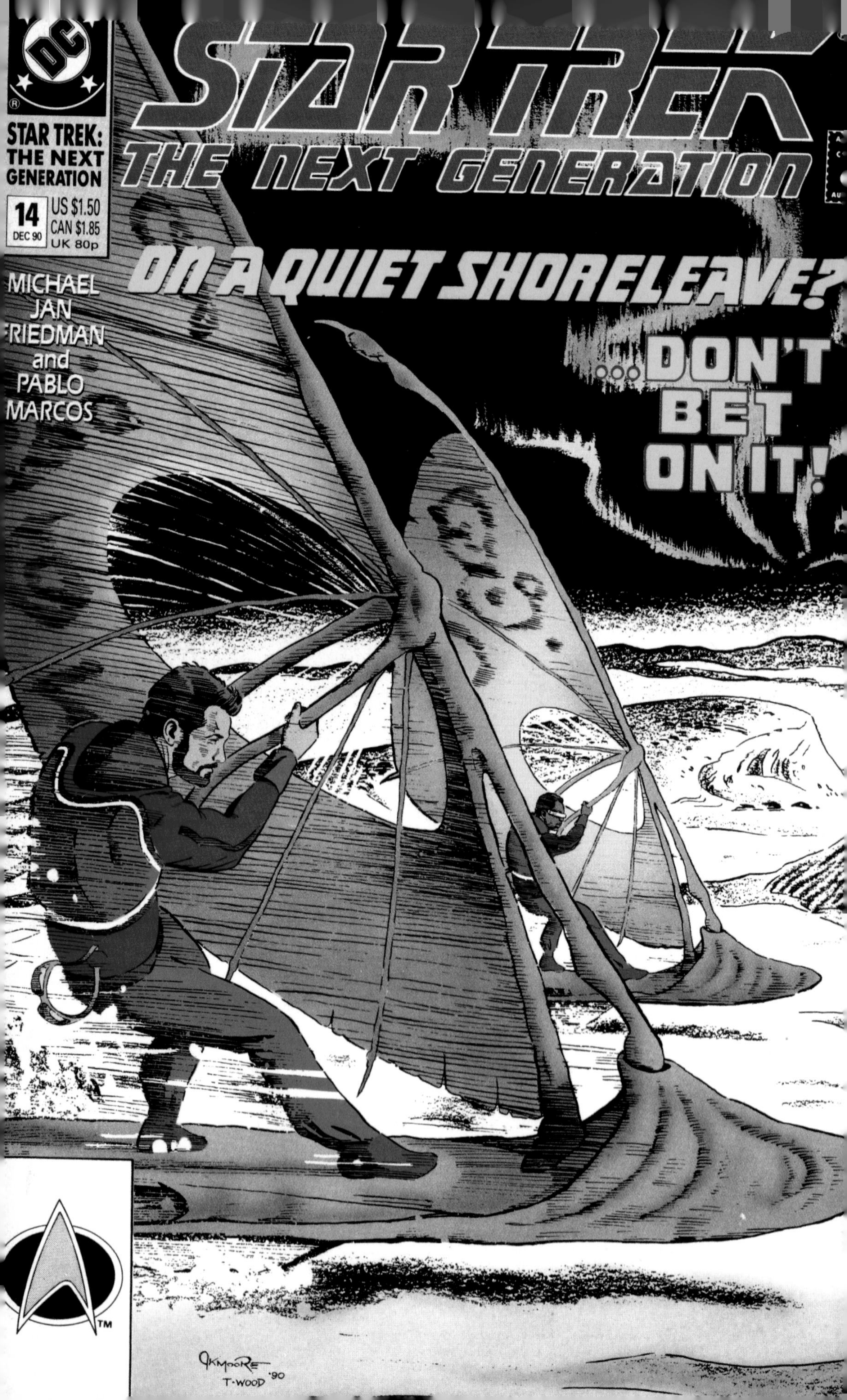
DC
STAR TREK
THE NEXT GENERATION
STAR TREK: THE NEXT GENERATION
14
DEC 90
US $1.50
CAN $1.85
UK 80p
MICHAEL JAN FRIEDMAN and PABLO MARCOS
ON A QUIET SHORELEAVE?
...DON'T BET ON IT!
TM
JKMOORE
T-WOOD '90

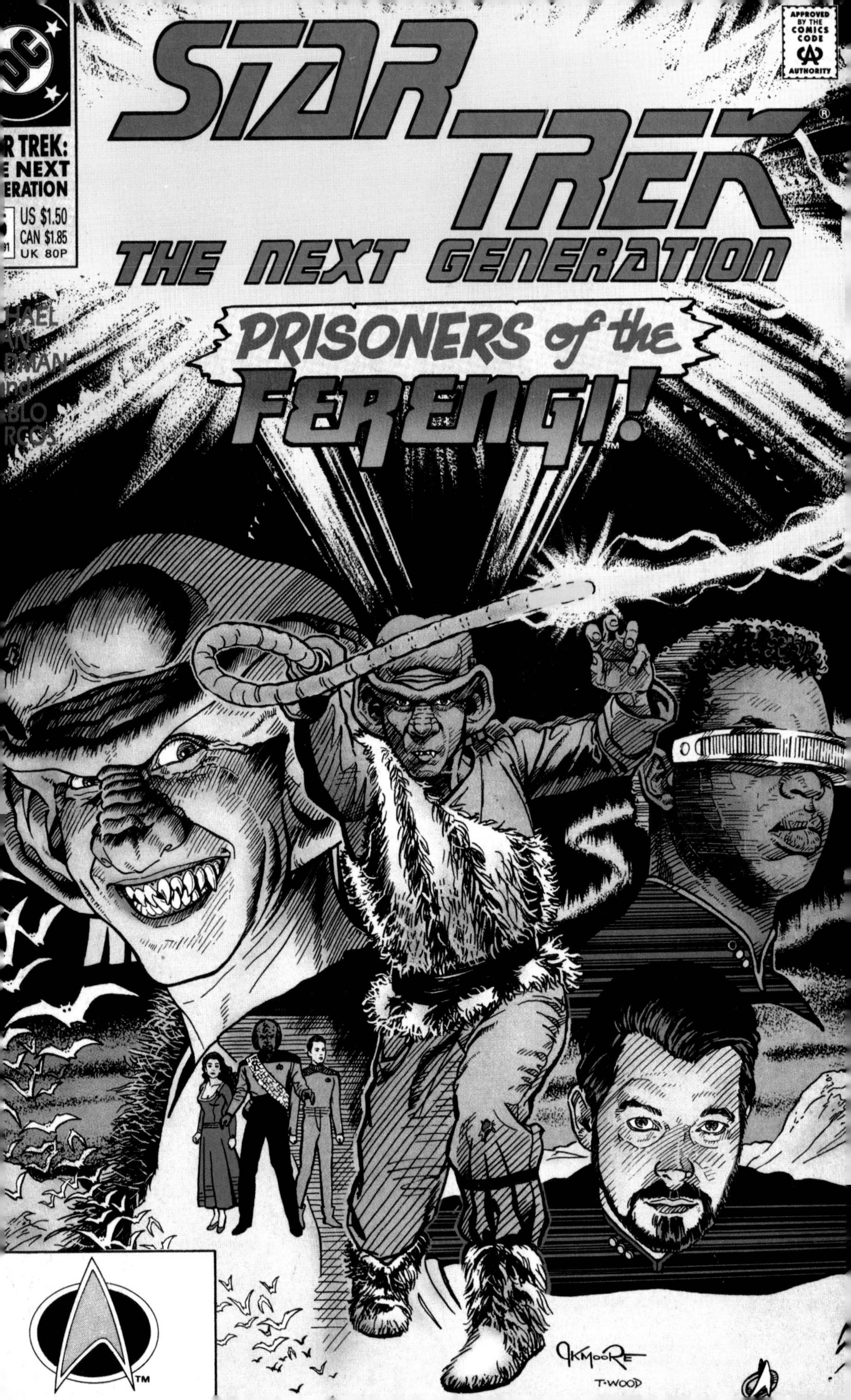

STAR TREK®
THE NEXT GENERATION
PRISONERS of the FERENGI!™
APPROVED BY THE COMICS CODE AUTHORITY
US $1.50
CAN $1.85
UK 80P
JKMOORE
T-WOOD

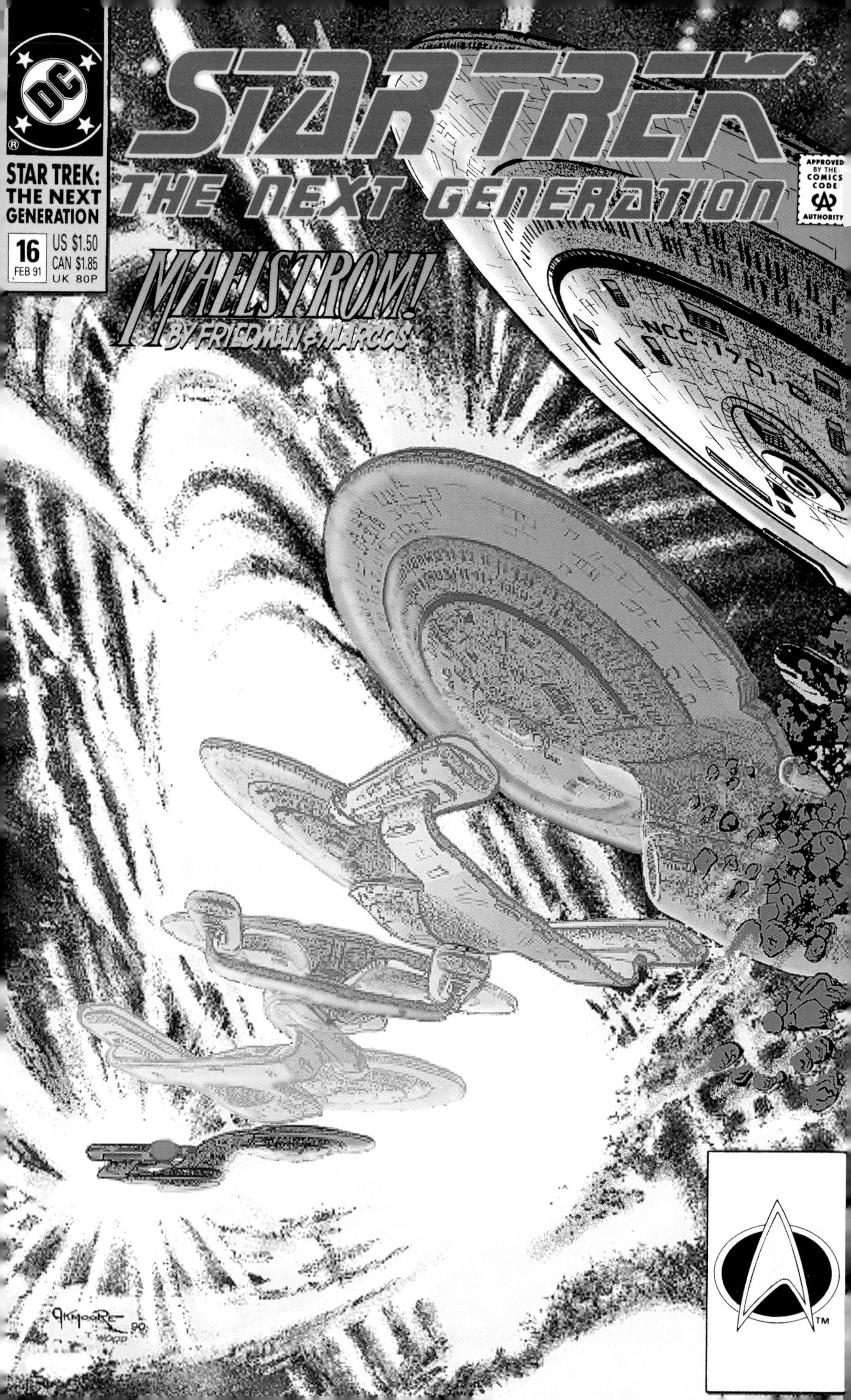
DC
STAR TREK: THE NEXT GENERATION
16
FEB 91
US $1.50
CAN $1.85
UK 80P
STAR TREK
THE NEXT GENERATION
APPROVED BY THE COMICS CODE AUTHORITY
MAELSTROM!
BY FRIEDMAN & MARCOS
NCC-1701-D
AKMOORE 90
T. WOOD

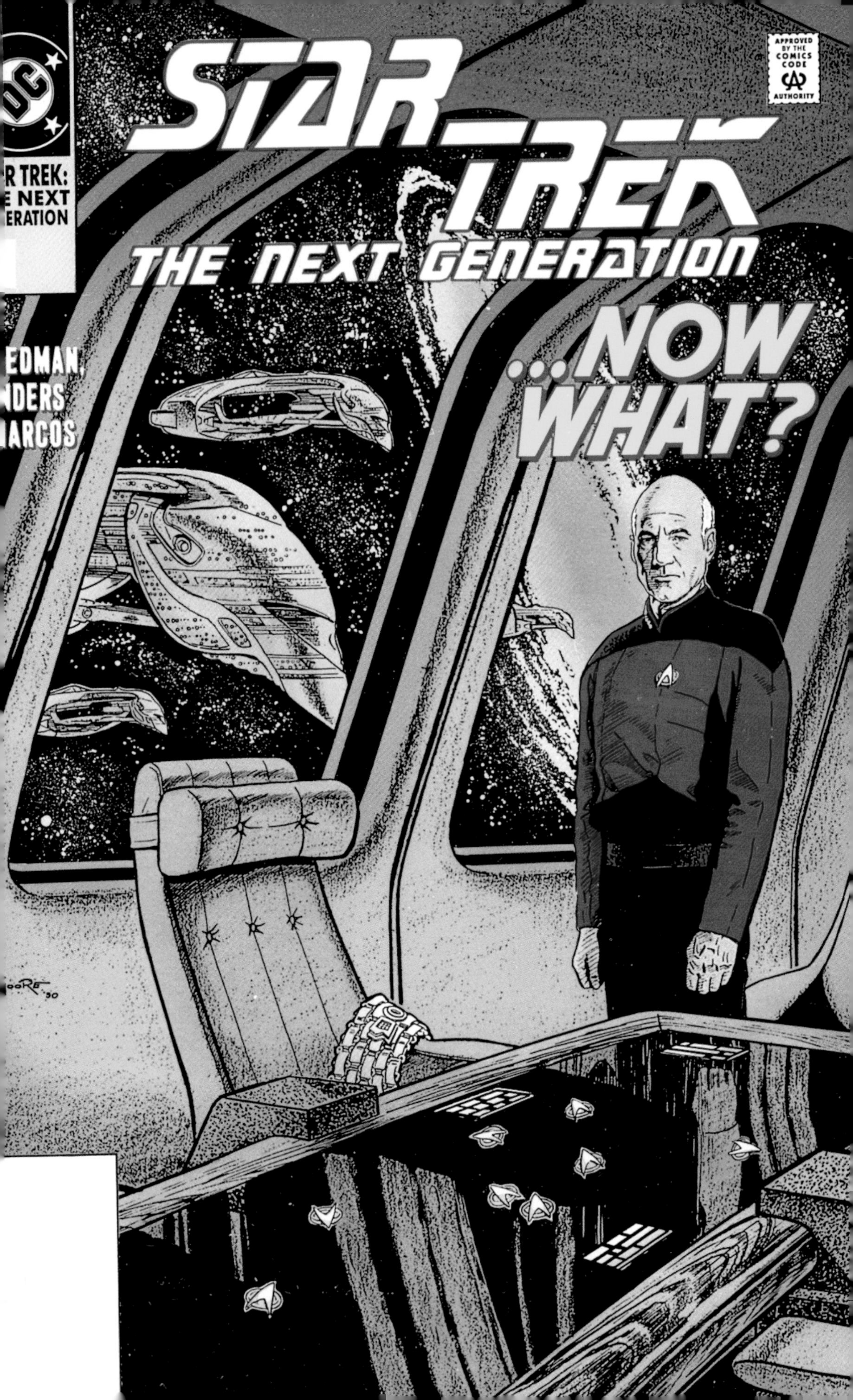
STAR TREK
THE NEXT GENERATION
...NOW WHAT?
APPROVED BY THE COMICS CODE AUTHORITY

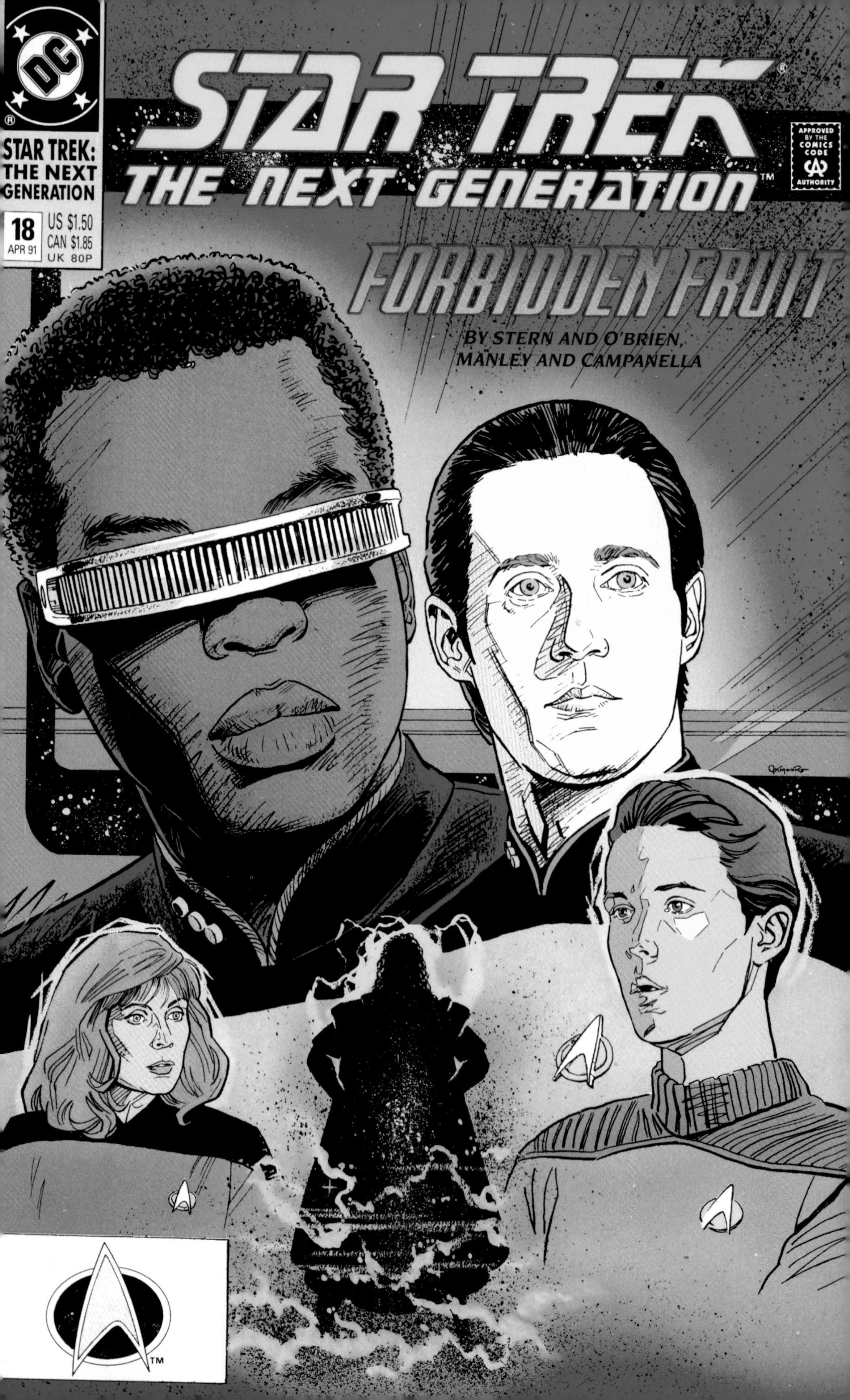
DC
STAR TREK
THE NEXT GENERATION
STAR TREK: THE NEXT GENERATION
18
APR 91
US $1.50
CAN $1.85
UK 80P
APPROVED BY THE COMICS CODE AUTHORITY
FORBIDDEN FRUIT
BY STERN AND O'BRIEN, MANLEY AND CAMPANELLA

CREATOR BIOGRAPHIES

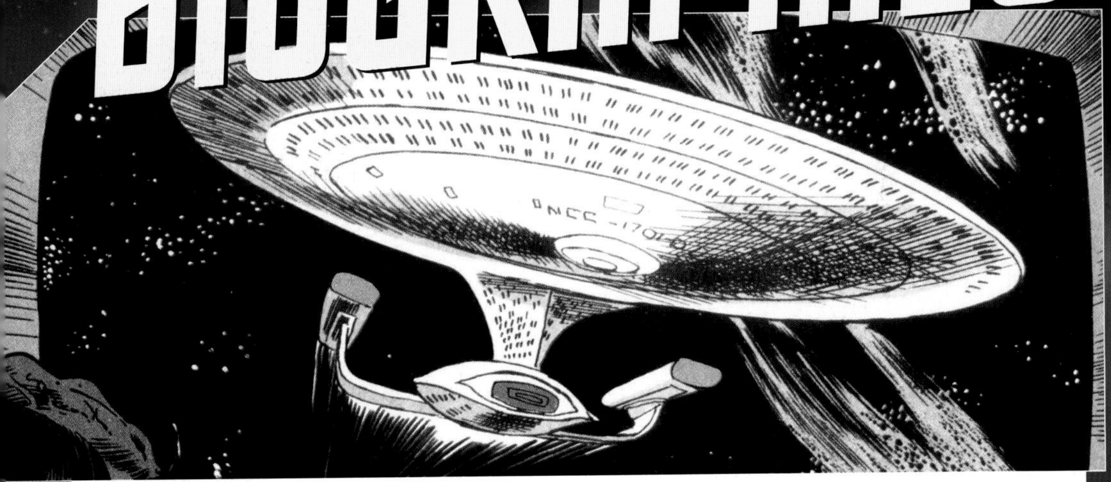

MICHAEL JAN FRIEDMAN

is a heavyweight when it comes to writing for the *Star Trek* universe, with thirty-seven original novels under his belt, an eighty-issue run on the *ST:TNG* DC comic; six *Star Trek: Stargazer* novels; and an episode for television (*Star Trek: Voyager*'s 'Resistance'). He has also written extensively for comics, lending his pen to *The Flash, Justice League Quarterly, Justice League Task Force, Outlaws, Darkstars*, as well various *Star Trek* annuals and mini-series. His most recent *Star Trek* novel, *Death in Winter*, was published in September 2005.

DAVE STERN

is another prolific and popular *Star Trek* editor and author, having written novels including *What Price Honor?, Daedalus* and *Daedalus' Children*. He has also written several other movie tie-ins, including *Lara Croft: Tomb Raider – The Cradle of Life*, and is currently working on a *Fantastic Four* novel, *The Baxter Effect*. Mike O'Brien is Stern's sometime writing partner.

PABLO MARCOS

is considered Peru's most popular comics artist. His career began in the early 1970s and continues to the present day. He has worked on a host of Marvel titles including *Fantastic Four, Daredevil, Avengers, Thor, Captain America, Captain Britain,* and *The Savage Sword of Conan*. For DC his art has appeared in high-profile titles like *Batman: Detective Comics, Green Arrow,* and *Star Trek: The Next Generation*. He is also known for his classic horror illustrations, which have appeared in *Vampirella, Eerie,* and *Creepy* magazines for Atlas and Warren.

KEN PENDERS'

work on *Star Trek* comics includes several issues pencilling *Star Trek: Deep Space Nine* and *Who's Who in Star Trek* in addition to his *Next Generation* issue collected herein. His other work includes *Advanced Dungeons and Dragons, The Jaguar* and a long run on *The Man From U.N.C.L.E.*

MIKE MANLEY

made his major-league comics debut with Marvel's *Darkhawk*, where his run lasted for over two years, and he has also illustrated *Batman, Conan the King, Dexter's Laboratory, Jon Sable: Freelance, Quasar* and *Superman Adventures*. He is currently working on online comics *Monsterman* and *G.I.R.L. Patrol*.

ROBERT CAMPANELLA

is a prolific inker with credits including *Aliens vs Predator, Batgirl, Batman, Catwoman, Cops, Doom Patrol, Green Arrow, Green Lantern, Outsiders, Robin, Stormwatch, Suicide Squad, Who's Who in the Legion of Super-Heroes* and *Wonder Woman*.

EXPLORE THE FINAL FRONTIER WITH THES
OTHER FANTASTIC STAR TREK BOOKS!
STAR TREK
TO BOLDLY GO
STAR TREK
DEATH BEFORE DISHONOR
STAR TREK
THE TRIAL OF JAMES T. KIRK
Star Trek - To Boldly Go
ISBN: 1 84576 084 0
Features interviews with
William Shatner and DeForest Kelley!
Star Trek - Death Before Dishonor
ISBN: 1 84576 154 5
Features interviews with
Leonard Nimoy and James Doohan!
Star Trek - The Trial of James T. Kirk
ISBN: 1 84576 315 7
Features interviews with
Nichelle Nicholls and Walter Koenig!
STAR TREK
THE NEXT GENERATION
THE HERO FACTOR
STAR TREK
THE NEXT GENERATION
THE BATTLE WITHIN
Star Trek: The Next Generation -
The Hero Factor
ISBN: 1 84576 153 7
Features interviews with
Patrick Stewart and Brent Spiner!
Star Trek: The Next Generation -
The Battle Within
ISBN: 1 84576 155 3
Features interviews with
Jonathan Frakes and Marina Sirtis!
™ & © 2006 CBS Studios Inc. All Rights Reserved. STAR TREK and Related
Marks are Trademarks of CBS Studios Inc. Titan Books Authorized User.
IN STORES NOW!

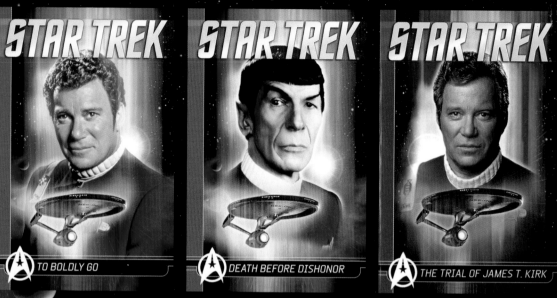

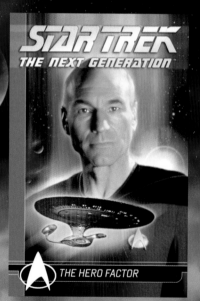

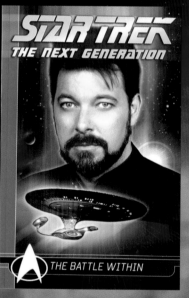